The Market for Rural Land

The Conservation Foundation is a nonprofit research and communications organization dedicated to encouraging human conduct to sustain and enrich life on earth. Since its founding in 1948, it has attempted to provide intellectual leadership in the cause of wise management of the earth's resources.

The Market for Rural Land
Trends, Issues, Policies

Robert G. Healy and James L. Short

The Conservation Foundation
Washington, D.C.

The Market for Rural Land:
Trends, Issues, Policies

Library of Congress Catalog Card Number: 81-67850
International Standard Book Number: 0-89164-065-7

Cover Design by Sally A. Janin

Typeset by United Graphics, Inc., Fairfax, Virginia

Printed by Universal Lithographers, Cockeysville, Maryland

The Conservation Foundation
1717 Massachusetts Avenue, N.W.
Washington, D.C. 20036

Contents

Chapter 3
The Supply of Rural Land   **77**

Chapter 4
How the Land Market Works   **93**

Chapter 7
Toward New Policies for Rural Land   251

Foreword

Something has happened in rural America. Perhaps the first inkling came in the late 1960s, when government tabulations revealed that manufacturing employment had started to grow more rapidly in the countryside than in metropolitan centers. About the same time, public perceptions of the countryside were changing—from images of poverty and backwardness to sometimes romanticized visions of the good life rural America seemed to offer: a slower pace, a less-polluted environment, an opportunity for individual self-expression. More recently has come a rather surprising finding of demographers that, starting about 1970, nonmetropolitan counties, including some far from the influence of any big city, were growing faster than metropolitan ones.

Farming, long dominant in the rural economy, has also been changing, both in character and in relative importance. Today, only 1 rural resident out of 10 lives on an operating farm. Even among farmers, more than half of aggregate income in most recent years has been derived from off-the-farm sources. The interstate highway system has vastly expanded the typical rural dweller's access to shopping, to medical services, and to places of employment. And housing in rural areas recently has been built at a rate more than twice that of urban areas. The popular mental image of rural American life, with its emphasis on farming and its expectation of stability or decline, increasingly is out of joint with reality.

The new rural change deeply affects two of the most fundamental concerns of The Conservation Foundation. It affects our interest as a conservation organization in safeguarding the long-term productivity of America's natural resource base. And it affects our interest as part of the environmental community in protecting natural systems and the scenic beauty of the American landscape. For about the same time that rural America began to change in new directions, our need for its traditional products—food, wood, water, and recreation—began to quicken. The massive increases in U.S. grain exports which began in 1973 put a sudden end to decades of farm surpluses. Extremely rapid rises in timber prices through much of the 1970s helped exacerbate fears that the average American family might soon be unable to afford a new single-family house. The explosion of interest in outdoor recreation activities of all sorts put great pressures on public lands and led many to wonder if private land could fill the gap.

Because of this conjunction of rural change and growing demands for traditional rural functions, The Conservation Foundation has recently devoted a great deal of attention to rural issues. We have published a book and held conferences on the future of American agriculture. We have researched the economics and politics of soil erosion. And we have undertaken projects aimed at understanding the appropriate roles of private and federal lands in rural areas.

This book is a major component of the Foundation's rural resources program. It is a highly original investigation of one of the driving forces behind rural change—the desire of millions of individuals to buy, sell, and hold rural property. The study of the rural land market is important in two ways. First, the land market is the arena where competing demands on land are expressed and where they contend with one another. Second, the market itself seems to affect the level and nature of demand, as when past increases in land prices raise expectations about the future and inflame speculation.

Despite the importance of the rural land market, it has never been given a book-length treatment. Healy and Short's study follows a grand tradition of Conservation Foundation research. It looks not just at the obvious problems of the present but tries to take a long look at those that are just emerging. It adopts a sober and analytical tone and aims at understanding behavior rather than identifying villains. It draws policy suggestions not from abstract theories but from the tentative, and often little known, experiments being undertaken in local jurisdictions around the country. And, despite treating a sometimes complex subject, it avoids jargon and speaks to the policymaker and interested lay person.

The Conservation Foundation is deeply grateful to the Richard King Mellon Foundation and to its donors of unrestricted support, who provided the funding for this project.

William K. Reilly
August 1981

Preface

This book was written out of curiosity. We are economists, one with a national conservation organization, the other a university professor of business administration. Each of us, from quite different perspectives, grew aware over the past decade that interesting things were happening to rural land. Each watched the great second-home boom of the late 1960s and early 1970s, the resulting social and environmental controversies, the subsequent bust. We read newspaper reports of the turnaround in rural population growth, the boom in farmland prices, and the increase in the size of farms. In travels around the United States, each of us saw great changes occurring in the way land was used, particularly changes in agricultural technologies and the sprawl of industrial, commercial, and residential uses over the rural landscape. At professional conferences, we heard discussions about the future adequacy of farmland and forestland and about new opportunities and techniques for rural real-estate investment.

Because we both have professional training in land economics, we were aware that the diverse forces affecting rural land were likely to have a measurable impact on the land market. But we also knew that the rural land market was in nearly all respects inadequately documented and understood. Landownership, prices, market trends, implications—all were subject to information gaps or lack of study. "Land tenure," a popular research subject during the 1930s and again briefly during the late 1940s, had been ignored subsequently by academic researchers and policy analysts alike. One land policy expert, summing up the state of knowledge in the mid-1970s, commented, "We know more about who owns Bolivia or who owned the Mekong Delta than about who owns the Corn Belt."

To be sure, there had been scattered pieces of good research, most of them dealing with the determinants of land prices in particular rural places. But, searching the literature, we less often found helpful information than complaints about the lack of it. Aside from general texts on land economics and on appraisal techniques, there was no comprehensive, book-length study of the rural land market. Particularly lacking, we thought, was a book that simultaneously examined trends, identified issues and controversies, and proposed appropriate public policies. There was also need for a work that would go beyond traditional fragmentation of rural research into the study of farms, the study of forests, and the study of rural development. Increasingly, we observed, these uses were in competition among one another for the use of rural land.

Our curiosity piqued, we decided to write a book about the rural land market. One of our early steps was to convene a meeting of experts on various subjects related to our study. We gathered 22 people from around the country to spend a day in Washington discussing land-market trends and the status of research. The participants included land economists, agricultural economists, foresters, land-use planners, real-estate dealers, advocates of land reform, appraisers, a geographer, and a demographer. We also corresponded with a number of experts who could not attend.

Two important things were learned at this meeting. First, although research on the rural land market had been neglected in the recent past, a fresh interest was rising among a number of people and agencies. This was subsequently reflected in a bounty of relevant studies and new data that were made available to us. Most notable has been the development of new government data sources—particularly a national landownership survey and new data on foreign ownership. Second, most of the people who attended our meeting did not know one another. People studying forestland do not generally interact with people studying cropland. Real-estate dealers and appraisers tend to be unfamiliar with relevant academic studies or debates over land policy. This encouraged us to cast our net broadly in the course of our study, for we became convinced that, although no one was an expert on the rural land market as a whole, there was a considerable body of information, widely scattered, on particular parts of it.

We also found early in our study that, if we wanted to learn about market trends, we would have to do case studies of small areas. We studied six rural places in detail, places representing a wide variety of types of land and types of land uses. The places we chose span the country, from New Hampshire to California. At each site, we talked to farmers, real-estate dealers, land investors, and new settlers. We also spent long days drawing statistical information from land records in the dusty vault or damp basement of the local county courthouse. Our findings are summarized in chapter 5, though the knowledge we gained in these local studies is woven throughout other chapters.

Our book is an attempt to summarize what we have learned about trends in the rural land market, their implications, and policy alternatives. We are aware that, despite all our work, there is much we do not know. Often, we were frustrated: our observations in a case-study area would suggest a hypothesis about some aspect of the land market, but no data were available with which to test its applicability to other areas. Similarly, we often wished that there had been more studies by others on which we could draw. We are confident that we have some useful new material to present, both to the land expert and to the general reader. We also hope that by essaying such a broad study and defining the area of what we know, we will encourage others to fill in the gaps.

In the course of our research, we found that land-market trends were raising a multitude of issues. These varied widely from place to place, but they generally fell into two categories. First, there were issues connected with the land-use impact of rising land prices, changing types of landowners, and changing parcel sizes. For example, in many areas people worried that the purchase of abandoned farms by urban residents and the division of farms into smaller parcels would severely constrain, if not eliminate, the possibility of future crop production. A second type of issue concerned the impacts of land-market phenomena, particularly of changes in the composition or "structure" of landownership, on the economy and society of rural areas. For example, we found that many people around the country were concerned about absentee ownership of rural land and the concentration of ownership—and, hence, of decision-making power—in the hands of a few individuals or corporations.

As economists interested in land planning and conservation, we felt more comfortable analyzing the first type of issue than the second. "Ownership structure" issues tend to be value-laden, often ideological, frequently controversial. Policy prescription, in particular, becomes difficult when there is no agreement on the goals to be sought. Despite this difficulty, we have resisted the temptation to concentrate exclusively on land-use issues. Land-market trends affect more than just the use of land. They also affect rural people and rural society. When we talked to people about rising farmland prices, for example, their greatest concern was for how young farmers could afford to buy land. Similarly, some of the strongest pressures on government to collect land-tenure data have come from people concerned with corporate and foreign ownership of land, not land use.

Organization of the Book

There are three major sections of this book. The first, which includes chapters 1, 2, 3, and 4, is a broad-ranging analysis of the workings of the rural land market. Chapter 1 defines what we mean by "rural" land, then examines three important trends that have been observable in the rural land market, nationwide, for a number of years. Chapter 2 analyzes sources of demand for rural land, including the changing motives for owning rural properties and the changing identity of rural landowners. Chapter 3 offers a similar treatment of the supply of rural land, emphasizing those factors that seem to be responsible for an observable sluggishness in how the quantity of land supplied to the market responds to changes in the prices offered. Chapter 4 describes the market itself, showing how land markets differ from the markets for other commodities, analyzing the fragmentation of the land market, and investigating the determination of land prices.

A second major section of the book is composed of chapter 5, which presents the results of our original research in six local areas around the country. The counties (or parts of counties) studied span the continent, and in them are represented a wide spectrum of types of land and types of land uses. They encompass exurban areas, as well as areas remote from cities, and include places notable for agriculture, forestry, grazing, outdoor recreation, and rural residential uses:

> *Loudoun County, Virginia* (outlying portion). Part of Virginia's "horse country," this exurban portion of the Washington, D.C., metropolis preserves a rural life-style for commuters and retirees.

> *Tyler County, Texas.* Located in the east Texas "piney-woods," Tyler County lies in the midst of some of the nation's most productive softwood timberland.

> *Hardy County and Pendleton County, West Virginia.* Located in a remote area of steep, timbered mountains and fertile agricultural valleys, Hardy and Pendleton

counties have seen their former isolation disturbed by urbanites seeking recreational properties.

Douglas County, Illinois. Almost exclusively agricultural, Douglas County is in the center of the midwestern Corn Belt, one of the most fertile farming regions in the world.

Plainfield, New Hampshire. Plainfield provides low-density rural living for persons working in small New Hampshire cities.

San Luis Obispo County, California. An area of dry, rolling grazing land, this county along the central California coast has become a magnet for persons moving out of crowded southern California cities.

Chapter 5 presents a portrait of each place in turn, describing land-market forces; documenting changes in prices, types of owners, and parcel sizes; and analyzing impacts on land use and on local society.

Chapters 6 and 7 form the book's third, and concluding, section. Chapter 6 discusses the present and potential policy issues raised by the workings of the rural land market. It concentrates on situations in which private and social interests diverge, so that the unfettered working of the land market creates problems for society. Chapter 7 describes and analyzes a number of policies that might help us to cope with, or even avoid, some of the problems described in chapter 6. The policies cover actions by federal, state, and local governments; actions by land-market participants; and new institutional arrangements.

Acknowledgments

Many people contributed to this book. First, we were privileged to have had three capable student employees who helped us with the field research. Mark Foley worked on the Texas and West Virginia case studies; Margaret Watkins worked on the Illinois study; and William Yancey worked on the New Hampshire study. The first two were associated with the project through internships sponsored by the Jesse Smith Noyes Foundation. Robert Peters, also a Noyes Foundation intern, helped with the initial literature search, while Peter Bross and William Jackson helped us compile and analyze some of the data we obtained in the field.

A number of land experts reviewed parts of our manuscript or provided us with unpublished results of their own studies. We would like particularly to acknowledge Nancy Bain, Raleigh Barlowe, Calvin Beale, Howard Conklin, Richard Forstall, Karl Gertel, Linda Lee, Frank Mittelbach, Frank Popper, Philip Raup, Franklin Reiss, Stephen Roulac, Robert Wilbur, and Gene Wunderlich. A large number of other people, including colleagues, employees of government agencies, and residents of our case-study areas were also helpful to us in many ways and on many occasions.

Finally, we would like to thank members of the staff of The Conservation Foundation who helped us with our work. William K. Reilly, the Foundation's president, encouraged us to begin the study and gave us moral as well as financial support during the course of the research. John H. Noble, vice-president, gave a painstaking critical review to each chapter, contributing a tremendous number of both organizational and substantive suggestions. Robert J. McCoy, senior editor, ruthlessly exposed sloppy writing. Other members of the Foundation's interdisciplinary staff gave us comments or answered questions from the diverse vantage points of law, political science, agricultural economics, and planning. Among them were Sandra Batie, J. Clarence Davies, Christopher Duerksen, Michael Mantell, and William Shands.

During the course of our research, the Foundation decided to make a film about the revival of rural population growth and its impacts on rural land and rural society. The result, *Growing Pains: Rural America in the 1980s,* was released in December 1980. It was filmed on location at our study sites in Tyler County, Texas; Plainfield, New Hampshire; and San Luis Obispo County, California. The two principal filmmakers, Janet Mendelsohn and Rob Whittlesey, taught us a great deal about both the techniques of film and the human side of the land market.

Finally, we wish to acknowledge Zeny G. Scott, who diligently served as project secretary during the course of the research and typed and retyped the several drafts of the manuscript.

Robert G. Healy
Washington, DC

James L. Short
San Diego, California

July 1981

CHAPTER 1

Introduction:
A Changing Market

There are about 10 acres of rural land for each American. If one ignores the vast holdings of federal, state, and local governments, there are still about 6 acres per person—just under 1.3 billion acres. This privately owned land produces nearly all of the nation's food and two thirds of its timber. It provides water, recreation, grazing, minerals, and wildlife habitat. It represents a large, and probably rising, proportion of the national wealth.

Each day, thousands of rural landowners buy or sell land or make decisions about its use. In doing so, they are principally motivated by personal preferences and by market forces, for government regulations on rural land are few.

We believe that forces now developing in rural places may profoundly affect the appearance of the American countryside, the distribution of rural wealth, and the long-term availability of rural land to provide food, timber, and recreation. These forces are given their first expression in the rural land market.

Understanding the land market is important because events in the land market precede, and often preordain, changes in the way land is used. Public concern about preserving the beauty and productivity of the rural land base usually focuses on the sometimes alarmingly brief period during which the use of land is actually changed. Our study, in contrast, looks at the much longer period during which landowners form expectations about future uses and institutional arrangements are created that commit land to a given use.

The expectations and institutional arrangements affecting land are frequently revealed in the land market long before any change occurs on the land itself. For example, the expectation that agricultural land will be put to urban or other developed use is usually reflected in the land's price years before a single building is constructed on it. The purchase of land by a mining or agribusiness enterprise may occur long before a visible change in its use. Potentially productive timberland may be split into recreational parcels too small to produce wood products economically; yet the land itself may appear unchanged.

Public policy generally deals with social issues only after they have become critical, despite the fact that, in retrospect, many problems can be seen to have roots in long-developing social trends. For example, concern over the burgeoning of U.S. suburbs was highest during the 1950s, years after a combination of widespread automobile ownership and readily available home mortgages had made suburban development all but inevitable. Similarly, the urban problems of the 1960s had their roots in agricultural innovations that decades before had begun to displace rural poor people toward the cities.

The workings of the rural land market have long been one of the great unknowns in land studies and in the formulation of land policies. The principal market trends have been recognized only piecemeal by the public and policymakers alike. Public consciousness of these trends, and the resulting call for policies, has been formed on the basis of personal observation or newspaper accounts, rather than serious studies. Until very recently, there has been little attempt to document land-market trends nationally, to show how they relate to one another, or to analyze how they affect important public interests.

Our book is an attempt to summarize what is known about rural land markets in the United States, to draw together new data and new studies recently done by others, and to present the results of our own original research. In the following pages, we explain how the rural land market works, investigate the implications of market trends, and explore what public policies, if any, are appropriate in dealing with present and future problems raised by the market's operations. First, we must define our subject.

What Is Rural Land?

According to the dictionary, *rural* refers to sparsely settled or agricultural areas, as distinct from settled communities. In practice, it seems easiest simply to think of rural land as whatever is not urban.

This convention is followed by the U.S. Census Bureau, which defines as urban all incorporated or unincorporated places with populations of over 2,500, as well as densely populated areas on the fringe of large cities.[1] According to provisional census counts, the United States in 1980 contained 167.0 million urban residents. Since the total population was 226.5 million, this left 59.5 million rural residents. At the time of writing, 1980 figures for the amount of urban and rural *land* were not yet available. In 1970, urban land totalled 35 million acres or about 1.8 percent of the nation's land area (excluding Alaska and Hawaii). If urban densities did not change, urban population growth between 1970 and 1980 would make the nation's urban land area in the latter year approximately 39 million acres, still leaving more than 98 percent of the nation's land rural.

Another way of looking at rural land is in terms of metropolitan and nonmetropolitan location. The government defines Standard Metropolitan Statistical Areas (SMSAs), consisting of a central urban core of at least 50,000 people, plus the county containing the core, and surrounding counties that are economically and socially integrated with the core county, according to specific rules. As of 1980, there were 286 SMSAs in the nation (excluding Alaska and Hawaii), covering 340 million acres and containing 164 million people. The remainder of the population, 61 million, lived in 2,500 nonmetropolitan counties. By no means all of the land within metropolitan boundaries is built-up or densely occupied—in fact, less than 10 percent meets the census definition of "urban." Moreover, millions of people in nonmetropolitan areas live in towns and even small cities, though these occupy only a tiny fraction of the nonmetropolitan land area.

The metropolitan/nonmetropolitan dichotomy has two advantages over the urban/rural distinction. First, proximity to a metropolitan center seems to have an influence both on land's use and land's value. Knowing how much land is metropolitan is thus advantageous in studying the land market. Second, data on urban and rural land and population are available only once every 10 years, when the census is taken. In contrast, a wide variety of demographic and economic data for metropolitan and nonmetropolitan areas is available every year. This enables us to track much more closely how these two types of areas are changing over time.

A third way of looking at rural land is in terms of land in farms. The 1978 Census of Agriculture defines a "farm" as any place selling $1,000 or more per year of agricultural products. The Census of Agriculture found that (again, exclusive of Alaska and Hawaii) 1,028 million acres of land met this standard. Land in farms, however, is of limited value in describing what we normally think of as "rural." For one thing, although some woodlands are included in farms, hundreds of millions of acres of woodlands are not. Neither are millions of acres of rural recreational land and land used for mining or held idle. Even more striking is the fact that, in contrast to habitation patterns of several decades ago, only a tiny minority of rural residents now lives on farms. Table 1.1 shows the long decline of the farm population as a percentage of the total rural population. Today, only 6.1 million rural people live on farms, that is, only 1 rural resident in 10. "Rural" and "farm" have not been synonymous for many years, and the difference is now greater than at any time in the nation's history.

Table 1.1

U.S. Farm, Rural, and Urban Populations, Selected Years, 1790-1980 (in millions)

Year	Farm	Rural	Urban	Total
1790	*	3.7	.2	3.9
1820	*	8.9	.7	9.6
1850	*	19.6	3.5	23.2
1880	22.0	36.1	14.1	50.2
1910	32.1	50.2	42.1	92.2
1920	32.0	51.8	54.3	106.0
1930	30.5	54.0	69.2	123.2
1940	30.5	57.5	74.7	132.1
1950	23.0	54.5	96.8	151.3
1960	15.6	54.1	125.3	179.3
1970	9.7	53.9	149.3	203.2
1980	6.1[1]	59.5[2]	167.0[2]	226.5

Source: USDA, *Rural Development Perspectives* (March 1980); U.S. Bureau of the Census, *1980 Census of Population*; USDA, *U.S. Farm Population, 1980*.

*Data not available.

1. Figure for 1980 based on current definition of "farm." Figure would be about 1.3 million higher if pre-1978 definition were used.
2. Provisional figure.

Conceptually, our own preference is to think of rural land as part of a continuum of metropolitan development. This enables us to consider simultaneously whether or not a piece of land has been urbanized and its location relative to metropolitan centers. Figure 1.1 shows the typical range of metropolitan development, from the central city of an SMSA, where average population density may

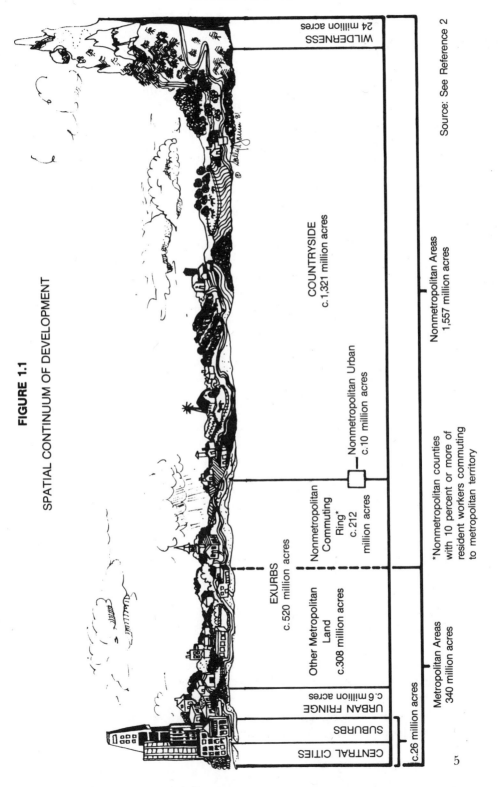

FIGURE 1.1

SPATIAL CONTINUUM OF DEVELOPMENT

CENTRAL CITIES

SUBURBS

URBAN FRINGE
c.6 million acres

c.26 million acres

Metropolitan Areas
340 million acres

Other Metropolitan
Land
c.308 million acres

EXURBS
c. 520 million acres

Nonmetropolitan
Commuting
Ring*
c. 212
million acres

*Nonmetropolitan counties
with 10 percent or more of
resident workers commuting
to metropolitan territory

Nonmetropolitan Urban
c.10 million acres

COUNTRYSIDE
c.1,321 million acres

Nonmetropolitan Areas
1,557 million acres

WILDERNESS
24 million acres

Source: See Reference 2

5

exceed 20 persons per acre, to federally designated wilderness areas, where government policy allows no human habitation. Using government data, we have attempted to estimate how much of the surface of the United States (excluding Alaska and Hawaii) lies in each of the categories along this continuum. Central cities and their contiguous suburbs occupy approximately 26 million acres, about two thirds of the nation's urban land. Traditionally the central cities contained most of the nation's manufacturing, offices, large stores, and entertainment facilities. But the suburbanization of affluent consumers and the building of urban freeway and beltway systems have caused many former central-city activities to be spun off to the suburbs. Some of the large suburbs now contain multistory office towers and huge shopping malls for economic activities that once would have been located only in the central city.

Beyond the suburbs is the "urban fringe." This land, presently outside the contiguous urbanized area of the city and suburbs, is, in the minds of the owners, committed to future urban use.[3] As Fuguitt puts it:

> ...the fundamental aspect of the rural-urban fringe, at least within the United States, is *transition*. The fringe is an area moving from rural to urban in land use, occupational structure and social organization. What is fringe today is most often city or suburb tomorrow.[4]

We would expect land values in the urban fringe to be set almost entirely by the land's expected urban-development value, rather than by its current rural use. Thus, typical prices would be at least several thousand dollars per acre. Some of this land may appear rural—it may even be farmed or used for grazing—yet this is only an interim use while owners await the land's "ripening" for urban development.

It would be convenient if we could locate the fringe geographically, as well as describe its characteristics. But it is not possible to forecast exactly how and in what direction the urbanized portion of a given metropolitan area will expand. On the basis of expected 20-year demand for urban land, we would guess that perhaps 6 million acres of land should be described as "urban fringe."[5] However, because landowners are often overly optimistic about the urbanization potential of their property, we suspect that the actual area that owners presently believe to be urban fringe may be several times as large.

Beyond the contiguously urbanized area and beyond its fringe are the "exurbs." Clawson has described some of their characteristics:

INTRODUCTION

> Suburbs of cities are usually thought of as being rather closely
> identified with the cities on whose outskirts they lie. Many suburban-
> ites commute to the central city for employment, some kinds of shop-
> ping are likely to be carried out in the city, and in general, the suburb
> is an integral though outlying part of the urban complex to which it
> is physically adjacent.
>
> The term "exurbia" can be applied to a less clearly defined type of
> land use and of living, more remote from the city and less closely
> integrated with it. There is no sharp, clear line between rather remote
> suburb and relatively near exurbia, or between suburban living loosely
> oriented to the city and exurban living much less dependent upon the
> central city....
>
> While acreage per dwelling unit in exurbia varies greatly, it is
> nearly always large even by suburban residential land use standards.
> Hence the land area involved is much larger than the numbers of
> units would suggest....
>
> The exurban type of settlement clearly has an urban origin. It was
> in the city that most exurbanites secured enough capital or a sufficient
> assured income to be able to afford exurban living, and it has been
> their attitudes toward city and suburban living which have led most
> people to locate in exurbia.[6]

If the inner edge of exurbia is difficult to distinguish from the
suburbs, its outer edge might best be defined by commuting patterns: it is possible, though not necessarily convenient, for a person
to live in an exurban area yet work in the central city or in a
suburb.[7]

Exurbs present a diverse appearance. They usually contain quite
a bit of agriculture, often with farm sizes smaller than the average
for the nation. There is sometimes a visible emphasis on vegetables,
dairying, and specialty crops. Exurbs often contain a large number
of suburban-type houses. At times, there may even be a scattering of
dense subdivisions, a phenomenon sometimes given the name
"buckshot urbanization." Yet urban services are generally not available; nor is the population density likely ever to be so great as to
warrant extension of these services. Despite the sometimes high
degree of metropolitan-core influence, the exurbs are still "beyond
the fringe."

In trying to estimate the amount of land that could be considered
exurban, we have combined the amount of land within SMSAs that
is neither now contiguously urbanized nor likely to become in the
next 20 years (approximately 308 million acres) and have added to it
the 212 million acres of land contained in nonmetropolitan counties where 10 percent or more of the employed workers commute to
jobs in metropolitan territory.[8] The total (520 million acres) represents 27 percent of the land area of the United States, a measure of

how widespread is the influence of large urban concentrations in the current U.S. land-use picture.

Beyond the exurbs is what we might call "the countryside." This is the land in the 1,900 nonmetropolitan counties where there is little commuting to SMSAs. These counties do contain towns, even small cities.[9] Unlike the large center cities of SMSAs, however, the urban places scattered across the countryside usually do not cast an influence on land use over a large surrounding region. Overall, this "countryside" area contains about 1,321 million acres.

Within the exurbs and countryside, approximately 550 million acres are owned by various levels of government, with the largest holdings those of two federal agencies, the Bureau of Land Management and the U.S. Forest Service. A considerable amount of land, much of it forest, is owned by state government. The federal government holds 50 million acres in trust for Indian tribes, and there are relatively minor holdings by local governments. The policies of government as landowner are particularly important in the western states, where federal ownership is very large. But the objectives of government, both in land management and in the acquisition and disposal of land, are quite different from those of the private owner.[10]

In this book, our interest will focus on the privately held land in the exurbs and the countryside. In the pages that follow, it is this 1.3 billion acres to which we will refer when we speak of "rural land." And it is this land that is traded in the "rural land market."

Land-market Trends

Three important long-term trends may be identified in the rural land market. We investigated these trends as they appear in national data and as they have been reflected in the six places where we undertook case studies (see preface and chapter 5).[11] As a result of our research we believe the rural land market in the United States has been characterized by: rapidly rising prices for all types of rural land; changes in the identity of rural landowners; and changes in the sizes of parcels. These trends have their roots as far back as the beginning of the post-World War II period, but they have accelerated greatly since the late 1960s.

Rising Prices

Perhaps the most dramatic of the new phenomena in the rural land market has been the rise in land prices. The best documented of the rises has been in the price of farmland.[12] Between 1970 and 1980, the average price of farmland rose by 245 percent. Comparing 1950 and 1980, the average price rose more than 900 percent. By contrast, during the same period, the general price level rose 231 percent. Every part of the United States participated in the long price boom, although the more heavily urbanized states and states in the Deep South did better than average before 1970, while the Corn Belt showed the greatest increases after 1973. (See Figure 1.2.)

Prices for grazing land in 11 western states have risen about as fast as all farmland prices, although since 1970 the rate of increase has been less than that for farmland. Prices of irrigated land in the West have gone up much more slowly, increasing less than 500 percent between 1950 and 1980.

Figure 1.3 compares the long-term performance of farmland prices with a general price index and with Standard and Poor's index of 500 common stocks. It shows that, during the 1950s and 1960s, farmland prices rose about twice as rapidly as the general price index, but not nearly as rapidly as did the stock market. Since 1970, however, farmland prices have continued to far outpace inflation, even as the stock-market average stagnated.

Timberland prices may have been rising even more rapidly in percentage terms than have farmland prices. Unfortunately, there is no source of national data on timberland sales. Anecdotal evidence, however, almost invariably points to high rates of increase. A New Hampshire researcher reports, for example, that "common talk among foresters is that forestland prices in New Hampshire have gone from $10 per acre to nearly $100 per acre in a single decade."[13] A U.S. Forest Service land buyer notes that low-grade timberland in Arkansas sold for $12 to $18 per acre in the early 1960s, was at $50 per acre by 1970, and by 1977 brought $150 or more an acre.[14] In Louisiana, appraisal reports indicate that prices of timberland and pasture were rising in the 1970s at an average compounded rate of 11.5 percent.[15] In Minnesota, where cropland prices have been soaring, prices of land in the wooded northeastern section have been going up even more rapidly.[16] A comprehensive study of forestland sales in Vermont found that per-acre prices rose from $163 in 1968 to $398 in 1973, then leveled off for the next four years.[17]

Trends in values of rural land used for outdoor recreation are difficult to estimate, because such land can range from waterfront on Cape Cod or Chesapeake Bay (sold by the front foot) to rugged wilderness in the Far West. The chief of land acquisition for the

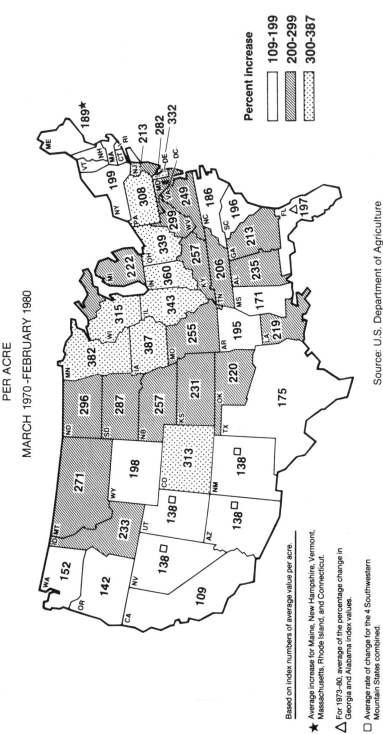

FIGURE 1.2

PERCENT INCREASE IN AVERAGE
VALUE OF FARM REAL ESTATE
PER ACRE

MARCH 1970-FEBRUARY 1980

Percent increase

109-199

200-299

300-387

Source: U.S. Department of Agriculture

Based on index numbers of average value per acre.

★ Average increase for Maine, New Hampshire, Vermont,
Massachusetts, Rhode Island, and Connecticut.

△ For 1973-80, average of the percentage change in
Georgia and Alabama index values.

☐ Average rate of change for the 4 Southwestern
Mountain States combined.

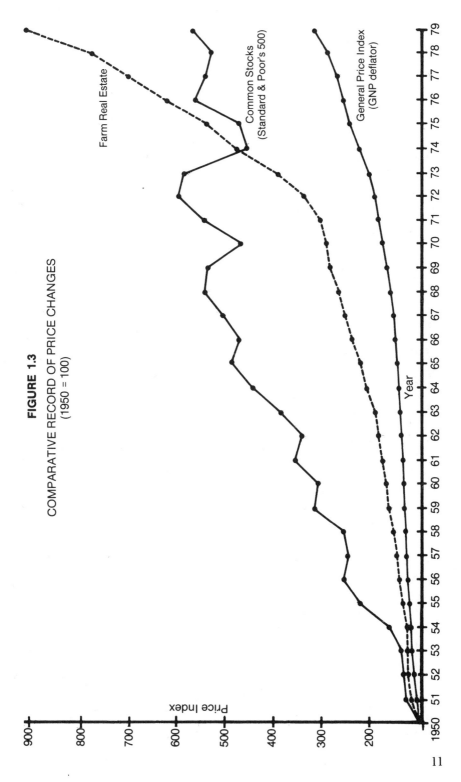

FIGURE 1.3

COMPARATIVE RECORD OF PRICE CHANGES
(1950 = 100)

National Park Service told a congressional committee in 1975 that land purchased by that agency was appreciating at an average of about 12 percent annually.[18] In 1979, a National Park Service research appraiser estimated that smaller recreational tracts were rising in price by perhaps 15 percent a year.[19] Several real-estate experts we interviewed pointed to the extremely high demand for water frontage, whether on the ocean or on inland lakes, and the consequent very rapid rise in the prices of such properties.

Perhaps the best approximation of the change in value of timberland and recreational land for a large area of the country can be found in the prices of land acquired by the U.S. Forest Service. The Forest Service acquires land with two distinguishable pools of funds. First is money appropriated under the Weeks Act, which has been used since 1912 to buy land for timber and watershed purposes, primarily in the 49 national forests east of the Rockies. In the pre-World War II period, millions of acres of cutover forestland, principally in the Appalachians, upper Midwest, and South, were purchased with these funds, at prices averaging less than $5 per acre. By 1979, the cost of such land was $235 per acre, a fifty-fold increase. The other source of funds is the Land and Water Conservation Fund (LWCF), used since 1966 to buy land primarily for recreational purposes, nationwide.[20]

Figure 1.4 compares prices of Weeks Act and LWCF land with those of farmland for the period 1969-79. The graph shows that both general timberland and recreational land have risen extremely rapidly during the 1970s, their percentage rates of increase dwarfing even those of farmland.

Figure 1.4 also gives some indication of how rural land prices have changed in comparison with prices of urban land. Unfortunately, there is no suitable series for such prices.[21] As a substitute, we have presented the National Association of Realtors' series on prices of existing homes, derived from a very large number of transactions around the country. Figure 1.4 indicates that home prices rose rapidly during the period in question, but not nearly as rapidly as did prices of the principal types of rural land.

It is difficult to predict the future course of rural land prices, although there have been some signs of near-term softness. Between February 1980 and February 1981, farmland prices rose by only 9.3 percent, the third slowest rise in a decade. This was slightly less than the rate of general inflation and well below the 12.5 percent rise in the stock market. The slowdown in the relative rate of

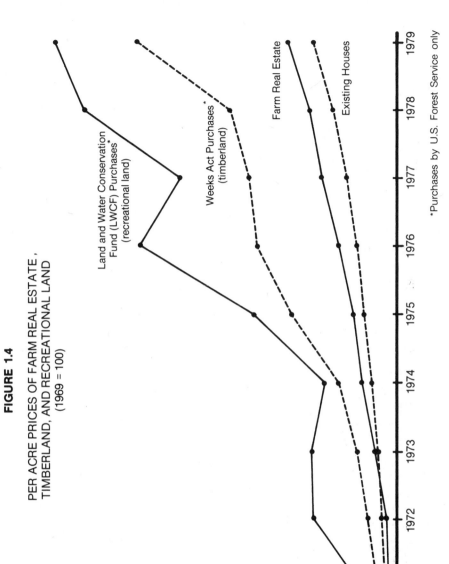

FIGURE 1.4

PER ACRE PRICES OF FARM REAL ESTATE,
TIMBERLAND, AND RECREATIONAL LAND
(1969 = 100)

Land and Water Conservation
Fund (LWCF) Purchases*
(recreational land)

Weeks Act Purchases*
(timberland)

Farm Real Estate

Existing Houses

*Purchases by U.S. Forest Service only

Price Index

900
800
700
600
500
400
300
200
100

1969   1970   1971   1972   1973   1974   1975   1976   1977   1978   1979

Year

increase in farm prices was most likely due to record-high interest rates and a very poor year for farm income. Land prices in the Corn Belt, which had performed extremely well during the middle and late 1970s, were particularly poor performers during this recent period, while California and the Mississippi Delta states showed high rates of increase.

Despite the near-term slowdown, many long-term forces seem to favor continued increases in land prices. Many of the demands for land that will be discussed in chapter 2 are likely to continue to increase; moreover, many of the factors of production that substitute for land (water and energy, for example) are expected to become increasingly scarce. Moreover, while rural land in the United States is currently expensive by the standards of our historical experience, it is still quite cheap compared to land of equivalent quality elsewhere in the world.

New Demands and New Owners

Accompanying the escalation of rural land prices, and contributing to it, have been new and more varied sources of demand for rural land, and new market participants. Some of the names now appearing on the landownership books in musty county courthouses are urbanites buying land for use or investment; others are corporations or real-estate syndicates; still others are local people now living in cities who have bought rural land for retirement or have acquired the land through inheritance. Some new owners have moved onto the land; many have not. A few are residents of foreign countries.

This changing composition of owners has occurred simultaneously with a significant broadening of the motivations for owning rural land—affecting not only new participants in the land market, but also many longtime owners. Because highway improvements have greatly improved the access of many rural areas to metropolitan centers, the possibility of future urbanization or nonfarm residential use is now a major force influencing the value of many rural properties. Because of fear of general price inflation, many investors are seeking to own rural land as an inflation hedge. Recreation and retirement demands for land have reached levels many times higher than in past decades.

As with most aspects of rural land sales, we simply do not have national statistics describing trends in the demand for land or in patterns of ownership. However, the U.S. Department of Agriculture's (USDA's) first nationwide landownership survey, taken in

1978, does give us a picture of ownership patterns at a single moment in time.[22]

According to USDA's national survey, more land is owned by farmers than by any other group in the United States. The total amounts to a half billion acres, or 38 percent of all privately held acreage. This is certainly not surprising, given the large amount of U.S. land that is devoted to agriculture. Nevertheless, it is interesting to note the study's finding that 44 percent of *farmland and ranchland* is owned by nonfarmers.

Next in importance among landowners are retirees, who hold 190 million acres, or 14 percent of all private land. Many in this group are probably retired farmers who either have leased their fields to tenants and continue to live on the farmstead or who have moved off the farm entirely to spend their later years elsewhere.

The remainder of U.S. land is owned by white-collar workers (12 percent); nonfamily corporations (11 percent); blue-collar and service workers (7 percent); family corporations (5 percent); housewives (3 percent); and "others," including estates (7 percent).

Because of the lack of studies showing how ownership patterns have been changing over time, we decided to make this kind of study a major component of our field research, comparing ownership patterns in 1954 with patterns in 1976. In five of our six case-study areas, discussed in chapter 5, we found that over the two-decade period there was a substantial increase in rural land owned by absentees, or in parcels purchased by new, formerly urban, residents, or both.[23] For example, in our Tyler County, Texas, study site, 31 percent of landowners in 1954 lived outside the county; by 1976, 58 percent were noncounty residents. In Loudoun County, Virginia, and Plainfield, New Hampshire, absentee ownership of rural land increased simultaneously with an influx of new, formerly urban, residents. In Hardy County, West Virginia, and San Luis Obispo County, California, we could not calculate the exact magnitude of ownership change, but there were many indications of significant activity by both newcomers and nonresident investors. The only study site where we did not encounter a changing mix of land-market participants was in our midwestern study site, Douglas County, Illinois. There, we found little residential demand for rural land and a high (43 percent of parcels, 47 percent of land area) but unchanging percentage of absentee ownership.

Beyond what we learned in our case studies, information on how ownership has been changing over time is either indirect or impressionistic.[24] One indirect, but probably reliable, indicator of the direction of change is the level of the farm population. It has fallen precipitously, from 23 million in 1950 to 6.1 million in 1980. Undoubtedly, many who left the farm sold their land to some local farmer. Nevertheless, there must be a large number of persons from farm backgrounds—including farm heirs—who no longer live on farms, but who continue to own farm property.

A second indicator of changing ownership patterns is change in the amount of land in farms, which reached a high point of 1.2 billion acres in the early 1950s, but has since fallen by more than 150 million acres. This change involves a land area half again as large as California.

Accompanying the decline in land in farms has been an even larger proportional decline in the amount of forestland owned by farmers. In 1952, farmers owned 172 million acres of woodland; by 1977, their holdings had fallen to 116 million acres.[25] In the early part of this period, much of the forestland going out of farmer ownership was apparently transferred to other nonindustrial private owners—businessmen, professionals, retired persons. But, since 1962, the decline in farm forests has not been offset by much change in other ownership categories. The decline thus represents a shift of land from forests to other uses.

A third indicator of change in patterns of rural landownership is the revival of growth in rural population that began around 1970. Between 1940 and 1970, rural population fell by 3.6 million people, the result of an exodus from farms to city and suburban employment. But during the 1970s, rural areas made up this loss and more, gaining 5.6 million residents. Even more impressive is the change in the number of rural housing units. Between 1960 and 1970, the number of urban housing units grew by 23 percent, while rural units grew by only 6 percent.[26] Then came a very dramatic reversal. Between 1970 and 1977, while urban housing units grew by 14 percent, those in rural areas increased by 35 percent. Demographic studies have indicated that the rural population revival has touched all regions of the United States, and rural places of all sizes.[27] Newcomers tend to have higher levels of education and job status than do the longtime rural residents. The influx of new people has helped change the composition of rural landholders and has injected new funds into rural land markets.

Changing currents in the land market are reflected, too, in the rates at which rural property is transferred from one owner to another. As with the distribution of ownership, the only national data available on changes in transaction rates over time are limited to land in farms. There has been a significant and rather steady decline in the total number of yearly transfers of farms, from 280,000 in 1950 to a record low of 85,600 in 1980.[28] But much of this decline is simply due to the ongoing decline in the total number of farms. If we look instead at rates of transfer per 1,000 farms, we find considerable stability in transfer rates, with transfers averaging 49 per 1,000 during the 1950s, and 45 per 1,000 during the 1960s. In no year during that period, in fact, did the rate go above 54 or fall below 44. In the 1970s, however, there were signs of more varied market activity. In 1973 and 1974, following the dramatic rise in grain prices associated with massive wheat purchases by the Soviet Union, the rate of farm transfer rose, reaching 56 per 1,000 in 1973 and 58 in 1974. Subsequently, transfers fell off sharply, reaching the very low level of 40 per 1,000 in 1979 and again in 1980.

An alternative look at transfer rates may be obtained from our case studies. We were able to count yearly numbers of rural property transfers for five of our six study sites, in two cases going as far back as 1950. Table 1.2 summarizes the results, which confirm our general impression that there has been a notable leap in market activity for rural land of all types, beginning in the late 1960s or early 1970s and continuing, only slightly diminished, to 1979. Despite considerable diversity in their locations and physical features, our study sites showed marked similarities in the way land transfers varied over time. In each place, there was an acceleration in the rate of transfer in the late 1960s or at the beginning of the 1970s. In each, a peak level of transfers was reached in 1972-73, followed by a generally sharp decline in the recession and energy-crisis years 1974-75. Since then, there has been considerable recovery in all of the study areas, with 1978 or 1979 market transfers in two of the five areas at higher levels than even in the early 1970s.

Taken together, these bits of evidence appear to us to indicate that the rural land market is no longer just an even flow of land from one generation of farmers or other users to another. Increasingly, the purchase and sale of rural properties is affected by a wider variety of market participants, motivated by both personal interests and events in the economy at large.

Changing Parcel Sizes

The changing composition of demand for rural land has also modified the size of parcel in which land is held. In some parts of the

Table 1.2
Rates of Property Transfer at Case-study Sites
(1969 = 100)

	Hardy Co., W. Va.	Loudoun Co., Va. (western)	San Luis Obispo Co., Calif.	Plainfield, N.H.	Tyler Co., Tex.
1979	198	118	162	161	
1978	176	127	170	161	134[1]
1977	181	131	200	140	122
1976	175	125	196	164	133
1975	164	97	153	146	92
1974	181	94	125	141	94
1973	185	142	133	201	99
1972	168	136	138	196	127
1971	137	118	134	160	110
1970	95	97	114	117	95
1969	100	100	100	100	100
1968	84	97		96	93
1967	88	91		123	85
1966	85			184	63
1965	78			114	77
1964				113	
1963				87	
1962				90	
1961				101	
1960	82			144	65
1959				110	
1958				84	
1957				104	
1956				99	
1955	78				50
1950	81				52

1. First six months, annual rate.

country, scale economies in farming have led to land consolidation; elsewhere, demand has been strongest for small-acreage parcels, causing landowners and land dealers to respond by dividing large parcels into smaller ones.

In the more fertile farming areas of the United States, the predominant trend has been toward expanding the size of farms. Between 1950 and 1979, the average size of a U.S. farm more than doubled, reaching 450 acres per farm. Even as small farmers were leaving the countryside, their neighbors were buying land to expand operations.

INTRODUCTION

At the same time, in other parts of the United States, rural land—particularly woodland and marginal cropland—was being divided. A relatively small, but often quite noticeable, number of acres were cut up into small lots for recreational development. A far larger amount was divided into the 5-to-40-acre parcels newly in demand by urban investors and people seeking homesites.

The size of parcel in which land is held has traditionally been mainly a result of custom (for example, the 40-, 80-, 160-, and 640-acre plots laid out in 18th- and 19th-century government land surveys) and of the economics of past land uses. As economic forces change, the size of parcels slowly changes to reflect them. Because the most desirable size of parcel for a second home, for timber management, or for modern farming is rarely the same as what was most efficient for the predominantly agricultural uses of the past, opportunities occur for changing parcel sizes.

Our case-study data reveal the enormous popularity of splitting large tracts of land into a number of small to medium-sized (5-to-40-acre) parcels. This practice has been encouraged by changes in both supply and demand. On the supply side, multiple-acre lot splits can often be created by a local real-estate agent or an individual landowner, without need for elaborate planning, legal or sales organization, and with minimal front-end costs. If fewer than 50 lots are created, no Department of Housing and Urban Development (HUD) property registration is required. And, in many cases, multiple-acre lot splits are not regulated by state or local subdivision laws. On the demand side, consumers appear to have become disenchanted with the small-lot recreational subdivisions so popular during the late 1960s, in part because consumers discovered that an unimproved 10-acre parcel may cost no more than an acre in a rural development project.

Price is another factor that has influenced parcel size. When land prices were low, people buying land for investment or recreation could afford the relatively large parcels that were used in agriculture. In fact, buyers still frequently approach the market with a better idea of the amount of money they have to spend than they do of the exact amount of land they require. As long a property taxes remain low, the consumer is happy to accept more land than he really needs. Rising land prices, however, mean that a given amount of money buys a smaller parcel, which in itself provides an incentive to break traditional-sized parcels into smaller ones. In the pages that follow, we will refer to the division of land into smaller parcels as "parcellation."[29]

19

Until very recently, the only thing that could be said with certainty about parcel size was that the average size of operating farms was climbing steadily. Newly available data from the USDA's national landownership survey, as shown in Table 1.3, indicate that the overwhelming majority of private land acreage in the United States appears to be held in ownership units large enough to permit efficient commodity production. For example, 94 percent of cropland is held in units of 50 acres or more. And for rangeland, where much larger management units are appropriate, more than 90 percent of the acreage is in units of 260 acres or more. Even if these units prove too small for efficient operation (and certainly a 50-acre farm or 260 acres of rangeland are not regarded as optimal in most parts of the country), the ownerships seem large enough to make consolidation into still-larger units feasible.

Nevertheless, some areas still bear watching. For example, 22 percent of private forestland is held in ownership units that are smaller than 100 acres. Foresters disagree on what constitutes the minimum parcel size for efficient timber management, but 100 acres certainly is small enough to make profitable management at least questionable. A combination of small parcels and owners uninterested in forest management implies that a very large amount of forestland may not be available for future wood production. Similarly, the fact that somewhat less than 6 percent of all cropland is held in parcels smaller than 50 acres becomes more striking when one recognizes that well over 20 million acres of land are involved. Considerable attention has recently been focused on the urbanization of farmland, virtually none on acreage where the production potential may have been severely limited by parcellation.

To help fill the void of data on how parcellation has been changing over time, we collected ownership and parcel-size information at our case sites for the 22-year period between 1954 and 1976. These data indicate that parcellation has been quite high during the last two decades, as shown in Table 1.4. The increase in total number of rural parcels over the 22-year period ranged from 16 percent in Douglas County, Illinois, to 266 percent in Tyler County, Texas. On an annual basis, this translates into compound changes ranging from 0.7 to 6.1 percent per year.

At all but one study site, there was an increase in the number of small holdings at the expense of large ones. The exception was Douglas County, Illinois, where the market was dominated by expanding farms. In the Texas and West Virginia counties, the greatest increase in number of parcels was found in the very smallest

Table 1.3

Land Use in 1977 by Size of Holdings, United States[1]
(excluding Alaska)

Size of Holdings[2]	Cropland	Pasture	Range	Forest	Other[3]	Urban & Water[4]	Total
Acres				Percent			
Less than 10	1.33	2.78	.88	3.30	5.09	33.02	3.43
10 - 49	4.41	9.37	1.60	8.43	9.58	11.90	5.77
50 - 69	2.32	4.67	.45	3.69	3.36	3.00	2.51
70 - 99	5.37	9.38	1.13	6.19	7.82	3.93	4.97
100 - 139	6.19	9.05	.92	6.65	7.22	3.19	5.20
140 - 179	10.77	9.10	2.20	5.65	5.32	3.78	6.66
180 - 259	10.86	12.09	2.39	7.73	5.93	4.56	7.62
260 - 499	20.62	16.71	7.64	10.78	10.79	8.68	13.61
500 - 999	16.86	11.71	10.99	8.06	8.95	6.37	11.90
1,000 - 1,999	10.20	6.07	12.75	4.87	6.47	4.75	8.69
2,000 - and over	11.07	9.07	59.03	34.64	29.49	16.84	29.66
Total	100.00	100.00	100.00	100.00	100.00	100.00	100.00

1. Data provided by Linda K. Lee, Oklahoma State University.

2. Landowner's total holdings within a specified county.

3. Includes farmsteads, other land in farms, strip mines, quarries, gravel pits, borrow pits, barren land, and all other land not defined elsewhere, including greenbelts and large unwooded parks.

4. Includes urban and built-up land, transportation uses, water, and miscellaneous land uses for which limited Soil Conservation Service data are available.

Table 1.4

Total Number of Land Parcels at Six Study Sites

Study Site	1954	1976	Annual Percent Change
Hardy Co., W. Va.*	2,186	3,688	2.4
Loudoun Co., Va. (western half)	4,034	6,425	2.1
San Luis Obispo Co., Calif. (rural portions)*¹	46,899	54,332	1.6
Tyler Co., Tex.*	3,080	11,264	6.1
Plainfield, N.H.	493	959	3.1
Douglas Co., Ill.* (northeastern quadrant)	841	972	0.7

*Adjoining or nearby parcels in single ownership counted as single parcel.

¹Data are for 1967 and 1977.

class size, that is, under 1 acre. (In Tyler, the increase was more than 1500 percent, from 351 to 5,745.) In Plainfield, New Hampshire, the greatest growth was found in tracts of 10 to 50 acres.

Despite the very dramatic increase in the number of small parcels, the number of acres affected has proved not to be great. In Tyler, for example, although the number of parcels with fewer than 10 acres rose more than 5.5 times, the percent of acres held in tracts of this size rose only from 2.0 to 5.6 percent. In Plainfield, the proportion of land area held in parcels smaller than 10 acres was 1.8 percent in 1954 and 4.0 percent in 1976.

The 10-to-25-acre parcels, on the other hand, showed more moderate growth in number, but increased their acreage more impressively. In Tyler County, they rose from 4.1 to 10.0 percent of total acreage; in Loudoun, from 5.3 to 10.7 percent; in Plainfield, from 3 to 8 percent.

Perhaps the most comforting aspect of these data, as we noted for the national-level data, is the finding that, despite the parcellation that has occurred, more than half of the area of each county is in holdings of more than 100 acres in size. The nation's land resource base has, at least for the present, not been fragmented beyond repair. But the direction of change, as well as the problems already evident in some local areas, indicates that parcellation should be viewed as a potentially serious threat.

INTRODUCTION

In the chapters that follow, we will return again and again to our three land-market trends—rising prices, changes in the identity of owners, parcellation—documenting their occurrence both in general and in specific places around the United States.

REFERENCES

1. An interesting variant of the usual urban-rural dichotomy is found in the Netherlands, where for census purposes municipalities are divided into "those of a predominantly rural character, those of a transitional character [the urbanized countryside], and those of a predominantly urban character [towns], with each major type being subdivided into from three to five categories." U.S. Census Bureau, *The Methods and Materials of Demography*, vol. 1 (Washington, D.C.: Government Printing Office, 1972), p. 158.

2. SMSA land areas are as defined in January 1980; central city and suburb land areas are Conservation Foundation estimates based on the 1970 census and partial data from the 1980 census; commuting-pattern data are based on inter-county commuting behavior in 1970; designated wilderness acreage is for 1980, according to data provided by the Wilderness Society, Washington, D.C. To minimize the complexity of Figure 1.1, we have assumed that all designated wilderness is in nonmetropolitan counties outside metropolitan commuting fields. There is also an unknown area of *de facto* wilderness, some owned by government, some privately owned. All data exclude Alaska and Hawaii.

3. There also, of course, are a great number of vacant parcels within the contiguously urbanized portions of cities and suburbs.

4. Glenn V. Fuguitt, "The Rural-Urban Fringe," *Proceedings of the Forty-first Conference of the American Country Life Association*, July 10-11, 1962, p. 89.

5. This very rough estimate assumes that, between 1980 and 2000, U.S. population will grow by 39 million (Census Series II projection); 55 percent will locate in central city and suburban portions of SMSAs, and the ratio of land urbanized to population growth will be .27 acres/person (the 1960-70 national ratio).

6. Marion Clawson, *Suburban Land Conversion in the U.S.* (Baltimore: John Hopkins University Press for Resources for the Future, 1971), pp. 53-54.

7. For example, Morrill defines as exurban, "non-metropolitan counties located within the large SMSA commuting zones." Richard L. Morrill, "Population Redistribution 1965-75," *Growth and Change*, vol. 9, no. 2 (April 1978).

8. Commutershed data based on special tabulations provided by Richard L. Forstall, Population Division, U.S. Census Bureau. The SMSAs are defined as of January 1, 1980, but commutersheds are based on patterns prevailing when the 1970 census was taken. Nonmetropolitan areas with more than 20 percent commuting to metropolitan areas accounted for 63 million acres; those with 10-19 percent, 149 million acres; those with 3-9 percent, 263 million acres; and less than 3 percent, 1,083 million acres. Over time, a number of the counties with the highest commutership will no doubt be added to SMSAs.

9. For example, Missoula, Montana (population 30,735), and Beaufort, South Carolina (population 8,651).

10. A rather considerable literature on government land management has emerged, and government managers have increasingly relied on long-range planning and economic analysis in their decision making. See, for example, Sally K. Fairfax and Samuel T. Dana, *Forest and Range Policy: Its Development in the U.S.*, 2nd ed. (New York: McGraw-Hill, 1980).

11. One of the coauthors also undertook intensive study of rural portions of San Diego County, California. That analysis investigated the environmental, economic, and natural-resource consequences of rapid population growth in San Diego's exurban land market. Findings of that study are presented wherever relevant in the present treatment. See James L. Short, "Dimensions of Land Use Change in Exurbia: Two Case Studies" (Unpublished study, funded by an environmental fellowship from The Rockefeller Foundation, The Conservation Foundation, Washington, D.C., July 1979).

12. U.S. Department of Agriculture, *Farm Real Estate Market Development*, various issues. In using this series, we follow the usual convention of using prices of "farm real estate" as synonomous with land prices. In fact, the value of structures has dropped over time, from 29 percent of total real-estate value in 1950 to 17 percent in 1980. Thus, the data presented here understate the rise in the value of bare land, which has, on a per-acre basis, risen nearly 1100 percent over the period 1950-80. We have chosen not to separate land and structure value both because of data limitations and because the two are physically inseparable.

13. O.P. Wallace, Sr., *Some Factors Influencing Forest Land Pricing in New Hampshire* (Durham, New Hampshire: New Hampshire Agricultural Experiment Station, 1973).

14. John F. Welsh, U.S. Forest Service, Atlanta, August, 1977.

15. Data from Joel H. Nitz, U.S. Forest Service, Pineville, Louisiana.

16. David Henneberry and Philip M. Raup, *The Minnesota Rural Real Estate Market in 1979* (St. Paul: Department of Agricultural and Applied Economics, University of Minnesota, 1980). Between 1969 and 1979, prices in this region rose by 581 percent, compared to 366 percent statewide. (The absolute price of land in the northeast, however, is still the lowest in the state.)

17. F.H. Armstrong and R.D. Briggs, *Valuation of Vermont Forests, 1968-1977* (Burlington: University of Vermont Department of Forestry, 1978). The authors attribute $57 of the $235 per acre increase to the fact that parcel size fell over the same period, from an average of 80 acres to 52 acres. Small parcels typically sell for more per acre than do larger parcels.

18. U.S. Congress, House, Committee on Interior and Insular Affairs, *Hearing, To Amend the Land and Water Conservation Fund Act*, 94th Cong., 1st sess., July 28, 1975, p. 44.

19. Interview with Peter Langer, National Park Service, Washington, D.C., September 1979.

20. Naturally, some timberland has recreational value, and some recreational land also could be used for forestry purposes. Nevertheless, it is fair to say that Weeks Act land is a reasonable sample of lower-priced forestland with no special recreational features. LWCF land typically sells for 3 to 4 times as much per acre as does Weeks Act land.

21. Perhaps the most likely candidate is the series of prices per square foot of land used in building new homes insured under the Federal Housing Administration's section 203(b) program. Unfortunately, over the 1969-79 period, limits on

the maximum mortgage that could be insured under the program changed in such a way that the type of home and regions of the country served by the program changed substantially from year to year. Thus, a comparison of yearly averages of land prices would be misleading.

22. James A. Lewis, *Landownership in the United States*, USDA Economics, Statistics and Cooperatives Service, Agriculture Information Bulletin No. 435 (Washington, D.C.: Government Printing Office, 1980).

23. A study of 10 counties in mountainous western North Carolina, an area much affected by recreational and retirement demands, tends to support our findings. During the period 1968-73, nonlocally owned land jumped from 28 percent to 36 percent of all private land, even as new migrants increased the number of locally owned small lots. The study also found that "prices for comparable tracts of mountain land appear to have increased anywhere from one hundred to one thousand percent" during the five-year period. William Cary, Molly Johnson, Meredith Golden, and Trip Van Noppen, *The Impact of Recreational Development in the North Carolina Mountains* (Durham: North Carolina Public Interest Research Group, 1975).

24. In addition to the USDA landownership study, there has recently been increased activity in studying ownership patterns for subnational areas. But there are few statistics on changes over time. For example, the Highlander Center, New Market, Tennessee, has recently conducted a major study for the Appalachian Regional Commission on absentee landownership in 80 counties, many of them with important mineral deposits, in Alabama, Kentucky, North Carolina, West Virginia, Tennessee, and Virginia. Another recent study is Nancy R. Bain, *et al.*, *Absentee Ownership in Rural Ohio: A Case Study in Athens, Gallia, Jackson, Meigs, and Vinton Counties* (Wooster: Ohio Agricultural Research and Development Center, forthcoming). Such cross-sectional studies provide valuable baseline information, but they do not indicate whether ownership patterns are changing, nor indicate the direction of change.

25. U.S. Forest Service, *An Analysis of the Timber Situation in the United States 1952-2030* (Washington: U.S. Forest Service, 1980), Appendix 3, p. 25.

26. U.S. Bureau of the Census, *Annual Housing Survey*, H-150-77 (various issues).

27. Recent statistics on rural growth within the broader context of national demographic change are contained in U.S. Department of Housing and Urban Development, *1980 President's National Urban Policy Report* (Washington, D.C.: Government Printing Office, 1980).

28. U.S. Department of Agriculture, *Farm Real Estate Market Developments*, various issues. The data include voluntary sales, estate sales, foreclosures, and other transfers, but voluntary sales account for most of the year-to-year variation.

29. *Webster's Third New International Dictionary* defines *parcellation* as "division into parcels." The term sometimes also appears in the planning literature as "parcelization."

CHAPTER 2

Demands for Rural Land

Throughout history, people have sought to own or control rural land. Behind this demand have been many motivations, including the desire to use land to produce crops or wood, the desire to build a dwelling on it, as well as the desire to benefit from future rises in land prices. Always important, too, have been the prestige and satisfaction derived from ownership for its own sake. This chapter, which examines the determinants of demand for rural land, will pay particular attention to how various sources of demand have been changing. Notably, there have been increased demands for rural residences, shifts in the profitability of various types of commodity production, and a new interest in rural land as an asset or a consumption good rather than as an instrument of production.

There also have been changes in the mix of buyers who are interested in purchasing rural properties. Controversy has developed over the allegedly expanded role of three specific groups: corporations, foreigners, and speculators.

Urban Conversion

All urban land was at one time rural. As late as the middle of the 19th century, some farmland could still be found on Manhattan Island. Within living memory, Los Angeles' San Fernando Valley was noted more for its citrus groves and vegetable plots than for densely packed homes and offices.

Changes in transportation technology and in patterns of settlement have in recent years greatly enlarged the amount of rural land that has potential for conversion to urban or other developed uses. For example, each of the interstate highway system's literally thousands of exits and interchanges in rural areas is the potential site of motels and gas stations. Miniature versions of suburbia have sprung up at the rural edges of some small and medium-sized cities. The spread of manufacturing plants to nonmetropolitan areas across the country has encouraged some landowners to view their property as a possible location for industrial facilities.

The demand for land for these purposes is perhaps best measured by the rate at which land is urbanized. One USDA study has shown that between 1967 and 1975 nearly 17 million acres of rural land were converted to urban or built-up uses.[1] Another 7 million were inundated by water, mainly as a result of reservoir projects. Of these 24 million acres, about 5 million had previously been cropland, 7 million forestland, and 12 million pasture, range, or "other" land. The estimated 3 million acres per year converted or innundated is sharply higher than a previous USDA estimate of about 1.1 million acres per year.

The spread of urbanization has sent ripples through the rural property market. Although the probability that a given property will be converted is low, the possible payoff can be very large. Land converted to commercial or industrial use typically commands several times its price for agriculture or forestry. One study found that raw suburban land suitable for residential building (in 259 cities) sold for an average of 19 times its probable value as farmland.[2]

A number of studies have looked at the relationship between rural land prices and nearby urbanization. The studies generally have found that, when other factors—such as parcel size and land quality—are held constant, the per-acre price of rural land varies inversely with its distance from towns and cities. For example, one study found "elevated plateaus" of higher than average farmland values around some of Minnesota's metropolitan areas.[3] Another study, using national data, found that farmland values in metropolitan counties were nearly twice as high as the average for all counties. Moreover, values in nonmetropolitan counties adjacent to metropolitan areas were higher than in those not adjacent.[4] Farmland prices also tend to be higher in the more densely populated states.[5] For example, New Jersey has both the nation's highest population density and its highest average farmland price.

The possibility of urbanization affects rural land *uses* as well as prices. Land with potential for future urban use may be held idle, perhaps because ownership has passed into the hands of nonfarming speculators or developers, or perhaps because urban uses on nearby land have created spillovers that make farming unprofitable. Land with urbanization potential may also be subject to the "impermanence syndrome," a condition in which farmers are unwilling to make long-term investments in agricultural structures or machinery because they expect their land will eventually be urbanized. According to the National Agricultural Lands Study, "even if urban growth stops long before it reaches many farms, the perceived impermanence of agriculture in areas near expanding centers gives rise to a pattern of disinvestment in farmland, buildings, fences, and other farm property."[6]

The geographic reach of speculation, spillovers, and the impermanence syndrome is uncertain. One study of urbanizing counties in the Middle Atlantic states found that land conversion and idling were "fairly localized," but the decline in dairying (a capital-intensive activity) relative to field crops was "far more widespread."[7] Rough estimates of the average number of acres of farmland that are idled for each acre urbanized have ranged from about half an acre to somewhat over one acre.[8]

The amount of land urbanized in the future will depend on how densely people choose to live, on the number of highways and water projects built, and on whether manufacturing firms still want to expand at rural locations. It will also depend on which regions grow fastest, since some sections of the country have more compact cities than do others. Studies of the amount of land converted per person added to the local population have found average land consumption varying from region to region, from as much as .48 acres per person to as little as .07 acres per person.[9] Therefore, one important factor influencing future land consumption may be the regional distribution of urban growth. Another will be the availability and price of energy, which will influence the distance commuters are willing to drive and, therefore, the residential locations they find acceptable.

Population Dispersal

Recently, demands for rural land also have been fueled by a revival of rural population growth. Starting around 1970, for the first time in decades, the population of nonmetropolitan areas began to grow more rapidly than that of metropolitan areas. The phenomenon has many causes and can be found virtually nationwide. "There is no real precedent for it," says Calvin Beale, chief demographer for the USDA. "It marks a turning point [for] our society."[10]

National statistics show that between 1970 and 1980 population increased by 15.4 percent in nonmetropolitan areas and by only 9.1

percent in metropolitan areas. The nonmetropolitan growth has been about evenly divided between natural increase (the excess of births over deaths) and gains due to migration. Nonmetropolitan areas no longer seem to be losing as many of the young people who in past decades would have left for urban areas. And, in a startling reversal of long-standing population trends, nonmetropolitan areas are attracting new residents from cities and suburbs.[11] The fastest growth, occurring in counties that border on metropolitan areas, is the result of "metropolitan overspill." One factor influencing this sort of growth has been the increased availability of jobs in the suburbs, which has created a new breed of long-distance commuter from homes or farms beyond the metropolitan limits.

It is the more remote rural areas, however, that have shown, if not the fastest growth, the most marked turnaround. After high and protracted net loss of population from people moving away during the 1950s and 1960s, even counties outside metropolitan commuting distances and with no city of more than 2,500 people are starting to grow. Interestingly, this growth is most likely to occur in remote counties that are rich in natural amenities. Many counties lacking such amenities are still losing population.[12]

A significant amount of rural population growth depends on the increasing availability of jobs in rural areas. For some time, manufacturing employment has been growing more rapidly outside metropolitan areas than within them. Between 1970 and 1976 manufacturing jobs in nonmetropolitan areas grew by 7.5 percent, and in metropolitan areas fell by 5 percent.[13] Nonmetropolitan manufacturing growth involves many diverse industries; one review found job growth in 18 out of 20 manufacturing sectors.[14]

Some of the new jobs in nonmetropolitan areas are in routine, labor-intensive industries that do not need the rapid interchange of information and commodities a big-city location provides. These "footloose" industries are thus free to take advantage of the relatively cheap and nonunionized labor as well as the abundant sites available in small towns and rural areas. Other nonmetropolitan manufacturing jobs involve the processing of locally produced food, wood, or minerals. In some cases, low tax rates or government subsidies have helped firms decide on a nonmetropolitan location.

There has also been an increase in other kinds of jobs in nonmetropolitan areas. Between 1970 and 1976 nonmanufacturing employment grew by 13.6 percent in nonmetropolitan areas, compared to 11.9 percent in metropolitan areas. Nonmetropolitan areas showed particularly sharp gains in mining, wholesale and retail trade, services, and government employment. Growth in mining jobs reflects attempts to find and extract fossil fuels under conditions of increasing scarcity, with much of the product ultimately "exported" to urban consumers. Much of the nonmetropolitan growth in trade, service, and government employment, however, is directly related to the demands of a growing, and increasingly sophisticated, rural population. In some ways, this latter type of employment has helped create its own demand; for the increased availability and variety of retail stores, and of professional and government services, have probably played a role in making rural areas desirable places to live, thus attracting still more people.

Overall, growth in nonmetropolitan jobs has helped make it possible for people of working age to migrate to rural areas and small towns and has helped keep rural young people from moving to the city in search of work.

In the future, dispersal toward rural areas of certain types of employment may be fostered by new communications technologies, including two-way cable television and video and audio teleconferencing. Such technological advances, long discussed but only recently becoming available commercially, should dramatically increase rural places' access to information.[15] Just as improvements in trucking helped decentralize routine manufacturing operations, the coming information revolution is likely to give knowledge-based activities greater locational freedom. In the future, people may be able to choose to work at home or in small-scale rural communications centers. Whether they do so, or continue to make a daily commute to a downtown or suburban office center, may in the future depend less on the needs of business than on the personal taste of the employee.

Many of today's migrants to rural areas are people of modest incomes who are less pulled by the amenities of the rural countryside than they are pushed by the high rates of crime, pollution, and congestion found in the central areas of many cities. Scholvinck found, for example, that newcomers to nonmetropolitan counties in New York were predominantly older people from the lower middle class who previously lived in urban areas within the state.[16] Moreover, in many parts of the United States it appears that the movement to exurban areas is motivated in part by the availability of housing that costs less than housing in the suburbs. Housing costs may also be one of the factors inducing rural young people to stay in their area of origin.

A persistent thread in the revival of rural population growth has been the "back to the land" movement. This movement, which draws inspiration from utopian writers such as Henry David Thoreau and B.F. Skinner, and from agricultural experimenters such as Scott Nearing and J.I. Rodale, has had an ideological impact that reaches far beyond its modest numbers of practitioners. It influences some people to move to rural areas and has given a perhaps larger group, including some former small-town dwellers, yet another rationale for low-density rural living. The number of people making a living from subsistence agriculture is probably quite small; many more try than succeed. Perhaps the highest degree of self-sufficiency can be realized by communal or cooperative groups, which have enough labor to permit the development of farm-related processing activities.[17] A somewhat larger number of people probably are partially self-sufficient, raising much of their own food, but also supplementing their income with casual labor, welfare or unemployment payments, aid from parents, and savings. Many persons whose rural residence really depends on the availability of an outside job or a retirement income still take great joy in raising vegetables or animals, home canning, heating with wood, and other subsistence-type pursuits.

Retired persons are another important factor in the movement to the country. Between 1960 and 1977 the number of persons over 55 and not in the labor force rose from 19.4 million to 29.6 million, increasing at a rate more than twice that of the total population. Retirees' income from pensions and Social Security benefits rose about sevenfold over the same period. Thus, retired persons are not only more numerous than ever but increasingly able to afford to indulge their locational preferences. For some, a move to the country is a return to an area from which they migrated decades before. For others, it represents a source of cheaper housing and relief from urban crime and congestion. Demographic studies have shown that rural counties with high proportions of retirees have grown significantly faster than the national average in recent years. Among the more popular retirement destinations are rural counties in the Ozarks, western North Carolina, Florida, northern Michigan, New Hampshire, Oregon, and California.

In addition to the effects of population dispersal *per se* on the demand for rural land, there is also some evidence—although virtually no hard data—that indigenous rural people as well as newcomers are adopting housing patterns that use more land. In the past, rural residents tended to live either at very low densities on individual farms or at fairly high densities in towns and villages. Lately, in response to a decline in the number of farms and the obsolescence of much of the small-town housing stock, longtime rural residents as well as newcomers have been stringing new houses along roads, converting old farmhouses to nonfarm residences, or moving into widely scattered low-density subdivisions. The total amount of land occupied by the dwellings themselves is not likely to be very large, but the generous size of the lots and the mixture of rural and residential uses point to an impact on the land that is disproportionate to the growth of rural population.

Demands for Commodity Production

The most tangible products of rural land are crops, livestock, minerals, and timber. In the early 1970s, prices of these commodities tended to rise more rapidly than the general price level. Fears of future resource scarcity made many people believe that the increases were not only permanent but augured a new era in which resource prices would rise faster than prices of manufactured goods and of services. The purchase of land was seen as a way of participating in this resource market.

Table 2.1 shows how prices of important commodities produced from rural land have changed over a recent 30-year interval, and compares the changes in product prices with that for farmland. With the exception of Douglas fir (produced entirely in the Far West), prices of commodities listed all have gone up far less than have farmland prices. Particularly notable has been the way in which farmland prices have outpaced those of corn, wheat, soybeans, and cattle, commodities that made up nearly half the value of all farm products sold each year.

Farmland and Farm Commodities

Over the past three decades, there have been tremendous changes in the way in which most agricultural commodities have been pro-

Table 2.1
Changing Commodity Prices

	1949-51 Average Price	1977-79 Average Price	Percent Change
Corn	$ 1.48/bu.	$ 2.23/bu.	+ 51
Wheat	2.00/bu.	3.04/bu.	+ 52
Soybeans	2.45/bu.	6.24/bu.	+155
Cattle	23.93/hwt.	49.67/hwt.	+108
Southern Pine Stumpage	27.00/mbf.	130.00/mbf.	+381
Douglas Fir Stumpage	17.63/mbf.	290.20/mbf.	+1,546
Crude Oil	0.43/mmBtu	1.65/mmBtu*	+284
Bituminous Coal	0.18/mmBtu	0.96/mmBtu	+433
Farmland	69.00/ac.	530.00/ac.	+668

Source: USDA, *Agricultural Statistics;* U.S. Department of Energy, Energy Information Administration, *Annual Report to Congress.*

*During this period most domestic crude oil was subject to federal price controls, which held its price well below world market levels.

duced. Some of these changes have had a significant impact on the demand for land to be used for farming.

First, there has been a great increase in yields of farm commodities per acre, particularly for grains. For example, corn yields have risen from an average of 39 bushels per acre in 1950-54 to 100 bushels in 1977-79. Wheat yields rose during the same period from 17 bushels per acre to 32, and soybean yields from 20 to 31. These yield increases mainly have been due to a combination of improved seed, greater use of purchased inputs, such as fertilizers and pesticides, and better farm management. Because many of the purchased inputs are quite costly, increased yields do not translate directly into higher net income for the farmer. But the combination of higher farm product prices and greater output per acre have clearly contributed to making farmland more valuable to the farmer.

Economies of scale, particularly in the use of machinery and in farm management, are another important change that has increased farmers' demand for land to be used in commodity production. Scale economies have made it profitable for farmers to increase the size of their operations by purchasing or renting additional land. Farmers may try to gain control of land immediately adjoining their "home base," or in certain cases within a radius of several miles.

U.S. Department of Agriculture data show that farm enlargement has been the dominant reason for farmland purchase in recent years, amounting in 1979 to 63 percent of all purchases, up from only 29 percent in 1954.[18] As a central Illinois extension agent put it, "If you're already farming 600 acres, you can pick up another 40 or 80 acres to add on, without buying any more machinery or hiring any more labor, and you can spread the machinery cost and depreciation over more acres."

Farm expansion demand has been further increased by structural or institutional factors.[19] Government price-support and crop-insurance programs have subtle features favoring large operations over small ones and may, therefore, have increased farmers' desires to expand.[20] Moreover, farm credit institutions tend to reinforce the demand for expansion. Thanks to the increase in their equity brought on by higher land prices, farmers who already own some property are able to borrow money and expand even more. Thus, the farmer who wants to expand often enjoys not only economies of scale, but relatively easy access to capital.

To evaluate how land's changing role as a commodity producer affects the demand for land, one must consider the interaction of physical productivity, prices of outputs, and prices of inputs. For farmland, we can examine net farm income per acre. This is the residual left after the farmer has subtracted from the value of crops sold his expenses for fuel and materials, for depreciation on machinery, and for hired labor. In effect, it is the return to his own labor, to his management skill, and to the land.

Figure 2.1 shows the behavior of net farm income per acre over the last three decades. Net income declined during the 1950s (from Korean War highs) and then showed little or no growth through most of the 1960s. Income was somewhat higher during the 1969-71 period, but farmers still were not even keeping up with the prevailing rate of inflation. Then there were three extraordinary years. Burgeoning export demand for U.S. wheat and feedgrains helped push farm incomes to record-breaking levels. Since 1974, however, net farm income has followed a somewhat erratic course, with a mixture of high- and low-income years and no evident trend.

Figure 2.1 also shows the course of farm real-estate prices over the same 30-year period. Land prices rose steadily throughout the 1950s and 1960s, despite almost static income per acre. In the 1970s, when farm income rose significantly, farmland prices began to soar. Subsequently, however, the two series again diverged. Since 1974, farm-

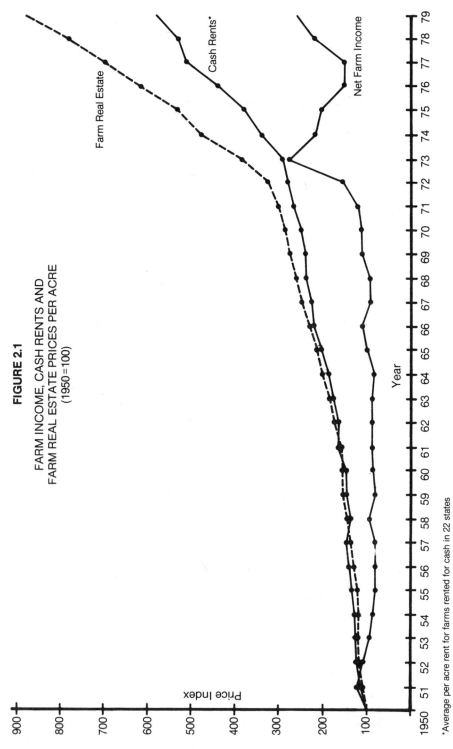

FIGURE 2.1

FARM INCOME, CASH RENTS AND
FARM REAL ESTATE PRICES PER ACRE
(1950=100)

*Average per acre rent for farms rented for cash in 22 states

land prices have continued to rise, even though net farm income has ceased growing.

Given the steady growth in farmland prices and the lackluster performance of farm income, the net result has been a significant decline over time in the ratio of farm income to farmland prices, illustrated in Table 2.2.

Table 2.2
Farm Income and Farm Real-estate Prices

	1950-59	1960-69	1970-79	1978-80
Net Farm Income (per acre in farms)	$ 11.11	$ 11.27	$ 21.94	$ 26.12
Average Farm Real-Estate Price (per acre)	87.00	146.00	338.00	563.00
Income/Price Ratio	.128	.078	.065	.046

Sources: USDA, *Agricultural Statistics*

These comparisons might lead one to conclude that, although the demand for land to produce farm income has certainly been an influence on land prices, the relationship has been weakening over time. However, in a recent article, Melichar contends that there are "important defects inherent in comparing operators' net farm income with land prices."[21] The most significant of these is that over the years there has been a substantial relative decline in the amount of labor used to produce crops. Thus, a steadily greater share of the return to farming should be attributed to "production assets," the largest of which is land. Expressed in these terms, Melichar finds the return to production assets has experienced significant growth since the mid-1950s, with an annual growth rate for the period 1954-78 averaging 4.25 percent. He concludes that farmland prices had to rise simply to maintain a more or less constant ratio with this growing return.

One way to isolate the contribution of land to farm product output is to consider the behavior over time of rents on farmland rented for cash. This indicator should measure what additional pieces of farmland were worth to farmers for the purpose of commodity production, particularly to those farmers seeking economies of scale through expansion. (We must caution, however, that each year only a small, and not necessarily representative, amount of farmland is rented for cash.)

Table 2.3 illustrates how cash rents have changed over time, using statewide averages for 22 states. The table shows that the behavior of farmland prices rather closely parallels that of cash rents. Unlike net farm income, cash rents per acre have continued to climb since 1975, as have land prices. Despite the almost continuous rise in cash rents, however, land prices have increased even more rapidly. In the period 1960-69 the ratio of cash rent to land price averaged .073. By 1978-80 the ratio had fallen to .046. Table 2.3 shows that the drop was particularly noticeable in the southern states, but that some reduction in the rent-to-price ratio was observed in each of the 22 states.

Table 2.3
Ratio of Cash Rent to Land Price
(farms rented for cash)

	1960-69	1978-80	Change
Mississippi	11.0%	5.3%	-5.7%
Georgia	9.8	4.7	-5.1
Virginia	8.0	3.7	-4.3
North Carolina	8.2	4.1	-4.1
Alabama	9.3	5.2	-4.1
Tennessee	9.2	5.1	-4.1
South Carolina	7.6	3.9	-3.7
Maryland	5.1	2.3	-2.8
Kentucky	7.7	5.0	-2.7
Wisconsin	8.2	5.7	-2.5
North Dakota	8.7	6.2	-2.5
Delaware	5.2	3.0	-2.2
Minnesota	7.4	5.3	-2.1
Pennsylvania	5.2	2.3	-1.9
Indiana	6.9	5.2	-1.7
Iowa	6.6	5.0	-1.6
Illinois	5.7	4.3	-1.4
Michigan	6.0	4.6	-1.4
Oklahoma	4.8	3.6	-1.2
South Dakota	7.1	5.9	-1.2
Ohio	5.5	4.2	-1.1
Missouri	7.0	6.0	-1.0
Average	7.3	4.6	

Source: USDA, *Farm Real Estate Market Developments.*

The rise in the price of farmland relative to its average income in producing commodities has occurred against a background of rising interest rates. During the 1950s the average interest rate on new loans made by the Federal Land Banks, a major source of farm credit, was 4.51 percent. In the 1960s it averaged 6.05 percent, and it averaged 8.29 percent in the 1970s. In 1980 the rate reached a record 10.39 percent.[22] Thus, people buying farmland have not only been accepting lower current yields in terms of the ratio of net income from commodity production to land price, they also have had to pay more in interest to finance their purchases.

It can be argued, of course, that national data on both farm income and land prices are too highly aggregated to make a comparison relevant. Nevertheless, rates of current yields that are far less than mortgage interest rates are almost invariably found in regional data and in individual transactions for all types of rural land. For example, Reiss found that in 1977 the average ratio of net rent to price of farmland in central and northern Illinois was 2.6 percent. The ratio was 3.7 percent for southern Illinois farmland. That same year, the average interest rate charged on farmland loans by banks in the Chicago Federal Reserve Bank District was 8.9 percent.[23] Similar examples abound.[24]

The demand for land for commodity production depends not only on the value of its current products, but also on demanders' expectations about the value of what the land will produce in the future. If people come to believe that productivity will increase, or that increases in world food demand will cause real prices of U.S. farm products to rise, the current price of land is likely to reflect that anticipation. Thus, although land might seem to have a low financial yield in terms of current output, it could have a more reasonable financial yield when future growth in the value of output is considered.

There is really no way to measure people's expectations. In chapter 4 we show how alternative assumptions about future increases in the yield from land can have a great impact on current prices. During the last several years, there has been much discussion both in the press and among experts about possible "limits to growth" and prospects for future food shortages. It is quite likely that these discussions have had a psychological impact on the expectations of farmland buyers.

Timber Production and Demand for Land

Changes in the net returns to timber growing are not as well documented as those for farming. There are not even good data on the yearly value of sales of uncut timber ("stumpage"). By making some "heroic assumptions," two Forest Service analysts have estimated the value of U.S. stumpage sales in 1977 at $6.4 billion, with $4.4 billion coming from privately owned land.[25] This compares with $2.9 billion (total) in 1972 and $1.3 billion in 1963.[26]

Since 1970, prices of wood products have risen greatly, with lumber prices increasing significantly faster than those for paper or plywood. Prices of stumpage have tended to go up even more rapidly than have those of manufactured wood products. This is especially true of large, easily handled trees of both softwood and hardwood species. The softwoods—mainly Douglas fir and southern pine—have been in great demand for new home construction; the premium hardwoods are used in furniture. An important new factor affecting stumpage demand in the Pacific Northwest has been rapidly growing exports of raw logs to Japan for use in home-building.

During recent years, technological changes have increased the value of certain sizes of trees and certain species. For example, development of processes for pulping low-grade hardwoods and for making them into particle board has created a demand for trees that were formerly completely unmarketable. Technological advances have made it possible to produce plywood from southern pine, a development that since the middle 1960s has created a major new industry in many parts of the South. "Chipping saws" and "whole tree chippers" have enabled loggers to salvage more of the wood fiber in a given tree by converting tops, bark, and branches into wood chips. These innovations have allowed the timber industry to maintain its output in the face of a dwindling stock of large, easily harvested trees.

The overall effect of recent trends in the demand for wood products and in wood-processing technology has been to increase greatly the value of premium-quality stumpage, to create new markets for formerly unsalable sizes and species, and to increase the profitability of growing new trees. Nonetheless, it appears to be a general belief among foresters and forest economists that income from wood growing is not sufficient, even under good management, to "carry" most pieces of forestland (that is, to pay a typical mortgage rate of interest on the land's market value). For example, Clawson notes that "[t]here is considerable evidence that land speculation and the purchase of forests for purposes other than wood production have pushed the price of forestland in many areas to levels so high that a purchaser cannot hope to grow wood and from wood growing alone make a good return on his investment."[27]

But there are many exceptions to this rule. Recent increases in timber prices have made it possible in some parts of the country for people who already own land to earn a respectable return on new investments in productivity-increasing forest practices, such as tree planting and thinning. Due to the high price of land, especially in smaller tracts, however, such investments would rarely generate enough income to pay off a mortgage based on the current market value of the land. In other cases it is possible to buy land covered with immature trees for little more than bare land would cost. Yet trees just below sawtimber age are typically increasing very rapidly in both size and market value.[28] Two knowledgeable New England observers, one a land dealer, the other a forester, agreed that annual returns of 8 to 10 percent on invested capital could be obtained by seeking out such undervalued properties.[29] Moreover, like agricultural land, forestland may be worth more to some buyers than to others. Timber companies may need a minimum land base to secure supplies for a new mill, to block out competitors, or to increase their power in bargaining with private suppliers for stumpage. Because of the potential processing profits, the companies are thus willing to buy land, even though the apparent return (yearly increment in stumpage value divided by the price of the land) is below the 10 to 15 percent per year they typically earn on their overall operations.

In some ways, one might expect timberland investors to demand higher percentage returns than do farmland investors. For one thing, without at least 1,000 acres of good-quality forest, it is difficult to generate a regular annual income from the sale of timber. Moreover, while weather or insects might cause a farmer to lose a given year's crop, forest fire or insect infestation can destroy or severely damage trees that took many years to grow. And, of course, wood prices are not held up by the price supports enjoyed by many farm commodities. On the other hand, forestland investors benefit from the fact that income generated by growing trees is usually taxed at capital gains rates, only 40 percent as high as rates applicable to net income from growing crops.

The long-term upward trend in wood prices—more dependable in the past than for most farm crops—may also incline buyers toward forestland. The price of lumber in constant dollars has, since 1800, "risen more or less steadily" at an average compound rate of 1.7 percent annually.[30] This would imply a doubling of 1980 prices around the year 2020.

Inflation Hedging

Distinct from anticipation of future land-use opportunities or commodity demands is a more general expectation that the price of rural land will rise at least as rapidly as the general level of prices. This expectation has been particularly strong in the past decade, which has seen higher than average rates of inflation and a corresponding scramble by investors to find ways to preserve the value of their capital.

Since 1950, the general level of U.S. prices[31] has risen at a compound rate of 3.9 percent per year. Since 1970, spurred first by budget deficits resulting from the Vietnam war and later by increases in energy prices, the inflation rate has averaged 6.6 percent per year. In response, investors have tried to place their funds in various commodities that will offer total returns at least equal to the rate of inflation. Precious metals, art objects, oriental carpets, and houses have been among their favorites—as has rural land. Common stocks, long considered an effective inflation hedge, have for a variety of reasons somewhat fallen from favor.

Gertel and Lewis[32] have compared the returns that investors have received from cash-rented farmland (in four states) and from the stock market (in 500 stocks included in the Standard and Poor's index) with rates of price inflation for various periods since 1940. In the case of both stocks and farmland, returns include current income, in the form of dividends or cash rents, and price appreciation over time. Table 2.4 indicates that during the post-1940 period both farmland and common stocks have been good hedges against price inflation, but with widely varying performance, depending on the time period considered. During the 1950s common stocks showed superior performance; during the 1940s and 1970s farmland had a clear edge. Although the rates of return for the entire 1940 to 1979 period were not markedly different between these two kinds of assets, farmland has exhibited two characteristics that seem to give it a real advantage as an inflation hedge. First, the total return to farmland was highest during the two periods of greatest general inflation, the 1940s and the 1970s. Second, inflation-adjusted returns to farmland (annual return minus annual inflation) were much more stable than those of common stocks. For example, in no decade did the inflation-adjusted farmland return exceed 10 percent—but it never fell below 5 percent. Common stocks, on the other hand, produced adjusted returns that varied between 17.0 percent annually, for their best decade, and –2.3 percent, for their worst.

Table 2.4
Total Annual Return on Investment
(percent)

Period	Farmland*	Common Stocks	Price Inflation
1940-1950	14.0	8.0	6.3
1950-1960	10.2	19.5	2.5
1960-1970	8.9	7.7	2.9
1970-1979	16.1	4.3	6.6
1940-1979	12.9	10.7	4.5

Source: Adapted from Karl Gertel and James A. Lewis, "Returns from Absentee-Owned Farmland and Common Stock, 1940-79," *Agricultural Finance Review*, vol. 40 (April 1980), pp. 1-11.

*Average return for cash-rented farmland in areas of Illinois, Kansas, Montana, and Mississippi.

In the very long run, the price of land will increase in tandem with the inflation rate only if prices for the products or services produced by the land continue to rise, or if the per-acre productivity of land continues to increase. But in times of rapid inflation, people's behavior can change. Investments perceived as a good inflation hedge tend to attract investor interest, making their price rise even faster than increases in their underlying "value" (as measured by their yield of income or services) would imply. The role normally played by land's productivity may become secondary to the simple expectation that land prices are going to rise even faster in the future.[33] Such inflation psychology leads people to "buy now before the price goes even higher."

Inflationary expectations have also characterized urban residential and commercial real-estate markets. Extremely low rates of current return, and even negative cash flows, have been commonplace for investors in urban rental properties. Yet, because of anticipated price appreciation, prices of these properties have risen dramatically.

Investor interest in all types of real estate is fueled by the fact that it is often possible to buy property with borrowed money at mortgage rates of interest that (after accounting for the fact that interest payments are tax deductible) are less than the rate of general price inflation. Eventually, the mortgage can be paid off in depreciated dollars and the property resold for a profit that is taxed at favorable capital gains rates. Inflationary expectations and the ready availability of farm mortgages provide persuasive explanations of why farmland prices have risen more rapidly than cash rents in recent years and why land prices have continued to increase even though crop prices have fallen from their 1973-75 highs.

Recreation and Amenity Demands

Americans have long looked to rural land for outdoor recreation, relaxation, and the enjoyment of natural and man-made amenities. Urban dwellers seem to be both "pulled" to the country by scenery and recreational attractions and "pushed" by a desire to escape from cities and suburbs that are perceived as crowded, noisy, or polluted.[34] People already living in rural areas also contribute to recreational and amenity demands.

In the past three decades, outdoor recreation has been growing extemely rapidly in both volume and variety of activities.[35] Although the rising average age of the population may mean that high growth rates for the more vigorous outdoor activities will not be maintained in the future, some of the fastest-growing outdoor pastimes, such as fishing and cross-country skiing, have a rather broad age appeal. Government projections anticipate a moderate increase in outdoor recreation demand over the next 20 years, with the greatest growth in winter sports, boating, camping, and freshwater fishing.[36]

Privately owned rural land serves recreation demands in two ways. First, some land, small in acreage but often scenically or environmentally critical, is used for commercial recreation sites. A nationwide survey found that there were 1.9 million acres in privately operated campgrounds, 1.1 million acres in recreational resorts, and 326,000 acres in ski areas.[37] Scattered evidence suggests that these commercial recreation sites are not expanding very rapidly at present, perhaps because of overcapacity created during the early 1970s and because of competition from greatly expanded publicly run facilities.[38]

Rural land also provides sites for second homes, which may be used as bases for engaging in recreation elsewhere (the chalet near a ski resort, for example) or as recreational sites in their own right (the cottage with its own swimming pond). It has been estimated that there are about 3.5 million second homes in the United States and that they receive some 700 million person-days of use annually.[39] Although second homes occur throughout the nation, especially in mountain and shoreline settings, in the 1970 census they were found in largest numbers in Michigan, New York, Texas, Wisconsin, and California. (Since 1970, Florida, North Carolina, and Colorado probably also joined that list.)[40]

Second homes are not a new phenomenon in rural areas. Traditionally, they have ranged from such manorial establishments as the Hearst Castle at San Simeon and Vanderbilt's Biltmore to shack-like hunting and fishing camps in Maine or Michigan. But since the 1950s, and particularly during the boom years 1965-73, second homes were constructed in unprecedented numbers for a massive middle-class market.

The way in which second homes were developed also changed. According to one major study:

> Prior to the 1960's, most recreational property occurred as individually scattered lots and second homes, but today's recreational land development is almost synonymous with large-scale subdivisions similar in design to most conventional suburban subdivisions, although typically with fewer improvements and facilities.[41]

For those who could not afford a unit in these developed recreational resorts, subdividers were eager to provide unfinished lots. At least 10 million had been subdivided by 1975.[42] Many of these unfinished lots proved to be useless for building purposes—too wet, too dry, too isolated, or too steep.[43] And, even where construction could occur, the rate at which owners have built in many recreational subdivisions is very low. For example, studies of remote rural subdivisions in Arizona, California, and Hawaii suggest that, based on past trends, it could take from 150 to 1,000 years for many to be fully built out, with a structure on each lot.[44]

In 1974 the high-flying recreational-land industry plummeted. The energy crisis joined with recession and with continuing revelations of consumer fraud to dry up demand almost completely. Meanwhile, soaring interest rates and tightened environmental regulations cut severely into developers' profits. Even a seemingly innocuous change in the standard accounting rules for reporting profits from land sales greatly reduced the attractiveness of the business.[45] Many developers, large and small, went into bankruptcy. Projects were abandoned, or the land was sold off in bulk. One observer called the recreational land industry "a no profit situation."

After 1977, however, there were signs of modest, but rather unfocused, activity. Surviving developers began to revive old projects, particularly if the projects were water-oriented or were close enough to cities to be marketed as primary homes. Some entrepreneurs began to specialize in purchasing failed projects—often for a sizable discount—and remarketing them under a new name or to a new market segment.[46] Other developers sold their inventory through "time-sharing," a concept by which a purchaser buys the long-term use of a resort unit for a specific unit of time (say, one week each year). Since such shares can be sold for as little as a few thousand dollars, people who cannot afford to buy a second home or condominium can afford to share one.

The head of a trade association for the land-development industry now describes the recreational sector of the industry as "reasonably healthy." He notes that many of his members have diversified into building residential subdivisions that sometimes mix primary and vacation homes within the same development.[47] Another land-development expert notes that, while traditional recreational development is again on the upswing, "it appears doubtful that demand will ever reach the peak years of 1969-1973, especially for unimproved lots or single family detached vacation houses."[48]

The current regulatory and market climates both tend to favor development of land suitable for immediate use, rather than the sale of unfinished lots for use in the distant future. "Resort development," says a trade journal, "was largely a matter of selling land ten years ago. Today's developers have to sell housing."[49] Operators of resorts have also begun to pay more attention to the profits to be made from hotels and recreational facilities oriented toward vacationers who are not necessarily interested in buying property.

The recreational-development industry is not at present a significant source of demand for rural land. Nor is it likely to be for some time to come. High inventories of unsold lots and the existence of many bankrupt or dormant projects mean that few would-be developers are looking for additional raw land to package and sell. In the case of the market for luxurious resorts and second homes, many of the choicest locations have already been purchased and partially developed. Thus, it is often easier for an entrepreneur to buy or expand an older development than it would be to start from scratch.

On the other hand, there is evidence that another kind of recreational demand for land is now having a significant effect on non-farm rural properties. (See case studies in chapter 5.) Even while the recreational-development industry was at its height, people were scouring the countryside individually in summer and on weekends in search of small and medium-sized parcels of undeveloped land. Their motivations were probably similar to those of people buying a lot in a development—investment, recreation, possible retirement. But they were perhaps more knowledgeable about the land market, and more committed to finding land in a particular location. Many of the psychological forces underlying this demand are still present—desire to escape urban crime and pollution, fear of inflation, desire for self-sufficiency and self-expression. As an East Texas land appraiser put it, "On any given day there are probably 10,000 people in Houston who would like to buy a little place in the country."

Many persons buying rural land for recreation talk almost mystically of the psychic benefits they receive from visiting it. As one Washington, D.C., resident who owns 70 acres in rural Virginia puts it, "I love the city and I like to live in the city, but I can only tolerate the stresses of the city by frequent periods of isolation." Another, holder of a pressure-ridden government job, describes his 37 acres as "an opportunity to enjoy a slightly less intense rhythm of life." Yet another, who drives off on weekends to his farmhouse in the West Virginia mountains, claims that "as soon as I get west of Hagerstown, I feel as though I've left the East Coast behind."

Some of the people who have bought country land and houses have also reaped more tangible benefits. Although the purchase of small lots in heavily advertised developments has almost always proved to be a very poor investment,[50] many of those who bought larger tracts of rural land privately in years past have had handsome rates of appreciation. The upshot seems to be a change in taste in favor of "do-it-yourself" development. Says a Boston land dealer, who specializes in northern New England properties:

> Even when you do a development, you have to be sure that it's not a "development." We have 1,000 acres in Waterville Valley [New Hampshire] and 100 lots. But we only sell 5 or 6 at a time because people don't want a development.

It is extremely difficult to give an overall estimate of the amount of rural land devoted to private recreation. In June 1979 there were some 6.9 million acres of recreational land registered with HUD's Office of Interstate Land Sales. Taking into account projects too small to be required to register, projects no longer registered, and recreational developments begun before registration was required (1969), we would guess that the total of subdivided properties is roughly twice that figure. To that must be added acreage surrounding more than 2.5 milion second homes built prior to 1970.

Probably dwarfing these figures, however, is the privately owned land that is held partly for recreation and partly for other purposes. For example, the amount of private timberland and farmland used for hunting each year undoubtedly reaches into the hundreds of millions of acres. In many cases, particularly on timberland, this recreational use may be the owner's primary motivation for buying. Also, the sharp increases in the price of home heating oil after the Iranian revolution in 1979 created new interest in the harvesting of firewood, particularly in the New England states. A University of Vermont forestry professor noted a "recent demand for woodlots by local people and some outsiders. They want twenty, thirty, or forty acres, not to build on but to harvest for firewood and eventually, for lumber."[51] Although production of firewood for personal use is probably not a sufficient reason to purchase rural land, it adds an additional motive for the recreation/amenity buyer. Firewood demand should have its greatest impact on medium-sized, multiple-acre parcels in hardwood growing areas.

Recreational motives might also be broadly viewed to include the "pride of ownership" lying behind so many purchases made ostensibly for investment. One southern observer, noting the widespread purchase of timberland in his region by doctors, lawyers, and other professionals, relates:

> You ask them, "Doctor, why did you buy that land?" He says, "An investment." Well, all of us like to give answers that make us sound like we are rational and businesslike. But if you dig a little deeper, one answer, time after time, comes back: "I don't feel whole until I own some land. My granddaddy owned land and I've got to have some land."[52]

Although far more difficult to quantify than demands for resource production, the recreational motive for owning rural land is widespread, varied, and growing.

Demand for Land by Governments

An important, but frequently overlooked, factor in the rural land market is demand by federal, state, and local governments. Together, they own about 31 percent of rural land in the United States, excluding Alaska and Hawaii. Most of this land is suitable for grazing, recreation, or the production of forest products; very little is cropland. Although by far the largest proportion is composed of remnants of the original public domain, and has been in government hands for generations, some of the government-owned land has been acquired by purchase or exchange in more recent years.

Perhaps the primary impact that government holdings have on the land market is to reduce the amount of land available for private ownership. This has recently become an issue in some of the western states, where federal agencies hold between 30 and 90 percent of all land. "We're like serfs," complains the president of the Idaho Cattleman's Association. "There's no way that we can control our destiny while Washington controls the land."[53] During the late 1970s such sentiments gave rise to a political movement, generally called the "Sagebrush Rebellion," in several western states. It demands the massive transfer of federal lands, especially those administered by the Bureau of Land Management, to state ownership. Some leaders of the movement have proposed that the lands be managed in perpetuity by the states; others have called for eventual sale to private owners.

Although most federal and state-owned lands in rural areas are available for such uses as timber harvest (under sale contract), mining, recreation and grazing, some uses are restricted. For example, commercial timber cutting is prohibited in designated wilderness areas and in national parks. Moreover, various regulations on *how* permitted uses are to be conducted often result in intensities of use very different from those characterizing private lands in the same region. Thus, timber harvest and grazing practices may be much more tightly controlled on public than on privately owned land.

The net effect of public landownership on private land values is unclear. On one hand, the fact that some of the most scenic recreation lands are owned by the government is likely to give a scarcity value to the limited supply of comparable private land. Similarly, the fact that some state and federal lands are set aside as wilderness areas raises the value of private timberlands. On the other hand, some government lands produce goods and services that are sold below cost, thus absorbing demands that would otherwise go to private lands. The best example is recreation: if free government lands were not so widely available, private landowners would be in a much better position to charge for recreational access.

Although much more important as landholders than as active participants in the land market, various levels of government do buy, and sometimes sell, land. During the 1960s, there was a spate of federal land purchases for the interstate highway system and for land to be inundated by federal reservoir projects. Since 1965, the National Park Service has spent more than $1.6 billion on land acquisition. In 1980 alone the agency budgeted $153 million for parklands, including $20 million for 10,000 acres of the Big Cypress National Freshwater Preserve in Florida, $23 million for land along Georgia's Chattahoochee River, $35 million in the Santa Monica Mountains in California, and $14 million for 19,000 acres of land and easements along the Appalachian Trail. State governments have also embarked on ambitious park acquisition programs, and there have been additions to the systems of national forests and national wildlife refuges.

Because of escalating land prices, government agencies have been finding it difficult to reduce the backlog of lands authorized for purchase but not yet acquired. For example, in July 1980 the National Park Service's backlog was $899 million for 501,000 acres (an average price of $1,794 per acre). In addition to recently authorized park areas, the backlog included $131 million for inholdings, including some privately owned lands in America's best-known national parks. Assuming even a modest 10 percent yearly rise in land prices, the Park Service would have to spend $90 million yearly just to stay even with the backlog. Although possible in past years due to steady increases in federal appropriations, staying even, much less making up the backlog, will be a mounting problem in times of budget stringency, including fiscal 1982, for which the executive branch requested only $45 million in new appropriations for land acquisition by all the major federal land-management agencies.

Governments are usually required by law to pay "fair market value" when they purchase land. Courts tend to be generous to landowners in interpreting this requirement, and many observers believe that governments pay prices on the high side of the market. This probably tends to push up values of land in areas where governments make substantial purchases. Moreover, landowners often seek to replace land sold to the government. Their demands, backed up by cash in hand, push up the prices of whatever land is available for private purchase. In rural East Texas, for example, timber companies are actively searching for land to replace the tens of thousands of acres of industry land purchased by the government when the Big Thicket National Preserve was created.

Demand by Corporations

The changing reasons for demanding rural land have frequently involved a changing mix of demanders. Three types of rural landowners have become quite controversial in recent years, in part because their activity in the land market has been widely (though sometimes erroneously) believed to be increasing. These owners are corporations, foreigners, and land speculators.

Corporations, especially railroads and timber companies, have been major owners of rural land for many decades. But worries about the extent of corporate landownership and about the land-management practices of corporations increased greatly during the 1970s. Interest in corporate ownership was heightened by the publication of Victor Ray's *The Corporate Invasion of American Agriculture* (1968), the reports of Ralph Nader study groups on corporate ownership in California (1973) and Maine (1974), and other books documenting widespread corporate holdings of rural land and alleging that social and environmental abuses had resulted.[54]

Discussion of corporate ownership has been much hampered in the past by poor data. Historically, virtually no data existed on any type of corporate landownership except for the holdings of timber companies, which were periodically monitored by the U.S. Forest Service. When data on corporate farming began to be collected regularly, beginning in 1969, it was difficult to distinguish family-owned farming corporations from other types of corporations. This was an important defect, for the incorporation of family farms has increased greatly in recent years, principally because the corporate form of ownership offers tax advantages and flexibility in transferring land to younger family members. The increase in family farm corporations inflated figures on total corporate involvement in agriculture and tended to increase public concern about a corporate takeover of farming.

The 1978 U.S. Department of Agriculture landownership survey offers new detail on the extent of corporate ownership, although it does not reveal how corporate holdings have been changing over time.[55] The survey reports 59 million acres of land owned by family corporations with 10 or fewer stockholders, 8 million acres owned by family corporations with more than 10 stockholders, and 151 million acres owned by "other corporations." The last category, which amounts to 11 percent of all privately owned land in the United States, is the most appropriate focus for a discussion of the extent of corporate ownership.

Of the 151 million acres owned by nonfamily corporations, 37 million are farmland and ranchland, about three fifths of which are in the West.[56] Another 69 million acres are commercial forestland owned by timber companies.[57] According to the USDA survey, the Northeast had the highest percentage of its land in nonfamily corporate ownership—18.1 percent. Corporate holdings were particularly large in Maine (45 percent of all land) and New Hampshire (25 percent). The West was second in corporate ownership (16.4 percent of all land), followed by the South (13.3 percent), and the North Central region (3.8 percent).

The amount of corporate ownership of land may also be estimated by looking at the holdings of individual large corporations. This is complicated somewhat by the fact that some companies do not release ownership data, while others do not distinguish land owned in fee simple from land that they control through timber leases, mineral leases, and ownership of mineral rights.[58] Fairly comprehensive data covering corporate holdings in 1975-76 were drawn together by Rural America, a public-interest organization. The data indicate that the 8 largest energy companies, 16 largest timber companies, and 4 railroads owned, or controlled, a combined total of 130.3 million acres.[59]

Scattered pieces of information on ownership are available for individual states:

> "[In California] 25 landowners [including Southern Pacific, Tenneco, Standard Oil of California, and Boise Cascade] held over 16 percent of the state's privately held land . . . twenty firms, including Southern Pacific, own about 43% of the state's private timberland.[60]

> . . . 80 percent of the land in Maine is held by absentee owners [and] . . . just 12 timber companies own 52 percent of that state's land.[61]

> In 1975 agribusiness corporations owned or leased nearly a third of [Minnesota's] 993,000 cultivated acres, and their share of Minnesota's agricultural land is increasing rapidly.[62]

In fact, the kinds of investments that large corporations make in rural land vary greatly from region to region. Corporate investment in agricultural lands is concentrated by and large in the western portions of the United States (for example, California, Colorado, Hawaii). Appalachia, on the other hand, shows a heavy concentration of landownership by large energy-related companies. And in parts of Maine, the Deep South, the upper Midwest (Michigan, Wisconsin), and the Pacific Northwest, corporate holdings often account for a high proportion of all timberland. Most corporate holdings were assembled long ago, when land prices were far lower than they are today.

Perhaps the most systematic way to investigate corporate holdings of rural land, and recent trends in those holdings, is to examine the use made of the land. Traditionally, corporations have owned rural land to produce "the three F's"—food, fiber, and fuel.

Food

Although interest in corporate farming dates back to the 1920s, there was no surge in corporate farming activity until well into the 1950s.[63] Relatively low land prices, farm price supports, a storehouse of new technology promoting economies of scale, and changes in tax laws—all increased the attractiveness of farming to corporations. IRS tax-return data indicate that between 1957 and 1975 the total number of corporations listing farming as their major activity rose nearly fivefold—from 8,200 to 39,600.[64] This growth was accompanied by an expanding scale of operations, so that it is now common to find much larger farms than in past decades.[65] Between 1940 and 1974 the average size of farms in the United States rose from 174 to 440 acres.[66] Indeed, the traditional, small, family farm is increasingly operated as a corporation for tax purposes and, due to certain economies of scale, tends to be larger than in the past.

Of greater concern than farm corporations to policymakers has been the farmland investment by large *nonfarm* corporations, which took place throughout the 1960s, and the effects this might have on the future of U.S. agriculture. The corporations involved included such giants as Tenneco, Purex, Ralston Purina, Dow Chemical, and Del Monte.

Many of these large nonfarm corporations did not remain in farming long.[67] By the early 1970s Gates Rubber, Purex, Ralston Purina, and others had pulled out of agriculture, citing management problems, low returns on their investments, and substantial operating losses. The corporations found that using the techniques of modern industrial management did not bring the cost savings that had been anticipated; economies of scale were small and more than offset by coordination costs. Many of the firms that remain in agriculture have stressed processing and distribution of "name brand" foods.

In 1977, as some of the large corporate investors were pulling out, two proposals were made offering an alternative means for bringing nonfarm capital into agriculture. These were the "Ag-Land Fund," proposed by Continental Illinois National Bank and Trust Company of Chicago and Merrill Lynch, Pierce, Fenner, and Smith, and the "Western Farmlands" investment syndicate, proposed in California. The basic purpose behind these proposals was the purchase of a diversified portfolio of working farms, which would then be leased back to local farm operators.[68] The concept was seen as a way of tapping pension funds and other large sources of nonfarm capital. Public and congressional opposition were sufficient to cause the withdrawal of both proposals before they were implemented. In 1980 a firm with similar syndication plans purchased several farms in Arkansas and California; Congress again held hearings but no action was taken.[69]

What role are large nonfarm corporations likely to have in the future demand for U.S. farmland? Lack of data allows us to do little more than speculate. Another round of nonfarm corporate investment similar to that of the 1960s would likely occur only if there were significant shifts in the returns to farming's basic factors of production—land, labor, and capital. Recent history does not suggest such a shift. And recent research argues that, with certain exceptions, scale economies and increased profits can be realized by well-managed, family-type farms at sizes substantially below those typically operated by large corporations.[70] The exceptions may be in poultry and egg operations, beef-cattle feedlots, mechanized orchards, citrus and nut groves, pineapple and sugar-cane plantations, and vegetables for canning and processing. This suggests that farmland investment by large corporations may continue its historic pattern of concentration in specialty-crop states like California, Florida, Texas, and Hawaii, rather than expand into areas producing corn, wheat, or soybeans.

Most agricultural experts appear to believe that, at current prices of farmland and current interest rates, the large nonfarm corporation is likely to find the returns from producing major crops intolerably low. One USDA report observes, "The available data . . . simply do not support the allegation of a takeover of farming by nonfarm corporate interests."[71] Don Paarlberg, a well-known agricultural economist, recently noted in a survey of agricultural policy that "[t]he surest prediction . . . is that the 1980s will see no takeover of agriculture by corporate farms."[72]

Fiber

Corporate demand for land for production of fiber comes primarily from the timber industry. Lumber and paper companies are among the largest corporate owners of rural land. Collectively, they own 69 million acres, or 14 percent, of commercial forestland—3.6 percent of all rural land.[73] But, compared with other nongovernment owners, their individual holdings are large and their impacts on local land markets can be substantial. The biggest paper company, International Paper, owns 8.5 million acres, most of it in Maine and the southeastern states. Weyerhaeuser, the largest lumber producer, owns 5.8 million acres, including, in the coastal region of Oregon and Washington, some of the nation's richest timberlands. Each of at least 14 other forest-product companies owns more than 1 million acres of land.[74] All of these companies control millions of additional acres through long-term timber leases.

The landownerships of the timber industry have not been static. Between 1950 and 1960 forest-product companies acquired land at a rate of 291,000 acres yearly. During the next decade the annual rate increased to 600,000 acres. Between 1970 and 1977 industry ownership rose by a *total* of only 1.8 million acres, or about 260,000 acres per year.[75] Despite these acquisitions, however, the timber industry's land "portfolio" was nearly its present size by 1950 (59 million out of 69 million acres). Thus, company holdings were put together in an age when conditions in both the timber market and the land market were quite different from what they are today. Since that time, three important changes have occurred.

First, the economics of timber supply have caused the industry to move from a dependence on "mining" its existing stocks of old-growth timber to a more agricultural approach that focuses on the ability of the land to produce new trees on a sustained-yield basis. The concept of forestry as agriculture is, of course, not new, but the practice of forest management has only recently begun to emphasize intensive, sustained-yield forestry. And, until recently, a reluctance to invest money in growing trees as a crop was economically quite rational. There has always been a vast supply of old-growth and unmanaged second- and third-growth trees. The size of these stocks relative to demand has tended to hold stumpage prices below levels that would justify much investment in intensive management.

The situation has been changing, however. Demand for timber products has been increasing. Industry stocks of old growth in the

Pacific states have been falling steadily. Nonindustry private lands, many of them ill managed, have frequently remained lightly stocked or stocked with inferior timber. National forests have the largest timber inventory of all, but the strength of environmental concerns, growth of recreational use of the national forests, and designation of wilderness areas have meant that the National Forest System may not increase significantly the rate at which its "old growth" is liquidated.

The net result of the current and prospective timber-supply situation is to make intensive forestry more attractive to industry than it has ever been.[76] And this has focused industry attention on increasing the productivity of the land it already owns and making sure that land it may acquire has the capacity to produce successive crops of new timber.

The second important change in market conditions has been the great increase in demand for forestland for purposes other than raising timber. Residential, recreational, and inflation-hedging demands have pushed land prices to record levels. The rise in these demands and the corresponding rise in land prices means that industry purchases of new land must be made at prices far higher than the average price of current holdings. There is little doubt that demands other than forestry are affecting the regional land markets in which many timber companies operate. Looking at prices of recreational land in his area, one forester in East Texas put it this way: "Can you afford to pay $1,000 an acre for land to grow timber on it? That's the question the timber companies are asking themselves."

A consulting forester in Alabama notes that forest-product companies have purchased less land recently "because of the high cost of land and the increasing proportion of capital that must be devoted to bare land cost." He observes that until the 1960s "it was often possible to buy land [in the South] for the price of the timber alone." One may speculate that the reduction in land purchases by timber companies since 1970 is, in part, a consequence of the great increase in rural land prices that has taken place since that time.

A third major market change is that exurban expansion and increased recreational demands have combined to attract timber companies into putting part of their present land base to different uses. Some timber companies jumped into recreational land development, mainly between 1967 and 1971. Often, they lacked an adequate understanding of the complexities of the real-estate business.

Most found the experience unprofitable, particularly after the 1973 oil embargo and recession dried up sales, and many shut down or greatly curtailed their development activities. Department of Housing and Urban Development records, examined in mid-1979, show that 10 of the 15 largest U.S. timber companies had registered a total of 177 development projects in 26 states. Virtually all of the registrations were dated before 1974. The most conspicuous casualty was Boise Cascade Corporation, which took only two years to become one of the nation's largest land developers (sales of $169 million in 1969), only to abandon the activity in 1971 at a loss of at least $150 million.[77]

As the economy emerged from the 1973-75 recession, timber companies took a newly cautious approach to developing those portions of their holdings not suited to timber production. One firm, which has extensive holdings in rural Georgia, created a subsidiary to develop properties it held around highway interchanges. Another company, hoping to develop the minerals that were thought to underlie its timberlands, spent nearly $500 million to purchase an oil company with the expertise to do so.[78] Champion International— using language similar to that of several other companies— announced that:

> . . . the company realizes that certain of its landholdings have a value substantially in excess of that of land primarily used for timber or pulpwood supply purposes. Approximately 51,450 acres of such land have been transferred to its wholly owned subsidiary, Champion Realty Corporation, which plans to sell such acreage for residential, recreational, commercial or industrial purposes.[79]

After reviewing their holdings, several firms have donated large areas of swamp, or other land not suited to intensive timber culture, to the Nature Conservancy or to other land-preservation organizations.

Overall, the timber companies are currently rather cautious participants in the land market. They tend to buy selectively, mainly to fill in gaps in their inventory of timber species or age classes, to replace land lost to government purchase,[80] or to assure a wood supply for a new mill. We have found little evidence that major timber companies are accumulating land strictly as an investment. Companies also do not appear to be selling productive land, except in a relatively few cases where it is directly in the path of suburban expansion. Rather, their major effort appears to be directed to raising the productivity of their existing land base, disposing of marginal properties, and investing substantial sums in growing more timber per acre.

Fuel

Despite the attention now being paid to national energy supply, we know relatively little about the landholdings and land-market activities of energy-related corporations. The scattered data that exist rarely distinguish between land owned in fee simple, mineral rights owned, and mineral rights controlled by lease. For example, one compilation showed that, in 1976, 10 major corporations involved in oil, gas, or mineral production owned or controlled more than 115 million acres.[81] Among the largest were Exxon, with 40.2 million acres, Standard Oil of Indiana, with 27.5 million, and Gulf Oil, with 12.5 million acres.

In the case of the oil companies, we suspect that the bulk of these holdings represent leases (which typically run for 5 to 10 years) rather than ownership interests. Nationwide, the total amount of private land, producing and nonproducing, under oil and gas lease was 329 million acres in 1978.[82] Many of these leases are likely to have been counted among the holdings of the oil companies. Moreover, an additional 113 million acres of public lands, nearly 10 million of them offshore, were subject to lease, and hence possibly reported among the company "holdings."

There is great variation in the degree of control that ownership of mineral rights or of a lease provides to a corporation. At one extreme, a coal company may have permanent ownership of the minerals under a piece of land, under a deed that allows it to enter the land at will, displace existing uses of the surface, and, where strip mining is profitable, substantially change the land's long-term usability for other purposes. At the other extreme, a mineral lease may merely give the holder a time-limited right to explore for oil and gas by diagonal drilling under a property, with no impact at all on the use of the surface.

Moreover, the severance of mineral and surface rights can easily mean that corporate holdings are double-counted. For example, between 1969 and 1977 the Standard Oil Company of Indiana held an option to drill on 7.5 million acres of land owned by the Union Pacific Railroad.[83] An attempt to measure corporate mineral holdings would be likely to count both Union Pacific's fee-simple interest and Standard Oil's option interest.

It is known that coal companies own substantial amounts of rural land in some parts of the country, notably Appalachia and the northern Plains states. In a few cases, the type of ownership interest is explicitly stated. For example, McAteer reported that, in 14 West Virginia coal counties, 25 corporate entities owned 905,000 acres in fee simple, surface rights on 374,000 acres, and mineral or timber rights on 1,106,000 acres.[84] This was about 44 percent of those counties' total land area.

Of the studies we examined, the broadest geographic scope was offered by a compilation that apparently mixed fee, surface, and mineral holdings for the Appalachian areas of Tennessee, Kentucky, Virginia, and West Virginia. It showed that the 20 top corporations with landowning interests in coal controlled 4.5 million acres. The largest were Consolidation Coal Company, with 784,000 acres, the Norfolk and Western Railroad, with 547,000 acres, and Georgia Pacific Corporation, with 402,000.[85]

Increases in prices of all fossil fuels have revived interest in exploration in many parts of the United States, including some places where mineral rights had little or no market value only a few years ago. The number of acres under oil and gas lease nationwide rose by almost 50 million acres between 1959 and 1978. Prices offered for leases have reportedly risen dramatically in the three years 1976-79, in most cases at least quadrupling.[86] In areas of the United States newly attractive to exploration, companies and independent lease brokers are ringing the doorbells of rural property owners, offering them cash bonuses for a lease, as well as royalties if drilling proves successful. For example, at our West Virginia case-study site (see chapter 5), oil and gas leases averaged fewer than 40 per year between 1970 and 1976. In 1977 exploration lease activity increased nearly fourfold to 144; in 1978 it increased again to 190. Nationally, major oil companies have large holdings, but significant amounts of "acreage" (as oil executives call the right to explore for oil) are held by a multitude of small to medium-sized exploration companies. In some cases, major oil companies are increasing their leaseholdings by buying smaller oil or timber concerns that are rich in "acreage" but short of exploration capital.

Unlike the case of oil leases, ownership of coal reserves frequently involves surface ownership, particularly where strip mining is contemplated. Because available data mix surface ownership, mineral-rights ownership, and leases, it is not possible to present national figures on coal-company landownership or on how it has been changing over time. At present, most large coal-producing companies control proved reserves sufficient for many decades of production at current rates. Although there is some acquisition of land or mineral rights from individual private owners (for example, in southern Illinois[87] and in northwest Colorado[88]), much of the recent land-related activity by coal-producing companies appears to have been centered on trying to acquire leases to federally owned, low-sulfur coal in the West, and on the acquisition of small operators by larger ones. Particularly notable has been the acquisition of coal-mining companies by major oil companies. The most recent available figures show that in 1976 oil and gas companies and their mining subsidiaries controlled 41 percent of the country's recoverable coal reserves (in tons), more than three times as much as is owned by the independent coal companies.[89] Most of the remainder is owned by railroads, steel companies, and electric utilities.

Finally, energy companies, or speculators planning eventual sale to an energy company, are seeking land or subsurface rights in some areas with potential for nonconventional sources of energy, such as oil shale, tar sands, or geothermal heat. Although most of the land now thought to have such potential is owned by the federal government, there have been reports of recent leasing activity involving oil shale on hundreds of thousands of acres of privately owned land in central Kentucky, southern Ohio, and southern Indiana.[90]

Demand by Foreigners

During the last several years, many people have expressed concern over foreign investment in U.S. rural land—particularly farmland.[91] There has been a good deal of controversy on this subject in rural areas throughout the country. Frequent media headlines carry an emotional appeal that has drawn attention to the phenomenon:

Foreigners Plowing Cash into Farmland
The Selling of California
Foreign Investors Flock to U.S. Farmlands
The Rich Foreigners: How Much of the South Are They Buying?

To be sure, there have been a number of highly visible purchases of rural land by nonresident aliens. The Prince of Lichtenstein owns a 10,000-acre farm in Texas' Red River area. A Saudi Arabian prince paid $5 million for entertainer Authur Godfrey's farm in the rolling hills of Virginia. French investors purchased 5,000 acres of

California's San Joaquin Valley—some of the most fertile acreage in the country. An Italian family bought 12,000 acres of Illinois corn land. German heirs to the Mercedes-Benz fortune have purchased a large cattle ranch in the picturesque Flint Hills of eastern Kansas.

These highly visible purchases notwithstanding, most experts agree that the amount of activity in the rural land market that can presently be attributed to foreign demand is, in the aggregate, quite small. But lack of accurate data, combined with anecdotal evidence that foreign ownership was rapidly increasing, led to passage of the 1978 Agricultural Foreign Investment Disclosure Act. The act requires foreign owners of agricultural land (defined to include cropland, grazing land, and timberland) to report both their holdings and any transactions to the U.S. Department of Agriculture.[92]

The most recent report under the act showed foreign ownership of 7.8 million acres, or slightly more than .6 percent of U.S. agricultural land.[93] In only four states did reported foreign ownership amount to more than 2 percent of the agricultural land: Maine (5.1 percent), Hawaii (2.4 percent), Utah (2.1 percent), and Nevada (2.1 percent). (The high figure in Maine is primarily due to ownership interests in forestland by a single Canadian timber firm.) Corporations, rather than individuals or partnerships, accounted for more than 80 percent of the foreign holdings. The largest of the holdings were by U.S. corporations and partnerships in which partial ownership interests were held by individuals or other entities from the United Kingdom, Luxembourg, Canada, West Germany, the Netherlands, and the Netherland Antilles. Individuals and corporations based in Canada, West Germany, the Netherlands, and the Netherland Antilles also reported significant holdings. Forestland accounted for 41 percent of foreign ownership, most of it land in Maine and in the southern states held by U.S. timber companies partly owned by foreign interests. Reported ownership by residents of OPEC nations was extremely small, although inspection of individual filings revealed that some holdings by persons from OPEC countries are attributed under the disclosure act to corporations or partnerships registered in the Netherland Antilles and other tax havens. The report indicated that, during the two-year period February 1979 to December 1980, foreigners made purchases of 1,740,544 acres and sales of 557,053 acres, for a net addition of 1,183,491 acres. Purchasers from the Netherland Antilles, Canada, and West Germany were particularly active during this recent period.

It has been estimated that only about 2 to 3 percent of the country's 1 billion acres of farmland changes hands in any given year and that generally more than half of those acres transferred are purchased by local farmers to enlarge their operations.[94] Tenants, retired farmers, local nonfarmers, and absentee owners make up the balance of a given year's transfers. Of the 21 million acres of farmland sold in 1980, foreigners' annualized net purchases of 600,000 acres amounted to about 3 percent.[95] This is about .05 percent (or one twentieth of 1 percent) of the nation's total stock of farmland. At this rate, it would take 20 years for foreigners to obtain even an additional 1 percent of this land.

Furthermore, not all purchases of farmland by foreigners result in permanent absentee ownership of land. Evidence from a 1979 USDA study showed that of the foreign purchases of farms since 1977 nearly one fifth were operated by those purchasers. An additional 12 percent were operated by professional farm managers, and 69 percent operated by tenants or renters. In the tenant-renter category, nearly half (46 percent) were operated by the previous owner or tenant, with the balance operated by new renters.[96]

To put foreign investment in perspective, between 1975 and 1978 the book value of all direct private U.S. investments abroad averaged nearly 4.4 times that of all similar foreign investments in the United States ($144 billion vs. $33 billion).[97] During 1979-80, reported purchases by foreigners of U.S. agricultural land were approximately $2 billion.[98] Overall, foreign investment in such properties as office buildings and shopping centers in *urban* areas in the United States is widely believed to be much higher than foreign investment, thus far, in rural land.

The extent of foreign investment varies widely among our own case-study areas. (The case studies appear in chapter 5.) Foreign holdings of rural land were zero or negligible in Douglas County (Illinois), Tyler County (Texas), and in Hardy and Pendleton counties (West Virginia). Plainfield (New Hampshire) showed no foreign owners, although there is a moderate amount of foreign investment in timberland in parts of New Hampshire not too distant. In Loudoun County (Virginia) foreigners owned more than 3 percent of the land in the county, with nearly all of the purchases made since 1975. In San Luis Obispo County (California), on the other hand, two extremely large foreign holdings of ranchland acquired in 1974-75 were liquidated in early 1980, without any gain, by their German owners.

Many foreign buyers appear to see U.S. land, particularly prime farmland, as a means of protecting capital against inflation, currency devaluation, and possible taxation or confiscation by their own governments. In this respect, U.S. land plays a role akin to that of gold in the wealthy foreigner's investment portfolio—an asset valued more for its intrinsic worth than for its ability to generate current income. As one California mortgage expert was quoted as saying of foreign buyers, "They don't want to get rich. They are rich. They just don't want to get poor."[99]

Until very recently, tax laws in the United States enhanced this capital-preserving attribute of rural land. Although foreigners have been liable for local property taxes, and for taxes on income generated from the land, under certain conditions they have been able to avoid paying U.S. tax on capital gains. And some foreign governments do not levy such taxes on their citizens.[100] Moreover, the ability to disguise the ownership of land through the use of nominee or corporate holders makes it possible for foreigners to invest funds that they might wish to keep secret from their own governments.

In 1980 Congress passed legislation extending capital gains taxes (at a minimum rate of at least 20 percent of the gain) to profits from foreign-owned real estate.[101] It remains to be seen whether taxes can be collected successfully from the foreign seller. The legislators rejected various bills to require that the buyer of U.S. property owned by a foreigner withhold tax on purchase payments, much the same way employers now withhold tax from employees' salaries.[102] Successful collection of capital gains taxes could somewhat dampen foreigners' demand for U.S. real estate.

Some observers have alleged that foreign buyers are willing to pay what local owners consider unreasonably high prices for rural land. For example, a real-estate agent in rural Virginia has commented:

> They [foreign buyers] come here and see these big manor houses and the rolling hills, and they just have to have some of it. . . . Why, what they paid for just plain old farmland . . . the most ridiculous price you can imagine.

Some U.S. owners have claimed that they cannot afford to buy additional acreage for farm expansion or that new farmers cannot afford to enter the market because foreign purchasers have driven up prices. And when farmers see land prices increase rapidly, even during uncertain swings in farm commodity prices, emotions can run high. An Illinois farmer and state representative put it strongly: "Land values go up even when farming isn't profitable, but we don't want *them* [foreigners] to benefit."[103]

To be sure, there is evidence that foreigners do pay premium prices, often in cash, for farmland, and any increased demand is bound to affect the price of land remaining in the local market. But documenting the impact that foreign purchases have on land prices is not easy.

First, the concept of "market value" in most rural areas is clouded by a number of issues: lack of accurate sales-price data; transfers of land between family members at prices not likely to reflect true market value; and the problem of comparing prices paid for land of differing quality.

Second, land markets, particularly rural land markets, are very localized. Thus, at least in the short run, foreign investors are not likely to have the intimate knowledge of the market necessary to obtain the very lowest local price, nor are they likely to understand fully the credit institutions that serve rural real-estate markets. Part of the premium prices paid could be a compensation for this general lack of information.[104] Moreover, prices of rural land in the United States are quite low by the standards of much of the rest of the world, possibly leading foreigners to show less resistance as prices rise. If foreigners do pay premium prices for land because they lack information, this is likely to persist only over the short run—that is, until information on market value filters through the various foreign investment networks, and foreigners become more familiar with the market. If foreign interest in U.S. rural land persists, U.S. real-estate brokers and others can be expected to provide increasingly sophisticated services, including market information, to foreign clients. There is no compelling reason to believe that foreign purchasers of rural land in the United States will continue over the long run to pay prices that are very much higher than those prevailing in the local market.

Third, if foreigners actually do pay more, this may be due to their desire for highly productive lands. As one account put it, "Foreign investors buy quickly, buy the best, and pay premium prices."[105] A 1975 study of foreign farmland purchases in Iowa, for example, found generally that foreign investors were careful buyers, willing to pay only what was considered a reasonable price for the land, and that the tracts purchased were top-quality farmland.[106] Finally, another researcher summed up the issue by noting that European investments in U.S. land were "not made for speculation, but forever."[107]

Speculation as a Source of Demand

Few land-market topics generate as much emotion as does the role of speculators. There is considerable disagreement about when speculative activity is taking place and even more about whether the speculator helps or hinders the efficient operation of the land market.

Land economist Raleigh Barlowe defines land speculation as "the holding of land resources, usually in something less than their highest and best use, with primary managerial emphasis on resale at a capital gain rather than on profitable use in current production."[108] A distinction is often made between "land speculation" (generally viewed negatively) and "land investment" (which has a positive or neutral connotation). The line between the two is a thin one, and there is considerable overlap. Both investors and speculators in land hope for a future sale at a profit. But in real-estate markets an *investor* generally expects benefits during the holding period as well as profits from the eventual sale of the property. The average of these returns over some period of time will be the result of the investor's analysis of risks, expected holding periods, transaction costs, the costs of holding, and available alternative investments. The *speculator,* on the other hand, can be said to have as his primary objective the profit he will make at time of sale; any benefits that might accrue during the holding period will be viewed as unexpected additions to the eventual returns from the sale. Speculators are more likely than investors to count on a change in the use of the land to provide the anticipated profits. As a consequence, speculators are likely to have shorter time horizons than investors.

It should be pointed out that the special characteristics of the real-estate market may blur any distinction made on the basis of length of holding period. For most commodities in which speculators are active, the market adjusts fairly quickly, the speculator's holding period is short, and the commodity is not altered while it is being held. But as Smith notes:

> Real estate markets often adjust slowly, the speculation cycle can be quite lengthy, and speculative activity is often combined with developmental activity. . . . [S]peculative holdings may be positive for a longer period of time and thus have a considerably longer than "temporary" influence on the price [of land].[109]

In this light, it seems difficult to distinguish clearly between the speculator and the investor without knowing the underlying motive for holding land. Perhaps the most easily observable distinction to be made in the case of rural land is between the buyer who intends to continue some productive use of the land (or to place previously vacant land into production) during the holding period and the buyer who merely holds land idle in anticipation of a future sale.

A person who has for many years been mostly concerned about the land's current output may at some point begin to pay primary attention to price appreciation. Many long-time rural landowners find themselves facing economic uncertainty, with no one in the family willing to continue to work the land. In such situations, the landowner may want to sell at the higher prices being bid by non-traditional buyers. As a result, it seems that many farmers have earned the label of "speculator" because they are waiting to sell their land at high prices to the newly arriving buyers from outside their local rural markets. More than once we have heard the traditional, long-time owner referred to as such. According to one rural resident in Virginia, "You can't draw a line between speculators and farmers. . . . When a farmer's land reaches a high enough price, he'll sell it, it's that simple." And in the words of another, "The farmer is more of a speculator than anyone else. When he's tired of farming or can't continue, he's not going to sell to another farmer anyway. . . . More than likely he'll subdivide it himself."

To be sure, many traditional landowners view their land as a "bank account" that they hope to tap upon retirement. But those who have used the land productively for so many years, often for generations, can hardly be called speculators just because economic conditions and views of the future have changed. The motives to sell may be the same, but the important motives at the time of original acquisition certainly do not fit a reasonable definition of speculation.

Assuming that some speculation does take place, does it perform any useful function? Some students of the land market take the position that speculation can contribute to a more orderly transition of land from one use to another, helping to smooth out market price fluctuations by maintaining a stock of land that is readily for sale.[110] Others hold the more critical view that speculation artificially inflates land prices because speculative holdings reduce the supply of land for immediate use. [111] Still others assert that speculation, even if it has the long-run effect of stabilizing price fluctuations, can trigger destabilizing behavior over the short run by non-speculators, such as the final users of the land. As these final users observe speculation and rising prices in the land market, one expert argues, they try to protect themselves by purchasing land earlier than they otherwise would, helping create a temporary excess demand.[112] This makes land prices, in the short run, rise to levels higher than they would reach in the absence of speculation.

Some will argue, of course, that distinguishing between speculation and investment is a mere academic exercise. But motives at time of purchase are a primary factor affecting the future uses of rural lands. Thus, whether the new buyers of rural land are speculators or investors is a useful distinction. When speculators are at work in a given area, a change in land use is in store. On the other hand, if investors are in the marketplace, existing uses may be more likely to continue, although perhaps not indefinitely.

A Mixture of Motives

We have seen that a broad array of types of demand for rural land can be isolated; some are growing rapidly. Yet rarely does the individual demander exhibit only a single motive. A recreationist may buy a plot of forestland primarily for amenity reasons. He may also at some time during his tenure sell off some timber. A farmer might own land primarily for its productive value. At the same time, he may be keenly aware of his land's usefulness as an inflation hedge.

The overview of demands that we have presented has highlighted demands for land for urbanization and for rural residential use; demands for resource production, particularly for cropland and high-quality softwood timberland; demands for land as a hedge against inflation; and recreational and amenity demands. Such demands affect large amounts of land, and they seem to have grown substantially during the past decade.

Next, we turn to the supply side of the land market. Poised against demand, and in many ways reacting to it, the supply of rural land makes its own contribution to determining how much rural land will cost, who will be able to own it, and in what size of parcel it will be held.

REFERENCES

1. U.S. Department of Agriculture, Soil Conservation Service, *Potential Cropland Study* (Washington, D.C.: Government Printing Office, 1977).

2. A. Allen Schmid, *Converting Land from Rural to Urban Uses* (Baltimore: Johns Hopkins University Press for Resources for the Future, 1968).

3. Rodney Christianson, Stephen Nelson, and Philip M. Raup, *The Minnesota Rural Real Estate Market in 1976* (St. Paul: Department of Agricultural and Applied Economics, University of Minnesota, 1977).

4. Tim B. Heaton, "Metropolitan Influence on United States Farmland Use and Capital Intensivity," *Rural Sociology*, vol. 45, no. 3 (Fall 1980), pp. 502-8.

5. The simple correlation, over 31 eastern and midwestern states, of 1976 per-acre farmland values and statewide population densities, was .875. The relationship remained strong and positive even when income per acre was held constant.

6. U.S. National Agricultural Lands Study, *Final Report* (Washington, D.C.: Government Printing Office, 1981), p. 31.

7. David Berry, "Effects of Urbanization on Agricultural Activities," *Growth and Change*, vol. 9, no. 3 (July 1978), pp. 2-8.

8. Raymond I. Dideriksen and R. Neil Sampson, "Important Farmlands: A National View," *Journal of Soil and Water Conservation*, vol. 31 (1976), pp. 195-97; Robert Coughlin, *et al.*, *Saving the Garden* (Philadelphia: Regional Science Research Institute, 1977), pp. 64-69; U.S. National Agricultural Lands Study, *Final Report*, p. 17.

9. Studies cited in Coughlin, *et al.*, *Saving the Garden*, p. 34.

10. Quoted in Jourdan Houston, "How're You Gonna Keep 'Em Down in New York After They've Seen Presque Isle," *Country Journal*, April 1977.

11. Outmigration from nonmetropolitan counties has fallen about 12 percent since the late 1960s. James J. Zuiches and David L. Brown, "Changing Character of the Nonmetropolitan Population, 1950-75," in Thomas R. Ford, ed., *Rural USA: Persistence and Change* (Ames: Iowa State University Press, 1978), p. 65. An excellent recent overview of nonmetropolitan population-growth data and a review of demographers' thinking on the matter may be found in Larry H. Long and Diana DeAre, *Migration to Nonmetropolitan Areas: Appraising the Trend and Reasons for Moving*, U.S. Census Bureau, Special Demographic Analyses CDS 8-2 (Washington, D.C.: Government Printing Office, November 1980). The authors observe that nonmetropolitan growth has not slowed since the 1974 energy crisis and that "nonmetropolitan areas in the aggregate are likely to continue, for a while anyway, to have higher rates of population growth than metropolitan areas."

12. Richard Lamb, "Intra-regional Growth in Non-Metropolitan America: Change in the Pattern of Change" (Paper presented to the annual meeting of the Association of American Geographers, April 1977). See also, Kevin F. McCarthy and Peter A. Morrison, *The Changing Demographic and Economic Structure of Nonmetropolitan Areas in the 1970s*, Rand Paper P-6062 (Santa Monica: The Rand Corporation, January 1979). Both studies showed higher growth rates in nonmetropolitan counties specializing in retirement and recreation.

13. Data cited in David L. Brown and Calvin L. Beale, *The Sociodemographic Context of Land Use in Nonmetropolitan America in the 1970s*, U.S. National Agricultural Lands Study, Technical Paper VI (Washington, D.C.: Government Printing Office, 1981), p. 20. For discussion of rural industrial growth, see Richard E. Lonsdale and H.L. Seyler, eds., *Nonmetropolitan Industrialization* (New York: John Wiley, Halsted Press, 1979) and Howard G. Roepke, "Industry in Nonmetropolitan Areas" (Paper prepared for the Association of American Geographers Con-

ference on Land Use Issues of Nonmetropolitan America, College Park, Maryland, June 23-25, 1980).

14. M.F. Petrulis, *Regional Manufacturing Employment Growth Patterns*, U.S. Department of Agriculture, Economics, Statistics and Cooperatives Service, Rural Development Research Report No. 13 (Washington, D.C.: Government Printing Office, 1979).

15. Writers have been discussing such communication advances for a number of years. At present, it appears that their introduction depends more on consumer acceptance and the solution of regulatory issues than it does on further advances in technology. See Starr Roxanne Hiltz and Murray Turoff, *The Network Nation: Human Interaction via Computer* (Reading, Mass.: Addison-Wesley, 1978); Robert Johansen, Jacques Vallee, and Kathleen Spangler, "Electronic Meetings: Utopian Dreams and Complex Realities," *The Futurist*, vol. 12, no. 5 (October 1978), pp. 313-20. For an account of how advanced communications could change rural living, see Alvin Toffler, *The Third Wave* (New York: William Morrow, 1980), pp. 210-23.

16. Johan B.W. Scholvinck, *Migration and Population Growth in Rural Areas of New York State*, A.E. Res. 79-1 (Ithaca: Department of Agricultural Economics, Cornell University, 1979).

17. Communes or "intentional communities," so heavily publicized in the late 1960s, still exist in some numbers, particularly in areas where marginal farmland is available at reasonable prices. One study guesses that they may have numbered as many as 25,000 or 30,000 in 1973. Judson Jerome, *Families of Eden: Communes and the New Anarchism* (New York: The Seabury Press, 1974), pp. 16-19.

18. U.S. Department of Agriculture, *Farm Real Estate Market Developments*, August 1980, p. 9.

19. U.S. Department of Agriculture, *A Time to Choose: Summary Report on the Structure of Agriculture* (Washington, D.C.: Government Printing Office, 1981).

20. Michael Boehlje and Steven Griffin, "Financial Impacts of Government Support Price Programs," *American Journal of Agricultural Economics*, vol. 61, no. 2 (May 1979), pp. 285-96.

21. Emanuel Melichar, "Capital Gains Versus Current Income in the Farm Sector," *American Journal of Agricultural Economics*, vol. 61, no. 5 (December 1979) pp. 1085-92.

22. U.S. Department of Agriculture, *Agricultural Statistics* (Washington, D.C.: Government Printing Office, 1979 and prior years), Table 678.

23. Franklin J. Reiss, "Trends in Returns to Farm Real Estate," in *Farm Real Estate*, North-Central Regional Extension Publication No. 51 (Champaign-Urbana: University of Illinois College of Agriculture, 1979), pp. 15-19; Board of Governors of the Federal Reserve System, *Agricultural Finance Databook*, April 1979.

24. For example, Scott claims that the long-run farmland capitalization rate has been relatively constant at about 3 percent and that it has been below the mortgage interest rate for the past several decades. John T. Scott, Jr., *Forecasting the Prices of Farmland for 1990*, Illinois Agricultural Economics Staff Paper No. 79 E-85 (Champaign-Urbana: University of Illinois, 1979).

25. Clark Row and Paul Teese, "Calculation of the Stumpage Value of 1977 Timber Removals in U.S." (Unpublished, U.S. Forest Service, Washington, D.C., 1980).

26. Robert Phelps, *Timber in the U.S. Economy, 1963, 1967, and 1972*, General Technical Report WO-21 (Washington, D.C.: U.S. Forest Service, 1980).

27. Marion Clawson, *The Economics of U.S. Nonindustrial Private Forests* (Washington, D.C.: Resources for the Future, 1979), p. 279.

28. For example, well-managed southern pines between ages 26 and 32 might be adding board feet of potential lumber at a rate of over 20 percent yearly. From yield data in Texas Forest Service, Circular 296 (1973).

29. Interviews with Richard Perkins, president, Land/Vest Inc., and John T. Hemenway, executive director, New England Forestry Foundation, September 1977.

30. U.S. President's Advisory Panel on Timber and the Environment, *Report* (Washington, D.C.: Government Printing Office, 1973), p. 39.

31. GNP deflator.

32. Karl Gertel and James A. Lewis, "Returns from Absentee-owned Farmland and Common Stock 1940-1979," *Agricultural Finance Review*, vol. 40 (April 1980), pp. 1-11.

33. Castle and Hoch have recently attempted to use expectations about future rates of land price increase in a model explaining current levels of land prices. In preliminary results, they find these expectations a relatively important component of farm real-estate values, though not as important as land income. Emery Castle and Irving Hoch, "Explanation of Farm Real Estate Prices, 1920-1978" (Unpublished, Resources for the Future, Washington, D.C., 1980).

34. For example, a survey of visitors and second-home owners in a recreational area in northern Michigan showed that both push and pull factors were prominently cited as motivating forces. Robert W. Marans, *et al.*, *Waterfront Living: A Report on Permanent and Seasonal Residents in Northern Michigan* (Ann Arbor: University of Michigan Institute for Social Research, 1976).

35. Probably the best measure of how rural recreation demand has been changing nationally is the visitation rate to federally owned recreation lands. Visits to the national parks rose from 13.9 million in 1950 to 62.0 million in 1977; national forest use rose from 39 million visitor-days in 1950 to 205 million in 1977. These figures represent very rapid growth during the 1950s and early 1960s (often in excess of 10 percent per year), then a slowing to rates of increase of less than 3 percent per year. *Statistical Abstract of the U.S., 1978*, p. 242, and U.S. Forest Service data. Due to changes in statistical procedures, long-term figures may not be exactly comparable, but the fact of rapid growth, then slowing, is indisputable.

36. U.S. Forest Service, "An Assessment of the Forest and Range Land Situation in the U.S." (Draft document, RPA assessment, U.S. Forest Service, Washington, D.C., 1978), pp. 85-86; 164.

37. National Association of Conservation Districts, *Inventory of Private Recreation Facilities, 1977* (League City, Texas: National Association of Conservation Districts, 1978).

38. For example, a 1977 edition of a national directory listed 8,283 privately operated campgrounds, only 16 more than it did in 1973. U.S. Forest Service, "An Assessment of the Forest and Range Land Situation," p. 109.

39. Richard L. Ragatz, *Private-Seasonal Recreational Property Development*

and Its Relationship to Forest Management and Public Use of Forest Lands (Report prepared for U.S. Forest Service Southeastern Forest Experiment Station, Asheville, North Carolina, 1978), pp. 34, 119.

40. The post-1970 growth in second homes will not be known exactly until housing figures from the 1980 census have been released. A recent estimate for Texas, where building has been particularly active, put growth at 30 percent (from 165,000 to 215,000) between 1970 and 1978. Bart Eleveld and Roger P. Sindt, "The Leisure Home," *Tierra Grande*, second quarter 1978 (Texas Real Estate Research Center, Texas A & M University, College Station, Texas).

41. U.S. Council on Environmental Quality, *Subdividing Rural America* (Washington, D.C.: Government Printing Office, 1976), p. 17.

42. *Ibid.*

43. INFORM, *Promised Lands* (New York: INFORM, Inc., 1977), vol. 1-3.

44. Larry K. Stephenson, "Primary Markets, Secondary Homes, Tertiary Locations: Subdividing the Southwest" (Paper presented at Association of American Geographers Conference on Land Use Issues of Nonmetropolitan America, University of Maryland, College Park, June 23-25, 1980), p. 6.

45. William K. Reilly, ed. *The Use of Land: A Citizens' Policy Guide to Urban Growth* (New York: Crowell, 1973), pp. 282-92.

46. See *Recreation Development Today*, February 28, 1978.

47. Interview with Gary Terry, executive vice-president, American Land Development Association, September 10, 1979.

48. Richard L. Ragatz, *Analysis and Overview of the 1979 ALDA Survey* (Paper prepared for the American Land Development Association, August 1979), p. 2.

49. "New Tactics to Sell the Changing Resort Market," *Housing*, vol. 35, no. 11 (December 1978).

50. Some profits appear to have been made, however, on second homes, especially in shoreline or winter sports areas.

51. Interview with Professor Frank H. Armstrong, January 24, 1980.

52. James M. Montgomery, "No Management or Some Management," in R. Dennis Child and Evert K. Byington, eds., *Southern Forest Range and Pasture Symposium* (Morrilton, Arkansas: Winrock International, 1980), p. 199.

53. "The Angry West vs. the Rest," *Newsweek*, September 17, 1979, p. 32.

54. Victor K. Ray, *The Corporate Invasion of American Agriculture* (Denver: National Farmers Union, 1968); Robert C. Fellmeth, *The Politics of Land* (New York: Grossman Publishers, 1973); William C. Osborn, *The Paper Plantation* (New York: Grossman Publishers, 1974).

55. James A. Lewis, *Landownership in the United States, 1978*, U.S. Department of Agriculture, Economics, Statistics and Cooperatives Service (ESCS) (Washington, D.C.: Government Printing Office, 1980). Regional data may be found in ESCS Staff Reports NRED 80-8, 80-11, and 80-12 (Washington, D.C.: U.S. Department of Agriculture, August 1980).

56. Lewis, *Landownership in the United States, 1978*.

57. U.S. Forest Service, *Forest Statistics of the United States, 1977* (Washington, D.C.: Government Printing Office, 1979). These holdings are reported for the "forest industry," which is generally, but not always, organized in corporate form.

58. As an oil-company official put it, "We don't disclose anything we don't have to." Quoted in Peter Meyers, "Land Rush: A Survey of America's Land," *Harper's*, January 1979, p. 60.

59. Rural America, "Corporate Invasion in Land Ownership" (Working paper, Rural America's Third National Conference on Rural America, Washington D.C., December 5-7, 1977).

60. Fellmeth, *The Politics of Land,* pp. 8-11.

61. Rural America, "Corporate Invasion in Land Ownership," p. 7.

62. Frank Popper, "Who Owns the Midwest? Who Cares?" *Acorn,* December/-January 1978-79, p. 6.

63. An excellent overview of this topic can be found in Philip M. Raup, "Corporate Farming in the United States," *Journal of Economic History,* vol. 33, no. 1 (March 1973), pp. 274-90.

64. Annual statistics of corporate income-tax returns from U.S. Internal Revenue Service, Department of the Treasury.

65. Kenneth R. Krause and Leonard R. Kyle, "Economic Factors Underlying the Incidence of Large Farming Units: The Current Situation and Probable Trends," *American Journal of Agricultural Economics,* vol. 52, no. 5 (December 1970).

66. U.S. Bureau of the Census, *Census of Agriculture, 1974,* vol. 11, part 2 (Washington, D.C.: Government Printing Office, 1977), p. II-3. Part of that increase has been due to changes in the census definition of a "farm," which has tended to exclude an increasing number of very small units. If we consider only units selling at least $2,500 worth of products yearly, average farm size rose from 407 acres in 1950 to 534 acres in 1974. Preliminary data from the 1978 Census of Agriculture show average farm size of 416 acres, but differences in data collection methods mean that the figure is not directly comparable to the 1974 results.

67. See Dan Cordtz, "Corporate Farming: A Tough Row to Hoe," *Fortune,* August 1972. A number of other references to the decline in corporate farming can be found in Kevin F. Goss and Richard D. Rodefeld, "Corporate Farming in the United States: A Guide to Current Literature, 1967-1977" (Unpublished, Department of Agricultural and Rural Sociology, Pennsylvania State University, 1978).

68. U.S. Congress, House, Committee on Agriculture, Subcommittee on Family Farms, Rural Development, and Special Studies, *Ag-Land Trust Proposal,* 95th Cong., 1st sess., 1977.

69. U.S. Congress, Senate, Select Committee on Small Business, *The Investment of Pension Funds in Farmland,* 96th Cong., 2nd sess., 1980.

70. See for example, J. Patrick Madden and Earl J. Partenheimer, "Evidence of Economies and Diseconomies of Farm Size," in A. Gordon Ball and Earl O. Heady, eds., *Size, Structure and Future of Farms* (Ames: Iowa State University Press, 1972); Warren R. Bailey, *The One Man Farm,* ERS Report No. 519 (Washington: Government Printing Office, 1973); Bruce F. Hall and E. Philip LeVeen, "Farm Size, and Economic Efficiency: The Case of California," *American Journal of Agricultural Economics,* vol. 60, no. 4. (November 1978), pp. 589-600.

71. Donn Reimund, "Form of Business Organization," in U.S. Department of Agriculture, Economics, Statistics and Cooperatives Service, *Structure Issues in American Agriculture* (Washington, D.C.: Government Printing Office, 1979), p. 133.

72. Don Paarlberg, *Farm and Food Policy: Issues of the 1980's* (Lincoln: University of Nebraska Press, 1980), p. 194.

73. By contrast, various levels of government own 28 percent of the commercial forestland; farmers own 24 percent; and "miscellaneous private owners" own 34 percent. Unpublished U.S. Forest Service data prepared for the 1980 Resources Planning Act assessment. Figures are for 1977 and exclude Alaska.

74. Information from annual reports and *Value Line Investment Survey*. The 14 are Boise Cascade, Champion International, Crown Zellerbach, Diamond International, Georgia-Pacific, Kimberly-Clark, Great Northern Nekoosa, Louisiana-Pacific, Mead, Potlatch, Scott Paper, St. Regis, Union Camp, and Westvaco. Here we follow the Forest Service convention of defining the timber industry as industrial manufacturers of wood products. Not included are firms—including such large landowners as the Southern Pacific and Burlington Northern railroads and some utilities—that sell stumpage to others for processing.

75. Pre-1977 data from U.S. Forest Service, *The Outlook for Timber in the United States* (Washington: Government Printing Office, 1974). Data for 1977 are from U.S. Forest Service, *Forest Statistics of the U.S., 1977* (Washington, D.C.: Government Printing Office, 1979). Between 1970 and 1977, the most notable increases in industry holdings were in New Hampshire (+19 percent), Louisiana (+18 percent), and Alabama (+10 percent). The most notable declines were in North Carolina (-23 percent) and Wisconsin (-18 percent).

76. For example, a national survey of industrial forest managers found that "applications of most techniques (especially growing-stock control, fertilization, and use of genetically improved stock) more than doubled from 1971 through 1974" with further increases expected. D.S. Bell, A.P. Brunette, and D.L. Schweitzer, "Expectations from Intensive Culture on Industrial Forest Lands," *Journal of Forestry*, vol. 75, no. 1 (January 1977), pp. 10-13.

77. Boise Cascade's experience is recounted in Herman Boschken, *Corporate Power and the Mismarketing of Urban Development: Boise Cascade Recreation Communities* (New York: Praeger, 1974).

78. In 1979 the parent company, International Paper, sold the oil subsidiary to Mobil Corporation for $800 million.

79. Champion International Corporation, 10-K statement, 1976. See also St. Regis Paper Company, 10-K, statement 1976; Westvaco Corporation, annual report, 1976; International Paper Company, 1st quarter report, 1977.

80. For example, large companies have lost land to government purchase for Redwood National Park, Voyageurs National Park, Big Thicket National Preserve, and the Tennessee-Tombigbee Waterway.

81. Acreage data are taken from form 10-K filings with Securities Exchange Commission, annual reports, Moody's Manuals, and other sources. Cited from Peter Meyer, "Land Rush: A Survey of America's Land," *Harper's* (January 1979), p. 47. The 10 companies are: Shell Oil, Union Pacific Corporation, Amax, Inc., International Paper, Diamond Shamrock Corporation, General Crude Oil, Standard Oil of California, Gulf Oil, Standard Oil of Indiana, and Exxon.

82. Calculated from data supplied by Independent Petroleum Association and U.S. Geological Survey.

83. Standard Oil Company (Indiana), annual report, 1977.

84. J. Davitt McAteer, *Coal Mine Health and Safety: The Case of West Virginia* (New York: Praeger, 1973).

85. John Gaventa, "Land Ownership and Coal Productivity," in Steve Fisher, ed., *A Landless People in a Rural Region* (New Market, Tennessee: Highlander Center, 1979), pp. 108-118. The data are described as "incomplete" and "subject to some error, though the pattern it establishes remains correct." In 1981 the Appalachian Regional Commission released a massive study of landownership patterns in 80 counties in six Appalachian states. The report contains a great deal of information about the extent of corporate ownership in those counties, as well as

statistical analyses indicating a relationship between corporate holdings (as well as absentee ownership and concentrated ownership in general) and various indicators of poverty and underdevelopment. The study was released too late for the findings to be incorporated fully into the text of our book. See Appalachian Land Ownership Task Force, *Land Ownership Patterns and Their Impacts on Appalachian Communities* (Report submitted to the Appalachian Regional Commission, Washington, D.C., 1981).

86. James Flanigan, "Acreage—the Newest Game in Oil," *Forbes*, September 1979, pp. 116-20.

87. David L. Ostendorf, "Food or Fuel: The Conglomerates Dig for a New Cash Crop," *The Progressive*, April 1979, pp. 44-46.

88. Allen D. Hertzke, "The Impact of a Growing Energy Industry on Agriculture: Northwest Colorado Case Study" (Unpublished, Cornell University, January 1977).

89. U.S. President's Commission on Coal, *Coal Data Book* (Washington, D.C.: Government Printing Office, February 1980), p. 123.

90. Jeff Hoover and Jack Doyle, "Synfuels vs. Agriculture" (Working paper, Environmental Policy Institute, Washington, D.C., 1980), pp. 58-59.

91. Kenneth Cook, "Foreign Investment in U.S. Farmland," Issue Brief #IB78064 (Congressional Research Service, The Library of Congress, Washington, D.C., September 1978).

92. The Act requires that the acquisition or transfer by any foreign person or other legal entity of any land in or to be used for agricultural purposes (including crops, timber production, livestock and poultry raising) be reported to the Secretary of Agriculture within 90 days of the transaction. A civil penalty of up to 25 percent of the fair market value of the owner's interest can be assessed for failure to report the transfer or acquisition.

93. J. Peter DeBraal and T. Alexander Majchrowicz, *Foreign Ownership of U.S. Agricultural Land, February 1, 1979 through December 31, 1980*, Economics and Statistics Service, U.S. Department of Agriculture, Agriculture Information Bulletin No. 448 (Washington, D.C.: Government Printing Office, 1981). National-level data are as of December 31, 1980; state data and ownership-by-country data are as of February 1, 1979.

94. U.S. Department of Agriculture, *Farm Real Estate Market Developments*, July 1978.

95. This calculation somewhat overstates foreign purchases as a percentage of total agricultural land sales, since some timberland not in farms was sold in 1980 but not included in the 21-million acre total.

96. Larry Walker, "Foreign Investment in U.S. Farmland" (Unpublished paper, U.S. Department of Agriculture, Economics, Statistics and Cooperatives Service, Washington, D.C., July 1979).

97. Figures supplied by U.S. Department of Commerce, Bureau of Economic Analysis.

98. J. Peter DeBraal and T. Alexander Majchrowicz, *Foreign Ownership*, pp. 37-38. The figure on value of foreign-owned land presented in that report must be adjusted downward somewhat to account for the fact that some foreign ownerships involve only partial interests.

99. Quoted in Hal Rubin, "The Selling of California," *California Journal*, December 1978, p. 409.

100. See Donald Abramson, Karl Gertel, and James A. Lewis, "Federal Taxation of and Incentives for Foreign Investment in U.S. Real Estate: An Introduction with Emphasis on Farmland," NRED Working Paper Series Number 47 (Washington, D.C.: U.S. Department of Agriculture, Economics, Statistics and Cooperatives Service, 1978).

101. Public Law 96-5499, signed December 5, 1980.

102. Bills under consideration in 1979-80 were HR 1372, HR1494, HR6007, and S208.

103. "Pastaville, Ill.: Farmland Investment in the U.S. by Europeans," *Newsweek*, May 22, 1978, p. 56.

104. Paul W. Barkley and LeRoy F. Rogers, "Problems Associated with Foreign Ownership of U.S. Farmland," in U.S. Congress, Senate, Committee on Agriculture, Nutrition, and Forestry, *Foreign Investment in U.S. Agricultural Land*, 95 Cong., 2nd sess., 1979.

105. *Ibid.*, p. 33.

106. Michael Boehlje, *et al.*, *Non-Resident Alien Investment Activity in Iowa Farmland, A Preliminary Analysis*, Economic Report Series (Ames: Department of Economics, Iowa State University, September 1975).

107. Cited in "Foreign Investors Flock to U.S. Farmlands," *Business Week*, March 27, 1978, p. 80.

108. Raleigh Barlowe, *Land Resource Economics*, 3rd ed. (Englewood Cliffs, N.J.: Prentice-Hall, 1978), p. 201.

109. Lawrence B. Smith, "The Ontario Land Speculation Tax," *Land Economics*, vol. 52, no. 1 (February 1976), pp. 1-12.

110. James Gillies and C.E. Elias, "Some Observations on the Role of Speculators and Speculation in Land Development," *UCLA Law Review*, vol. 12 (March 1965), pp. 789-99.

111. Bruce Lindeman, "Anatomy of Land Speculation," *Journal of the American Institute of Planners*, vol. 42, no. 2 (April 1976), pp. 142-52; Jack E. Adams and Bruce Lindeman, "Speculation in Undeveloped Land," *Appraisal Journal*, vol. 47, no. 2 (April 1979), pp. 218-26.

112. Smith, "The Ontario Land Speculation Tax."

CHAPTER 3

The Supply of Rural Land

It may seem odd to speak of a changing supply of land. After all, the amount of land within the borders of the contiguous United States has been essentially fixed since the Gadsden Purchase in 1853. What is constant, however, is only the *physical amount* of land in the sense of surface area. Given enough time for adjustments to be made, the supply of land in an *economic* sense varies considerably.

The economic supply of land can vary in two ways. First, there can be variations in the amount of land available for particular uses, such as farming, forestry, or recreation. Land supply in this sense depends heavily on the natural characteristics of land, on technological and economic opportunities for using it, and on institutional constraints.

Second, there can be variations in the amount of land offered for sale. The amount offered for sale naturally depends on the prices that those demanding land are willing to pay, but it is also very much influenced by the desires and values of existing owners and by various demographic factors affecting these owners.

The supply of land for particular uses and the supply of land for sale are interrelated. Suppose that a new use for rural land is developed—for example, using land to produce biomass for conversion into liquid fuel. Some current landowners will react to this new opportunity by going into the biomass business. Other owners will not. The latter may be too old to go into a new business, or may lack requisite capital or skills, or may simply find change unacceptable. Their land will not be supplied to the new use unless it is eventually sold to some new, more entrepreneurial, owner. Thus, the impact that a new or newly increased market demand will have on land prices and land uses depends not only on current owners' willingness to change uses but also on their willingness to offer their land for sale to others.

Land Supply for Alternative Uses

At present, privately owned rural land in the United States is about evenly divided among cropland, forests, and range or pasture. The proportion of land in each use varies from one part of the country to another. Cropland dominates the Midwest; the Pacific Northwest specializes in forests and rangeland. These differences in use are mostly due to the differing natural characteristics of the land. Yet these characteristics can often be altered so as to increase the supply suitable for a given use—although sometimes this is very expensive or difficult technologically. Swampland can be drained, forests cleared, and arid land irrigated. Moreover, although the location of a parcel of land cannot be changed, it is very common for surrounding uses to change in ways that profoundly alter the parcel's "locational" advantages. Thus, extension of a railroad or an expressway may greatly increase the supply of land easily accessible to a city center.

Physical and Technological Factors

Historically, man-made changes in the physical character of the U.S. land base have been enormous. They have included felling the original hardwood forests of the eastern states, plowing the midwestern prairies, and irrigating large areas of the Southwest. This kind of physical change still occurs to a surprising extent. Between 1967 and 1975 some 270 million acres (about 19 percent of all nonfederal land) were converted from one major category of use to another, mostly shifting back and forth among crops, pasture, and forest, but with significant conversion to urban uses.[1]

Frequently, several kinds of offsetting land-use shifts may occur simultaneously. For example, between 1967 and 1975 some 24 million acres of rural land, mostly agricultural, were converted to urban, built-up or reservoir uses, a loss rate of nearly 3 million acres each year.[2] Yet production lost from this land was more than offset by an increase in the amount of existing cropland used for crops, which rose from 333 million acres in 1969 to 376 million in 1977.

Some of the major past changes in land use have come in response to shifting patterns of demand for various products or services. As new demands raise the prices people are willing to pay for a particular use, landowners are induced to increase the quantity of land supplied to that use. At times, the quantity supplied can be increased relatively easily. For example, when export demand for

U.S. grain increased sharply during the 1970s, the supply of land to this use adjusted rapidly. This was possible because idle cropland and pastureland could easily be planted in wheat, corn, or soybeans.

More fundamental land-use shifts—say, from soybeans to rice, or from hardwoods to pines—often require substantial capital investment in special equipment, machinery, irrigation, fertilizers, and so on. These shifts also often require that the landowner acquire new production or management skills. Because of the need for capital investment and for the development of new skills, it may take some time before the quantity of land available for the new use is actually affected.

Changes in the amount of land that is available for a given use may also occur because of a technological change or because of major government projects. Such developments have historically been responsible for many of the most important physical changes in the U.S. rural land base. The supply of land suitable for residential development, for example, was greatly expanded when advances in transportation technology and improvements in metropolitan highway systems facilitated development of lands on the fringes of cities. Federal water projects, complemented by the invention of new types of irrigation equipment, have opened millions of acres of formerly arid western land to crop and pasture uses. New methods of controlling livestock diseases have greatly expanded the amount of southern land usable for grazing. In the future, it is possible that improved drilling and mining technologies (their development induced by higher energy prices) will increase the supply of land available for energy-related uses.

Technological change can expand the supply of forestland by increasing productivity per acre. One possibility is through "supertrees," genetically selected varieties that grow to maturity more rapidly than average, or that produce higher-quality wood. Increased fertilization of forestland can also increase output, while new methods of pest control show promise of reducing insect and disease damage to growing trees.

Yet there are limits to what technology can do to overcome the natural limitations of land. Nowhere is this more clear than in the increased concern over the retention of adequate supplies of naturally fertile cropland to meet future domestic and worldwide demands for food.[3] As one observer has put it, "There are two ways of increasing food supply. One is by increasing yields, and the other is by increasing the cropland area."[4] For the past several decades,

79

increased yields have mitigated the effects of increased food demands on the amount of land devoted to crops. Since about 1920, in fact, the percentage of land in crops has remained roughly constant while we relied on increases in output per acre to supply growing demands for products. But, according to researchers, we may have reached an important crossroads in the evolution of food production. The chief of the Soil Conservation Service notes that "... yields per acre have continued to increase, but at a decreasing rate, suggesting that available agricultural technology may have reached the point of diminishing returns."[5]

There are many reasons for the growing uncertainty over increased yields. Climatologists have suggested that the phenomenal yields of the 1950s and 1960s were as much a consequence of favorable weather conditions as they were of the application of heavy investments in agricultural technology. According to one observer, "These analysts are concerned about the possibility that we may now be entering a period of more erratic weather patterns which could adversely affect agricultural production."[6] Climatic shifts can decrease agricultural productivity in some parts of the country and increase it in others. This raises the question not only of how much cropland will be required for food and fiber production, but, importantly, of where it is located.

Higher costs of energy are another limiting factor. In the past, soil deficiencies were largely overcome and yield increases achieved through heavy reliance on relatively cheap fertilizers, pesticides, irrigation, and other measures. Now, however, high-cost energy means higher prices for all energy-related inputs. Crosson and Brubaker conclude that "real prices of energy, fertilizer and irrigation water, the key ingredients of land saving technologies, are likely to rise to the end of the century, in contrast to their behavior in the two decades prior to the early 1970s."[7] Rising prices, or even physical scarcity, will make these ingredients less desirable as a means of overcoming land's natural limitations for agriculture.

In the future, if technological progress slows, or if land-saving inputs become more expensive, physical and natural attributes will become more important as determinants of the value of land. For example, if irrigation water becomes costly, land that receives abundant natural rainfall will become more valuable. As noted above, the supply of land in the sense of surface area is fixed. Technology can improve many of the physical attributes of land, and can even substitute other inputs for land, but it cannot extend the physical supply of land indefinitely.

THE SUPPLY OF RURAL LAND

Institutional Factors

The supply of land for different uses is also affected by land-use controls, tax regulations, and other institutional factors. Historically, land markets in the United States have operated under the dominance of the fee-simple ownership system. Under this system, a landowner has the legal right to use his land as he sees fit, subject only to certain public interventions, such as eminent domain and the police power, intended to protect the rights and welfare of the general public. Earlier in our history, little restraint was exercised on the private use of land, particularly rural land. As one researcher has noted, "A person could cut his forest without thought or care about growth of a new forest—and many did; or a farmer could farm without concern over soil erosion—and many did."[8]

In the first half of the 20th century, a small number of public and community institutions, including local weed-control districts, drainage and irrigation districts, and soil conservation districts, began to affect the use of rural lands. During the 1960s and 1970s, the environmental movement focused attention on the effects of land-use change on environmental systems. Most recently, the rapid conversion of rural lands to nonrural uses has highlighted the concern of many over possible future shortages of land to meet increasing food and fiber demands. Both environmental protection and resource conservation have been reflected in legislation affecting the use of land. The institutional effects on the rural land supply have come from three levels—federal, state, and local.

The Federal Level. Federal influences on land use are generally indirect, but can be quite significant. One count found that approximately 137 federal programs had an impact on land use, the most prominent being the Department of Housing and Urban Development's planning grant programs, the 1972 Coastal Zone Management Act, the Clean Air Act, the Water Pollution Control Act, the Rural Development Act, and the Department of Agriculture's soil conservation programs.[9] Also important is federal tax policy, although most tax measures (for example, tax subsidies to agriculture, or deductibility of property taxes and mortgage interest from taxable income) operate more on the demand for land in various uses than they do on the land supply. Despite some congressional sentiment for greater federal activism in such areas as preservation of agricultural land, it is likely that any federal land-use policy will continue to recognize the primacy of states and local government in direct regulation of land use. One research study characterized current and anticipated federal initiatives as "federal . . . legislation to encourage states to exercise states' rights."[10]

The federal government directly affects land supplies by its extensive holdings and new purchases of land for the National Park System, National Wildlife Refuges, and National Forest System. The result in some local areas is to reduce the supply of land available for uses other than those desired by federal policy. The use of an area's remaining privately owned land may be affected, as demands for certain uses are met by a reduced supply. Another result may be an increase in the price of private land. This occurred in one of the areas we studied—Tyler County, Texas. There, land purchases by the federal government for the Big Thicket National Preserve reduced the local land supply, which was already limited by the large holdings of the area's timber industry and under pressure from population growth.

The State Level. Under the U.S. Constitution, ultimate authority over the use of private land is retained by the states. Traditionally, states have delegated their regulatory powers to local governments. Since about 1970, however, there has been an increase in statewide regulations affecting the use of "critical areas," "environmentally sensitive" lands, and other rural lands.[11] Many states now have programs for coastal zone management and mining. Particularly relevant to the rural land market have been programs aimed at stemming the conversion of farmland to nonfarm uses. For example, nearly all of the states have passed legislation to reduce taxes on property used for agriculture.[12] Other states are experimenting with exclusive agricultural zoning, or with agricultural districts, which offer tax and other advantages to farm operators.

In theory, such programs should raise the amount of land supplied to uses considered socially desirable—or at least keep that supply from declining. Most research tends to agree, however, that tax incentives alone are not great enough for the voluntary retention of agricultural lands when significant development pressures exist.[13] Regulatory programs, in contrast, such as Hawaii's state agricultural zoning or California's coastal land-use controls, are generally believed to have affected land supply, although the impacts have not been precisely measured.

The Local Level. It is at the local level that the supply of land is most affected by institutional controls—generally in the form of zoning or subdivision regulations. For the most part, rural land use remains relatively unregulated compared to land use in urban areas. But, in response to heightened competition among land uses, zoning, subdivision controls, and local planning are becoming increasingly familiar in rural areas.

One major impetus has been the creation, usually with federal aid, of regional planning agencies that serve several rural counties. Another has been the insistence by a number of state governments that all localities improve their land-use regulations. In some states, this has been achieved by requiring that local land-use goals, and regulations to achieve these goals, be established in accordance with region-wide general plans. But perhaps the greatest spur to local land regulation has simply been local recognition that rural jurisdictions are no longer immune to growth and its problems.

Land-use regulations, whether state or local, affect the supply of land in three major ways. First, they can change the amount of land legally available for a particular use. A county might, for example, designate a limited amount of land fronting on highways for commercial use. If the amount designated is less than the amount that would have been supplied in an unregulated market, prices of land enjoying the commercial designation would rise.[14] Meanwhile, the price of land suitable for commercial use but not designated as commercial would be likely to fall. Similarly, a county might zone a large portion of its area as exclusively agricultural. If some of this land would otherwise have been supplied to other, more intensive uses, the regulation would depress the price of the land.

Second, land-use controls may specify minimum parcel sizes for particular uses. A county might decree that no rural building lot may be less than five acres in size. This would prevent owners of some larger parcels from splitting them into smaller ones, thus limiting the total number of building lots that could be supplied. As a result, land sellers would find their per-acre prices lower than before, while buyers would face the prospect of having to buy more land than they otherwise might have purchased. Zoning officials can easily create an "oversupply" of one permitted use or size of parcel relative to the demand for it, lowering the land's market price, while driving up the price of other lands for which there is a greater demand than the amount permitted by zoning.[15]

Third, land-use regulations may determine the way in which land is used for a particular purpose. This would occur, for example, if a county or state decreed that all new rural houses must be hooked up to sewer lines at the builder's expense. Such a law would lower the price of land far from existing sewer lines relative to that of land that could be most cheaply connected.

Tax policies are another institutional factor potentially affecting the supply of land for alternative uses. Local property taxes are one of the costs of holding land and, if sufficiently high, may motivate landowners to change uses. In most truly rural jurisdictions, however, property-tax levels are quite low compared to taxes in urban jurisdictions, and probably do not have much effect on land use.

In one rural West Virginia county, for example, a local attorney and real-estate agent told us about a 310-acre tract he purchased in the late 1960s for about $20 per acre. At an assessment rate of $1.67 per $100 of value, his property taxes on the 310 acres amount to only $100 per year. He estimated the land to be worth a total of about $77,000 if divided into three parcels. And further out in West Virginia a county assessor provided the following scenario:

> In 1966, a 26-acre parcel was valued for taxes at $200. With the county's assessment rate of $0.75 per $100 of value, the owner paid $1.50 per year in property taxes. The land was sold in 1976 for $11,500, and sold again four months later for $14,000. The property continues to be carried on the assessment rolls at $200, and the new owners are still paying a total tax bill of $1.50 per year.

Even in the Midwest, where rural property taxes may be several dollars per acre per year, rates are generally low compared to the land's agricultural income.

It is in rapidly changing rural and exurban areas, where pressures are strong for conversion of land to nonrural uses, that property taxes can have a significant effect on the supply decisions of owners. In many instances, owners of properties that have been reassessed to reflect sharply increased market value claim that they will be forced to sell to developers or speculators because current uses do not generate enough cash flow to pay the taxes. The tax burden can be sufficient to cause either the conversion of land to more intensive nonresource uses or sale of the land to someone who can pay the taxes out of nonland income. For example, in some parts of southern California where the fresh-flower industry provides an important part of the agricultural output, yearly property taxes incurred by some landowners have amounted to more than three times the annual revenues generated from leasing the land to flower growers. Economic pressures to convert this land to housing are intense.[16] At the same time, however, owners of land with urbanization potential are often most reluctant to submit to the contractual limitations imposed by many of the state programs offering preferential assessment to farmland.

The Supply of Land for Sale

A second way to look at land supply is to consider the amount of land that is made available for sale over any given length of time. This is almost impossible to measure directly, but can be described in terms of the amount of land actually transferred (which is, by definition, the quantity supplied at the then-current market price). The amount of land transferred in any one year is typically quite small compared to the total quantity of land. On the New York Stock Exchange, the amount of common stock sold yearly has recently averaged 21 percent of the total amount of listed securities outstanding. By contrast, since 1970 the number of farms transferred yearly averaged less than 5 percent of the total number of U.S. farms. And only two thirds of those transfers were voluntary sales, as distinguished from gifts, foreclosures, or estate settlements.[17]

The low rate of land turnover reflects the intensity of the desire of current owners to keep their land. This desire, in turn, is a function of the owners' demographic characteristics and their expectations. At any given time, the current owners expect their parcels to provide them with certain resources or benefits. Thus, they exert a "reservation demand" to hold land for the services it provides. Over time, as new sources of demand arise, current owners of the resource have to decide whether to make their land available to the market. Each existing owner has a "reservation price," the minimum price at which the temptation to sell overcomes his desire to hold his land. Differences between the reservation prices of owners and the prices being bid by new demanders are negotiated in the land market, and, if the two coincide, a transaction results. If reservation prices are high and the demand for land is increasing, transactions are likely to take place at steadily rising prices.

The reservation demand for land is somewhat different from the reservation demand for other goods. If the owner of 100 shares of General Motors stock is offered a price only slightly higher than the current market price, he is likely to offer his stock for sale without hesitation. Commodities such as securities have little sentimental value and, in any case, can be replaced easily. On the other hand, a farmer who is offered a good price for his land can take advantage of the offer only if he is willing to find a new place to live, and perhaps a new source of livelihood. Seldom, particularly on the rural-urban fringe, can he find a replacement parcel that is similar in most respects to what he owns. As one researcher put it:

> For farmers on the fringe, the fact that a specific parcel of land is irreproducible in supply has important consequences. Farmers cannot reproduce the land parcels they offer up to the market for sale. Their decision to sell may require not only a change in location but the sacrifice of a desirable lifestyle as well.[18]

Another factor heightening the strength of reservation demand is the owners' personal attachment to their land. As one rural lawyer noted:

> People in this county look on land as something almost sacred. They will pass it on to their children and maybe even tie it up so the children can't sell it.

An elderly landowner, asked what would induce her to sell the 300 acres she and her husband owned, responded strongly:

> Absolutely nothing. No way would we sell. It's in our will that the place will stay in our family as long as there's a Thompson alive. The children wouldn't part with it either. It's been paid for for years, so there would never be a reason to sell it.

Even newer, urban-oriented owners of rural land may quickly develop such an attachment to their land that they become very reluctant to consider offering it for sale, regardless of the price offered. A former high government official explained that "nothing conceivable" would cause him to sell all or part of the 600 acres of rural West Virginia land that he purchased some 10 years ago:

> Now the land is not being put to its highest and best use, I guess, in public terms. Sometimes we feel a little selfish about it...[But] we've no interest in what's happening to the land values, except that it will increase our taxes some. But when you expect to hang onto it for your own lifetime, and hope that your heirs will be of the same mind, land values are not matters of importance. We would under no conceivable circumstances and at no price imaginable sell it.

People who hold rural land solely for investment do not have such ties of residence, or livelihood, or even sentiment. Nevertheless, they must also consider that it may not be easy to replace the parcel they have sold.

Reservation demand is also affected by expectations of future price movements. Experience with past increases is likely to induce landowners to believe that prices will continue to rise in the future. Unless death, retirement, or some other personal reason intervenes, landowners are likely to believe that their land will appreciate in the future at least as fast as an alternative investment. Thus, the inducement to sell as the price goes up may be dampened if price rises incline owners to be even more optimistic about the future. An official of Japan's National Land Agency believes this to be true of Japanese farmers on the urban fringe, who, he says, "tend not to sell in response to price increases because they believe the price will go even higher. And as prices go higher they are able to generate whatever funds they need by selling off only a small portion of their land."[19] Similarly, a study of rural areas outside Sacramento, California, found landowners "overly optimistic about their ability to achieve an exceptionally favorable sale."[20]

Demographic Factors

One of the most notable factors affecting the supply of rural land for sale is that the landowner's personal circumstances will often take precedence over economic forces in the decision to sell land. For example, in many rural land markets the supply of land is controlled by a few long-time landowners who are reluctant to place land on the market. Estate sales and sales associated with the illness or retirement of the owner are major sources of land supply, but these have more to do with demographics and life cycles than with market phenomena and prices. In one rural Virginia area, a real-estate broker commented, "Divorce and death are the big things here...divorce is how we got our farm." A recent survey of farmland owners in three Vermont counties found that health and age were the two most important reasons for selling land. Ranking only third was the price response, "received a good offer for the land."[21] Nationally, sales by estates and by retired farmers accounted for one third of all farmland sales in 1979-80.[22]

The death of a landowner is particularly important in motivating land sales, because of estate taxes. For many estates that include valuable landholdings, total federal and state tax liability exceeds the liquid assets in the estate.[23] Heirs may be forced to sell all or part of the land component just to pay the taxes. Federal legislation passed in 1976 lessened this pressure for some farmland owners by permitting heirs who remain actively engaged in agriculture to pay estate taxes on use value rather than market value. Another provision of that law gives some farm heirs up to 15 years to make estate tax payments.

To reduce the estate tax burden on their heirs, some rural landowners deed over a portion of their property during their lifetime, under a provision of tax law allowing tax-free gifts of up to $3,000 per recipient per year. Some farmers have placed their land into a trust or a corporate entity solely to facilitate such a gradual transfer.[24] Thus, the supply of rural land available in the market at any given time may often be as much a function of the age of landowners and the extent of their estate tax planning as of current prices being offered by buyers in the market.

It is often difficult to predict whether economic or demographic factors will predominate when an owner must decide whether to sell a piece of land. But, considering the land supply as a whole, both factors are clearly important. For example, one study investigated the supply response of owners of vacant parcels of five or more acres on the fringe of two North Carolina cities.[25] The researchers found that, over a 10-year period, the greater the proportion of nearby land that had already been developed, the more likely it was that a parcel would be sold. This finding would tend to support the proposition that the supply of land to the market does respond to demand. But the researchers found that demographic factors were also important: land was more likely to be sold if it was owned by an absentee owner, or by a retired person, or by a person who had held the land either for a very short time or a very long time.

A recent major study of the land market at the fringe of six U.S. and Canadian cities also found both demographic and economic factors were important determinants of land supply. It reported that:

> The evidence suggests that personal factors to a large extent determine whether a particular parcel is sold and which land is available for purchase at any given point in time. It also appears that as development becomes more imminent, the opportunities for capital gains resulting from rising land values, as well as the cash flow difficulties caused by increasing property taxes, induce some owners to sell or subdivide that would not have otherwise.[26]

The tension between economic and noneconomic motivations is often reflected in the ambivalence expressed by many long-time landowners when they are asked how they—or their heirs—would react to an offer to buy their land. We asked one elderly Virginia farmer what he intended to do with the land he had purchased in 1929 for $75 per acre:

> I'll probably keep it until I die, then pass it on to my wife if she outlives me....I don't know, though, depends on the market. I've given some of it to my kids, and they'll probably keep it until someone comes along who wants it more than they do."

A West Virginia real-estate broker noted that the reluctance of farmers to sell melted when newcomers were willing to pay what he called "extortion prices" for land—far above what it was worth for farming or forestry. Finally, in rural California a local title-insurance executive smiled as he noted the willingness of many to pay such high prices:

> People come in here every day and ask, "What's my land worth? What price should I ask?" I ask them if they *have* to sell it, and if they say no, I tell them, "Put any damned price you want on it. Some people will think you're crazy, but someone will come along and think it's a steal."

Overall Supply Response

Overall, the response of the rural land supply to changing demand conditions perhaps can best be described as "sluggish." The supply of land for particular uses is by no means completely predetermined by the physical characteristics of land. But it is limited by the fact that major supply increases for new uses often require substantial capital investment or technological change. The supply of land offered for sale in the market is also severely limited—by the strong reservation demand of present owners.

These two forces interact. Current owners often lack the capital to make productivity-increasing investments and the skills needed to take advantage of technological change. Yet these owners are frequently reluctant to sell land to people more willing and able to make changes in use.

The amount of time allowed for supply to adjust thus becomes a particularly important consideration in describing rural land supply. Given enough time, some of the technological and financial barriers to land use can be overcome. And, with time, old landowners will pass on and new owners, whether part of the family or from an urban center, will gain control of rural properties.[27] But it takes time for the land supply, both for new uses and for the sale market, to adjust fully to rapidly changing demand prices. Institutional factors may further limit the rapidity of adjustment.

We do not mean to suggest that the supply of land, even in the short run, is completely unresponsive to changes in the price offered. But we do believe that the dramatic rises in rural land prices over the past two decades have depended not just on the pressure of new and more varied demands, but also on the sluggishness of the rural land supply.

Prices act as a market signal for the allocation of land resources among uses and among users. If these signals are distorted over the short run due to the sluggish nature of supply, the result can be higher land prices, which then set a floor price for future rounds of bidding in the land market. Only if the supply of rural land were to become more "elastic"—that is, were to respond more to market prices than to the peculiar and personal circumstances of individual owners of the supply—could we expect rural land-use change to occur with relatively stable prices.

REFERENCES

1. U.S. Department of Agriculture, Soil Conservation Service, *Potential Cropland Study*, Statistical Bulletin No. 578 (Washington, D.C.: Government Printing Office, 1977).

2. *Ibid.*

3. A review of the constraints on expanding U.S. agricultural production can be found in Sandra S. Batie and Robert G. Healy, eds., *The Future of American Agriculture as a Strategic Resource* (Washington, D.C.: The Conservation Foundation, 1980).

4. Lester Brown, "Viewpoint," in Charles E. Little, ed., *Land and Food: The Preservation of U.S. Farmland* (Washington, D.C.: American Land Forum, Spring 1979), p. 27.

5. Norman A. Berg, "Viewpoint," in Little, ed., *Land and Food*, p. 19.

6. Little, ed., *Land and Food*, p. 24. See, generally, John Gribben, *Forecasts, Famines and Freezes: Climate and Man's Future* (New York: Walker and Co., 1976).

7. Pierre Crosson and Sterling Brubaker, "Resource and Environmental Impacts of Agriculture in the United States" (Unpublished, Resources for the Future, Washington, D.C., December 1980), p. 77.

8. Marion Clawson, *America's Land and Its Uses* (Baltimore: Johns Hopkins University Press for Resources for the Future, 1972), p. 28.

9. Susan L. Kendall, "Existing Land Use Programs," Urban Land Institute *Environmental Comment*, vol. 22, no. 6 (1975).

10. W.E. Anderson, *et al.*, "Perspectives on Agricultural Land Use Policy," *Journal of Soil and Water Conservation*, vol. 30, no. 1 (January/February 1975), pp. 36-43.

11. For a review of state land-use controls, see Robert G. Healy and John S. Rosenberg, *Land Use and the States*, 2nd ed. (Baltimore: Johns Hopkins University Press for Resources for the Future, 1979).

12. Thomas F. Hady, "Differential Assessment Programs for Agricultural Land," in Soil Conservation Society of America, *Land Use: Tough Choices in Today's World* (Ankeny, Iowa: Soil Conservation Society of America, 1977), pp. 114-21.

13. See Robert Coughlin, *et al.*, *Saving the Garden* (Philadelphia: Regional Science Research Institute, 1977).

14. In many areas, however, the amount of land zoned for commercial or industrial use is far greater than any conceivable demand could support.

15. Several interesting zoning scenarios are presented in William K. Reilly, ed., *The Use of Land: A Citizens' Guide to Urban Growth* (New York: Crowell, 1973).

16. From data compiled through interviews in San Diego County, California, as part of The Conservation Foundation's California Coastal Commission study.

17. U.S. Department of Agriculture, *Farm Real Estate Market Developments*, various issues.

18. Michael Knute Bertelsen, "Supply Response and the Land Conversion Process in the Rural-Urban Fringe" (Ph.D. dissertation, Department of Agricultural Economics, Virginia Polytechnic Institute, 1979), p. 3.

19. Remarks of Mr. Sekikawa, deputy director of land price division, Japan National Land Agency, at a U.S. Department of Housing and Urban Development seminar, Washington, D.C., November 14, 1980.

20. David E. Hansen and S.I. Schwartz, "Landowner Behavior at the Rural-Urban Fringe in Response to Preferential Property Taxation," *Land Economics*, vol. 51, no. 4 (November 1975) pp. 341-54.

21. Robert L. Bancroft, *et al.*, *Attitudes Toward Preserving Agricultural Land in Vermont*, Miscellaneous Publication 93 (Burlington: University of Vermont, Agricultural Experiment Station, 1977).

22. U.S. Department of Agriculture, *Farm Real Estate Market Developments*, August 1980.

23. There is some evidence that this claim, frequently made by heirs, is exaggerated. A study of 179 Illinois estates containing farmland showed average land value of $226,000; estate tax due of $68,000; and average liquid assets of $74,000. In 17 percent of the cases, the heirs sold the land. Harold D. Guither, *Death, Taxes and Transfer of Farmland* (Champaign-Urbana: Department of Agricultural Economics, University of Illinois, 1979). On the other hand, Sutherland and Tedder have argued that estate taxes pose special problems for people who have inherited forestland. See Charles F. Sutherland, Jr., and Philip L. Tedder, "Impacts of Federal Estate Taxation on Investments in Forestry," *Land Economics*, vol. 55, no. 4 (November 1979), pp. 510-20.

24. It is easier to make a yearly transfer of a partial stock interest than it is to make a transfer of an acre or two of land.

25. Edward J. Kaiser, *et al.*, "Predicting the Behavior of Predevelopment Landowners on the Urban Fringe," *Journal of the American Institute of Planners*, vol. 34, no. 5 (September 1968), pp. 328-33.

26. H. James Brown, Robyn Swaim Phillips, and Neal A. Roberts, "Land Markets at the Urban Fringe: New Insights for Policymakers," *Journal of the American Planning Association* (Forthcoming, 1981).

27. The 1978 USDA landownership survey found that 28 percent of currently owned land had been acquired in the period 1960-78; 26 percent in 1960-69. Regionally, in recent years the highest land turnover has been in the Midwest, the lowest in the Deep South.

CHAPTER 4

How the Land Market Works

Supply and demand have little meaning unless they can be expressed in markets. No matter how eager the buyer, or how desperate the seller, their wishes will not affect either the price or use of land unless buyer and seller are aware of each other and have the opportunity to make a transaction. The term *market* describes where and how buyers and sellers of a commodity get together to make exchanges.

The land market has no central institution, like the stock exchanges in New York or Chicago's commodity exchange. Rather, a land market occurs in any of the varied spots where buyers and sellers get together to exchange money for land.[1] Some rural parcels are traded at auction, some through real-estate brokers, others through direct contact between buyer and seller. Land may be "put on the market" by formal advertisement or listing, or may be sold only after a buyer has taken the initiative and sought out a potential seller. Thus, the land market is not a single entity but encompasses an array of places and mechanisms.

How Land Is Traded

There are four principal ways by which rural land is transferred from one owner to another: (1) nonmarket transfers, such as by gift or inheritance; (2) sale by private agreement; (3) sale through a real-estate broker; and (4) sale at auction by oral or sealed bid.[2]

Nonmarket transfers account for a significant proportion of total land transfers. The 1978 USDA landownership survey found that 21.2 percent of all privately owned acreage had been acquired through gift or inheritance.[3] Another 16.6 percent had been purchased from relatives, presumably by private agreement, and often at lower than market prices. Altogether, just 62 percent of the current stock of land has been acquired by its owner through purchase from a nonrelative.

We do not know what proportion of rural land is transferred by each of the three major methods of sale. The relative importance of each varies somewhat according to the type of land and the part of the country where the transaction takes place. Certainly, sales by private agreement occur for all types of rural land. A farmer who wants a parcel of land adjoining his property may be able to negotiate with an aging neighbor to buy it. Often, the buyer may have leased the land in years past. Such neighbor-to-neighbor transactions are advantageous to the buyer in that he is likely to have first-hand knowledge of the capabilities and limitations of the parcel. On the other side, the seller avoids paying a real-estate broker's commission and sometimes gains flexibility in timing the sale. Private sales are also likely to occur between owners of rural recreational properties. The bulletin board at any large place of employment, for example, will probably contain one or more advertisements for a country lot or second home. Other private sales take place by direct advertisement in newspapers or magazines (*Country Journal, Country, Yankee*) that are likely to be read by people seeking rural property.

Real-estate brokers sell some farms, and probably the bulk of timber, recreational, and development land. Typically charging the seller a 6 to 10 percent commission, the broker may be a local, general-purpose agent who sells everything from homes in town to commercial buildings. Or he may be a specialist in rural properties. Of the specialists, some deal only in a small geographic area; others deal in regions or nationwide. One large brokerage in Boston, for example, sells country properties throughout northern New England.

Two national real-estate firms, United Farm Agency (Kansas City, Missouri) and Strout Realty (Springfield, Missouri), have for many years produced illustrated catalogs of available country properties.[4] Published semiannually in editions of hundreds of thousands, and advertised in popular magazines, the catalogs list commercial farms, hobby and recreational farms, and country homes. Actual sales are made by affiliated local real-estate brokers, who also provide the listings. Each firm has more than 600 affiliates nationwide.

Another national organization is the Farm and Land Institute, part of the National Association of Realtors. Its 8,000 members exchange information about available rural properties in a variety of ways, including state, regional, and national "marketing sessions." In 1980, the Institute began a computerized listing service, enabling the 100 members who subscribe to gain instant access to one another's listings via telephone-linked computer terminals.[5] It is impossible to calculate the proportion of all rural land sales made through such regional or national mechanisms. Probably it is fairly small.

Firms specializing in farm management and in forest management also frequently act as real-estate brokers. One firm, based in the Midwest, but selling land nationwide, has advertised farmland and grazing land in European publications, seeking to attract overseas investors, for whom it will select, manage, and resell properties. Some of the large forest-management companies in the Deep South have promoted a similar service. One is reported to be trying to have all of its foresters registered as real-estate agents.

Another important means of buying and selling rural land is the auction sale. Auctions tend to occur most frequently when demand is strong and many potential bidders can be expected to attend. Often, auctions are used to settle estates. Typically, an auctioneer handles properties in several counties, advertising individual sales through handbills, mailings, and newspaper advertisements. The sale sometimes involves not only land, but also buildings, farm machinery, sawmills, and even household goods. The auctioneer usually is paid some proportion of the value of the property sold— between 1 and 3 percent is a common figure. This gives the auctioneer an incentive to publicize the sale widely and to try to encourage buyers to bid vigorously against one another, driving up the final price.

Land auctions are generally thought to set the local "market price" for particular types of land. Auctions tend to attract knowledgeable local buyers, and some outsiders, and offer participants a chance to see publicly what their neighbors are willing to offer for land. Oral auctions are best suited for small to medium-sized parcels of relatively standardized land, the kind that will attract more than a handful of serious bidders. Larger parcels—very large timber tracts, for example—are more likely to be sold by sealed bid among a nationwide list of large investors, such as timber companies. Advertisements often are placed in trade journals or in financial papers like *The Wall Street Journal* in an effort to gain the attention of the widest possible audience.[6]

Financing Land Purchases

Borrowed money is the lifeblood of all real-estate markets. Because real estate "wears out" slowly, or not at all, lenders have traditionally been willing to make loans for a relatively high proportion of a property's value and to allow repayment over very long periods of time. This happens in the rural market as in other land markets, although the types and sources of financing are rather different from those for urban homes or commercial properties.

The 1978 USDA landownership survey asked people who had bought land during 1975-77 how they had financed their most recent purchase.[7] Only 17 percent of the acreage purchased had been bought in an all-cash transaction. Most commonly the purchase was financed by the seller (37 percent). In some cases, the seller would take a mortgage on the land, just as a bank does in most home sales. For 18 percent of the acreage purchased, however, the seller used a "land contract." Under this arrangement, while the buyer makes installment payments, the seller retains title to the land. The buyer may use the land in the interim, but he does not receive title until he has made either the entire payment or a stipulated portion of it. Other common sources of finance found in the survey were Federal Land Banks (16 percent), commercial banks and savings and loan associations (19 percent), government-agency loans (4 percent), and insurance-company loans (2.8 percent).

Thanks to data series collected for many years by the U.S. Department of Agriculture, we know most about the role of financing in the farmland market.[8] The percentage of sales of farmland in which debt was incurred has more than doubled over the last three decades, rising very steadily from 44 percent in 1944 to 90 percent in 1979. On average, farmland purchasers borrow 79 percent of the purchase price, up from 73 percent in 1970 and 58 percent in 1944. The increasing use of credit combined with rapidly rising land prices has resulted in a soaring debt for farm real estate. In 1979 that debt stood at $72 billion, having doubled in the previous six years. Nonetheless, real-estate debt amounts to only 12.3 percent of the market value of farm real estate. The debt is very unevenly distributed. Most farmers, having bought their land years ago at low prices, owe little or nothing. Others, particularly younger farmers, or those with rapidly expanding operations, owe a great deal.[9]

Sellers are the most common source of loans for purchases of farmland, although this source has been falling slightly in relative importance in recent years. Seller financing has some advantages for both parties to the sale. The major attraction for sellers is a tax break. If deferred payments are accepted from the buyer, the seller pays capital gains tax only as payments are received, rather than immediately on completion of the sale.[10] Moreover, many farmers consider this a convenient and secure retirement annuity.

Seller financing also offers some flexibility to buyers. For example, sometimes a buyer can obtain a favorable interest rate or repayment schedule in exchange for agreeing to pay a higher per-acre price for land.[11] At other times, buyers may find that institutional financing is not readily available (either because of personal circumstances or the economy in general), making a mortgage or land contract from the seller a desirable alternative. Buyers do face certain risks when purchasing under a land contract. Because the seller retains title, for example, he may under some conditions pledge the land as security for further debt. Buyers can protect themselves from this kind of risk by retaining the right to approve any new loans against the property or by recording the sale contract as a public record.

Second in importance to sellers in financing farmland purchases are the Federal Land Banks. Although these 12 banks and their 540 local Federal Land Bank Associations were founded with federal money in 1916, they are now cooperatively owned by their borrowers. The banks raise money by selling bonds in national financial markets, then relend the proceeds to farmers. (Interest on the bonds is subject to federal, but not state, income tax.) At the end of 1979, the Federal Land Bank Associations had more than 548,000 loans outstanding, for a total value of $31 billion. This represented a recent, dramatic rise in the participation of these institutions in the farm mortgage market.

Insurance companies, on the other hand, which once financed as much as a quarter of all farm real-estate purchases, have decreased in importance in recent years. In part, insurance companies have found more attractive rates of return in lending for urban commercial projects; in part, they have faced stiff competition from the Federal Land Bank Associations. Commercial banks and savings and loan associations have captured about 13 percent of the farm mortgage market, a share that has held steady for many years.

The terms of loans made for the purchase of farmland, and for other rural land, differ greatly from lender to lender. Some loans (by banks and insurance companies, for example) may be for periods of

15 years or more. On the other hand, loans made by the seller of the property may be for only a few years. Payments may be level over the life of the loan, or the buyer may pay only interest for a few years, then face a lump sum "balloon payment" of the balance. Interest rates may be fixed over the term of the loan or may, as is the practice of the Federal Land Bank Associations, vary according to current market interest rates.

Information is sparse on how purchases of rural land other than farmland are financed. Individuals' purchases of timberland are often made with cash or seller financing. Timber companies tend to finance through bank loans, insurance company loans, or bonds, and a given loan is not necessarily secured only by a single piece of property, but by the overall credit of the company. One student of the timber industry has noted that over the years large companies have been encouraged by lending institutions to add to their timberland base. Apparently, banks feel more secure in lending for a new sawmill or paper mill if a large tract of land is also part of the package.[12]

People buying lots in large recreational developments often are financed by the seller under a land contract. The buyer may benefit from such contracts insofar as they sometimes extend for a period of several years.[13] But the buyer does not receive a bank appraisal, which might point out the embarrassing difference between the lot's appraised value and its selling price. Moreover, if there is a default on any payment, the seller (the developer) may be legally entitled to resell the land to someone else and keep all payments made on the contract to date of default.[14]

Financing for second homes is more varied, with some loans arranged through the developer, some through local banks, and some through the buyer's own, generally urban, bank. Bank mortgages are easier to get for rural second homes than for vacant building sites. Even so, such mortgages typically entail a shorter term, higher downpayment, and higher interest rate than does a regular home mortgage. Buyers, therefore, sometimes refinance their primary residence, using the "cashed-out" equity to make a cash payment for the vacation home.

The purchase of raw land with development potential offers many opportunities for creative approaches to financing. Lindeman has described how chains of speculative transactions, each based on seller financing, have artificially inflated land prices.[15] Development land is sometimes also financed through limited partnership syndications, in which a single organizer (the "general partner") secures equity financing from individual investors whose liability is limited to the amount of their investment.[16]

Economic Characteristics of the Land Market

In economic terms, a market (or market area) is defined as "the area within which the price of a commodity tends toward uniformity, allowance being made for transportation costs."[17] Economists are in the habit of analyzing actual markets by comparing them with an ideal "perfectly competitive" market. The ideal type is characterized by *many buyers and sellers, homogeneity and divisibility of the product, and perfect information*. The present market for gold is a reasonably good approximation of a perfectly competitive market: there are tens of thousands of active buyers and sellers around the world; the product is standardized (homogeneity); one can buy by the ounce or by the ton (divisibility); and price and other relevant information are spread almost instantaneously on financial wires and sophisticated private information systems.

More or less the same situation obtains in markets for the common stock of large companies, for grains, and many metals. The "market areas" for these commodities are nationwide or even worldwide.[18] The market price for a share of General Motors stock or an ounce of gold will scarcely differ in the smallest American town, in New York, London, or Sydney. Whenever there are short-term or localized imbalances of supply and demand, the operation of competitive markets is aided by the activities of a group of very active speculators, called arbitragers, who buy and immediately resell commodities so as to profit from momentary price differences. In their attempts to profit from such transactions, arbitragers tend to eliminate price discrepancies rapidly.

Recent analysis of securities markets has paid great attention to the "efficient market hypothesis," which holds that "new information is widely, quickly, and cheaply available to investors, that this information includes what is knowable and relevant for judging securities, and that it is very rapidly reflected in securities prices."[19] This hypothesis, which has been given much empirical support in studies of the price behavior of listed common stocks, implies that, if some important new event influencing the prospects of a firm were to occur (or even be suspected), the price of the firm's stock would make its full adjustment almost instantly. The same kind of adjustment behavior is likely to characterize other highly competitive markets.

How Land Is "Different"

The rural land market is quite different from the perfectly competitive ideal. The reasons for this stem directly from some basic characteristics that distinguish land from other commodities.

First, land is fixed in location. A Minnesota farmer cannot buy a piece of Tennessee cropland and take it home. He must use it where it is. Thus, many potential bidders, particularly if they want to use the land themselves, will not bid on land outside a quite limited geographic area.[20] Moreover, a potential seller cannot move his land to another area where there may be more buyer interest. Land's fixed location greatly restricts the number of potential buyers and sellers.

Second, land is not homogeneous. It is probably saying too much to claim that each piece of rural land is unique—a drive across Iowa cornfields or Georgia pine plantations would provide some excellent counterexamples—but differences among parcels, even within the same locality, can be large. Land can differ in fertility, in climate and rainfall, in slope, in the kind of vegetation it contains, or does not contain, in road access, and in scenic beauty, to note just a few possibilities. In many cases, a parcel includes structures that account for a significant portion of the parcel's total value. Also contributing to differences among parcels is the way in which each is situated in relation to existing land uses. One parcel may be on the edge of a city; another may abut a national forest; still another may have nothing but farms for neighbors. Each of these factors can have important impacts on the value of land and on the most probable uses of land.

The great differences among individual parcels of land magnify the importance of information in the land market. An investor who orders 100 shares of General Motors common stock through his stockbroker has a firm understanding of what he is buying; all of the 288 million shares of General Motors common stock are identical. A land buyer, on the other hand, must be concerned about soil quality, access, water supply, the soundness of structures, local zoning regulations, and a host of other characteristics of the individual parcel and of the local economy. In general, the closer a bidder is to a given parcel, the easier it will be to get such information. Thus, even for the person who does not intend actually to occupy the land, the rural land market is localized. And even the local buyer must devote quite a bit of time to gathering information if he wishes to make an informed offer.

Land is also typically sold in relatively expensive units. Although it is nearly as simple to buy 10 shares of common stock as it is to buy 10,000, land typically comes onto the market in parcels selling for thousands or tens of thousands of dollars. Land is certainly divisible, as our discussion of parcellation amply illustrates (see chapter 1), but it is not easily divisible, nor infinitely so.[21]

In some cases, the cost of land severely limits the potential number of buyers. A 19,000-acre tract of timberland in northwest Louisiana was recently put on the auction market for a minimum bid of $20 million. At that price, only large forest-products companies would be willing or able to purchase it.[22] Similarly, a 204-acre tract of good farmland near Champaign, Illinois, could not be split because of drainage problems. Normally, neighboring farmers would have been eager to bid on the land, but the more than $500,000 required to purchase it was simply beyond their means. Eventually, the land was bought by an Italian-controlled corporation. Even for smaller parcel sizes, the cost of land is such that at any given moment only a few members of a community may be willing or able to purchase it.

Land is also subject to certain transfer costs that are not applicable to other assets. Each time land is sold, legal costs must be incurred to prepare new transfer documents and to search the title. Property taxes must often be prepaid; moreover, sometimes special transfer taxes are levied by state or local government. Fees for surveys and for mortgage placement must sometimes be paid. Brokerage fees, generally paid by the seller, tend to be much higher in percentage terms than those applied to the transfer of stocks or bonds. In addition to the monetary costs of transferring land, the process tends to be time-consuming: purchase or sale certainly does not approach the speed or convenience of trading a share of stock. The combination of high transfer costs, the high price of individual pieces of property, and imperfect information flows means that arbitragers are tempted to act only when there are very large price discrepancies from parcel to parcel or from place to place.

These characteristics have made land markets not only distinctive, but difficult to study, which is why much less is known about rural land markets than about securities markets or commodities markets. Since each piece of rural land is different, and the yearly rate of turnover is relatively low, it is difficult to obtain an accurate measurement of price behavior by inspecting sales records. Because land is fixed in location, sales and ownership records have historically been kept at the local level, often in a form that is inconsistent from place to place. And because the characteristics of land vary from place to place (for example, Iowa cropland is, on average, very different from California cropland), it is difficult to know whether variation in prices between places is due to differences in land quality or to the imperfect transfer of information. These and other factors have severely inhibited quantitative research on the operation of land markets, particularly beyond the local level.

Segmented Markets

Taking into account the special characteristics of land, and the trading behavior observed in actual land markets, we can say that the rural land market is *a series of interconnected local markets, segmented geographically and by type of land, and joined together by fitful and imperfect flows of information and capital.* The rural land market is not a perfectly competitive national market; nor is it a series of balkanized local markets, in each of which the price of land is completely independent of the price in any other.

Geographic Segmentation. In the main, competition between local buyers and sellers sets the price of rural land. Yet if the price in a given locality becomes unusually low, outsiders will eventually take an interest, bringing new money to the market and driving up the price.[23] The availability of unusually cheap recreational land in the Ozarks and in northern New England during the 1960s, for example, caused urban bidders to enter the market, paying more than local people could afford or were willing to pay. Similarly, high prices for cash-grain land in the Midwest have caused a few farmers to consider selling out and moving their operations to cheaper, but nearly as productive, land in the Mississippi Delta states.[24] People involved in the transfer process, such as bankers, auctioneers, appraisers, and real-estate agents, probably play a leading (but as yet unstudied) role in the transmission of price information and the elimination of gross disparities in prices of similar parcels.

It is likely that growing sophistication of real-estate investors and real-estate brokers, along with growing population mobility, is slowly increasing the flow of information about rural land, making the market more unified and "national" in scope. Today's farmer, for example, is likely to be more highly educated, better read, and more widely traveled than were previous generations of farmers. He is accustomed to selling crops in national and international markets and therefore has an incentive to learn about crop production in other parts of the country. Participation by foreign investors and by national corporations, although limited in extent, is another force tending to break down the localization of land markets.

One researcher points out that land investors can significantly raise their return for a given level of risk by geographically diversifying their investments. He observes:

> Although land investments historically have been highly regional by nature, the scope of the real estate market—increasing in size and sophistication—is opening new possibilities toward a truly national market in which diversification offers significant risk-reduction possibilities.[25]

But even with sophisticated buyers and sellers and computerized listing services, the factors that make land "different" will still work strongly toward localized land markets.

Localization and the informality of information flows mean that the rural land market is probably fairly slow in reacting to new information. But changes in important conditions affecting land eventually do get reflected in land prices. Announcement of a new highway or industrial plant, an increase in the price of farm crops, or the boom-and-bust cycle of the range-cattle industry all make land prices in the affected regions rise or fall.

The adjustments seem to take time. For example, almost immediately after the announcement in mid-1972 of an agreement boosting U.S.-Soviet wheat trade, farmland prices in grain-producing areas of the Midwest began to quicken their rate of increase. But prices continued to rise vigorously over the next four years, even though grain prices fell back sharply. It appears that, unlike securities markets, the rural land market requires a certain amount of time to digest new information and to reflect it fully in land prices.[26]

Segmentation by Type of Land. In addition to the geographic segmentation of land markets, there is also evidence of separate, but interconnected, markets for various types of land. It is our hypothesis that there are three basic rural land markets: an agricultural land market, a timber/recreational land market, and a development land market. Each is characterized by a particular group of potential buyers and by a distinct pattern of information flows between buyers and sellers. Thus, when a piece of cropland or grazing land is auctioned off on the steps of a rural county courthouse, the bidders are likely to be quite different from those who would attend the auction of a piece of timberland or be interested in the sale of a rural parcel with potential for development as a housing subdivision or a shopping center. Figure 4.1 shows graphically how these three markets for privately owned rural land are distinct, yet inter-connected.[27]

FIGURE 4.1

THREE PRINCIPAL RURAL
LAND MARKETS

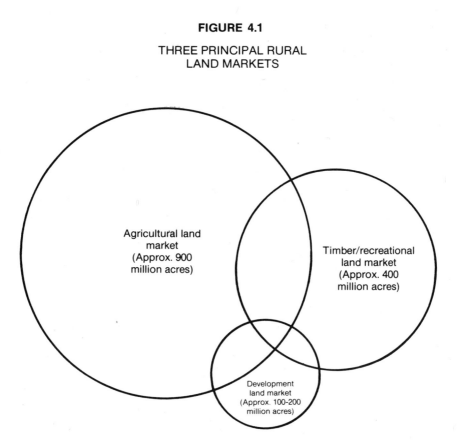

Agricultural land
market
(Approx. 900
million acres)

Timber/recreational
land market
(Approx. 400
million acres)

Development
land market
(Approx. 100-200
million acres)

The three types of land markets are differentiated by natural characteristics that make it difficult or expensive to convert land from one use to another, by the kinds of expertise needed to manage various types of land profitably, and by the sizes and prices of parcels that typically come on the market.[28]

Agricultural land can be converted to timberland by planting or by simply waiting for trees to grow. And some timber tracts can be converted to cropland or pasture by clearing—although it is expensive. Moreover, about 95 million acres of woodland are part of operating farms and are thus likely to come to the market along with agricultural land. But, in general, timberland is too steep, too wet, or too infertile to be very useful as farmland, while most cropland is too valuable to warrant growing trees on it.

The skills needed to be a successful farmer are also rather different from those needed, for example, to operate a forest. To reap the full benefits of a good tract of cropland, the buyer must either actively farm it or find a tenant for it. A timberland owner, on the other hand, can live in the city, visit his land only occasionally, and secure the same financial return as he could if he lived on the property. Thus, different types of land tend to appeal to different groups of buyers.

Cropland is generally not as suitable for recreational use as are other types of rural land. The best cropland tends to be flat and well drained, with few scenic views and few streams or natural bodies of water. Cropland and good-quality pastureland are also usually too expensive to attract buyers whose major interest is hunting, hiking, snowmobiling, or other recreational pursuits. Potential buyers of recreational properties are therefore more likely to show up at sales of timberland or marginal farmland than they are when land currently used for commercial crop production is being sold.

Land with development potential can come from either agricultural land or timberland. Timberland is usually cheaper and possibly more scenic, but agricultural land tends to be more economical to service with roads and sewers.[29] Only a small fraction of either type of land will likely be developed. The explanation, in most cases, is accessibility. For land near growing population centers or with highway frontage, some bidders will be speculating on the possibility of development. Land that is otherwise nearly identical but that is more remote will not draw a single bidder interested in development, and will generally sell at a far lower price.

A final characteristic distinguishing the three land markets is the average size of parcel and average size of transaction. Table 4.1 shows some characteristics of land sales during 1977-79, classified according to whether the probable use five years from date of sale was likely to be agriculture, forestry/recreation, or development (rural residence, subdivision, commercial, industrial).[30]

Land with development potential tends to sell in the smallest-sized parcels but for the highest prices per acre. Most types of development simply do not require parcels as large as those needed for most resource-based uses. And developers are typically able to pay much more for land than are farmers or forest operators.

Table 4.1
Characteristics of Land Sales by Types of Land

Probable Use	Size of Parcel	Price per Acre	Price of Parcel
Agriculture	332 ac.	$629	$209,000
Forestry/recreation	229	427	98,000
Development	146	943	138,000

Source: USDA, *Farm Real Estate Market Developments.*

Agricultural land tends to sell in relatively large parcels and, because it is generally flat and fertile, for fairly high per-acre prices. The combination of parcel size and high prices means that the typical transaction for agricultural land involves a large total amount of money. One notable exception to the tendency to transfer large parcels is found in the Corn Belt. Much of the land there is quite uniform, and farmers can rather easily farm several scattered fields, creating a demand for smaller parcels to be added to existing farms. Moreover, the high per-acre price of this exceptionally fertile land means that an entire farm unit sells for several hundred thousand dollars. There is thus some tendency to sell land in parcels of 20 to 80 acres rather than in the larger units common to farm sales elsewhere in the country.

Forest and recreation land probably shows the greatest variation in size of sale. Sales can be as small as a few acres or as large as tens of thousands of acres. Because wooded land tends to be of poorer quality than farmland, prices per acre are generally much lower than for farmland. Parcels heavily stocked with merchantable timber can sell for as much as several thousand dollars per acre, but generally no more than a few hundred dollars are attributable to the value of the land itself.

There is a small amount of empirical work that tends to support the existence of market segmentation by type of land. Crowley studied three rather different rural areas in Oregon: a grain-farming area, an urban-influenced county in the populous Willamette Valley, and an urban- and recreation-influenced area in mountainous southwestern Oregon. He found that "six property characteristics were of varied importance in explaining differences in land prices among areas studied."[31] For example, income per acre was a significant determinant of value in the grain area but not in the urban-influenced area. Crowley interprets his findings as "evidence supporting the existence of several types of agricultural land markets."

Using similar methods, Barrows and Dunford found that the determinants of land values in northern Wisconsin counties (mainly recreational) were significantly different from those in southern Wisconsin counties (agricultural and urban).[32] Chicoine, studying land in exurban Chicago, found that sale prices of farmland located within 35 miles of the metropolitan center were determined differently from prices of farmland lying at a greater distance from the city.[33]

These studies, among the very few that have examined the market for more than one kind of land, lend credence to the market segmentation theory. But much more research is needed before market segmentation can be described with confidence. More work is needed, for example, on how different types of buyers obtain information, on determinants of interregional variations in prices of nonfarm rural properties, and on the costs of converting rural land from one use to another. It is to be hoped that the recent improvement in national data on rural landownership and land use and the increased interest in the rural land market in general will begin to motivate researchers to do more imaginative empirical studies of how rural land markets actually operate.

Partial Rights. Besides geographically segmented markets and the three major types of landownership markets we have just described, there are also separate markets for certain partial rights in land. A land transaction involves more than physical space. It involves a set of legally defined ownership rights. Lawyers refer to this set as the "bundle of rights." The transfer of land from seller to buyer may convey all of the rights in the bundle or merely a portion of them. For example, mineral rights are very often split from surface rights. Once divided, surface and mineral rights may be resold in entirely separate transactions.

In arid parts of the West, water rights have become increasingly important as a component of land value. In Utah, for example, the water rights attributable to an acre of irrigable land—rights that can be severed from the land and used elsewhere—are worth as much as 10 times what the land would be worth without water rights. Other rights can be severed permanently from the land through easements. For example, a utility company may purchase the right to run a high-tension line over a farmer's land, or a pipeline beneath its surface, or a conservation group can acquire a scenic easement.

Leases and rental agreements make it possible for a landowner to allow his land to be used without giving up his ownership interest. Agricultural leases typically run from year to year, either on a cash-rent or share-of-crop basis; timber leases may allow a timber company to use an owner's land over a period of 30 to 60 years. Other common leases involve grazing rights, oil and gas rights, and hunting rights. A landowner may also sell someone an option to buy his land, good for a limited period at a specified price. An option allows the owner to use the land, but gives the buyer of the option the opportunity to capture any future appreciation in land value.

The most important of the markets for partial rights is the farmland rental market, which presently affects about one third of all farmland.[34] Most cropland is rented on a share-of-crop basis (usually the landlord gets between one quarter and one half the net product), but cash rentals appear to be growing.[35] The income that can be generated by renting land can be quite significant. Although poor-quality grazing land is rented for only a few dollars per acre per year, the best quality Corn Belt cropland can command as much as $150 per acre.

Like the landownership market, the rental market is localized. The most common type of lessee is a farmer who already owns some land, but who is unwilling or unable to pay the high prices needed to buy more. By renting, the farmer foregoes the benefit of future price appreciation, but is able to devote more of his capital to machinery and operating expenses. Naturally, the farmer is not interested in renting land that is too far removed from his own base of operations. It is simply not economical to move his equipment more than a few miles. One study has found the mean distance from the farm headquarters to scattered (owned and rented) fields in Oregon's Willamette Valley was 7.5 miles; an Illinois study found most rented fields "within five miles of the base unit."[36] As a result of this limitation, the number of farmers who are likely to offer to rent a given piece of land is limited. Nevertheless, opportunities to rent can create lively competition among neighbors, particularly in the more fertile farming regions.

In addition to limited geographic scope, the farmland rental market is characterized by poor information, informal lease arrangements (many rental agreements rest on a handshake), and frequent nonmarket dealings among relatives. As a result, the relationship between land price and cash rent may differ widely from farm to farm.

Partial rights in land for minerals and water are not necessarily transferred when a parcel changes hands. For example, of land sold during 1975-77, mineral rights were retained by the seller on 37 percent of the acres sold; water rights were retained on 2 percent of acres sold.[37] These rights were most likely to be retained in areas where they had significant economic value: mineral rights were most frequently retained on land sold in the Northern Plains and Mountain states, where interest in coal and oil production is high, and water rights were most frequently retained in the Mountain states, where water is scarce.[38]

The market for mineral rights is of long standing, but little is known about its workings. It is likely to be much more imperfect than, say, the cropland or timberland market, because the extent of a given mineral deposit and the cost of extraction are subject to more uncertainty than are crop- or wood-producing ability.

Water rights are best defined and most frequently traded in places where water is scarcest and where there is the most competition for water use. In some areas of the Mountain and southwestern states, potential industrial and municipal water users are now actively purchasing water rights with the intention of eventually using the water off-site.[39] When the rights are exercised, the land from which the rights have been severed will revert to desert. If economic growth in these areas continues, it is likely that water-rights markets will be even more active, and perhaps more formally organized.

The Determination of Land Prices

The price at which land is sold is ultimately determined by what buyers are willing to offer for it and by what sellers are willing to take. There is no fixed relationship between land's characteristics and its price. Ill-informed urbanites may pay $5,000 for an acre of desert, despite the fact that the acre's value in use is virtually nil. And a farm may be sold very "cheaply" relative to its productivity value simply because an estate needs to raise money quickly and few local bidders are interested.

Because land prices are determined in the market, the easiest way to estimate the value of a given parcel of land is likely to be investigation of prices of other, similar properties that have recently been sold. This technique is widely used by appraisers and by tax assessors, as well as by prospective market participants who are trying to decide how much to ask or offer for land. But since land differs so much from parcel to parcel, a similar property may be difficult to find. Moreover, such analysis is of little help in deciding whether land in one area is a bargain in comparison with land elsewhere, or whether the current level of land prices is high or low in relation to land's "value."

Are there theories or generalizations that can explain land values and thus give us an indication of what market prices might be? One such theory is based on the assumption that the demand for land depends on the uses to which land can be put, and that these form a rough hierarchy. At the bottom of the use hierarchy might be grazing, the kind that uses several acres of land to support a single animal. Somewhat higher on the scale might come forestry; then growing wheat or other small grains; then more intensive grazing (typically done on improved pasture); then corn, soybeans, orchards, and the more profitable specialty crops. At or near the top would most likely be nonagricultural uses: rural housing, industrial plants, suburban housing. Table 4.2 suggests the sort of land values that each of these activities can support.

Table 4.2
Land-use Hierarchy

Use	Typical Land Value (per acre)
Urban Uses*	$5,000-50,000+
Orchard, Specialty Crop	2,000-7,000
Rural Residence	1,000-5,000
Corn, Soybeans	1,000-4,000
Developed Pasture	300-1,000
Wheat, Small Grains	200-500
Forestry (bareland value)	100-600
Rangeland Grazing	50-200

*Urban uses include various intense land uses, including housing subdivisions, industry, and commercial establishments.

If a given piece of land is physically capable of supporting more than one of the alternative uses in the hierarchy, the use that can pay the most determines the land's market value. For example, much of the agricultural land in the southeastern states would make highly productive timberland; yet it is devoted to corn and soybeans. This is not because forestry is unprofitable, but because corn and soybeans are more profitable. Corn and soybean farmers can offer more for the land than can timber investors, so their offer determines the price of the land and determines its use.

Capitalization-of-income Theory

A more sophisticated version of the idea of competing uses is the capitalization-of-income approach. It emphasizes that land is a capital good that yields future streams of benefits in various uses. These benefits may be monetary (net farm income, for example) or they may be nonmonetary (the owner's enjoyment of outdoor recreation on the land). The value of a piece of rural land can be approximated by calculating the present discounted value of its expected future income or services in each use, a process called *capitalization.** The use with the highest capital value determines the highest price that a demander will offer for the land.

Assume, for example, that an acre of good-quality farmland can be expected when planted in corn to yield the owner a perpetual net income of $100 per year. If one discounts future income to the present using a 10 percent rate of interest (capitalization rate), this land would be valued for farming at $1,000 per acre.[40] (The formula for the calculation is explained in footnote 40.) A 5 percent capitalization rate would raise the value to $2,000 per acre; a 15 percent rate would lower it to $667 per acre.

The model applies equally well to other uses, although the arithmetic can become more complex. For example, forestland may yield cash income only when it is cut—say, every 10 years. Thus, the future income that is capitalized is not composed of steady yearly increments but is a series of large chunks occurring at 10-year intervals. Alternatively, a forest's income stream can be looked at as the yearly value of wood growth, whether or not the wood is cut. Recreational properties produce an income stream only if they are rented out; otherwise, the "yield" on such a property is the enjoyment gained by the owner in using the property himself, plus the capital appreciation he may obtain by eventually reselling it.

---

*Capitalization is based on the premise that receipt of *future* flows of benefits has some *present* worth to the recipient. This present value is not the simple sum of all future benefits, but rather a *discounted* amount that takes into consideration the fact that $100 received a year from now is a less desirable commodity than $100 today. For example, one may wish to "discount" next year's $100 by 10 percent.

We can make the income-capitalization model more realistic by modifying it to account for expectations about future increases in the land's productivity and expected future inflation. Consider the case of good midwestern farmland. If an acre yields $100 net farming income at present, then the simplest income-capitalization model predicts that a potential buyer capitalizing future income with a rate of 10 percent could be expected to offer no more than $1,000 per acre. But suppose the buyer expected that improvements in productivity and rising world food demand would cause real income per acre to rise by 2 percent a year indefinitely. In that case, he would raise his bid to as much as $1,250.[41] One farm economist has likened farmland to a "growth stock," a security that commands a high price relative to its current earnings or dividends because its holders are looking forward to continued growth in the earnings and dividends.[42]

Moreover, suppose the buyer also expected that inflation would continue indefinitely at a rate of 6 percent per year, and that this inflation (as well as 2 percent yearly real growth) would be reflected in the income stream available from the land.[43] In that case, he might offer as much as $5,000 for the property in our hypothetical example. It is likely that one of the reasons for the present high level of land prices is that people expect high rates of inflation. Interest rates on farm mortgages have also risen, but they appear to have risen less rapidly than did people's expectations about future inflation rates.[44]

Another reason for farmland prices to be higher than values calculated from average crop income is that land prices are set by what land is worth to individual buyers and sellers in the market, not on the basis of value to the average farmer. Suppose that an aggressive, efficient midwestern soybean farmer can get 38 bushels of soybeans per acre, rather than the average of about 32. If he sells the beans at $6 per bushel, the six additional bushels will increase his net income by $36 per acre per year. Assuming a capitalization rate of 10 percent, the efficient farmer should be willing to bid up to $360 more per acre than will average farmers.

Similarly, consider the farmer who bids on property that adjoins his existing operation or lies near it. Because he can farm a certain amount of additional land without spending any more on structures or equipment, he might produce a given amount of crop for

$20 per acre per year less than could someone without the advantage of proximity. The farmer could pay (again, at the 10-percent capitalization rate) as much as $200 per acre more than another farmer to buy the land.

The capitalization-of-income approach can also be modified to account for the fact that values of some rural parcels are influenced by the possibility of future urbanization or development. Consider our initial example of land yielding $100 per acre in agricultural income and selling for $1,000. Now assume that this land is within commuting distance of a city, and there is a possibility (say, one chance in 10) that in five years it will be bought by a housing developer for $10,000 per acre. Thus, the potential buyer can expect to receive not only current income, but also a future windfall. At a capitalization rate of 10 percent, the buyer might be expected to pay up to $1,559 for such a parcel.[45] It might be argued, incidentally, that one reason why land prices are so high is that both buyers and sellers chronically overestimate the probability of future development.

A model for determining land value would not be complete without accounting in some way for risk. Our simplest model merely assumed that land produces a steady yearly income stream, say $100 per acre per year indefinitely. In the real world, the income to be derived from land can fluctuate radically from year to year, reflecting weather, insect and disease damage, and year-to-year variations in commodity prices. Rather than producing a steady income stream, agriculture, and to a lesser extent forestry, may produce a succession of fat years and lean years. In general, investors are willing to pay somewhat more for a steady and predictable income stream than they will for one that has the same total value with erratic fluctuations. Thus, yet another reason for the steady increase in the prices of U.S. rural land over the years may be that government programs of crop insurance and forest-fire protection have reduced the financial risks of crop failure, while price-support programs have reduced risks of fluctuations in crop prices. Moreover, government price supports have been adjusted periodically to help farm income keep pace with general price inflation. This implicit "indexation" may have improved the ability of farm income to track inflation, an advantage that is likely to be capitalized into land value.

Accessibility Theory

Land value is also sometimes explained in terms of accessibility—that is, by the parcel's location relative to centers of population, or to major markets for the land's products, or to other desirable destinations. This theory is not incompatible with the capitalization-of-income approach, but differs in the emphasis given to location rather than productivity. Its usefulness as a separate theory stems from the fact that urban uses (which are very much influenced by location) are strong competitors for land; yet it is difficult to establish *a priori* the income that such uses would yield for a given parcel.

Transportation costs money, whether one is considering the movement of crops to market, the daily commute to work, the delivery of raw logs to a sawmill, or the recreationist's weekend journey to his second home. Location theorists refer elegantly to "the friction of space." Real-estate dealers make the same point when they speak of "the three determinants of urban land values—location, location, and location."

The most common version of the accessibility theory of land values posits that there is a land-value gradient, a mathematical relationship between distance from an important population center and the price of land. Even casual observation shows that the influence of cities on land values extends far beyond city limits. Most economists believe that the land-value gradient looks something like the curve depicted in Figure 4.2, with land values falling off as distance from the center increases, but at a diminishing rate.[46] It is also generally observed that land-use intensities (the amount of capital applied per acre of land) and population densities also fall off as distance from the center increases.

The gradient probably continues to decline well into the suburbs. Beyond some point, however, distance from cities is likely to have little impact on land values from one parcel to another slightly more distant. But distance still apparently has explanatory power when very large increments of distance are considered. For example, there seems to be a distinct regional land-value gradient in New England, such that the price of forestland in southern New England (the part of the region closest to major metropolitan population concentrations) is considerably higher than that of forestland in the more remote northern states. The same observation can be made when areas are compared within a single state—for example, northern and southern Vermont. Moreover, the opening of interstate highways in New England during the 1960s caused land values in newly accessible northern areas to show extremely high rates of increase.[47]

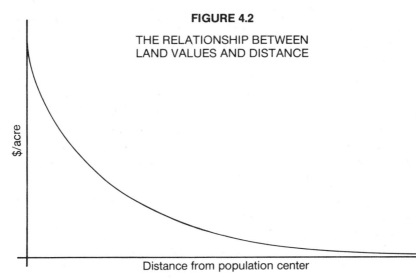

FIGURE 4.2

THE RELATIONSHIP BETWEEN
LAND VALUES AND DISTANCE

$/acre

Distance from population center

The existence of a land-value gradient was originally attributed to the influence of distance on the costs of hauling agricultural products to market. Until the middle of the 19th century, the price of farmland was primarily determined by the cost of transporting the product by horse-drawn wagon. So costly was this mode of transportation that, until the invention of the canal and later the railroad, vast acreages of fertile midwestern land were virtually "worthless." At that time, a land-value gradient based on wagon-transport costs would probably have worked very well in explaining the prices of rural land in different parts of the country.

Today, modern modes of transportation mean that the locational advantages enjoyed by one piece of farmland over another are probably the smallest they have ever been. Strawberries and tomatoes grown in California compete successfully with local produce in East Coast supermarkets, and American grains are exported all over the world. Timber products are also commonly shipped long distances from point of production to market. Although costs of transporting crops do still play a role in determining land values, an equally relevant factor is likely to be the land's accessibility for residential or recreational uses. Modern transportation has greatly

115

increased the commuting circle that surrounds our cities and towns, and hence has caused a quantum jump in the area of land where there is an urban influence on land values. Moreover, given the widespread availability of private automobiles, highway improvements, air travel, and increased leisure, no attractive part of the country is now so remote that it is unaffected by recreational demands.

The net effect of transportation changes on land values would be expected to be (1) a value gradient that continues to decline with distance from regional centers, even when the distance has become very large, but (2) an overall flattening of the gradient, so that value falls off more slowly with distance than was true in years past. A recent study of the distribution of farm real-estate values nationwide provides strong evidence for the existence of a land-value gradient and some indication of a flattening, although the latter has occurred only recently. In 1974, the average per-acre value of farm real estate was highest in metropolitan counties, lowest in nonmetropolitan counties not adjacent to metropolitan areas. Moreover, among the nonmetropolitan counties, farm real-estate values were highest in those with an urban area of more than 10,000 persons and lowest in those with no urban area. The study reported a decline in the gradient's slope between 1969 and 1974, although it was neither large nor persistent enough to allow strong conclusions to be drawn.[48]

Although accessibility theory emphasizes distance to population concentrations, the theory can be made more general by considering other relevant destinations. For example, a very important component of the value of a piece of recreational property may be its distance from the shore of a body of water. Properties that lie immediately adjacent to a lake may sell for several times as much per acre as properties lying 100 yards distant, while the latter may sell for several times as much as properties two or three miles from the lake. Distance to roads is another important determinant of a parcel's accessibility, and hence its value.

Empirical Observations

Constructs such as the accessibility theory or capitalization-of-income theory are useless unless they can help to predict actual market prices. Over the years, a number of empirical studies have tried to determine the actual contribution that various factors make to land prices. Some studies have looked at how land prices are affected by differences in the characteristics of land from parcel to parcel or from state to state ("cross-sectional" studies). Others have tried to explain how land prices have varied over time ("time series" studies).[49] In both cases, measures of income and accessibility have usually been tried as explanatory variables.

Empirical studies of land values have given fairly good coverage to cropland and land on the urban fringe; spotty treatment to recreational land; and have paid virtually no attention to the determination of prices for productive forestland. Only a handful of studies have considered more than one type of land and attempted to see whether, for example, the forces influencing the price of cropland in an area are the same as those influencing the price of forestland.

Cross-sectional studies typically find that land prices are positively affected by land quality, population density, proximity to urban centers, amount of road frontage, and (for land with recreational potential) the presence of amenity features such as lakes or streams.[50] Prices are generally negatively affected by high property taxes. In many cross-sectional studies, the single most important variable explaining the per-acre price of land is parcel size.[51] The general rule is: the smaller the parcel, the higher the per-acre price. This phenomenon, which might be called "parceling value," stems from a variety of causes. Small parcels appeal to a wider market than larger ones, and are more likely to be sought for homesites or for other development. Small parcels often also have a greater percentage of road frontage than do larger ones, and frequently contain a smaller percentage of steep, wet, or otherwise unusable land. Some studies have found that parceling value exists over a wide range of parcel sizes. Others have found that above 60 acres or so there is little or no relationship between parcel size and per-acre price that cannot be fully explained by differences in land quality.[52]

Time-series studies of rural land prices are plagued by the fact that many of the forces affecting land values are themselves highly correlated with time, and hence with one another.[53] This tends to produce models with an apparently high degree of power to explain land price behavior over time, but in which it is difficult to distinguish the influence of one time-related variable from that of any other. The rate of general price inflation, for example, may be found to be very closely related to land prices—but so is farm income, which is itself influenced by general inflation.

Among variables that are frequently found to be positively related to the behavior of land prices over time are rates of farm enlargement, net farm income, levels of government price supports for crops, productivity per acre, and expected capital gains. Generally negatively related to land prices are property taxes and the yearly rate of property transfer. The latter is a measure of supply, and the negative relationship simply means that, the smaller the amount of land available for sale, the higher will be the price.

A potentially valuable type of empirical study, but one which has rarely been done, is comparison of cross-sectional studies of prices at two widely separated moments and examination of any changes in the explanatory power of individual variables. For example, one might expect that, if rural residential demand for land were increasing, one would find the influence of parceling value would become increasingly significant when cross-sectional studies of two successive time periods were compared.

As an experiment, we examined the determinants of farmland prices for 31 states in the eastern half of the country, using cross-sectional data for 1960 and then for 1975. In 1960, 51 percent of the variation among states in average farmland price could be accounted for simply by differences in farm income per acre.[54] In 1975, differences in farm income explained only 35 percent of the price variation. This finding suggests that factors other than current agricultural income (such as inflation hedging or urbanization potential) may have become increasingly important as determinants of rural land values.[55] In fact, looking at changes in price per acre between 1960 and 1975, about two thirds of the variance among the states was explained by changes in population density.[56] Changes in net farm income per acre had little explanatory power. This type of analysis might be profitably applied to county data on farmland prices within a single state or for the nation as a whole, preferably using more sophisticated measures of both agricultural income and urbanization potential.

Changing Markets

Chapters 1 through 4 have endeavored to present a broadbrush portrait of the market for rural land—how it works, what underlying forces are determining demand and supply, and how prices, ownership, and parcel sizes are changing in response. It is a complex picture, one in which the plans and expectations of millions of individual owners are interacting with changing technologies, social patterns, and economic conditions.

One way to study these forces is by looking at how they are working themselves out in specific localities, which is what is done in the case studies in the next chapter. In a real sense, we had no choice but to study local areas. Because the United States is such a large and diverse country, there is a tremendous variation from region to region and from locality to locality in the dominant types of land and the competing land uses. Although many of the forces affecting the market—inflation, for example, or changing agricultural technology—have their origin at the national level, their expression and their impacts may be quite different from place to place. The local segmentation of the land market also pushed us toward a case-study approach. Finally, and most important, the paucity of national-level information on the rural land market meant that, if we wanted to measure market trends or analyze their impacts, we would have to visit specific local areas and collect data for ourselves. The chapter that follows reports on what we learned.

In the areas we studied, we found a great variety of situations in which at least some people were dissatisfied with the outcomes that the local land market produced. The issues included both complaints about the way rural land was being used—or in some cases not used—and dissatisfactions with the ownership patterns that were emerging. These issues, and possible solutions, will be further analyzed in chapters 6 and 7.

REFERENCES

1. Similarly, Barlowe notes that "what is often referred to as the real estate market is really a conglomerate concept made up of thousands of smaller markets that operate in different areas and deal with different types of properties." Raleigh Barlowe, *Land Resource Economics*, 3rd ed. (Englewood Cliffs, New Jersey: Prentice-Hall, 1978), p. 352.

2. See Donald L. Uchtmann, "Land Sale Methods," in *Farm Real Estate*, North-Central Regional Extension Publication No. 51 (Champaign-Urbana: University of Illinois College of Agriculture, 1979), pp. 31-34. A less common, but nevertheless interesting, type of transfer is the exchange of one property for another. By exchanging rather than selling properties, owners are able to postpone paying tax on their capital gains.

3. James A. Lewis, *Landownership in the United States, 1978*, U.S. Department of Agriculture, Economics, Statistics and Cooperatives Service (Washington, D.C.: Government Printing Office, 1980), p. 12.

4. Eric Broudy, "The Selling of America: Strout and United Farm," *Country Journal*, vol. 5, no. 7 (July 1978).

5. The computerized listing service may be particularly useful in structuring tax-free exchanges of properties among multiple parties.

6. One midwestern land expert tells of the auction of six pieces of expensive Illinois farmland. Although the sale was advertised in the *Wall Street Journal*, each of the parcels was bought by someone living within six miles of the property.

Nevertheless, the lawyer handling the sale believed that national advertising had brought in enough outside competition to force up the final sale price. Interview with Professor Franklin Reiss, Champaign-Urbana, Illinois, July 1979.

7. This survey included urban land, but, since the figures cited here are based on number of acres rather than dollar value of the land, they are overwhelmingly weighted toward rural transactions. Unpublished data from the national land-ownership survey supplied by U.S. Department of Agriculture, Economics and Statistics Service, April 1981.

8. U.S. Department of Agriculture, *Farm Real Estate Market Developments,* August 1979; also see Thomas L. Frey, "How Land is Being Financed and the Characteristics of Financing Methods," in *Farm Real Estate,* North-Central Regional Extension Publication No. 51 (Champaign-Urbana: University of Illinois College of Agriculture, 1979), pp. 20-30.

9. One commentator attributed the 1978 demonstrations by farmers in Washington, D.C., to discontent among farmers who had incurred debt to buy land, and then were squeezed by falling farm product prices. See Ben Weberman, "Who Gets Hung?" *Forbes,* May 1, 1978, p. 40.

10. Until the requirement was removed in 1980, a downpayment of no more than 30 percent was required for a sale to qualify for such treatment.

11. One study found seller contract financing associated with about a 5 percent increase in the land's selling price. See Robert D. Reinsel, "Effect of Seller Financing on Land Prices," *Agricultural Finance Review,* vol. 33 (July 1972), pp. 32-35.

12. Interview with Gordon Enk, Institute on Man and Science, March 1978.

13. A study of lot buyers in 42 subdivisions in the Colorado mountains found that 67 percent of properties purchased were financed by the developer, with nearly all of the repayment periods between 5 and 14 years. Herbert Hoover, *Impacts of Recreation Subdivisions in the South-Central Mountains of Colorado* (Washington, D.C.: U.S. Department of Agriculture, Economic Research Service, December 1976). INFORM's study of 19 large subdivisions in Florida and the West found that "all developers studied are marketing the lots at their subdivisions via some form of installment-contract sales in which the purchaser makes a small downpayment and pays for a lot over a period of years." Leslie Allen, Beryl Kuder, and Sarah Oakes, *Promised Lands,* vol. 2 (New York: INFORM, 1977), p. 5.

14. Allen, *et al., Promised Lands,* vol. 2, especially pp. 45-47.

15. Bruce Lindeman, "The Anatomy of Land Speculation," *Journal of the American Institute of Planners,* vol. 42, no. 2 (April 1976), pp. 142-52.

16. See Michael Boehlje, "Limited Partnerships and Investment Trusts for Real Estate Ventures," *Journal of the American Society of Farm Managers and Rural Appraisers,* vol. 38, no. 1 (April 1974), pp. 73-80.

17. See George Stigler, *The Theory of Price,* 3rd ed. (New York: Macmillan, 1966), p. 85.

18. This statement assumes that there are no artificial constraints on the market, such as import taxes or exchange controls.

19. James Lorie and Richard Brealey, eds., *Modern Developments in Investment Management* (New York: Praeger, 1972), p. 101.

20. This does not deny, however, that there are many nonlocal purchasers of land, including an increased interest in U.S. rural land markets by foreign investors. Like many other issues, the localization of the land market is relative. As we

noted in chapter 2, there are many factors that are making foreign investment in U.S. land markets attractive relative to existing alternatives in the foreigners' own countries. The fact remains, however, that the rural land market is quite localized.

21. Land can be, and sometimes is, divided into smaller parcels for purposes of sale. But the very act of parcellation tends to change the nature of the commodity. One practice common in land auctions is to offer a piece of land as parcels, then to solicit single bids for all the parcels together. A bidder willing to bid more than the sum of single parcel bids can buy the entirety.

22. In fact, the land was sold to a lumber company for $27 million in cash. The high per-acre price can be explained by the large amount of mature timber on the land.

23. One example of how outsiders are drawn to places with low land prices is a book that uses government data on farmland prices to identify states in which the price of land is unusually high or unusually low in relation to population density. The book is priced at $275 per copy. See Gerald S. Gilligan, *A Price Guide for Buying and Selling Rural Acreage* (New York: McGraw-Hill, 1974, 1976).

24. See Jack Bickers, "Why the Southern Land Boom May Be Just Beginning," *Progressive Farmer*, vol. 93, no. 7 (July 1978), pp. 15-17.

25. Samuel C. Hadaway, "Diversification Possibilities in Agricultural Land Investment," *Appraisal Journal*, vol. 46, no. 4 (October 1978), pp. 529-37.

26. In a very interesting recent study, Vining and Hiraguchi applied the efficient market hypothesis to urban land price data from Tokyo. They hypothesized that the price of a particular parcel at any given time should reflect all relevant information about future possibilities. Therefore, although a parcel's price might rise rapidly because of a change in circumstances (for example, announcement of a new highway), after the initial instantaneous adjustment its price should again "vibrate randomly." In Tokyo, however, the researchers found that land parcels rising rapidly in one year also tended to rise rapidly in subsequent years. This would imply an imperfect, or at least a lagged, adjustment to changing circumstances. D.R. Vining, Jr., and H. Hiraguchi, "Some Evidence from Japan on the Efficiency of Land Markets," *Environment and Planning A*, vol. 9 (1977), pp. 975-84.

We applied this idea to U.S. farmland prices for the years 1970-77, a time in which changing product and input prices would be expected to change both the absolute level of land prices and the relative prices of land in different parts of the country. Using data on farmland price changes for U.S. states for successive one-year periods, we found that states with high rates of price increase in one period also had high rates of increase in subsequent periods. The simple correlation between successive years ranged from +.074 (in 1971-72) to +.616 (in 1975-76). Three of the six correlation coefficients were statistically significant at the .01 level. Interestingly, the successive years with the greatest year-to-year similarities in price-change patterns were the pairs 1973-74, 1974-75, and 1975-76. This was the period during which land values were increasing most rapidly on average nationwide. They also were years in which the land market was digesting new information about energy prices and crop export possibilities. These data can be interpreted in three ways. First, the land market might have been reacting to a single piece of information (new farm export opportunities, for example) with a significant lag. Second, the market may have been encountering successive pieces of information that were correlated with each other, and reacting to the information relatively quickly. Third, farmers may have been increasing their bids for the purchase of new land after past price increases had raised the value of their existing holdings, and hence their borrowing power.

27. Compare the similar diagram in William D. Crowley, Jr., *Farmland Use Values versus Market Prices in Three Oregon Land Markets,* Economic Research Service Report ERS-550 (Washington, D.C: Government Printing Office, 1974). Barrows and Dunford distinguish three distinct rural land markets in their study of rural Wisconsin—agricultural, urban, and recreational. Richard Barrows and Richard Dunford, *Agricultural, Urban and Recreational Determinants of Farmland Values in Wisconsin,* Research Bulletin R2764 (Madison: University of Wisconsin, College of Agricultural and Life Sciences, 1976).

28. Cropland and grazing land are combined under the heading "agricultural" because in many parts of the country it is relatively easy to shift land back and forth from one such use to another.

29. Government figures show that, between 1967 and 1975, 4.8 million acres of cropland (1.1 percent of the total cropland base) were converted to urban use. Urban conversion also affected 4.4 million acres of forestland (1.0 percent); 3.2 million acres of pasture and rangeland (0.6 percent); and 4.2 million acres of "other" land (7.3 percent). U.S. Department of Agriculture, Soil Conservation Service, *Potential Cropland Study* (Washington, D.C.: Government Printing Office, 1977), p. 16.

30. The data pertain only to sales of farm property, more than 90 percent of which is sold for agricultural use. Nevertheless, the inferences drawn with regard to prices and parcel sizes for each type of land are consistent with our own observations of markets in several parts of the country.

31. Crowley, *Farmland Use Values versus Market Prices,* p. vii.

32. Barrows and Dunford, *Agricultural, Urban and Recreational Determinants of Farmland Values.*

33. David L. Chicoine, "Farmland Values in an Urban Fringe: An Analysis of Will County, Illinois, Market Data" (Ph.D. dissertation, Department of Agricultural Economics, University of Illinois, Champaign-Urbana, 1979).

34. There is no exact measure of the percentage of farmland operated by someone other than its owner. One estimate, based on data from the 1974 Census of Agriculture, is that 32 percent of acreage in farms is rented from nonfarmers, plus another 5 to 7 percent rented from other farm operators. Bruce Hottel and David H. Harrington, "Tenure and Equity Influences on the Incomes of Farmers," in U.S. Department of Agriculture, *Structure Issues of American Agriculture* (Washington, D.C.: Government Printing Office, 1979), p. 97. The 1978 USDA landownership survey reported 252 million acres of farmland (27 percent of the total) were rented from a nonoperator landlord. Robert Otte, "Farm and Ranchland Ownership in the U.S., 1978" (Unpublished, U.S. Department of Agriculture, Washington, D.C., 1981).

35. See Bruce B. Johnson, *The Farmland Rental Market—A Case Analysis of Selected Corn Belt Areas,* USDA Economic Research Service, Agricultural Economics Report No. 235 (Washington, D.C.: Government Printing Office, 1972); Franklin J. Reiss, Edward N. Ballard, William H. Brink, and William R. Harryman, *Farm Lease Practices in Three South-Central Illinois Counties in 1980,* University of Illinois, Department of Agricultural Economics, AE-4491 (Champaign-Urbana: University of Illinois, 1980).

36. George A. Van Otten, "Changing Spatial Characteristics of Willamette Valley Farms," *Professional Geographer,* vol. 32, no. 1 (1980), p. 68; Johnson, *Farmland Rental Market,* p. 52.

37. Unpublished preliminary data from the national landownership survey, subject to revision, provided by U.S. Department of Agriculture, Economics and Statistics Service, April 1981.

38. Mineral rights were retained by the seller in only 5 percent of sales in mineral-rich Appalachia, probably because the rights had been severed long before and were owned by third parties.

39. See for example, *Wall Street Journal,* December 28, 1977.

40. The capitalization formula for a level perpetual income stream is

$$V = \frac{A}{r}$$

where A is the yearly income flow and r is the capitalization rate. We prefer to capitalize income at the long-term mortgage interest rate, a rate that approximates the "cost of money" to the potential land buyer. Since land is typically purchased with a mixture of borrowed funds and equity funds, a more appropriate (but more difficult to calculate) rate would be a weighted average of the mortgage interest rate and the capitalization rate applicable to the purchaser's own funds. Additional adjustment could be made to account for such factors as the tax deductibility of interest payments.

41. The applicable capitalization formula is

$$V = \frac{A}{r-h-g}$$

where V is land price, A is the current net land income, r is the capitalization rate, h is the yearly rate of real increase in income, and g is the yearly increase in income due to inflation. Thus if A = $100, r = .10, h = .02, and g = 0 (as in our first example), V = $1,250. If r = .10, h = .02 and g = .06 (as in our second example), V = $5,000. See David Boyce, Janet Kolhase, and Thomas Plaut, *Estimating the Value of Development Easements on Agricultural Land: Methods and Empirical Analysis* (Philadelphia: Regional Science Research Institute, 1977). See also James O. Wise, "Modifying the Income Approach to Farm Appraisal," *Appraisal Journal* vol. 40, no. 2 (October 1977), pp. 505-510. The potential investor may not be willing to offer this high a price, even if his expectations are strongly held, for his current cash flow may fall too far short of the required mortgage payment. As Reiss points out, "higher future incomes [from land] are no help in meeting present payments when equity is low and interest payments are high." Franklin J. Reiss, "Decision Making in the Farmland Market," *Journal of the American Society of Farm Managers and Rural Appraisers,* vol. 40, no. 2 (October 1976), p. 42.

42. Emanuel Melichar, "Capital Gains versus Current Income in the Farming Sector," *American Journal of Agricultural Economics,* vol. 61, no. 5 (December 1979), pp. 1085-92. See also Robert D. Reinsel and Edward I. Reinsel, "The Economics of Asset Values and Current Income in Farming," *American Journal of Agricultural Economics,* vol. 61, no. 5 (December 1979), pp. 1093-97.

43. See footnote 41.

44. The mortgage rate of interest consists of three elements: the "real" (inflation adjusted) return to the lender, an allowance for expected inflation over the

life of the mortgage, and an allowance for the lender's risk. It appears that, in recent times of rapidly accelerating inflation, real-estate lenders initially did not raise interest rates rapidly enough to compensate themselves fully for the inflation that other market participants, including land buyers, anticipated.

45. We can calculate the expected value by the formula

$$V = (1-p)\ UV + p\ (DV)$$

where UV is the land's agricultural value (capitalized value of a level perpetual income stream); p is the probability that the land will be sold for development in year t; and DV is the land's present value if development occurs, consisting of the capitalized value of yearly income from year 0 to year t, plus the discounted value of its sale price as development land in year t.

46. See Edwin S. Mills, *Studies in the Structure of the Urban Economy* (Baltimore: Johns Hopkins University Press for Resources for the Future, 1972), esp. pp. 34-58.

47. Armstrong's data on Vermont land values by county seem to bear out these observations. Frank H. Armstrong, *Valuation of Vermont Forest, 1968-74* (Burlington: University of Vermont Department of Forestry, 1975).

48. Tim B. Heaton, "Metropolitan Influence on United States Farmland Use and Capital Intensivity," *Rural Sociology*, vol. 45, no. 3 (Fall 1980), pp. 501-508.

49. A good recent review of such studies may be found in Chicoine, *Farmland Values in an Urban Fringe.*

50. Among the more accessible cross-sectional studies is E.C. Pasour, Jr., "The Capitalization of Real Property Taxes Levied on Farm Real Estate," *American Journal of Agricultural Economics*, vol. 57, no. 4 (November 1975), pp. 539-48.

51. This statement does not hold when the data set does not cover the full range of parcel sizes—for example, studies limited to parcels 20 acres or larger.

52. Scattered evidence suggests that timberland is subject to parceling value for a wider range of parcel sizes than is farmland. That is to say that a 1000-acre timberland parcel may sell for less per acre, all other considerations equal, than a 500-acre parcel.

53. Among the more accessible time-series studies is Robert W. Herdt and Willard W. Cochrane, "Farmland Prices and Technological Advance," *Journal of Farm Economics*, vol. 48, no. 2 (May 1966), pp. 243-63.

54. This means the coefficient of determination (R^2) in a linear regression of value per acre on income per acre was .51. Similarly, gross rent per acre explained 29 percent of the interstate variation in farmland price in 1960, only 7 percent in 1975.

55. We also hypothesized that land's inherent capability to produce, rather than what it is currently producing, might be increasingly important as a determinant of value. We found, however, that the percentage of a state's land considered "prime" explained about 9 percent of land value variation in 1960, about 3 percent in 1975.

56. In a multiple regression with the dollar change in land value (1960-75) as the dependent variable, change in population per acre was significant at the .01 level and explained 65 percent of the variance in the dependent variable. Also significant in explaining the land price change was the level of land prices in 1960. Neither change in farm income per acre nor change in property tax per acre was significant at either the .01 level or the .05 level.

CHAPTER 5

Rural Places: Case Studies
of Local Land Markets

Rural America's landscape varies widely in climate, topography, and ecosystems and in such man-made characteristics as transportation corridors, settlement patterns, and distance to major urban centers. The six places we selected for intensive study and data collection—counties or parts of counties—collectively provide a representative sample of characteristics found in many rural places.[1]

In chapter 1, we noted that three trends—a rise in prices, a change in parcel sizes, and the emergence of new demands for land and new types of landowners—were occurring in rural areas across the country. These trends have been documented at each of our study sites. There are differences from place to place, however.

As can be expected, the magnitude of the impact of urbanization will differ according to an area's proximity to metropolitan centers. Rural areas accessible to large population concentrations typically exhibit stronger increases in land prices, more parcellation, and a greater diversity of ownership types than do more remote areas.

Moreover, both within and between the areas we studied, there are differences in the land itself. Generally, in the land market, the term *productivity* refers to the outputs obtained from a parcel of land minus the costs to produce those outputs. Whether the outputs are corn, coal, timber, or good views, some sites will be more naturally productive than others. The land's productivity in alternative uses is a powerful determinant both of how the land will be used and how the local land market will reflect broad national phenomena.

We chose six areas for intensive study: Loudoun County, Virginia (outlying portion); Tyler County, Texas; Hardy County and Pendleton County, West Virginia; Douglas County, Illinois; Plainfield township, New Hampshire; and San Luis Obispo County, California. Together, they illustrate a continuum of remoteness,

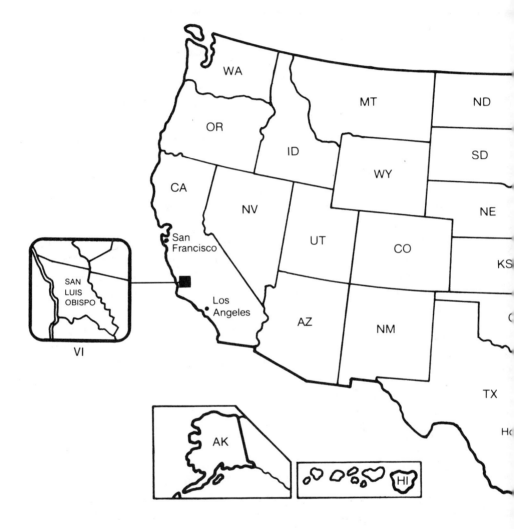

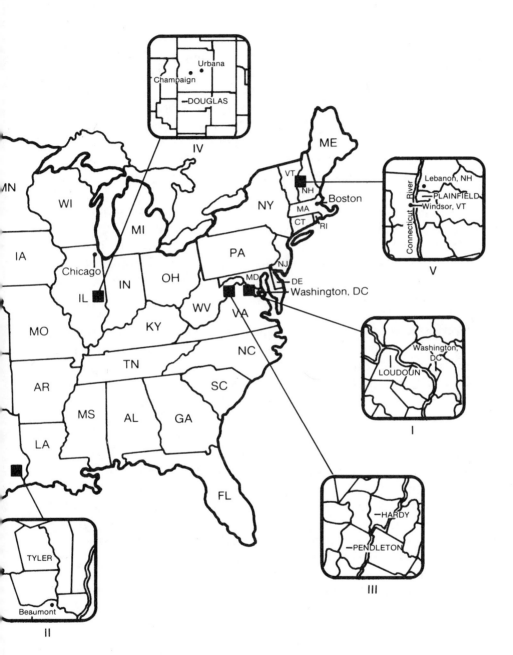

ranging from places just beyond the metropolitan fringe to places quite distant from any metropolis. And they include examples of both fertile and marginal farmland, hardwood and softwood timberland, and land in demand for recreational and rural settlement.

In choosing these sites, we used a series of clear but flexible guidelines. First, each area had to be truly "rural." Built-up areas, except for very small villages, were excluded. Moreover, open areas where land values were significantly influenced by nearby urban development were also excluded. Loudoun County lies within a metropolitan statistical area, but the portion of the county selected for study is, both on paper and on visual inspection, very rural, and it is an hour and a half commute to central Washington, D.C.

Second, each area had to be representative of its regional land market. Thus, in type of land and in the sources of demand for land, Hardy and Pendleton counties are similar to at least seven other counties in the Potomac Highlands area of West Virginia. Tyler and Douglas counties are representative in many ways of other rural counties within about a 50-mile radius.

Third, each area had to illustrate a nationally common type of land or type of land-market trend. Douglas County exemplifies hundreds of other counties where commercial farming is still the dominant land use. Tyler County does the same with respect to softwood timber. Loudoun County has much in common with other exurban jurisdictions around the country, while Hardy County is like many areas experiencing the effects of widespread interest in outdoor recreation. Plainfield and San Luis Obispo represent, among other things, the many rural areas experiencing substantial population growth from an influx of new people.

It was simply not possible for us to cover every region of the country with six case studies. We believe, however, that we do cover most of the important phenomena in the rural land market nationwide. For example, the Great Plains land market appears to be characterized generally by farm expansion and the other trends described in our Douglas County case study, while many rural areas in the Rocky Mountains and Pacific Northwest are experiencing residential and recreational growth (and accompanying land division) similar to that found at several of our other study sites, particularly Tyler County and San Luis Obispo County.[2]

Finally, although virtually every county in the United States is in some sense "unusual," we avoided selecting rural places with highly exceptional scenic qualities (for example, Aspen, Colorado), with unusually large recreational developments (Flagler County, Florida), with recent mineral discoveries, or with major public-works projects.[3] In selecting a county within a particular region, we generally did *not* select the one that appeared to have *a priori* either the most, or the least, land-market activity.

The areas we chose to study ranged in population from about 1,700 persons (Plainfield, New Hampshire) to well over 100,000 (San Luis Obispo, California). Most of the areas are growing rather rapidly in population. The selection process itself pointed up the increasingly blurred distinction between urban and rural areas. Except in the Great Plains and the Rocky Mountain West, few rural counties are really remote from metropolitan centers. Interstate highways, originally built to link the large cities, have dramatically increased the accessibility of many rural places. Thus, our case studies have been chosen to include examples from all parts of the spatial continuum outward from the metropolitan fringes.

I

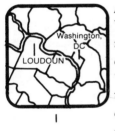 *In the still rural western half of* **Loudoun County, Virginia** *on the edge of the Washington, D.C., metropolis, formerly agricultural land is in great demand for large-lot residential parcels and for "hobby farms." Fertile cropland areas have provided excellent soil conditions for septic systems and have sprouted suburban-style houses on 10-acre lots. Beyond the homesite and perhaps a garden, the remainder of the parcel will be virtually unused by the new owner. Between 1954 and 1976, the mean size of a rural parcel in Loudoun County dropped by more than a third, from 47 to 31 acres. The drop appears to have resulted from a decrease in parcels of greater than 50 acres, and a substantial increase in those 10 to 25 acres in size. Accompanying the urban demand and the parcellation have been extremely high rates of land price increase, to the point that, at present, land prices throughout the county are far higher than can be justified by the land's productive capability. Local officials have shown increasing concern about controlling rural growth, but have not yet found a formula likely to preserve commercial agriculture in the face of a strong residential demand for land.*

Approximately 40 miles from central Washington, D.C., and within the expanding metropolitan shadow of the nation's capital, lies Loudoun County, Virginia (1980 population 57,244). Steeped in the early history of the United States, Loudoun's is a landscape of farms and small towns at crossroads. It is Washington's gateway to the Blue Ridge Mountains and to the rural Virginia Piedmont, Virginia's famed "hunt country."

Loudoun's location has led to substantial population growth in recent years. Between 1970 and 1977 the county population grew 57 percent. And in 1978 half of the households had lived in the county less than five years.[4] Most of this new growth has been in housing tracts sprawling across the eastern, essentially suburban part of the county closest to Washington.

Our case study focuses on the western half of Loudoun County, roughly that portion west of Leesburg, the county seat. In eastern Loudoun, the effects of population growth and the consequent subdivision of land into smaller and smaller parcels are unmistakable. Given the strong growth and change that have occurred, the political, planning, and land-use issues are more suburban than exurban or rural. To the west, the picture remains, for the present, one of rolling countryside dotted with cornfields, cattle and horse farms, and old secluded houses. Nonetheless, pressures exist, and changes are occurring—changes similar to those affecting exurban areas across the nation. As one newspaper account put it:

> For an increasing number of people who want an authentic slice of country life within commuting reach of Washington, D.C., Loudoun is the next best thing to Walton Mountain.[5]

Between 1970 and 1977 the population of western Loudoun County increased approximately 21 percent, ranging from 46 percent in the north to 5 percent in the south.[6] This growth pressure has become an emotional issue among rural landowners, especially when it comes to taxes. For example, a post office—a very small, two-story wooden structure with no bathroom—was bought for $2,000 at the beginning of 1977. Only 18 months later it was assessed on its "commercial potential" as being worth $29,090. The disbelieving owner mused, "They've got to be kidding.... The only thing that has ever been sold in the building—besides stamps and postal money orders—has been penny candy."[7]

Population growth has also put pressure on Loudoun's agricultural base—an important part of the economy and landscape. According to the Census of Agriculture, in 1974 the county ranked

13th in Virginia in value of total farm products sold, and 5th in value of livestock and livestock products sold. Some of the finest horses in the country are bred in Loudoun County. Major cash crops include hay, corn, and soybeans.

U.S. government soil maps show that a preponderance of the area in which we undertook our case study has "high potential" for cropland use.[8] But prices and population pressures add an air of uncertainty to this agricultural potential. Between 1950 and 1978 the average value per acre of farmland (including buildings) rose from $147 to $2,110.[9] One owner, now farming 170 acres he bought some 13 years ago noted:

> If I'd sell this [land], it would never go back to agriculture....[A] man would be silly to try to [buy land to] farm at these [land] prices. I only know of one farmer in the area that's attempted to do this, and he's doing it by selling off pieces every year.

Others see even less future for the area's argiculture. An elderly, now retired, farmer whose roots in the area reach back to 1870 told us:

> You can't farm on this land [any more] and make any money at it...and while we'd like to keep Loudoun a farming area...well, borrowing money for [land that costs] $3,000 to $4,000 per acre, you can't make any money; the interest will eat you up. The young people just can't do it....I don't know what will happen when all these old farmers die off.

Between 1954 and 1974 the total acreage of Loudoun County farms decreased by 70,000. The number of farms also decreased sharply, mirroring nationwide trends. In 1954 there were 1,438 farms in Loudoun; in 1974 there were 714, only 502 of which had sales of $2,500 or more. Extrapolation of these trends has led many to be pessimistic about the future of agriculture in the county.

Preliminary figures from the 1978 Census of Agriculture, on the other hand, indicate some contrary trends. They show that the number of farms rose from 714 in 1974 to 837 in 1978, while the amount of land in farms rose by about 7,000 acres. The increase in acreage is too small to be meaningful, and may be simply a statistical quirk. But two developments should be noted. First, there has been a large increase in harvested cropland, particularly for corn and hay. This appears to reflect the response of landowners to the relatively high grain prices prevailing in the last decade. Even much of the land that is being held for future development in the eastern half of Loudoun County has been planted to crops in recent years, although its continued high price indicates that housing, not farming, is expected to be its ultimate use. Second, while there has been a continuing decline in the number of farms of over 180 acres, there has been a 40 percent increase in smaller farms, especially those below 50 acres. This appears to reflect the desire of part-time and hobby farmers to raise a few acres of crops or to graze some cattle. Their motivation may be enhanced by the income-tax advantages available to farmers and by a preferential property-tax assessment that is available to farmers who own as few as 5 acres (8 acres if there is a house on the property).

The Exurban Land Market

For most of Loudoun County's long history, land-market activity was quite unremarkable, with changes in land prices depending mainly on the changing fortunes of agriculture. According to one account:

> [By 1800] one could purchase a two-to-three-hundred acre tract with improvements [in Loudoun County] for about $8 per acre. In the next hundred years, land "skyrocketed" to approximately $30 per acre. With the exception of the depressions in the 1890s and 1930s, land values have continued a very slow climb. By 1938, a good farm could be purchased for $70-80 per acre, and by 1950-55 an operating farm could be purchased for less than $100 per acre.[10]

Until quite recently, even land with considerable scenic value was very inexpensive, and market interest was slight. In the words of a Loudoun County real-estate agent, "For 20 years prior to the '60s land prices probably didn't change [a total of] 10 percent. The price was $300 to $500 per acre for anything you wanted. Then the big change hit."

During the 1960s, retirees and urban commuters began to look with interest on the residential possibilities of Loudoun County. The supply of land for sale did not expand to meet the new demand, and land prices began to rise at a steady pace. But the real demand surge came after 1970. In 1973 land sales in western Loudoun County were 46 percent above what they had been in 1970. Price increases also accelerated. Per-acre prices of 10-acre parcels rose at an annual rate of 17 percent between 1969 and 1973.[11]

This strong surge in market activity during the early 1970s resulted, in part, from metropolitan population spillovers promoted by high housing demand and made possible by the growth of employment in Washington and its suburbs. Similar rises in sales appear to have occurred in other exurban areas about the same time.

For example, real-estate sales in two rural portions of San Diego County were observed to have risen by 240 percent between 1970 and 1973.[12]

The subdivision activity in western Loudoun County was aided by soil conditions. During the early and middle 1970s, an acute shortage of sewage-treatment capacity throughout the Washington, D.C., suburbs led homebuilders to seek lots suitable for septic-tank systems. The eastern part of Loudoun has packed subsoil conditions, which make it difficult to meet the percolation standards needed to obtain health department permits. Western Loudoun, however, is characterized by what has been called "good perking soil."

Western Loudoun County also exemplifies the land market's sensitivity to overall economic conditions. In response to the economic recession and fuel shortages of 1973-75, land sales dropped sharply in 1974, back to pre-1970 levels. Interestingly enough, while sales dropped, land prices rose nearly 29 percent over their 1973 level. The market rebounded between 1975 and 1977, as did real-estate markets across the country. A drop in transactions during 1978 and 1979 reflected high interest rates, fuel costs, and general recession. The reduced rate of transfers, however, was not nearly as drastic as during the 1973-75 period. In 1979, real-estate transactions in western Loudoun were still 30 percent higher than their 1967 level, and, although sales were below peak 1973 levels, prices remained high and rising.

Nonresident Ownership

A focus on title transfers alone, while a necessary first step in understanding an area's land market, does not indicate *who* is buying the land. In general, real-estate sales in exurban places seem to be dominated by buyers who are changing their primary places of residence— moving to the country. Thus, one might expect nonresident land-ownership in exurbia to have increased less than in rural areas farther from the metropolitan commuting range. Nevertheless, our case-study evidence indicates that nonresident ownership in western Loudoun County has increased at an even greater rate than the growth in resident population.

Between 1954 and 1976 the total number of individual parcels in western Loudoun increased by 59 percent. During the same time, the number of parcels owned by people residing outside the county increased by 118 percent, exactly twice the overall rate of parcel increase. Based on our estimates, nonresidents owned slightly more than 21 percent of western Loudoun's land parcels in 1954, and nearly 30 percent in 1976. In both periods, the majority of nonresident owners resided in the Washington, D.C., area.

A moderately important influence on the Loudoun County land market is demand by foreign investors. As of 1980 foreigners owned 3.7 percent of all land in the county, and their holdings were growing rapidly.[13] Of the 30 holdings, totalling 12,000 acres, only 2 (a mere 87 acres) had been owned by foreigners in 1975. In 1976-78, foreigners bought 3,124 acres, and in 1979 added 7,262. In the first several months of 1980, foreigners bought 1,690 acres in seven separate transactions, spending $5.5 million, or $3,270 an acre. More than three quarters of the foreign holdings were held by corporations or trusts based in the Netherlands Antilles, a Caribbean tax haven. At least some of these represented Arab investors, including a Saudi Arabian prince, who bought the 2,000-acre Arthur Godfrey farm in 1979.

People familiar with the Loudoun County real-estate market observe that most of the foreign owners appear to be interested in keeping the land in farming, rather than speculating on potential residential development, at least in the short term. Most of their holdings are operated by hired farm managers, or rented to local farmers, although the current returns are very low in relation to the price paid for the land. Perhaps an important motivation for the foreign investors is the security of the investment, including the possibility of being able to migrate in case of trouble in their own countries.

Parcellation of Land

Obviously, increased numbers of owners and a fixed land base will lead to more parcels and smaller average holdings. What this means for resource management continues to be debated, however, as there is little agreement on the extent of production efficiencies and economies of scale for different sizes and uses of parcels.

Our data for western Loudoun County reveal a clear trend toward landownership in smaller parcels. Between 1954 and 1976 the mean size of parcel dropped by more than a third, from 47 to 31 acres, principally the result of a decline in ownership of parcels of more than 50 acres and an increase in ownership of parcels of 10 to 25

acres. Interestingly, the substantial increase in the number of hold
ings in the 10-to-25-acre category was largely the result of nonresi
dent purchases. Owners from outside the county increased their
holdings of parcels in this category by 361 percent, while resident-
owned parcels increased by 70 percent. It is likely that much of the
increase in holdings of 10 to 25 acres has occurred since 1970,
although we do not have annual data. By 1971, Loudoun subdivision regulations prohibited building on unsewered parcels of fewer
than 10 acres, even though zoning permitted 3-acre parcels. The
effect seems to have stimulated purchases of parcels of 10 acres or
more, created by subdividing larger parcels.

Unfortunately, 3-acre minimum zoning and 10-acre minimum
subdivision regulations are not likely to work in concert to preserve
the rural character of the county. As one owner of a 270-acre farm
put it:

> [Ten acres is] a ridiculous size for anything unless you want to be a
> "gentleman farmer" and run a few horses ... too large for a house, so
> small you can't raise crops on it.

And a real-estate agent echoed:

> Ten acres is the biggest waste of land there ever was. It's hard enough
> to keep *three* acres mowed. And from a seller's view, you can get nearly
> as much [due to parcelling value] for a three-acre tract as you can for
> ten acres anyway.

Despite continuing parcellation, the land resource base of western Loudoun County has not, at least for the present, been fragmented beyond repair. The fact is that in 1976 two thirds of the land
area of western Loudoun remained in parcels of more than 100
acres, and the percent of total acres in parcels of more than 300 acres
had dropped only slightly since 1954.

Loudoun's Future

Under the pressures of exurban growth, the landscape of western
Loudoun County is being affected in complex ways. Attempts to
preserve the historic rural character of the area through controls
over land use are likely to conflict with the desires of those who view
growth and change more positively, perhaps in terms of personal
economic benefits. Many existing landowners, for example, want to
be able to sell their land to whomever they choose for the best price
they can get, and incoming suburbanites may not be favorably
disposed toward being told what they should or should not do with

their newly acquired parcels. True, some new landowners, having moved to western Loudoun because of the bucolic nature of the area, are willing to restore a 150-year-old farmhouse to keep that character. But just down the road, the large, single-family brick house that another newcomer builds on 10 acres will look much like the dwelling he recently vacated in the nearby Washington suburbs. Meanwhile, the county's agricultural base is potentially threatened by both activities.

In addition to zoning and subdivision controls, other attempts are being made to preserve Loudoun's agricultural land. Since 1972, the county has given preferential tax treatment to land kept in agriculture. As of 1978, approximately 205,000 acres were part of this tax program—nearly 62 percent of the entire county. However, an owner can participate in the tax program with as few as 5 acres. Some 52,000 acres that have been zoned for agriculture were not in the program in 1978; these excluded acres "represent property that has been subdivided and is out of production as well as some woodland areas."[14]

Some people feel the fact that even very small parcels can qualify for the use-value assessment program has actually encouraged the breaking up of land, and one real-estate agent called the program "a speculator's dream." Many Loudoun County residents are beginning to question whether the results of the program are worth its price—annual losses in tax revenues of nearly $500,000. And the county's newly adopted Resource Management Plan notes:

> While it is evident that the tax structure under preferential assessment relieves, to a degree, the financial tax burden placed on agricultural landowners, it is also evident from research that land use taxation does not inhibit the conversion of land from agricultural to nonagricultural uses. Obviously, the county is not in a position to preserve agriculture at all costs.[15]

In addition to the use-value assessment program, Loudoun County has adopted a plan that allows areas of agricultural land or forestland to qualify as an agricultural district. The area must be at least 500 acres, but not all owners within the district need participate. Creation of an agricultural district assures participants of use-value assessments for the life of the district, regardless of what other ordinances are passed or rescinded in the county, and also places some restrictions on the application of eminent domain. Through mid-1980, five districts had been adopted, amounting to some

50,000 acres. Loudoun's agricultural districts do not, however, change any zoning or subdivision requirements currently in existence. Thus, there is nothing to prevent the subdivision of land in a district should the owner desire it. The districts are mainly an attempt to protect the lower use-value assessments against pressures later on to rescind the tax program in the face of development or arguments about foregone tax revenues. As a local planner put it, "The ag-district gives the farmer a few breaks, and asks nothing of him."

Attempts to regulate rural land-use change through land-use controls can have the unintended effects of causing land prices to increase because controls restrict the land supply. In Loudoun, this has led to charges of "elitism" against county planning officials. Only the rich, it is claimed, can now afford the benefits of exurbia's countrified life-style. Yet Loudoun clearly must plan for its new growth, lest it lose forever the very tranquility and rural character that have made it so attractive, not only for incoming urbanites but also for long-time county residents.

Loudoun County is grappling with these issues in a number of ways: in 1979, a comprehensive Resource Management Plan was adopted; the county has a 10,500-acre historic preservation district, one of the largest in the United States; agricultural districts and use-value assessments are expected to continue; subdivision amendments are being studied to distinguish more clearly between rural and urban land-use areas; density bonuses are being analyzed to foster cluster-type development that would be compatible with agriculture and open space; and planned development around towns and villages is being encouraged as an alternative to scattered rural subdivisions.

Many of these measures are adaptations of planning tools designed initially in response to urban-fringe problems and applied under economic circumstances uniquely urban. Their application to the diverse problems of exurban Loudoun County will surely require a better understanding of the area's land markets and the complexity of changes now occurring. One problem is that there are no rural land-use models, and most planners who are practicing in areas like Loudoun have been schooled in urban-oriented planning programs. One rural sociologist notes that the planning curriculum in most universities "focuses heavily on urban problems and urban regions, with little special attention to the uniqueness of rural communities or environmental systems with low population density."[16] He goes on to state:

> Possibly the greatest shortcoming of many professional planners who attempt to work in rural areas is their inability to understand and empathize with value systems of rural residents and the character of social, political and economic organizations.[17]

Exurban areas like Loudoun County, which are neither truly urban nor completely rural, are likely to be among the principal laboratories in which rural planning tools will be developed.

There is yet another side to the growth and planning issues facing Loudoun County. Growth brings problems, but it also produces the resources, through increased tax revenues, to help deal with that growth. Loudoun's planning staff has grown from 2 to 14 persons since the mid-1960s; a new county administrative complex was completed in 1977; and the county is now developing a computerized planning data bank. Such improvements do not come cheaply. The county budget for all land-use and planning-related functions was approximately $500,000 for 1979. As the county's Planning Director put it:

> We're experimenting here and doing things people say can't be done in this state...and a lot of our proposals have been turned down. ...We do very detailed studies to support our proposals and this is costly and time consuming. Because of very limited resources, other places have not been able to do this.

There is no indication that the growth pressures in Loudoun County will let up, or that the land-use issues will become less complex.

II

Tyler County, Texas, *lies in the heart of the East Texas "pineywoods," one of the most productive areas in the country for growing softwood timber. It is to just such areas that the lumber and paper industries must look to offset the declining stock of old-growth timber in the Pacific Northwest. But the timber industry must compete for land with a host of new land buyers, who find that the peace (and low cost) of living in the country can more than offset a long commute to the refineries in Beaumont or the relatively low wages offered by a scattering of new rural industries. Recreation*

seekers and retirees also have found the pineywoods of interest; subdivisions of lakeside lots have been created to accommodate their homes and trailers. Between 1954 and 1976, the number of Tyler County landowners with holdings of fewer than 5 acres increased from 868 to 6,962. Some land has been taken off the private market by the federal government, which has purchased more than 10 thousand acres in the county as part of the creation of the Big Thicket National Preserve. For the present, the Tyler County landscape continues to consist mainly of a sea of industry-owned pine trees. But forces are in motion in this once-sleepy rural region that make new uses increasingly strong competitors for land.

Stretching from the Red River on the north nearly to the Gulf of Mexico on the south, the East Texas Pine-Hardwood Region—the "pineywoods"—encompasses some 11.3 million acres of commercial forestland. The area covers 48 counties of rolling, densely timbered land, a sharp contrast to the popular rangeland and ranch image of rural Texas. Within the region are four national forests, several state parks, and numerous rivers, lakes, and reservoirs. The natural amenities of the pineywoods have been attracting increasing numbers of retirees, commuters, vacationers, and weekenders from large metropolitan areas in Texas and Louisiana, and from the oil fields and industrial areas of the Gulf Coast.

Our research in this region focused mainly on Tyler County, located about two hours' drive northeast of Houston, an hour north of Beaumont, and about 40 miles west of the Louisiana state line. Tyler is at the heart of the pineywoods and serves as the northern gateway to the newly created Big Thicket National Preserve.

Tyler County had 16,164 residents in 1980, nearly two thirds of whom lived outside the small county seat and four other very small unincorporated towns. The county is characterized by large expanses of dense forests, occasionally broken by smaller plots devoted to beef cattle, poultry, and crops such as corn, hay, and melons. It contains Lake Steinhagen and numerous streams; in fact, it has more miles of running streams than any other county in Texas. Tyler County's gently rolling terrain, which varies only between 100 and 400 feet above sea level, serves as a transitional zone between the coastal plains and upland forest portions of the East Texas region.

In many ways, Tyler County is representative of the East Texas region in general, without reaching the extremes of development pressure found in those counties closest to Houston. At the same time, as in many places across the United States, the rural traditions and landscapes of the county are being challenged and changed by new landowners and new activity in the land market. Prices are rising rapidly and ownership of land in increasingly smaller parcels is commonplace.

The economy of Tyler and surrounding counties has long been dominated by the timber industry. Tyler County's forestland is split between pure southern pine (45 percent) and mixtures of pine-hardwoods or pure hardwood types. The county ranks second among Texas' 254 counties in its proportion of "prime" (site index 85+) timberland.[18]

Commercial forest covers 90 percent of Tyler County, with some 141,000 acres, or 26 percent, held by private, nonindustrial owners. According to U.S. Forest Service information, in 1975 some 389,400 acres of the county (roughly two thirds of the land) was owned by the timber industry. One report states that total timber production contributes about $24 million annually to the Tyler County economy.[19] Most of the industry-owned land (approximately 300,000 acres) is held by four timber companies.

At one time, small towns in the county grew and declined with the successes and failures of the local sawmills, which in turn mirrored both the state and national economies, particularly housing markets. Now, local independent sawmills have given way to larger corporate operations.

Timber dwarfs the other productive use of the area's land base—agriculture. Nonforested farmland in Tyler County consists of only 16,000 acres of cultivated cropland, and 13,000 acres of cropland used for pasture.[20] Between 1964 and 1974, the number of farms in the county dropped by nearly half, and the land in farms decreased by nearly 60 percent.[21] As in many other rural places, it is difficult to earn a living solely from the farm, and few Tyler County residents today do so. Employment in agriculture dropped between 1950 and 1970 from 20 percent to 5 percent of the work force.[22] A member of one of the county's founding families described his situation this way: "My partner and I own a farm but try to make our living practicing law."

Recreation and tourism also contribute to Tyler County's economic base. Hunting, fishing, camping, boating, hiking, and visits to the Big Thicket Preserve and Alabama-Coushatta Indian Reservation have contributed significantly to jobs and income in the area.

Residents of the county seat note that it is difficult to get from one side of town to the other on weekends because of the congestion caused by boats, trailers, and camping vehicles.

Finally, the county has tried to stimulate industrial growth. A county development corporation has been formed to solicit new business and industry, and more than 400 acres of land have been purchased and cleared for an industrial park on the fringes of the county seat. An additional 80 acres are being cleared to facilitate other industrial improvements.

Many Tyler County residents, having seen hard times as rural areas generally declined, now look forward to economic growth. A local school official indicated, "We're proud to have the people come up here; we need some more people." And a local resident whose family goes back generations in the area, when asked if the county was prepared for new growth, replied, "You're damned right!" Confrontation is taking shape, however, between the enthusiastic advocates of economic growth and the many newcomers who have only recently begun to move to Tyler County as an escape from the pressures of urban life.

Population Growth

Like many rural places, Tyler County has in recent years begun to experience a marked turnaround in population trends. Census counts indicated a loss of population during the 1940s and 1950s, average annual increases of 1.6 percent during the 1960s, and an average annual increase of 2.6 percent during the 1970s. Tyler's rate of growth in the most recent decade was more than two and a half times as fast as that of the U.S. population as a whole and was slightly faster than that registered by the state of Texas.

Part of this growth has been due to retirees. Census figures for Tyler County indicate a constant increase since 1940 in the over-65 age group, with a 3.8 percent annual growth between 1960 and 1970 (1980 figures are not yet available). This increase has important implications for such public services as health care and transportation. At the same time, many retirees are settling in Tyler County with some degree of prosperity. Speaking about the changing rural environment of the area, one resident noted:

> This is a fairly prosperous area, with lots of Beaumont retirement people here. [With their retirement money] they build the best house they've ever had. Some have even come up here [to retire] and gone into the real-estate business; made more in a couple of years than they ever did as workers in Beaumont, and can now retire with ease.

141

Tyler's new arrivals also include pilots based in Houston, an architect who runs the local country club, a former Boston symphony musician, a Gulf Coast tugboat captain, and urban executives. One woman, who became a successful local real-estate agent, returned to the area where she grew up so that she and her husband could raise their children where "people were friendly," and where, unlike the cities in which they had lived, they could expect a "helping hand when needed." A former law-school administrator who had grown up in East Texas returned to escape the hectic pace of urban life. Now commuting 50 miles to work in Beaumont, he commented, "I'd rather be 10 minutes from beautiful woods than 10 minutes from a good restaurant."

The East Texas Land Market

The renewal of population growth has been felt strongly in the East Texas land market. The large timber companies in the area find themselves competing with real-estate developers for land needed to accommodate production expansion or to replace what has been lost to right-of-way and utility easements. With population growth has come an increase in sales of land in smaller and smaller parcels., And as the demands mount on the supply of privately held noncorporate land, the expected but often unwelcome result is rapidly rising land prices.

Sales and Parcellation of Land

Subdivision activity in Tyler County, although not a new phenomenon, dates back only to the late 1940s. By 1954, the number of subdivisions recorded could still be counted on one hand. However, mirroring the national real-estate market, including our other study sites, a substantial increase in activity occurred in the late 1960s. From 1950, when real-estate transactions in Tyler County were only 574 for the year, sales rose moderately to 855 in 1965. By 1972, however, real-estate transactions had doubled their 1966 levels. Land sales fell off during the recession of 1973-75. But in 1976 there were nearly 2,100 land sales in the county, including more than 600 in a 3,000-lot "resort city" subdivision.

These title transfers alone do not indicate that land was being broken up into smaller and smaller parcels. What does shed light on parcellation, and on the growth pressures facing the pineywoods, is an increase in the number of landowners—since the land base is essentially fixed. Between 1954 and 1976, the number of landowners in Tyler County (exclusive of the county seat) more than tripled, rising from 3,072 to 11,264. Combining this with market transactions, one quickly observes that the major parcellation of land in the county occurred only rather recently.[23] One concerned resident, himself a new arrival, has stated, "The biggest environmental problem in this whole area is all the real-estate development being carved out of the county."

Even more notable are changes in the size distribution of landholdings. Between 1954 and 1976, the number of landowners with total holdings of fewer than five acres increased more than 700 percent—from 868 to 6,962. During the same period, the number of owners of one acre or less skyrocketed to an estimated 5,745, more than 16 times the number in 1954! Our estimates indicate that in 1976 the average lot size in rural subdivisions in Tyler County was slightly less than one third of an acre; excluding ranchettes of two to five acres, the mean lot size drops to just under one quarter of an acre. Clearly, small-lot subdivision has come to the East Texas pineywoods. One real-estate developer voiced his philosophy by saying, "We make the lots small and sell them in mass. . . . Let's face it, you can sell a lot more Fords and Chevies than Cadillacs." Nonetheless, parcellation is not highly visible at ground level. Often one has to drive a substantial distance off the main roadways to reach subdivided properties. And, if corporation-owned timber acreage, public land, towns and built-up areas are excluded, only 7 percent of the remaining acreage is taken up by holdings of 10 acres or less.

Between 1954 and 1976 purchases in *all* size categories increased. In fact, holdings in the largest classes (100-plus acres) increased by 45 percent, from an estimated 400 to 580. This increase was not due to the creation of large parcels, but to the division of, say, a 500-acre parcel into three or four units. Even disregarding the huge number of less than one-acre lots, there was a substantial drop in the median size of holding over this period—from 24 to 15 acres. Naturally, given the phenomenal tripling of new owners by 1976, the number of large-acreage holders dropped as a percent of all owners. Nevertheless, large land parcels *do* remain in Tyler County. Holdings of 100 acres or more in 1976 accounted for 58 percent of private, noncorporate rural land. As noted below, whether or when these large landholdings become available in the market is a significant issue for the region's timber industry.

Nonresident Ownership

While the total number of landowners in Tyler County tripled between 1954 and 1976, the number of owners residing outside the county increased nearly sevenfold. Based on our estimates, in 1954 nonresident owners made up 31 percent of total owners, increasing to 58 percent in 1976. Fully 92 percent of the absentee owners reside in the state of Texas but outside Tyler County. Of these state residents, 42 percent live in the three metropolitan areas of Dallas, Houston, and Beaumont/Port Arthur. The number of out-of-state owners increased more than sixfold (from 79 in 1954 to 527 in 1976), but they represent only 8 percent of the nonresident owners in the county.

The total estimated acreage owned by nonresidents rose from nearly 59,000 acres in 1954 to more than 107,000 acres in 1976, with substantial changes in the distribution of holdings. In 1954 more than a third of the nonresidents owned 50 acres or more. By 1976 only 9 percent had holdings that large. Far more typical in 1976 was the nonresident owning less than one acre. Over the 22-year period, the number of such owners rose 43-fold, from an estimated 86 to 3,718. We believe that similar patterns exist in nearby counties. In fact, the situation may be even more pronounced as one moves southwest toward Houston.

As already noted, recreation is an important part of the economy in this area of Texas, and much of the nonresident demand for small lots and tracts of fewer than 10 acres appears to be for recreation—hunting, fishing, boating, hiking, camping. Although some purchasers have bought individual parcels scattered through the woods, many have purchased parcels in one of several large-scale recreational developments. One such development, the Wildwood "resort city," overlaps the boundary between Tyler and Hardin counties. Begun in 1965, Wildwood has 3,000 mostly tiny (50' x 150') lots, though some range up to an acre or more. All lots have been sold, and some have been offered on the resale market for prices ranging between $4,000 and $20,000. However, as of 1978, only 300 of the 3,000 lots had been improved by their owners with some sort of permanent or temporary structure. Wildwood has its own security system, "Millionaires' Island," and a golf course; there are plans for a country club and private airstrip. When asked why only 300 owners had improved their lots, a real-estate salesman said that people just liked to come for the weekend or longer to enjoy the clean air, to pitch their tent (or stay in the apartments that have been built at Wildwood), and go fishing or boating. Many owners who have made no improvements are likely holding the land as an investment.

Hunting is one of the most popular recreational activities pursued in the pineywoods. Indeed, the desire to secure hunting rights for exclusive use has been a significant factor impelling non-residents to purchase rural acreage there. The number of signs posting land against hunting is evidence of how jealously these private rights are then guarded. Most of the land owned by timber companies is open to hunting—partly for good public relations, partly because companies fear vandalism or even arson if they post the land. One firm advertises "We want to be a good neighbor" and has opened to the public for hunting and fishing more than 159,000 acres of its holdings in 15 East Texas counties. Frequently, companies try to control use, and raise some money toward administrative costs, by leasing hunting rights to private hunting clubs.[24]

The Big Thicket National Preserve

One of the most widely talked about new forces affecting the land market in the pineywoods has been the federal government's purchase of land for the Big Thicket National Preserve, established by Congress in 1974.[25] The Thicket will contain a total of more than 86,000 acres in a series of disjunct units and stream corridors located in seven southeast Texas counties. By mid-1979, 95 percent of this land had either been acquired through purchase, was being acquired through condemnation, or was in the negotiation stage.[26] All or part of four units of the Thicket—about 12,600 acres—are located in Tyler County.

The purpose of the Big Thicket is to preserve the highly varied ecosystems found in the region. Scientists have termed it a "biological crossroads." But many people in the region, particularly at the outset, expressed reservations over the project. The prevalent theme was that the Thicket was removing land from an already limited supply under pressure from population growth. Some people felt it was not clear whether the project would economically benefit the region as intended.

There now seems to be an attitude of general acceptance of the Thicket as the sort of inevitable change that may, after all, be beneficial. Nonetheless, when 86,000 acres of land are removed from a market already sluggish in its response to increased demand pressures, a natural result will be an increase in the price of land.

The Supply of Land

On the supply side, several factors are at work that appear to impede response to newly increased demand. First, "available" land in Tyler County is already quite limited. Removing from total county acreage the land already held by the timber industry (389,400 acres), the land already in urban or other nonrural uses (8,000-plus acres), and federal land (12,629 acres, including the Big Thicket), the remaining rural acreage only amounts to about 30 percent of the county, or roughly 177,000 acres. Assuming acres of pasture and cropland remain about the same (at 29,000 acres), expansion of timber-producing lands and lands needed to satisfy expected population growth are competing for some 148,000 acres.[27]

Under normal competitive market conditions, land would be allocated to the most profitable use. But conditions in Tyler County are not normally competitive. A relatively small number of families owns much of the remaining noncorporate land, and seldom are any of these lands placed on the market. What is offered for sale is often from estates or sold for other personal reasons not connected with the market demand. Combining the sluggish supply and few large tracts with the expansion and replacement demands of the timber companies and pressures from new population growth, the result is that, as one local real-estate broker put it, "land prices are going up by the minute."

Land prices began their rapid increase in the late 1960s. One local appraiser estimated that land values have been inflating about 13 percent annually since 1970, while a land dealer just down the street gave a more conservative estimate of 8 to 10 percent. Accounts of actual transactions indicate both estimates are on the conservative side. Annual value increases of 14 to 16 percent dominated the market transactions of which we were aware.

The following example of a succession of transactions involving a single rural property is illustrative. In 1960 a local real-estate broker bought 160 acres bounded on two sides by timber-company land for $100 per acre. Within the same year he sold it for $250 an acre in four 40-acre tracts. In 1965 two of the tracts were sold for $300 an acre. In 1970 the other two were split into 10-acre parcels and sold off at $600 per acre. The broker is now buying back 22 acres of this land, which adjoins his own property, for $1,500 per acre and is thinking about breaking it up into half-acre homesites.

Some Special Effects on the Timber Industry

The rising land prices in East Texas have particularly affected the timber industry. Purchases of new timberland have slowed as the price of land continues its upward movement to levels not justified by the production of timber. One forest manager told us that, because of the pressures of population growth, his company had not been acquiring much land in the area for several years. And another forester noted the problems of both price and parcellation on his firm's general policy:

> There's not much left to buy.... At $800 to $1,000 an acre you just can't grow timber...[and] if you can't get a good-sized tract it's not worth the effort.

Our estimates of timber-industry landholdings in Tyler County indicate that the companies have increased their total acreage by approximately 80,000 acres since 1954.[28] It is likely, however, that most of this was acquired prior to the strong real-estate market of the late 1960s.

Somewhat surprisingly, at first glance, the timber companies do not seem to be worried about the problems of growth and current activity in the real-estate market. When asked how these factors affected the industry's current and future plans, three different industry representatives gave quite similar responses. One said, "We don't really relate our changing technology to real-estate activity." Another indicated, "[We have] no major problem with the [population] influx as long as companies can continue to control their lands." And the third felt, "[The county's growth] has no real effect on the timber industry."

On the other hand, this apparent lack of concern may be due to the fact that timber companies are themselves in line to participate in some of the profits in the land market. One of the major timber companies has developed several subdivisions in the general piney-woods region, ranging from low-priced, small-lot tracts to half-acre lakeside properties that sell for $20,000. A company representative noted, "...we got into the [development] game because it looked lucrative."

It is hard to imagine Tyler County, even in the distant future, as other than a major timber producer. Its geographic location has given it great natural advantages for that use—a combination of soils and climate that can bring a pine tree to maturity in half the time required in northern climates. But geography has also placed Tyler County within driving distance of the fast-growing metropolitan centers of the Gulf Coast and blessed the county with the kind of scenery that recreationists and retirees demand. The resulting competition between timber and development is likely to be the dominant theme in the county's history in years ahead.

III

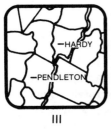

III

In **Hardy County** *and* **Pendleton County, West Virginia,** *poor transportation networks and lack of employment opportunity meant decades of population decline. But in the late 1960s abundant opportunities for hunting, fishing, and hiking began to attract the attention of urban recreationists. Land prices were extremely low because of lack of local demand, and many urbanites found that because of this they could afford more land than they ever thought possible. As new demand forced land prices up, investment interest quickened. Local and out-of-town developers alike were eager to accommodate the new money, creating medium-sized parcels and speculative lots out of abandoned farms and woodlands. New owners are frequently interested in environmental amenities, but they appear to be doing little to upgrade the area's forest resource, badly degraded by decades of exploitative "high-grading," which left only crooked trees and unsalable species. Although urban buyers have been of some help to the local economy, they have also created animosity—for example, by posting against hunting on land formerly open to the local community.*

The Potomac Highlands region is a string of rural counties lying on the Virginia-West Virginia border and providing the headwaters for the Potomac River. Little affected by the mining and industrialization that has sullied some other parts of West Virginia, the area is notable for its excellent hunting and fishing, for its white-water canoeing streams, and for the presence of hundreds of thousands of acres of mountainous national forest land. Early transportation routes, and the heavy settlement that accompanied them, tended to bypass the region, leaving it with the somewhat isolated character it retains today. Yet that isolation is fast diminishing. The Potomac Highlands lie only two to five hours by car from the land-hungry metropolitan populations of Washington, D.C., Baltimore, and Pittsburgh.

Revival in the "Back Country"

Our research efforts in the Potomac Highlands focused on two adjoining counties located near the center of the region: Hardy County (1980 population 10,051), which lies three hours due west of Washington, D.C., and Pendleton County (1980 population 7,935), which is four hours away. Both counties are dominated by forested mountains, the highest peaks of which tend to be within the George Washington or Monongahela National Forests. The bulk of the land is privately owned and is also heavily forested. There is a considerable acreage of farmland lying along major stream valleys, which makes agriculture more significant in the economy than is usual in mountainous West Virginia. Nearly one fifth of the land in each county is devoted to nonforest agricultural use, mainly corn, hay, and cattle pasturage.

A casual visitor will be struck by the area's seeming isolation and self-containment. No interstate highway lies within the borders of Hardy and Pendleton counties; nowhere is there any outlet of a fast-food or motel chain; between them, the two counties possess a single traffic light. The landscape consists of a handful of compact, not particularly prosperous towns; large fields of corn or grazing sheep and cattle; and unbroken expanses of forested mountains, with a mixture of hardwood species predominating. Few physical signs of growth are apparent. Although population is now increasing, neither county has as many residents as it had in 1940. As one local history put it (in 1963), "Even if urban man were burned off the earth, life in this back country probably would go on."[29]

Beginning in the late 1960s, there was a marked quickening in the land market of this "back country." For residents of Washington, D.C., or Baltimore, the Potomac Highlands were close enough for weekend recreation, yet so rough and underpopulated as to seem almost frontier-like. And the land, by urban standards, was unbelievably cheap. During this period, a Washington museum curator bought more than 300 acres in the highlands for just under $100 per acre. "It was impulse buying," he recalls. "Coming from the city, I was impressed with the beauty of the land. I just didn't discuss the price." He was surprised and delighted when he learned that $30,000 bought such a huge piece of property.

There were many similar experiences. Some of the urbanites sought river frontage; others looked for solitude on land so steep and hard to reach that the locals chortled. A few, hoping to hedge against urban social upheaval, wanted land fertile enough to support subsistence crops. The creation in 1965 of the 100,000-acre Spruce Knob-Seneca Rocks National Recreation Area in the mountainous Monongahela National Forest helped fix popular interest on the Highlands as a recreation destination. Local white-water canoe races and traditional music festivals began to draw crowds of visitors from the cities.

Changes in the Land Market

Real-estate transactions in Hardy County averaged 270 per year for the 15 years between 1950 and 1965. In 1966 an upward trend began, leading to annual transactions in 1971 that were 75 percent higher than the 1965 level. After dropping off during the 1974-75 recession, land sales rose strongly in 1976 and 1977. By the end of 1979, title transfers were double what they had been only a decade earlier (671 in 1979 compared to 339 in 1969). Interestingly, market activity seems not to have been greatly reduced, at least initially, by the high interest rates, and high cost of fuel and energy, during the 1978–79 period. Data for the first few months of 1980 do indicate, however, that a slowdown in transactions was occurring.

Along with this activity, the Highlands have experienced three trends that many other high-amenity rural areas have witnessed: sharp increases in land prices, increased ownership of land by nonresidents, and subdivision of land into smaller parcels.

Evidence of the increase in prices can be seen in Hardy County, for example. Mountain forestland that could have been had for $50 to $100 an acre in the mid-1960's now commands $350 to $500. Good cropland sells for up to $2,200 per acre on the infrequent occasions when it comes onto the market. Accessible residential tracts of fewer than 10 acres can seldom be found for less than $1,000 per acre. Most of the price appreciation in recreational land took place before 1973. Since that time, according to local land dealers, appreciation has been just a little faster than the rate of inflation, leveling off with the poorer economic conditions of 1980.

As to ownership by nonresidents, examination of county court-house records reveals that by 1975 28 percent of the privately owned land in Hardy County was owned by persons or corporations with addresses outside the county. Of these owners, more than 40 percent lived in metropolitan Washington or Baltimore. In Pendelton County, an hour or more farther from these metropolitan areas, only 16 percent of the land was owned by noncounty residents, and many of those owners were from elsewhere in West Virginia.

The third trend, subdivision, has been exacerbated by the rise in land prices. When land was cheap, newcomers to the Potomac Highlands bought whatever parcels came onto the market. As prices rose, particularly for the most scenic and buildable tracts, the prices of larger parcels began to exceed what the average buyer could afford to pay. The predictable result was what local real-estate agents call "land-busting"—the division of land into tracts of sizes that might appeal to urban purchasers.

During the late 1960s and early 1970s, local entrepreneurs, along with a scattering of outsiders, carved tracts of mountain land into developments. Sometimes these had recreational facilities or model homes; most often, however, the improvements were nothing more than a large "Welcome" sign and a system of steep dirt roads. Invariably, the development was given an evocative name like Sherwood Forest, Resortland, Land of Spruce. (The land was carried on county record books under such names as Hinterland, Inc., Oldfields Limited Partnership, Hidden Lake Joint Venture.) In locations closest to metropolitan areas, or in tracts along the Potomac or Shenandoah rivers, lots tended to be small and numerous. Farther away, larger parcels predominated, most of them between 5 and 20 acres, but some as large as 50 acres.

After 1974, most of the small-lot subdivisions in the Potomac Highlands became inactive. Leaning signs, ill-maintained roads, and a lack of new building attest to their near-moribund state. In some cases, the lots were all sold, and the owner no longer wanted to pay for maintenance; in other cases, lots are still for sale, but are not actively promoted. One real-estate dealer, speaking of a nearly bankrupt small-lot development, noted, "We got some free information from it. People just aren't interested in that kind of planned development." He continues to specialize in undeveloped parcels of several acres or more.

Records in Hardy County's cavernous turn-of-the-century court-house underline the impact that subdivision has had on the land. In

1954 rural land in the county was held in 4,625 separate parcels; by 1976 it was held in 6,613 parcels, an increase of 43 percent. The number of owners shows an even greater change. In 1954 there were 2,186 separate ownerships; in 1976 there were 3,688—a growth of 69 percent. In 1954 there were 145 parcels that contained more than 300 acres; these parcels totalled 114,000 acres, or 30 percent of all land in Hardy County. In 1976 there were only 116 parcels of this size, and they totalled 72,000 acres. The greatest growth between 1954 and 1976 was of parcels with fewer than 10 acres, which more than doubled in number. Also increasing substantially were parcels of 10 to 24 acres and 50 to 99 acres. Parcels of 25 to 49 acres and those larger than 100 acres registered declines.

Parcellation data are not available for Pendleton County. Because of its greater distance from metropolitan centers and lower proportion of nonresident ownership, we believe that it has experienced a lower rate of parcellation than has Hardy County.

Population and Economic Growth

The heightened activity in the land market of the Potomac Highlands comes at a time when the region is experiencing a modest quickening of population growth. Hardy and Pendleton counties each suffered a steady loss of population between 1940 and 1970. By 1970 Hardy County had 18 percent fewer people than in 1940; Pendleton County had lost 35 percent of its population. During the last decade, however, population trends have turned around. Between 1970 and 1980, Hardy County grew in population by 13.5 percent and Pendleton County by 12.9 percent. This was actually a bit faster than the rate of population increase for the nation as a whole (11.4 percent).

The turnaround in population trends did not result from agricultural growth. Between 1974 and 1978, the number of farms in Hardy County fell from 486 to 463; the amount of land in operating farms decreased by almost 10,000 acres (to 154,000 acres). Nearly all of this decline was in pasture and farm forests, not in cropland. The good-quality land along the river valleys continued to be cultivated, but—as owners died or moved away—rougher, less-productive lands have been sold to nonfarmers.

In contrast to agriculture, two other sectors do show some signs of economic growth. The first is associated with recreation, tourism, and retirement. Newcomers make modest contributions to the local economy, whether they come for a day or build a home. Motels, restaurants, sporting-goods stores, real-estate dealers, and banks receive the first benefits of this influx, but the new money eventually filters throughout the local economy.

Also, since about 1960, the region has enjoyed a moderate amount of manufacturing growth, mostly in industries employing low-wage, low-skill labor. Because these industries rely on outside demand for their products, they are easily affected by economic circumstances beyond local control. Hardy County's major non-farm employment comes from two plants processing locally raised chickens and from a factory making wooden kitchen cabinets. Declining housing demand outside the region in 1980 caused the cabinet factory to lay off about 15 percent of its employees. In less-developed Pendleton County, the only major nonfarm industry is a shoe factory, which employs some 400 local residents. In 1978, construction began on a hydroelectric dam in an adjoining county, causing a slight economic boom. A later decision by the utility firm (which served residents outside the state) to cease construction for at least two years threw Pendleton into a recession. Unemployment rose to 17 percent, the highest since the mid-1950s.

The nonfarm economic climate in the Potomac Highlands area remains fragile, even though growth has occurred. Out of West Virginia's 55 counties, Pendleton and Hardy ranked 1st and 12th, respectively, on the state's 1979 list of most distressed counties. Newcomers are entering the Highlands land market; as a local county official remarked, however, "They certainly aren't coming in for jobs."

Effects on Forestland and Mineral-bearing Lands

Although the Potomac Highlands area is more than 75 percent forested, its timber industry is not nearly as prominent as it was around the turn of the century, when the cutting of West Virginia's virgin hardwood forests was at its height. Much of the standing timber is now of low quality, the result of generations of "high-grading" (cutting only the best trees and most salable species) and subsequent neglect. Timber companies are slowly expanding their holdings, but they still own only a small proportion of the private forestland in the region. National forests contain significant acreages of commercial timberland. However, recreational and environmental constraints are likely to prevent the national forests from becoming really important factors in the local timber market. If future lumber and wood-pulp output is to be increased in the Highlands, nonindustrial private holdings must play the central role.

The ongoing purchase of forestland by new kinds of owners presents both opportunities and obstacles to improving forest management. On one hand, newcomers often have higher levels of income and education than did the previous owners, and this might predispose them to try to learn more about forest management. The West Virginia district forester for the Highlands notes that newcomers come to him for advice. "They say, 'I don't know anything about this. Help me.' The old-timer owners, especially farmers, have had an attitude of 'We're going to do it ourselves.' They don't ask for my advice." New owners may also be more prone to pay attention to the condition of tree cover than were previous owners, who were typically local farmers more interested in their cultivable bottomlands than in their forested slopes. Many newcomers also are very conscious of environmental quality and might be willing to spend money to foster wildlife, or to improve timber stands, even if there were no immediate monetary return.

On the other hand, the newcomers' initial motivation to acquire land has usually been either recreational use or capital gain, not commodity production. Many of the new urban owners lack any knowledge of forest ecology and forest management. It is quite common to find owners in the Potomac Highlands who believe they are "protecting" the forest by never cutting trees, blissfully ignorant of the fact that their land's timber stock is so poor that heavy selective cutting would be the principal way to improve both timber quality and aesthetics. Even if the new owners are aware of opportunities for timber management, they may conclude that the time and trouble involved do not make it worthwhile.

Parcellation of land puts additional obstacles in the way of timber management. Small-lot subdivisions do not have much impact: in Hardy County, an estimated 3,450 lots of fewer than 10 acres (in 1976) accounted for a total of only about 10,000 acres, or less than 4 percent of the county's total private land area. Potentially more serious is the proliferation of medium-sized parcels, which account for a significant number of acres. In Hardy County, we estimated that parcels of 10 to 50 acres took up 11 percent of all the privately held land in the county; those of 50 to 100 acres, another 21 percent. Parcels of this size cannot be written off as potential timber producers, but the economic possibilities are likely to be somewhat different from what they would be if more of the land were held in very large parcels.

The arrival of new owners in the Highlands also raises issues of public access to land for recreation. The area is extremely popular with hunters, fishermen, and canoeists. In one recent year, three Highlands counties led the state in number of deer killed. As many as 15,000 hunters have descended on Pendleton County during the first three days of the autumn deer season, tripling the county's population. Although many hunt on the extensive national forest lands, there is considerable pressure on private land as well. According to a West Virginia game warden, practically all of the private land in his jurisdiction is posted. Some land is posted specifically against hunting; on some land fishing, camping, and hiking are prohibited as well.

During the late 1970s, the search for domestic sources of energy led oil and gas companies to drill exploratory wells in Hardy and nearby counties. Although there had been some activity in oil and gas leases in Hardy County during the mid-1960s, a substantial increase in such leasing activity occurred beginning in 1977. Throughout the first half of the 1970s, exploratory leases for oil and gas averaged fewer than 40 per year. In 1977 they numbered 144; and in 1978, 190. During 1978 more than 140 leases were taken by a single company said by some local residents to be speculating in hopes of selling the acquired rights to larger energy companies. Several natural gas wells drilled in Hardy County have proved unproductive, but interest has been spurred by the 1979 completion in nearby Mineral County, West Virginia, of a test well with an extremely high daily gas yield. We have no information on the acreage involved with oil and gas exploration activity, but it certainly has the potential for changing the area's landscape should the explorations prove positive.

Conclusion

For decades, the Potomac Highlands lay just beyond the edge of the eastern megalopolis, bypassed by transportation routes and left behind by a changing national economy. But recent years have seen a new demand for the Highlands' main indigenous resources— cheap, scenic land and a willing, low-wage labor force. Like Tyler County, the Highlands has welcomed the long-needed influx of economic activity. But possible impacts on local life-styles and on

155

the productive use of agricultural land and forestland make it likely
that quickening growth will bring problems as well as benefits.

IV

IV

The flat, phenomenally fertile land of **Douglas
County, Illinois,** *is typical of the Corn Belt, one
of the world's most productive agricultural areas.
Although there is very little urbanization pressure, and no recreational demand, Douglas
County farmland sells for between $3,000 and
$4,000 per acre. This area differs from our other
study sites insofar as the strongest bidders in the
land market in Douglas County in recent years have been expanding local farmers, eager to borrow on the appreciated value of their
holdings to finance new purchases. As a result of farm expansion,
the number of farms has fallen over the years, and average farm size
has crept upward. Coupled with a very rapid increase in land
values, this has resulted in an enormous rise in the value of the
average farm. In 1978, the average value of land and buildings on a
Douglas County farm was more than $700,000. Young farmers have
difficulty competing in such a land market; it is often said, "The
only way for a young person to get a farm is to inherit it or marry it."*

East Central Illinois, which consists of several counties centered on
Champaign-Urbana, lies close to the center of the Corn Belt. Good
climate, innovative farmers, and the inherent capacity of the rich
black prairie soil to respond to management for intensive agriculture have established and guaranteed the region's farm economy for
the past 100 years. Average farmland values, at $3,000 to $4,000 an
acre, are among the highest in the United States.

Once agriculturally diversified, East Central Illinois is now a
region where farmers concentrate almost exclusively on grain production, with most of the land planted in corn or soybeans. The
full-time farm operations average 300 to 400 acres, with some reaching over 1,000 acres. Outside of the Champaign-Urbana metropolitan area and the various small towns, almost all land in the region is
in farms, and most of that is cultivated for crops. Because of favorable weather patterns and soil fertility, crop failures are very rare.
The farmers are efficient, optimistic, and willing to take risks. Over
the years, those whose operations were too small, or who were afraid

to expand and adopt new technology, have been forced out of business by competitive pressures. The result has been fewer farmers, but generally prosperous ones. In the words of a local tax assessor, "The farmers around here are wealthy. They own the banks." Today, a net worth of $1 million is "not uncommon at all."

Douglas County (1980 population 19,785), like most of the East Central Illinois region, is flat, low-lying, and largely bare of trees. Because of wet soils, the county did not develop agriculturally until the late 1870s, when "men of some capital" bought and drained the swampland farmed unsuccessfully by their predecessors. Completion of the Illinois Central Railroad in 1855, as well as subsequent lines, also helped make prairie agriculture viable. Corn and soybeans produced in the region are still moved to market by train.

With draining, about 96 percent of Douglas County is considered prime agricultural land, according to USDA definitions, a higher proportion than in any other Illinois county. Per-acre yields—about 135 to 140 bu/acre (bushels per acre) for corn and 34 to 38 bu/acre for soybeans—are very high, though not exceptional for the East Central region. Average farmland values have in recent years been among the highest in the state of Illinois, except for those in counties immediately surrounding Chicago.

Interstate 57 bisects Douglas County and brings the area within commuting distance of Champaign-Urbana. As a result, some residential and commercial development has occurred in and near the small towns with ready access to I-57, although the land-use changes have occurred slowly, and to a limited extent. In the early 1970s some residents were sufficiently concerned about nonfarm development in Douglas County to draft a countywide zoning ordinance, including provisions for agricultural zoning. Politically unpopular and ill timed, the measure never came up for discussion. Many residents simply feel there is no need for zoning. As the county tax assessor explains, "The county has always had farming. The farmers aren't going to leave." In fact, nearly 90 percent of all land is in farms, though farm families account for less than 20 percent of the population. Moreover, the amount of land in farms, reported by the USDA Census of Agriculture, actually increased by 5.5 percent from 1969 to 1978.

In the nonfarm sector, two plastics manufacturing firms and an undergound coal mine are the principal local industries. They employ a large number of people, including some who commute from Indiana. These three industries have not created major new demands for housing beyond municipal bounds, nor have they affected the value of land sold for farming purposes. This can be contrasted with other nearby counties, where proximity to urban areas such as Champaign-Urbana and Decatur has forced farmland prices up.

The farmers in Douglas County are like farmers throughout the East Central Illinois region, although local USDA field staff say they are "more progressive" and "more professional" than their counterparts elsewhere. "About 80 to 90 percent of the farmers here have on-the-farm storage facilities—that's more than in any other county in Illinois," commented one staff member. He believes that up to one third of Douglas County farmers hedge against crop price fluctuations by buying or selling contracts on the commodity futures market, and another 10 percent actively speculate in commodities.

In many ways, Douglas County farmers have to be sophisticated operators, for they must manage substantial assets. In 1978, the average Douglas County farm's land and buildings were valued at $777,000—up more than 100 percent in just four years. The average farmer's machinery was worth another $66,000. There are, moreover, a high percentage of tenants and many absentee landlords, both of which have been traditional in the more fertile parts of Illinois. Tenant farming has stimulated a "stiff competition" for the land and prods the county's farmers to build up reputations for being efficient producers, so that rentable land will be made available to them. The farmers' optimism and their competition for the land find expression in the rural land market.

Aspects of the Land Market

The most dramatic feature of the rural land market in Douglas County, and throughout the region, is the high per-acre price farmland commands. East Central Illinois farmland values are based primarily on the soil's productivity, the buildings, if any, and the amount of tillable land. Within the same county, fertile soils in a topographically flat area may sell for four to six times more than less-productive soils in "broken," or stream-crossed, rolling terrain. Prices paid also vary according to tract size, with smaller tracts (say, 40 acres) bringing higher per-acre prices.

Although highly fertile land has always commanded a premium price, the feed-grain export boom which began in the early 1970s gave an added stimulus to the land market. Land that at farm sales in 1968 averaged $800 per acre sold 10 years later for $3,000 to $4,000 per acre, a rise of 300 to 400 percent. Much of this rise occurred after 1973. Similarly, the average Federal Land Bank loan increased from $39,500 in 1972 to more than $100,000 in 1977, largely due to the "skyrocketing price of land."[30] As one local real-estate broker relates, "1973 was the last year you could buy land at $700 to $750 an acre. . . . Farm profits have some little bearing [on the price], but mostly it's the farmers. They want to own it [the land]."

To the farmer, landownership traditionally has meant job security and a home. Today, the advantages of large-scale farming make control of land resources even more attractive. Operators of larger farms have more land over which to spread the high fixed costs of farm production, such as machinery, and can use additional land, up to a certain point, without acquiring more equipment. The demand for land is very strong, but also very localized, for a farmer who wants to expand his operation. The typical farmer's limit of interest in new land seems to be a distance of less than 10 miles from his base of operations. There is also a lively demand for renting farmland. One Douglas County farmer jokes that, "If I had a heart attack today, I suppose that by six o'clock there would be five or six people coming by to ask my widow if they could rent the farm."

Often, only the larger farmers may have the equity and income to bid for land at its current high market price. Take, for example, the actual case of a farmer buying 80 acres at $3,810 per acre. His annual payment on the purchase amounts to $21,800. Net income on the 80 acres after property taxes, costs of production inputs, and depreciation is $6,300. To make up the difference between this net income and his annual mortgage cost, this particular buyer will rely on his net income of $55,600 from the other 500 acres he farms and the 128 acres he owns.

A nonfarmer buyer of the same land could support the same investment with nonfarm capital, but, because net earnings from the tract would be split with a tenant, the amount he would have to raise each year to make up the difference between earnings from the land and annual payments on it would be $3,150 more than the farmer's amount. Locally, this difference is considered to be enough to discourage nonfarm investors from buying. In either case, a buyer's profits lie in the capital gains. If the 80 acres at $3,810 per acre appreciate by 13 percent, as was true of Illinois farmland in 1978, the capital gains after one year would be $39,624. Anticipation of substantial capital gains is itself one of the reasons behind rising farmland prices.

Prices are forced up also by the limited amount of land coming onto the market each year. Pointing to his listings, one real-estate dealer explained, "In the early '70s, I had two and a half columns of farms for sale here. Now farm listings are scarce," in part because the farm economy has picked up within the past few years. The demand is strong; the supply is limited. Historically, only 3 or 4 percent of the county's farmland turns over annually, much of it transferred within families and never coming onto the market.

Already, farmland prices in Douglas County are well above what the land's productive capacity under current product prices and interest rates warrants. According to an agricultural economist at the nearby campus of the University of Illinois, "This means that if the current returns on land [traditionally 3 to 4 percent] don't rise, land prices will either decline or increase less rapidly than they have in the past."[31] He predicts that, in the future, farmland prices will probably continue to rise, but more slowly and more in keeping with the prices of farm products. Assuming some inflation continues, he believes that land currently selling at $3,500 per acre may be selling for $5,000 to $5,500 per acre by 1990.

Most of the people we interviewed in East Central Illinois share a cautiously optimistic assessment of future farmland values. Some experts, however, are more pessimistic. The fact that land values have continued to rise despite declining farm profits, in Illinois as elsewhere in the country, suggests that farm buyers are anticipating substantial capital gains on their investments in land. If farmers' expectations decline, farmland values probably will decline as well.[32] There is the possibility, too, that tightening credit policies will reduce farmers' buying power. Because so little land comes on the market each year, however, it takes only a handful of optimistic farmers to keep farmland prices high.

The existence of a continuing, albeit blurred, tie between farm income and land prices began to be illustrated in late 1979 and early 1980, when the national inflation rate jumped at the same time that farm income began to fall. Taken by itself, the acceleration of inflation—and particularly of expectations about future inflation—would be expected to increase investment demand for tangible assets, such as farmland. But farmers, who in recent years have been the main investment buyers, found that their costs of production were going up far more rapidly than were the prices of their crops. Although interest rates on farm real-estate loans remained low relative to the inflation rate, farmers in Illinois and around the nation became reluctant to borrow. And because of the deteriorating cash-flow position of farmers and a modest rise in delinquencies on existing loans, banks were more reluctant to lend.

The net result was that the farmland market in East Central Illinois simply dried up. When transactions did take place, land that would have sold for $4,000 an acre in 1978 sold for $3,400 to $3,500. Except for the occasional distress sale, however, there were few transactions. Most potential sellers chose not to place their land on the market until prospects for farm income had improved.

Patterns of Ownership

A conspicuous feature of the East Central Illinois land market, compared with the land markets in our other case studies, is its stability of ownership patterns. Between 1954 and 1975, the number of owners in the four eastern townships of Douglas County where we gathered our data increased by only 15.6 percent.[33] The average size of holding fell 14 percent, from 124 acres to 107 acres, while the median size remained stable, at 80 acres.[34] In percentage terms, the biggest changes were increases in the number of holdings under 5 acres and from 25 to 50 acres. But the predominant ownership size, in terms both of number of holdings and total acreage involved, was the medium-sized holding of 50 to 300 acres. These holdings were dominant in 1954 and increased slightly during the 22-year period we studied. They reflect the continued dominance in Douglas County of the medium-sized, family-operated commercial farm. Holdings of more than 300 acres decreased somewhat, from 58 in 1954 to 49 in 1976.

Comparison of the 1954 and 1978 Censuses of Agriculture reveals that this long-term stability of ownership masks some important but offsetting changes in land tenure arrangements. Countywide, there has been a decline in the number of farms, from 1,304 in 1954 to 851 in 1978. The size of the average farm operation rose from 193 to 317 acres. More than 30 farming operations are larger than 1,000 acres. Some formerly small farms have grown bigger by land acquisition, but much of the net growth in farm size has come from some significant changes in farmland rental patterns. In 1954 there were 627 tenant-operated farms, most of them small. By 1978, however, this number had plummeted to 228. The number of full-owner farms had also fallen. The only growth came in farms where the owner owned part of the land and rented part; these rose from 323 in 1954 to 353 in 1978. Thus, land that had been formerly cultivated as a single farm by a single tenant was increasingly becoming part of an operation in which a large-scale farmer would own some parcels and rent others, perhaps from several absentee owners.

Although the number of nonresident owners in our study area rose by 21 percent from 1954 to 1976, the amount of land held by nonresidents increased by only 1.5 percent. Moreover, some of the land held by nonresidents may be owned by farmers in adjacent counties who have expanded into Douglas County. On the other hand, the number of out-of-state owners rose by almost two thirds during the study period and their holdings were almost 11 percent of total acreage in 1976.

For decades, people with money to invest have bought land in the East Central Illinois area and rented it to farmers. Since the precipitous rise in farmland prices beginning in 1973-74, however, the number of nonfarmer investors dropped to the point where local farmers accounted for 80 to 95 percent of the new transactions. According to a real-estate broker in a nearby farming county, "Back in 1973, locally I'd say about 40 to 50 percent of the land went to professional investors. But the romance lies in profits, and the profits just aren't there now." As a local nonfarmer investor explains:

> Just last February I had $30,000 to invest. I put it in some triple B-rated bonds. They yielded a return of 12.9 on my money. If I put it in farmland, in the first place, that isn't enough to buy 40 acres.... I could maybe have made a down payment on another piece of land, but I also think the land will go down in price, and the bond looked a little more attractive to me at this time.

When interest rates are high, investors can get a better return on a bond or other liquid investment than they can on farmland, which traditionally returns only 3 to 4 percent. This is especially important for investors who depend on their investments for current income. On the other hand, there seems to be some interest among nonfarmer investors in buying land for farm-management purposes. Investors who actually participate in farming, as distinct from those who simply rent out their land, are able to enjoy certain tax advantanges. In fact, the ability to write off farm operating losses against nonfarm income may actually give these operators a tax advantage not enjoyed by full-time farmers. If the price of farmland were to fall significantly, this sort of investment interest may revive.

Demands for multi-acre rural residential parcels are significant in the East Central Illinois market only in areas where rolling topography, streams, or comparatively poor soils make the land marginal for farming. There, rural land may be sold in 10-acre lots for homesites. In addition, farmland adjacent to growing urban areas is being bought for residential and commercial development. In such cases, however, the developer may have to find land for a farmer to replace what is sought for development, sometimes in a ratio of more than one new acre for each removed. This means that the expansion of towns can increase farmland demand farther out.

Farmers in East Central Illinois buy farmland not only to spread equipment costs and increase their incomes through farm enlargement, but to provide space for their children, a number of whom seem eager to return to farming after finishing college. Like non-farm people, farmers also want to invest their savings and to protect themselves against inflation. But as a long-time loan manager in the area explains:

> Farmers traditionally haven't known much of any other way to invest money. The farmer knows land; he understands land. He usually gets his best buy in land when he buys it at home and he knows what he's getting, and this is where he wants to invest his money.

The supply of available farmland is too limited for farmers in Douglas County to forego an acquisition if they can secure enough credit to finance it. They have seen continually rising farmland prices, which they themselves have pushed upward in their anxiety to own land. And once they have acquired land, the equity makes it easier to finance additional purchases.

Second to farmers, heirs are probably the most typical farmland buyers. Commonly, land sold for estate purposes is reacquired, in part or in full, by one or more of the heirs or by relatives. According to one such buyer:

> About a year and a half ago, I bought 37 acres which had belonged to my wife's family. I bought it from her grandfather's sister out in California, so we could keep it in the family. My wife owns some other land nearby.... The future? Oh, it [the land] will be in corn and soybeans.... I plan to pass it on to my kids.

An extension agent described another situation where the mother, "who's about 100 years old," was giving away all but 78 acres of a

600-acre farm. If they could raise the capital, two of the heirs were expected to buy the land from the third, to keep the land in the family and to invest their savings.

An additional participant in the Douglas County land market is the coal industry. Almost all of the coal in Douglas and adjacent counties is subsurface; coal companies acquire it by lease and mine it without disturbing the land surface (although sometimes there is subsequent subsidence). Where coal is close to the surface and subsidence is likely, coal companies will purchase the land outright. Only one coal company, a subsidiary of Houston Natural Gas Corporation, owns land in Douglas County—831 acres as of 1978, 202 fewer acres than in 1954. In adjacent Edgar County, two coal companies (Peabody Coal Company and Meadowlark Farms, a subsidiary of Amax Coal Company) own 3,541 acres. Coal companies in both counties are continuing to acquire mineral rights.[35] According to a real-estate broker, "To the coal companies, and to industry, price isn't so much an object if the location is right. They'll pay almost anything."

The Sellers

Land is placed on the market in Douglas County mainly for two reasons—the owner's death, or his retirement. Seldom do farmers sell their land because they can no longer afford to farm or no longer want to farm. Probably the most common reason for selling land is to settle an estate. As a local real-estate dealer recounts:

> [Heirs] can get better investments elsewhere. One fellow who lived in Pennsylvania had two daughters, and owned 270 acres here. He died and his daughters inherited the land. One of them had never seen it. They had no personal feeling for the land, so they're selling it.

Land division among heirs is a common reason for farmland sales. Often, several children inherit a farm. If the amount of land each inherits is small, there may not be enough net rent returned from farming to prevent a nonfarming heir who needs the money from selling. On the other hand, if each heir gets a sufficiently large parcel, then he can earn enough net rent to make a forced sale unnecessary.

The significant liberalization of rules governing inheritance taxes on operating farms, brought about by the 1976 federal tax reform act, has greatly increased farmers' interest in estate planning. Farm financial advisers and agricultural extension staff in East Central Illinois find their seminars on the subject well attended and their publications in demand. If estate planning is more widely adopted in the future, the supply of land that annually comes on the market may decline. For example, some farmers now incorporate their operation, then give it to their children in yearly tax-free increments, thus reducing eventual tax burdens on their estate and eliminating some of the financial pressures that now force heirs to sell.

Aside from cases where parcels must be sold off for estate or tax or personal financial reasons, what comes on the market generally is an entire farm. High land prices, however, mean that the auctioneer or real-estate broker handling the sale will very likely split the farm into parcels small enough to be affordable to expanding neighboring farms.

Farmland Issues

Patterns of landownership and trends in land-market activity have important implications for the future of Douglas County's highly productive farmlands.

A Speculative Bust?

Many farmers and other market participants in East Central Illinois experienced the depression of the 1930s; thus, they view today's farmland market through cautious eyes. Having watched land prices rise rapidly following a World War I boom in prices of farm commodities, one long-time farmer remarked, "It was like land would go up forever, and we'd better buy. Just somewhat as it's doing today." And, he then reminded us, by 1933 farmland nationwide was selling for less than half its price in 1920.

In East Central Illinois, those who now buy land are older farmers with capital or farmers who already own land. Most of the farms that have changed hands in Douglas County recently are mortgaged, and some residents suggest many of the younger buyers may be in over their heads. The younger buyers are less cautious about extending themselves, possibly because they have more of their lives ahead of them to invest in their farms and to pay off debts, possibly because they have never experienced economic disaster. The newly purchased land cannot pay for itself, or even cover annual interest payments. Only supplementary income from other land or off-farm sources makes acquisition economically feasible. The buyer's hope is that eventually income per acre will rise, and the new land will begin to support itself.

Local bankers discount the likelihood that an economic squeeze would bankrupt many farmers who have borrowed to buy land. They point out that even at $3,000 or $4,000 per acre, a farmer's debt is likely to be only a few hundred dollars per acre when averaged over his total holdings. Nationwide, although Federal Land Banks will lend up to 85 percent of land's appraised value, the average loan-to-appraisal ratio in 1978 was only 58 percent.[36]

Rental Lands

Changes in farmland rental patterns raise several potential issues relevant to the future of agricultural production in East Central Illinois. First, landlords generally prefer to rent their land to larger-scale farmers, who are perceived as being better equipped for farming. This tendency complements existing land-market and technological forces favoring very large-scale farming.

Another concern is that absentee landlords may be more susceptible than are farmers to pressures for land-use conversion. Douglas County farmers have banded together in a coal-leasing association to prevent coal-mining interests from destroying their land as farmland, even if the preservation of farmland means no mining. But the absentee landlord, whose financial and personal interests are not confined to the farming operation, may be more interested in a coal company's offer.

A third facet of land rental is the effect it may have on traditional landlord-tenant relationships. Traditionally, the landlord and tenant shared certain production costs and management responsibilities. The crop was divided, usually equally. Now, families farming 1,000 or more acres may be working with four or five different landlords. This situation favors a switch to cash rents, freeing the landlord from operational responsibilities and production costs and giving the farmer complete control over the farm. But cash rentals are not popular with most farmers. They require that the farmer buy all farm inputs and take the consequences of a bad year as he would the profits from a good year. Some tenants may be unable to meet the cash-flow demands created by this kind of system. Cash leases may also heighten the sense of insecurity among tenants and could discourage them from making long-term capital investments in the land. Although cash-rented farmland can be found in Douglas County—and at rentals exceeding $100 per acre per year—the total amount is still small. But it is potentially a major problem on the horizon.

A fourth concern about farmland rental is the relationship between tenancy and land management. There is historical evidence that tenants have been considered notoriously negligent about caring for land. An 1877 Illinois newspaper account characterized tenants as, for the most part, "untrustworthy, dishonorable scoundrels...playing dirt with the landlords." A real-estate agent in Central Illinois wrote an absentee owner in 1882, "I think if you don't conclude to move back into your farm here you had better sell it, for you know that our tenants don't keep a farm up as they ought."[37] We did not find many people in East Central Illinois who accepted the hypothesis that rented lands generally are poorly managed. Most believed that the competition for rented lands in that region is fierce enough that a landlord who hears his tenant is not conscientious can easily find a replacement. As one older farmer points out, "Most tenants prefer to farm good soil, so they're going to care for it." In Douglas County, tenant farmers have sometimes received Conservationist of the Year awards.

Finally, a landlord's willingness to invest in land-conservation programs depends largely on his or her financial position. One study of "lady landlords" in West Central Illinois indicates that these older women, often widows of farmers, are, as a group, reluctant to take on any debt for farm improvements, to the point where tenants interviewed felt the farms and their outputs were suffering.[38] About 34 percent of the rented tracts in East Central Illinois are owned by women.

Corporate and Foreign Ownership

Corporate and foreign ownership of farmlands is an emotional issue in the East Central Illinois region. But inspection of reports filed in Washington under the Agricultural Foreign Investment Disclosure Act revealed a single parcel in Douglas County—154 acres of cropland inherited by a Canadian woman. Interviews with real-estate professionals indicated that foreign holdings were negligible throughout the region. Nevertheless, in June 1979 the Illinois legislature passed a bill requiring foreigners to disclose any agricultural or forestland holdings. Illinois already had a law requiring foreigners who acquired land by purchase or inheritance to dispose of it within six years. In recent years, bills to restrict corporate ownership of farmlands have been introduced in the Illinois legislature, but none has survived intensive lobbying by coal, manufacturing, and local development interests.

Air Pollution and Mining

Two additional concerns, perhaps limited to certain areas of the county, are the long-term effects of industrial air pollution and of mining on agriculture. The two plastics manufacturing firms emit chemicals that have caused crop burns within a three-mile radius. Also, some land mined for coal has subsided. Because the land is naturally low-lying, draining land that has subsided is nearly impossible.

Concluding Comments

Compared with the land markets in Loudoun County and Tyler County, Douglas County's seems little affected by urban influence. There is no recreational demand for land, as in West Virginia. But Douglas County farmers have themselves created a lively competition for land, and have bid up its prices beyond what current productivity can justify. Outside nonfarmer investors have been priced out of the market. Nevertheless, absentee ownership in Douglas County is among the highest found in our case studies. This is not because outsiders have increased their purchases of land, but because retiring farmers who move to other areas tend not to sell the land. The result has been a traditionally high rate of absentee ownership, which has changed but little over the past 25 years.

V

The township* of **Plainfield, New Hampshire,** *lies in the scenic valley of the upper Connecticut River. The township participated in the century-long decline of New England agriculture, and over the years its landscape changed from being predominantly cleared fields to one that is mostly forested. There are now few full-time farmers left. But growth is picking up, as persons working in factories and professions in small New England cities recognize that Plainfield is an attractive area for low-density rural settlement. In 1977, Plainfield again equaled the all-time population peak it had first reached in 1860.*

---

*Officially, "Town of Plainfield." In New England, the basic unit of local government is the "town," a subcounty unit that includes both urban and rural territory. (The urban portion of a New England town is usually referred to as the "village.") Because this terminology is likely to confuse many readers, we have substituted the term "township," which is technically incorrect, but more descriptive of Plainfield's predominantly rural character.

RURAL PLACES

Ironically, the population revival comes at a time when New England agriculture is experiencing a modest recovery of its own. Plainfield residents must decide how to preserve the area's rural look and its agricultural potential in a situation in which the vast majority of landowners no longer have a direct tie to the soil.

For more than 200 miles, the upper Connecticut River divides Vermont and New Hampshire. About 60 miles above the Massachusetts border, where the river passes the small cities of Windsor, Vermont (1980 population 4,077), and Lebanon, New Hampshire (1980 population 11,052), there is a very long-settled part of the United States, with many communities established before the Revolutionary War. The region's settlement took two forms—dispersed farmsteads, where the river valley's relatively fertile soils were cultivated, and small towns and cities, where manufactured goods were produced with the aid of water power. Over the years, the region has had cycles of agricultural and industrial prosperity and decline, and shifts in both its agricultural products and its manufactures. Since the decline of the sheep industry in the 1890s, the landscape has changed from being predominantly cleared fields to one that is mostly forested. But the mix of rural and small-town living has remained characteristic, not only of the upper Connecticut River valley but of much of nonmetropolitan New England.

Recently, some of the old towns in the upper valley have begun a modest industrial revival. New activities such as education and health care have also created employment, most notably in the expansion of Dartmouth College (in Hanover, New Hampshire) and its associated university hospital. A century-long decline in farming has recently stopped, and rural settlement of a different type has begun to increase. Some rural residents are commuters to jobs in surrounding towns; others are hobby farmers or part-time farmers seeking to revive older patterns of land use; still others are looking for outdoor recreation in the forests or on the ski slopes.

People have always found the field and forest landscape of the upper Connecticut River valley attractive. Retirees and vacationers are not a new phenomenon in the area. But the region's growth was given a tremendous boost in the late 1960s by the completion of two interstate highways, which intersect in the town of White River Junction, Vermont, just north of Windsor and across the river from Lebanon. Interstate 91, completed in 1965, significantly reduced the travel time for thousands of vacationers coming from southern New

England and New York City to ski at Vermont resorts. Four years later, Interstate 91 was crossed by Interstate 89, which connects Boston with Montreal.

The highway completion had an immediate impact: a surge in the value of land adjoining the intersection. In the late 1940s, a small-time sawmill operator had purchased 300 acres of farmland in White River Junction for $14,000, less than $50 an acre. When the interchange between the two highways was built on a corner of his land, he began selling off parcels for roads, motels, and other commercial developments. He is said to have gained over $1 million in profits. By 1977 prime development land near the junction of the interstates was selling for $100,000 an acre.

The new highways also helped quicken industrial and recreational growth in the region. This had two impacts on the rural land market. First, the improved access made it much easier for recreation seekers to make weekend trips from New York and cities of southern New England. Given the greatly increased popularity of skiing, the result was a major boom in resort and second-home development throughout central and southern Vermont and New Hampshire. Second, job growth in manufacturing and in Dartmouth's classrooms and hospital created a demand for new permanent homes, and many of the new employees welcomed the chance to live on a few acres in a rural setting.

The revival of growth in the upper Connecticut River valley is reflected in the number of dwelling units found in seven adjoining townships in Vermont and New Hampshire. Between 1965 and 1975 the number of dwellings increased by 23 percent, with more than three quarters of the growth taking place in 1970-75.[39]

The Plainfield Study Site

Plainfield township, New Hampshire (1980 population 1,751), is typical of the rural portion of the upper Connecticut River valley. Founded in 1761, the township sent more than 50 men off to fight in the American Revolution. During the 19th century, it was a center first of mixed agriculture and then of the sheep industry. One 95-year-old Plainfield man recalls that, when he was a boy, he could climb to the top of any hill in the area and shout and have 3,000 sheep hear his voice. But turn-of-the-century changes in the wool tariff doomed the sheep industry, and wheat and and dairy farmers found it hard to compete with larger operations in more fertile parts of the United States. Slowly, farms were abandoned; the brighter and more ambitious young people moved away. By 1930, Plainfield had barely more than half as many people as it had had in 1860.

In recent years, Plainfield has been growing again, like so many rural places where it is pleasant to live, and it has been growing at a steadily increasing rate. Between 1940 and 1960, population increased by only 101 persons. But during the 1960s Plainfield added 252 residents; between 1970 and 1980, another 428. By 1977, Plainfield again equalled the peak population it had first attained more than a century before.

Plainfield township is still very lightly settled, with about 18 acres of land for each resident. It is predominantly rural, with a few houses clustered in tiny villages, and the remainder either older farmhouses set well back from the road, or new dwellings on smaller parcels, hugging the road suburban-style. The land is mainly forested, broken by occasional pastures and corn fields. Nearly every house has a garden and a huge pile of firewood for heating.

There are no industries or shopping centers in Plainfield—the largest employer is a private school for boys—and many residents commute to jobs in Hanover or Lebanon, a drive of 15 to 30 minutes. Occupationally, the residents are a mixed group. There are a number of relatively affluent professionals, including Dartmouth faculty and physicians working at the Dartmouth hospital or at the large Veterans Administration hospital in White River Junction. But there are also large numbers of skilled blue-collar workers, who work in Lebanon's manufacturing plants, and people who hold nonprofessional jobs (secretaries, carpenters, nurses' aides) at Dartmouth. Only a handful of full-time commercial farmers is left, but there are many part-time farmers, and even more "hobby farmers." As might be expected, some residents are "over-educated" for their current job—having simply decided to go back to the land to farm or to enjoy the country atmosphere.

Involvement with the land varies. Many of Plainfield residents keep a few cattle or sheep; some strive as much as possible for self-sufficiency. Old farmhouses are in new demand, and many reflect painstaking restoration. But other people live in what one Plainfield resident calls "little suburbia"—new, cheaply built frame houses set at 200-foot intervals along the main roads. These people may raise a home garden, but they have little involvement with agriculture.

The Changing Land Market

Until the early 1960s, Plainfield's land market reflected slow population growth and the bleak prospects of the local agricultural and forest industries. In Plainfield, as elsewhere in northern New England, farms could be bought for under $100 an acre and timbered hillsides for $10 to $25 an acre. But improved access, changing tastes, and a new interest in land as an investment have brought some dramatic changes in the demand for land.

Market Forces

One of the most significant of the new forces affecting Plainfield's land market has been the desire of newcomers, including former urban residents, to live in a rural setting. Northern New England has been a particularly attractive destination for such people because of its cheap land, pleasant scenery, and relatively easy access to centers of education and culture. Some new residents are interested in communal living and subsistence farming, but there has been a high turnover of such groups in this region of rocky soils and harsh winter climate. A broader group of people coming to Plainfield and similar places do not want to be farmers but appreciate the advantages of rural living. Among this group is a young doctor, who moved to a Plainfield farm, but works in the White River Junction Veterans Administration hospital. He voiced his values as follows:

> When for years my wife and I lived in Boston and Washington and Denver, we were always more interested in doing the things you do in the country. We felt it was not a good idea to bring up a child who thinks that milk comes from a supermarket rather than from a cow that eats grass.

Also contributing importantly to the demand for rural land in Plainfield are people in their 50s who plan to work for a few more years and then retire to a quiet place removed from urban problems. Potential retirees often have had a substantial income and equity outside the region, and thus are able to pay fairly high prices for land. The upper Connecticut River valley area is particularly attractive to such people because its proximity to Dartmouth means that shopping and cultural events are more available than in other rural areas, as are excellent medical facilities.

Outdoor recreation has also become an important factor in the land market of northern New England. Although Plainfield contains no resort or second-home developments, it is within a few miles of the Mt. Ascutney ski area, in Vermont, and the Whaleback ski area, in New Hampshire, as well as a scattering of smaller second-home and condominium developments. Also within a few miles are very large resort and second-home projects at Quechee, Vermont ("Quechee Lakes") and Grantham, New Hampshire ("Eastman"). These developments, veritable "new towns" that cover 5,500 and 3,500 acres, respectively, provide year-round recreational attractions and cater to both weekend visitors and to retirees seeking a permanent residence.

The ski and recreation boom in northern New England reached its high point in 1970-72 and suffered a major setback during the recession and energy crisis in 1974-75. Developers found their revenues limited by falling demand and tight money at the same time that environmental restrictions were raising development costs. In 1970, Vermont passed its Environmental Control Act ("Act 250"), which required a state permit for any subdivision of more than 10 lots; New Hampshire did not pass a comprehensive state land-use law, but local health and zoning requirements were stiffened. Combined with a level of demand that continued to be only moderate for resort-type units and a backlog of unsold lots in existing projects, the Vermont and New Hampshire laws discouraged devlopers from undertaking new ventures. Since 1975, recreational development in the region has mainly consisted of the slow expansion of existing projects.

Still another source of demand for land in Plainfield is investment interest. As accessibility to northern New England improved and winter sports burgeoned, urban investors began to look anew at the bargain-priced rural acreage available there. Rising demand for land pushed up land prices, and this generated speculative demand. During the late 1960s and early 1970s, investors were typically most interested in potential profits from developing or subdividing larger parcels. The investors were encouraged by the fact that per-acre prices were—and to some extent remain—much lower for large tracts (200+ acres) than for the 5-to-40-acre tracts that are most in demand as building sites. More recently, investment interest has also focused on potential timber value.

In 1967, 609 acres of former sheep and cattle pasture in Plainfield were purchased by an investor living in Washington, D.C. He paid

$174 per acre for the land. A local real-estate broker looks after the property and gradually has been selling off medium-sized parcels for $1,000 per acre. The tract is only four miles from a new shopping mall and industrial park in Lebanon, and could provide beautiful rural homesites for the new employees. It is unlikely that this land will ever again be used for significant agricultural production; in fact, one 40-acre parcel was sold to another nonresident investor who, in reselling a 20-acre portion, wrote a covenant into the deed banning commercial farming from the parcel forever. The land is assessed as farmland under New Hampshire's use-value assessment program and taxed at the rate of $1.13 per acre per year.

Another land investment in Plainfield was made by a Boston real-estate firm specializing in rural properties. A former dairy farm of 590 acres had been sold to a local speculator in 1961, who in turn sold the house, logged off the best timber, and later resold the parcel to the Boston firm. The latter then apparently sold undivided shares in the parcel to individual investors, using the "limited partnership" form of ownership. In 1978, the partnership subdivided the land into 15 lots ranging from 14 to 53 acres. One 23-acre lot sold for $16,000 to a local man for use as a house lot; most of the other lots are still for sale and are listed with local real-estate agents. The partnership has not applied for use-value taxation and thus pays yearly property taxes in excess of $4,100, or about $7 per acre per year.

Trends in the Land Market

The changing currents in Plainfield's land market are closely reflected in rates of property transfer. During the period 1956-69, property transfers averaged 77 per year. But then the demand began to climb—to 82 parcels in 1970, 112 in 1971, 137 in 1972, and 141 in 1973. In 1974 transfers fell back to only 99; since that time, they have averaged 108 per year. A quite similar pattern of transactions could be observed in West Windsor, Vermont, just across the Connecticut River from Plainfield. West Windsor has experienced more purely recreational development than has Plainfield, mainly because it contains the Mt. Ascutney ski area. West Windsor's land boom began a bit earlier than Plainfield's, with transfers rising sharply during the period 1967-69. Transfers then stayed at a high plateau until 1974, when they began to decline, although not to pre-1966 levels.

Along with increased rates of transfer in these areas has come an increase in nonresident ownership. In 1954, the proportion of nonresident owners (defined as persons not living within the township) was 48 percent in Plainfield and 18 percent in West Windsor. By 1976 nonresident ownership had grown to 60 percent and 43 percent, respectively.

Plainfield and West Windsor differed significantly in 1976 in the median size of parcels held by nonresidents. In Plainfield, residents owned parcels much smaller than nonresidents (5 acres median size for residents versus 25 for nonresidents). In West Windsor, however, the residents tended to own larger parcels than nonresidents (10 acres median size for residents versus 5 for nonresidents). The reason for this difference is that nonresidents in West Windsor primarily are seeking sites for recreational homes close to the ski area. Often such parcels are relatively small. In Plainfield, most of the nonresident landowners are investors hoping to subdivide their land for new year-round homesites. Although most of the nonresident owners in both towns are individuals, in each town several real-estate investment companies have bought parcels of over 200 acres with the intention to develop them.

An interesting group of nonresident owners are those who live within 30 miles of Plainfield or West Windsor. In 1954 most of these nonresidents were farmers or timber companies using their lands for production. However, in 1976 this group of owners consisted mostly of real-estate brokers, builders, professional people, and retirees who held their land for its investment value.

One reason for Plainfield's high proportion of nonresident ownership in both 1954 and 1976 is that a private hunting club, the Blue Mountain Forest Association, owns 3,160 acres (12 percent of all land in Plainfield). This land is part of 22,000 acres—an entire mountain—owned by the association since the early 1900s. The association's game wardens stock the forest, which is enclosed by an eight-foot fence, with elk, wild boar, and other game. Hunting rights are reserved exclusively for 30 members, most of them from out of state, who pay up to $30,000 to join the club and substantial annual dues. Since some logging is done in the Blue Mountain Forest, the association qualifies for preferential property-tax assessment, a concession that has reduced the assessed value of its holdings in Plainfield from $668,000 to $110,000. Officials in Plainfield and other townships containing land owned by the association object strongly to the loss of revenue, but they have been unsuccessful in challenging the legality of the low assessment.

Concerning foreign ownership, there have been a number of newspaper reports in recent years of rural land purchases in northern New England by foreigners, particularly Canadians, South Americans, and Western Europeans. Some investment was said to be concentrated on operating dairy farms in the Champlain Valley of western Vermont; in other areas timberland management companies were said to have arranged syndicates including foreign investors to buy large tracts of forestland. Our inspection of land records revealed no direct ownership of land in Plainfield or West Windsor by foreigners. However, some foreigners are part of the investment syndicates and timber firms owning land in other nearby areas.

As in other parts of the United States, in northern New England heightened interest in rural land has been accompanied by the subdivision of land—much of it former farmland—into smaller parcels. The median parcel size in Plainfield fell from 23 acres in 1954 to 8 acres in 1976. In West Windsor, median parcel size also plummeted, from 55 acres in 1954 to 7 acres in 1976. Particularly notable in both towns was a decline in the number of acres in parcels of 100 to 300 acres and a corresponding increase in acres in parcels of less than 50 acres.

As was the case in most of the other areas we studied, although the amount of land in larger parcels (100+ acres) declined over time, even in 1976 about half of the land in both Plainfield and West Windsor was held in parcels of this size. Moreover, the amount of land in parcels larger than 300 acres was virtually unchanged over the 1954-76 period in both towns. This mainly reflects continued holdings of steep forestland, often by timber companies or institutions. Many of these large parcels are on hillsides that were pastures 50 to 100 years ago, but are now overgrown with so many trees that they are useful only for timber or recreation, not as farmland.

Our findings on parcellation confirm, and are consistent with, those of a study of five townships in the nearby Ottauquechee region of Vermont. That study found that between 1968 and 1976 there was a 34 percent increase in the number of land parcels, with the majority of the new parcels being six acres or less in size.[40] The study noted a 24 percent increase in permanent residences, a 27 percent increase in vacation homes, and even larger increases in mobile homes, commercial establishments, and miscellaneous vacant parcels. During the same period, the study found, the number of farms declined.

Of the various market trends evident in Plainfield, the most spectacular has been the rise in land prices. We could not obtain comprehensive data on this phenomenon, because sale prices depend so much on the characteristics of individual parcels, including such factors as parcel size, fertility, amount of cleared land, and availability of a building site. But the historical record of the 175-acre "Atwood-Farnsworth" farm in Plainfield is illustrative. The property was purchased by Francis and May Atwood in 1937 at a cost of $13 per acre. They developed a successful dairy farm, which town records show was sold to Henry and Eldora Farnsworth for about $50 an acre in 1961. In 1972, the farm was subdivided into 11 parcels and sold at auction for an average price of $500 per acre, a tenfold increase in 11 years. None of the new purchasers was a farmer, nor was any at that time a Plainfield resident. In 1975, one 13-acre parcel was resold for $1,000 per acre and the following year a 17-acre parcel sold for $900 an acre. By 1978, several nonresident owners were offering to sell their parcels for $1,000 per acre.

Land prices in Plainfield have generally followed the pattern indicated by the Atwood-Farnsworth farm. Prices were very low and increased only slowly during the 1950s and early 1960s. Then, in 1967-73 came a very rapid escalation in values, sometimes by several hundred percent. Since the 1974-75 recession, rates of price increase have moderated, although prices are still rising for both farm- and forestland.

Plainfield's record of price increase is roughly similar to that reported for New Hampshire farmland by the successive Censuses of Agriculture, although farmland prices appear to have increased less in the 1960s than prices of other land, and to have increased somewhat more in the years since 1974. In 1954, the average price per acre for farm real estate in New Hampshire was $86. Ten years later, the average had increased to $125. Then prices took off, reaching $218 per acre in 1969, $564 per acre in 1974, and $912 per acre in 1978.

One interesting feature of northern New England's land market is the very large disparity that one observes between the per-acre prices of small parcels (fewer than 40 acres) and very large parcels (more than 1,000 acres). The small parcel will often sell for $500 to $1,000 per acre, while the very large parcel can sell for much less, often not much more than the value of its standing timber. Thus, a 5,200-acre parcel in south central Vermont was sold in 1979 to a small timber company for $117 an acre; a very scenic 6,500-acre New Hampshire property (formerly the Bretton Woods resort) was sold in 1979 to the U.S. Forest Service for $325 an acre; and 6,000 acres of western Massachusetts timberland were sold in 1978 for only $234 an acre.[41]

The disparity in prices between small and large parcels in New England is due to several factors. The large parcel is more likely to contain significant amounts of steep, rocky, or flooded land, which is of little economic value. Moreover, the small parcel, often former farmland, is likely to have a greater percentage of cleared area, an important consideration given the difficulty and expense of clearing a hardwood forest. Finally, tracts of different sizes appeal to different groups of buyers, with the small tract appealing to a large potential market of recreationists, homebuyers, or individual investors, while the large tract is a feasible purchase only for a small number of timber companies and investment syndicates.

Impacts of Change in the Land Market

Rural residential growth in the upper Connecticut River valley has thus far had a mixed impact on the region's agriculture. Some developers have put trailer parks and groups of single-family houses on good pastureland, and the sale of individual house lots along town roads has raised farmers' expectations about the future value of their road frontage. Yet even before this new demand appeared, the area's agriculture had been in a decline and its timber business static. In most cases, new demands for land did not force farmers out of business but merely provided an outlet for land that otherwise would have been idled.

Moreover, new residents have been among those engaging in part-time commercial farming and in hobby farming. Although these kinds of farmers have not produced a great deal of food, they have kept land open that might otherwise have been abandoned to the encroaching forest. More importantly, they have helped create a new constituency for a local agriculture—politically, by supporting such pro-agriculture policies as use-value assessment and direct farmer-to-consumer marketing, and, economically, by providing enough of a market to keep feed stores and implement dealers in business. Similarly, newcomers have been among those promoting wood energy and improved forest management.

However, by splitting land into ever smaller parcels, and by scattering houses across the landscape, new residents may be putting an obstacle in the way of future expansion of farming and forestry. Recent interest in wood energy may signal improvement in New England wood markets, and the high cost of trucking in food from outside the region has raised hopes for some recovery in agriculture. Fragmented parcels, scattered settlement, and high land prices mean that the large-scale methods that characterize modern farming elsewhere in the country will be very difficult to apply in the upper Connecticut River valley. On the other hand, topography and climate have probably already made these methods inapplicable in the region. The future, therefore, may indeed lie in part-time farming and more intensive use of smaller plots.

In the long run, parcellation may have its greatest impact on forestry. According to the report of a Vermont Governor's Committee:

> When a large wooded property is checkerboarded or maneuvered into strangely-shaped 10 to 15-acre lots, the resource is so fragmented as to have no long-term commercial value. Problems with relatively small ownerships, the profusion of utility and boundary lines, complications regarding driveways and access to each property, and securing agreements among a sufficient number of owners can seriously encumber the area's resource and make it extremely difficult to ever harvest timber again.[42]

Also posing difficulties for the productive use of farm- and forest-land is increasing absentee ownership. To be sure, some absentee owners, particularly those buying very large parcels, have invested in professional timber management. Others have allowed free use of their open land for grazing. But, too often, absentee-owned land lies idle—ignored by its owner and unavailable for local users.

One portion of the Atwood-Farnsworth farm, for example, was purchased by a New Jersey man, who moved to Plainfield in hopes of establishing a part-time farming operation raising high-quality beef. This new resident owns only 9.7 acres, and he has been unable to persuade the absentee owners of adjoining parcels to enter into long-term leases for grazing and silage production. In fact, some of the surrounding parcels are already becoming naturally reforested.

One Plainfield resident, herself a newcomer and a hobby farmer, has stated that:

> A distinction [should] be made not between oldtimers and newcomers but between those who are using the land productively and those who aren't. A developer who's bought a big tract to keep awhile and then chop it up and make a killing should be taxed if the land isn't being used.

This sentiment lies behind the use-value approach to land taxation, which is intended to tax rural land used for farming and forestry at rates much lower than land held for development. Yet many use-value assessment laws currently do not do much to encourage productive use. Both New Hampshire (1973) and Vermont (1978) have passed such laws: both give tax preference for open land, and impose a 10-percent penalty if land in the program is later developed. But Vermont's requirement that the land actually be used productively is much stiffer than New Hampshire's. Thus, both states require that forestland be managed if it is to qualify for especially favorable tax treatment,[43] but New Hampshire also allows relatively low assessments of "unmanaged forest and farm land" and "inactive farm land."

Like Hardy and Pendleton counties in our West Virginia case study, Plainfield and surrounding rural towns have experienced conflicts over recreational use of private land. According to one long-time Plainfield resident:

> When many people come up here from southern New England or New York and buy land, the first thing they do is go to the hardware store and buy "No Trespassing" signs. This has really violated an ages-old trust between neighbors here.

Even without the posting, increased population in Plainfield means that hunters and snowmobilers are more likely than ever before to produce disturbance or even danger to residents.

Newcomers also want high levels of public services, posing a difficult problem in a state that relies heavily on the local property tax for public finance. Says one old Plainfield farmer:

> The folks who have moved onto the farms seem to want to live back in the country. But some of the other people who have moved in closer to the village and other parts of the town want better roads and a general face-lift of the community. They've been to town meetings and they've raised our tax rate considerably.

Individually, newcomers have been well accepted in Plainfield, which prides itself on being a neighborly community. But oldtimers and newcomers alike are not eager for further population growth. A survey of Plainfield residents taken in 1973 found that 50 percent wanted the area's population to stay the same or decrease over the next 10 years. Only 5 percent wanted to see the population double. Most wanted Plainfield to remain a "rural" area, neither reverting to agriculture nor becoming a commuter suburb.[44]

In an attempt to come to grips with its growth, Plainfield enacted a zoning ordinance described by some as "among the strictest in the state." It raised minimum lot sizes in most of the township from 1 acre to 3.5, 7, and 15 acres. But this type of large-lot zoning has not stopped sprawling rural population growth, and may have actually increased the amount of land affected by it. The same is also true of most rural areas with this type of zoning. As one Plainfield resident put it:

> It seemed at the time to be the right thing to do. But what in fact happened is that instead of losing one acre of meadow, we lose 7 acres at a clip—and then the 7 acres has a house in the middle of it and is forever lost to agriculture.

The upper Connecticut River valley region is a rural area experiencing population growth because of growing nonfarm employment opportunities and the desire of newcomers for a country life-style. The new growth has strengthened the economy of this long-stagnant region, yet it threatens to change its character in the direction of the very suburbanization that many of the newcomers have been fleeing. Ironically, the revival of growth comes at a point when, for the first time in more than a century, there seems hope for revival in the traditional land-based activities of farming and forestry.

VI

San Luis Obispo County, California, *is located in the center of the so-called "San-San Gap," the last long stretch of unurbanized coastline between San Diego and San Francisco. The county's dry grazing land has long been dominated by cattle ranches that are large enough to compensate for low productivity per acre. But now the open landscape of San Luis Obispo, reminiscent of southern California earlier in this century, is in great demand by retirees, hobby farmers, and other refugees from crowded metropolitan centers. Land prices have soared and ranchers are paper millionaires. Some have already subdivided. Between 1969 and 1977 the number of holdings of fewer than 5 acres rose 55 percent while those greater than 100 acres fell 22 percent. And the county must also contend with thousands of tiny unserviced rural lots, subdivided decades before, and only now in demand by new settlers. Local officials have implemented some of the strictest rural zoning in the country, but find it difficult to hold the line in the face of the large disparity between the land's commercial agricultural value and its value as rural homesites.*

San Luis Obispo County (1980 population 154,732; unincorporated portions 60,168) lies along the central California coast, midway between Los Angeles and San Francisco. Early in the century, publisher William Randolph Hearst inherited nearly 250,000 acres of land in the county and built the famous "Hearst Castle" at San Simeon. It was here, too, in the 1920s that thousands of acres were subdivided, planted in almonds, then sold to eastern urbanites by land salesmen dressed in cowboy garb, who advertised lots measuring 25 x 150 feet as "piece[s] of California gold." Now, people from all parts of the United States find retirement havens among the county's coastal communities; youthful migrants and college students influence the area's culture and life-style; a 30-year-old planning department grapples daily with the problems of rapidly changing land use.

The County

With more than two million acres of rolling grazing land, hillsides covered with fruits, nuts, and new plantings of California grapes, and rugged coastal vistas, San Luis Obispo County is, by southern California standards, quiet and remote. Although the county lies virtually in the center of "San-San"—a 600-mile swath of coastal megalopolis stretching from south of San Diego to north of San Francisco—it provides a long break in California's continuous stretch of coastal urbanization, thus leading one researcher to describe the county as being the center of the "San-San Gap."[45]

San Luis Obispo is separated by the Santa Lucia Mountain Range into a narrow coastal section to the west and vast inland acreage to the east. The immediate coastal area, bathed by ocean breezes and often blanketed by fog, gives way to rolling, straw-colored hills dotted with cattle and solitary California live oaks. On the eastern side of the Santa Lucia Mountains, the land is almost desert. Throughout the county, agricultural productivity influences land values less than does scenic quality. For example, along the coastal terrace, six acres are required to support a single cow, yielding the owner a yearly rent of perhaps $15 an acre. Yet a tract of land here costs several thousand dollars an acre, with property taxes running from $40 to $60 per acre per year. Says the deputy county assessor, "A guy doesn't buy coastal land here to raise cattle; he buys to raise cattle and later sell the land."[46]

San Luis Obispo is experiencing the pressures of rapid growth and land-use change. Prior to the 1950s, most Californians regarded San Luis Obispo as only a fuel stop between Los Angeles and San Francisco, commonly referring to it as "cow country."[47] Then, the county's population began to grow rapidly: from less than 52,000 in 1950 to 81,000 in 1960; then up to 106,000 between 1960 and 1970; another 46 percent between 1970 and 1980. The county's 1970-80 growth was more than two and a half times California's overall rate of increase for the same period. Nearly 90 percent of San Luis Obispo County's growth stemmed from migration, including a large number of retirees. Even more dramatically, population in rural portions of the county more than doubled between 1970 and 1980, while residents of urban areas increased by slightly less than 28 percent.[48]

For many years, growing government employment dominated the county's economic life, mainly because of state facilities: California Polytechnic State University, a 14,000-student school that dominates the city of San Luis Obispo; the California Men's Colony, a penal institution; and regional offices of state government. In fact, government accounted for nearly a third of nonfarm employment in 1977.[49] The largest recent *increases* in nonfarm employment, however, have been in those types of jobs servicing the growing local population. For example, over half of those employed in nonfarm occupations work in retail trade, services (including tourist-related services), and construction, and jobs in these three areas have more than doubled since 1965.[50] Increases like this suggest that employment changes are responding to, rather than stimulating, the county's population growth—and this is true in many nonmetropolitan counties where newcomers seek amenities more than jobs. Manufacturing remains a relatively minor part of the nonfarm economy, engaging only 5 percent of nonfarm employment in 1977, although manufacturing jobs have increased more than twofold since the mid-1960s. The small role of manufacturing is due, in part, to the distances from large urban markets, and also to the fact that local government does not encourage industrial plants to locate in the county. Buffered by a dependence on public-sector employment and strong growth in the services sector, San Luis Obispo County has been somewhat insulated from the sharp fluctuations in jobs felt in many other counties where growth is more dependent on increased industrial employment. Unemployment rates for the county during the 1970s were consistently below those for California as a whole.[51]

The Rural Land Market

Population growth and the structure of San Luis Obispo's economy are clearly affecting the rural land market. Compared to our other case-study areas, San Luis Obispo County is large, containing some 2.1 million acres. Nearly a fifth of this land (about 401,000) acres is in public ownership, most of it mountain land owned by the U.S. Forest Service or desert administered by the federal Bureau of Land Management. Excluding that land and the the land in the county's seven incorporated towns (nearly 21,000 acres as of 1978), the rural land market contains some 1.7 million acres of privately owned land. This is several times the size of the rural land area in our other study sites.

For the most part, population growth, both urban and rural, has occurred in the county's western half, which is cooler in summer and scenically attractive. The eastern half of the county, due to its arid and rugged landscape, has not experienced as much population growth. As we shall note later, however, this does not mean that the land market in the eastern half has been inactive.

New rural settlers in San Luis Obispo County tend to be pulled by scenic and recreational amenities and pushed by what they perceive as a deterioration in the quality of life elsewhere. Says an orthopedic surgeon who moved to a rural parcel: "I grew up in New York. It was sort of like living in the middle of a zoo. I now live on 40 acres because I can afford to. If I could afford 80 acres, I would live on 80 acres." Speaking in a similar vein is a California state research geologist, who bought 14 acres in rural San Luis Obispo in 1974. Previously a resident of Los Angeles, his job permitted him to live anywhere in the state: "I came here for health reasons. The smog was literally killing me."

A minority of newcomers intend to use their land for commercial agriculture. One young couple with whom we spoke saved for many years to buy 40 acres, which they have since planted in avocados and vegetables; another family moved from Los Angeles and raises purebred rabbits for medical laboratories. Many people like this find it difficult to survive without taking at least a part-time job in town. On the other hand, some very wealthy individuals also participate in agriculture, seeking the pleasures (and tax advantages) of growing wine grapes. A large number of newcomers, who have mainly come seeking rural homesites, at least dabble in farming. The above-mentioned state geologist, for example, observes that, "We intend to put in 200 apple trees. It's a tax write-off. When we eventually get so old that we sell the place, we will be selling an apple orchard, not just a residence."

Since the late 1970s, San Luis Obispo has maintained about 1.5 million acres of land in agriculture. Of this amount, more than 1.3 million acres have been devoted to cattle grazing, a use of land prevailing throughout the entire county.[52] Placing a distant second to cattle grazing were the 160,000 acres devoted in 1979 to field crops—primarily wheat, barley, and alfalfa—concentrated in the dry, eastern half of the county. Thus, in area, the beef-cattle industry dominates San Luis Obispo, just as it did in the early days of the Mexican ranchos, when tens of thousands of unfenced acres set the tone for a feudal and pastoral life-style.

Value of production on San Luis Obispo's agricultural land is a different matter. While occupying only minimal amounts of land, some intensive uses are impressive contributors to total agricultural revenues. For example, in 1979, vegetables—mainly lettuce, celery, and broccoli—were grown on less than 2 percent of the agricultural land (that is, about 25,000 acres), concentrated in the fertile, irrigated portions of the county's coastal strip. Yet the market value of vegetable production was virtually the same as the cattle industry's: 32 percent of total agricultural sales. Similarly, fruits and nuts, which doubled in acreage after 1975, still occupied only some 13,600 acres in 1979, less than 1 percent of the agricultural land. But these crops produced nearly as much revenue as did field crops, which occupied nearly 11 percent of the agricultural acreage in 1979. Acres devoted to specialty crops such as avocados, lemons, and wine grapes increased more than tenfold from 1965 to 1979, though the total number of acres involved remains very small (less than 1 percent of total agricultural land). The growing importance of these more intensive uses of San Luis Obispo's agricultural land can be partially attributed to rising land values, which have resulted from a general increase in demand for land. The lands are often cultivated by new rural settlers. Some of the new production is replacing that of southern California farms lost to urbanization.

This discussion would not be complete without mention of San Luis Obispo County's active participation in California's 1965 Land Conservation Act, commonly known as the Williamson Act.

One of the first legislative programs of its kind in the United States, the Williamson Act was designed to provide property-tax reductions to landowners who contracted with county governments to keep their land in agriculture (the act was later broadened to include open-space land). In 1969, San Luis Obispo established its own program of agricultural preserves which would be given preferential tax treatment. By 1978, nearly 60 percent of the county's agricultural land was either in agricultural preserves or under Williamson Act contracts. These 890,000 acres amounted to 42 percent of the entire county.[53]

Trends in the Land Market

The market for rural land in San Luis Obispo County is changing. In many ways, the changes parallel those found at our other case-study sites, although the amount of population growth and the attendant demand for land are greater than in the other areas we studied.

Land Transactions

There was a surge in land sales in San Luis Obispo beginning in the late 1960s and continuing through the generally strong real-estate markets of 1972. This is similar to what happened at our other case-study sites. For the five years between 1967 and 1972, land sales increased an average of 15 percent each year, with the largest jump occurring between 1967 and 1968, when transactions rose by more than 38 percent. The drop-off during the recession of 1974-75, however, was much less dramatic than at our other sites. The reduction in market activity did not last long, and sales fell by only 10 percent in the process. In fact, by 1975 real-estate sales countywide had increased nearly 23 percent over 1974 levels.

By 1977 the county reached a level of market activity higher than that in any of our other study areas when compared to our base year of 1969. Real-estate sales in San Luis Obispo in 1977 were exactly twice their level in 1969. The 1979-80 recession and high interest rates struck harder at the San Luis Obispo land market than did the previous economic downturn. By mid-1980 real-estate activity had fallen by twice as much as it had in the previous recessionary period, though total property sales remained higher than in all but the peak years of 1976-77.

As we noted earlier, San Luis Obispo is protected somewhat from severe economic fluctuations because of its employment structure. This, combined with the county's attractiveness for retirees, may help account for the lesser impact of the 1974-75 recession on the real-estate market. The more severe effect of the 1979-80 recession is difficult to interpret, although the unusually high mortgage interest rates that accompanied it may have been one factor.

New Parcels

As San Luis Obispo County's population has increased, so has the number of its land parcels, a trend common to all of our case-study sites. We could not obtain a reliable sample of landownership records that would make possible a comparison of 1954 and 1976 (as at other sites), but we did collect this information for an eight-year period, from 1969-77. During this time, the number of privately owned rural-land parcels increased 16 percent.[54] (These data exclude the county's incorporated towns as well as major urbanizing growth areas that had not yet been incorporated.) Although the percentage change is below that of all but one of our other study areas, because of the sheer size of San Luis Obispo County the absolute numbers are quite high—changing from 46,507 parcels to 54,037 over the eight years, or an average of more than 940 parcels each year. The fact that, in contrast to other study areas, the number of parcels did not keep up with or exceed the growth in population is most likely due to San Luis Obispo County's unusually strict rural zoning and subdivision controls, which we describe below.

As at other sites, ownerships of smaller rural-land parcels showed impressive gains in numbers at the expense of both medium- and large-acreage ownerships.[55] The number of holdings that were less than 5 acres rose 55 percent, while those greater than 100 acres decreased 21 percent. Ownerships between 5 and 25 acres rose 22 percent, and those between 25 and 50 acres dropped by 11 percent. Because of the sharp increase in very small ownerships, the median size of rural landholdings fell from 18 acres to only 7 acres.

Changes in the size distribution of acres owned present another view of San Luis Obispo's rural land market. Even though acreage in small holdings increased greatly in percentage terms, the number of acres involved was still quite small when compared with that held in larger holdings, including some extremely large ranches that have not been subdivided. Moreover, one fifth of the land in the county is zoned for minimum parcels of 640 acres. Thus, the increase in small holdings has not fractured the county's land base overall. Only 3.3 percent of San Luis Obispo County's private rural land is held in ownerships of less than 25 acres, and 87 percent remains in ownerships of more than 100 acres.

Rising Land Prices

As a result of population growth in San Luis Obispo County's rural areas, combined with the effects of parcellation just noted, there has been a dramatic increase in land prices. Much of the county's ranch- and farmland has had average price increases of 12 to 15 percent per year for the past 20 years, though the decade of the 1970s showed the strongest price appreciation. In areas near the county's incorporated towns, rural land prices have risen as much as 500 percent in the last 10 years. In such areas, tract sizes drop to 20-acre lots for "hobby farms" and prices range from $10,000 to $15,000 per acre. Even closer in, on the fringes of the towns, land that sold 20 years ago for $1,500 per acre was split during the 1970s into 5- and 10-acre "estate lots" which now sell for $25,000 per acre.

While land price increases generally have been strong throughout the county, there is substantial diversity among San Luis Obispo's rural land markets. The county's cooler and amenity-filled coastal strip provides a contrast to the drier farmlands of the north-central and south-central areas. And these, in turn, differ markedly from the poorer quality ranch and grazing lands of the arid eastern portions of the county.

For the most part, what evidence we could gather on changing land prices does not apply to land immediately adjacent to the coast. Comparable evidence of rising coastal land prices was lacking for two reasons. First, California's Coastal Commission (established in 1972 to protect the state's coastal environment) has imposed severe restrictions on coastal-area development, limiting the market turnover of land. Second, much of the coastal land area in the county is owned by only a handful of very large landowners, again resulting in limited turnover of parcels in the marketplace. Referring to the limited real-estate activity in the coastal areas, a county assessor noted that "even the Hearst family, with all its money, would have a hard time developing anything of any size in the coastal part of the county."

Farmland in the north-central and south-central areas has turned over more rapidly over the years, and our interviews furnished some evidence of how land prices have increased in these markets. Farm-land in the north-central areas rose in price by about 10 percent annually during the 1950s and 1960s, and by 1970 was selling for $1,000 per acre. Then, as a local university professor put it, "Around 1971 things in the real-estate market really popped." More intensive agriculture (for example, almonds and wine grapes) combined with the county's surge in rural population to drive land prices even higher. Acreage prices for farmland rose to $3,000 to $4,000 by the end of the decade—an appreciation rate of about 15 percent per year.

In San Luis Obispo's south-central rural land markets the *rate* of price increase has been more dramatic, but this appears due to the low level of land prices of earlier years. According to a county planner, the southern end of the county throughout the 1950s and most of the following decade was an economically depressed area made up of eucalyptus groves, with a substantial amount of squatting by migrant farm workers. Land in 10-to-40-acre parcels sold for as little as $100 an acre even as late as 1960. Then, during the 1970s, rural subdivision activity picked up and 40-acre-tracts with subdivision maps on file now sell for $3,000 to $4,000 per acre.

In contrast to other areas of the county, San Luis Obispo's vast eastern acreage is characterized by very arid soil conditions and rugged topography. Relatively poor grazing land interspersed with some dry farming predominates in this part of the county. Here, land prices have remained relatively stable, generally keeping up with inflation but providing little if any appreciation above this. As one county official put it, "With respect to land values out there, water's the name of the game . . . [but] you need big chunks of land to get water. There are stretches of 500 acres with only one water hole for the cattle." He added that, "If you could improve the water and access out there, you'd be talking about a million dollars for 500 acres."

New Faces and Old Subdivisions

In San Luis Obispo landownership by nonresidents was among the highest in our six study areas. By 1977 more than 40 percent of the rural ownerships and 55 percent of the county's rural acreage were owned by people residing outside the county. The fact that the percentage of land owned exceeds the percentage of nonresident owners reflects the presence of some extremely large nonresident holdings, such as the Hearst Corporation's 120,000 acres.

We have no specific data on *changes* in the types of owners who have been buying land in San Luis Obispo. Available data did not permit us to compare the numbers of nonresident owners at two points in time. Anecdotal evidence suggests that for many years the county's land market has been influenced greatly by buyers from other parts of California, mainly from the Los Angeles and San Francisco metropolitan areas. It is interesting to note that there are significant differences in the amount of land held by noncounty residents from the northern and southern parts of the state. Our data show that in 1977 fully 37 percent of the nonresident landholdings were owned by residents of the Los Angeles area. These holdings, however, amounted to only 16 percent of the acreage held by all nonresidents. On the other hand, San Francisco area residents accounted for only 17 percent of the nonresident ownerships, but held nearly 50 percent of the land owned by nonresidents. It is likely that this distributional difference is due mainly to large acquisitions (for example, the Hearst holdings in northern portions of the county) made when San Francisco was the major economic influence and source of capital in California. Recent pressures on the land market seem to have come more from the southern part of the state, and the purchases have been in smaller parcels than in earlier years.

Owners from outside California accounted for only 14 percent of the holdings and 15 percent of the acreage held by nonresidents. For a time, foreign investors held a large amount of low-priced grazing land on the eastern side of the county. The land, in several large tracts totaling 86,000 acres, was acquired by German investors in 1974 and 1975 for approximately $240 per acre. Much of the purchase price was financed by the seller. In January 1980, the Germans invoked an option in the sale contracts permitting them to return the land to the original sellers in return for the downpayment and cancellation of accrued interest owed. Although the price of the land had risen moderately over the six-year period, the investors were said to be disappointed in the land's price performance relative to prevailing interest rates.

Other out-of-state owners appear to hold part of the legacy of the subdivision and land-promotion schemes of earlier years. "Paper subdivisions"—subdivision maps filed with the county but never developed—play a colorful (and troublesome) part in San Luis Obispo's land-market history. A former county official, pointing to a map showing a large portion of the north-central county, noted,

"There was a period around 1918-24 when 40,000 acres out there were planted in almonds, and 'drugstore cowboys' went back East to sell 5 acres of 'almonds and independence'... and lots of people went for it."

Evidence from the county assessor's office indicates that one 350-acre tract was subdivided in 1915 into 5-acre parcels and planted in eucalyptus trees. These lots were sold to out-of-state buyers who speculated eucalyptus would be used as an alternative to other hardwoods in making furniture. The subdivision lay dormant for 60 years—few pieces of furniture were ever made from eucalyptus—until in 1975-77 a portion was resubdivided and resales were made. Prices by then were in the range of $4,000 to $5,000 per acre. In the north-central area, the county planning department counted out-of-state ownerships within 42 undeveloped subdivisions created between 1915 and 1936. Of more than 2,800 lots created, 13 percent were owned in 1977 by people who resided outside California.[56]

Premature subdivisions of the more recent past have also added to the stock of unused lots. In fact, the public reaction to them was a major factor moving the county to adopt the relatively strong rural planning policies now in force. One such project was "California Valley," located in the arid and desolate easternmost portion of the county. In 1963, nearly 90 percent of the wells analyzed in the area failed to meet U.S. Public Health Service standards, and even today little potable water is available. Described by a county planner as an area of "cheap desert land in the middle of nowhere," California Valley was a classic example of land promotion gimmickry. Originally a 26,000-acre ranch on which 5,000 head of cattle grazed, the land was purchased in 1960 by a southern California development group for $25 per acre, then subdivided into 7,200 lots of 2.5 acres. These lots initially sold for $895 each, with $10 down and $10 a month payments. Tents were erected in a carnival-like atmosphere, and Hollywood stars were flown in to promote the project to buyers who came from all areas of the United States. A long-time county resident looked back remorsefully on this celebration and said, "Many of us here in the county felt like the Indian, participating in the destruction of his own way of life."

Nevertheless, most of the project had sold out by 1963, with more than 380 miles of dirt roads built by the developer, who is estimated to have made a $6 million profit over the three years. A perusal of ownership records indicated that perhaps more Californians bought a piece of their own "gold" than did persons from out-of-state. A participating real-estate agent told us that many people who bought lots thought that even though the land purchase might not benefit them at the time, "for only $10 down, maybe the kids will enjoy it.... [It was] just the romance of owning 2.5 acres of land. Why, the first thing they'd do is go out and put a fence around it."

But whether or not the "kids" will enjoy using their land is debatable. Only three years after the project's roads were laid out, they were described as "rutted now by spring rains and totally unacceptable by San Luis Obispo County standards."[57] A large number of the lots are currently on the delinquent tax list. Tax sales have been frequent in the past few years. And few fences are really guarding anything. By 1979 only about 50 houses had been built on the lots, and prices for lots that did occasionally sell ranged all the way from $325 (at a 1977 tax auction) to $1,500 each. Occasionally, small-scale attempts are made to revive buyer interest in the lots. In 1978 a local newspaper carried an advertisement promoting the land as suitable for growing the jojoba plant, an oil-bearing bush touted as a cure for the energy crisis: "Join the Jojoba Bonanza in California Valley—lots starting at $2,000."

It may be many years, if ever, before buyer interest in California Valley booms again. But sales of lots in old developments in less arid parts of the county began to show new life in the late 1970s. As the county assessor told us:

> We still have a bunch of those old 25-foot lots up in back country which you can't get to. They're picking up again in some sales, and are bringing $2,500 to $3,000 apiece. People are buying them and holding on, assuming their grandkids will benefit... it's still too expensive to get utilities there now, but they still sell.

Although San Luis Obispo County now has 10-acre or greater minimum zoning on much of its rural lands, many of the early subdivisions were in lots of 2 to 5 acres. The Planning Department finds it difficult merely to eliminate the old subdivision maps due to the property-rights questions involved. Indeed, the "paper subdivision" remains an important land-use issue in San Luis Obispo County.

Other Demands on the County's Land

Applications for construction of single-family homes in unincorporated portions of San Luis Obispo County rose dramatically during the 1970s—for example, 285 in 1970; 1,703 in 1977; and 1,030 in recession-influenced 1980.[58] Much of this increase has occurred not on city-sized lots in unincorporated towns, but on 10-to-20-acre "ranchettes." This again raises the issue of converting land from larger, more efficient parcels to smaller, less efficient ones in terms of production value.

Permits for mobile homes in rural areas have also increased sharply. Although records have been kept only since 1974, such permits for units not in mobile-home parks are estimated to have averaged 70 per year during the early 1970s.[59] By 1979 nonpark permit applications had increased fourfold over these levels.[60] Until 1980 a county ordinance required that rural mobile homes (other than those in designated parks) be situated on parcels of 10 acres or more. With mobile homes providing an increasingly popular alternative to high-priced, single-family homes, this requirement had the controversial effect of further increasing conversion pressures on some rural lands. As we heard in one county office, "The point is, if you want a mobile home here, your choice is between a tiny [park] space and 10 acres. Even at $3,000 an acre, most people would prefer the 10 acres." In 1980, the 10-acre minimum zoning for nonpark mobile homes was invalidated by state legislation. Mobile homes can no longer be excluded from places houses are allowed, whether in rural or urban areas.

Responding to Changes: Commitments, Conflicts, and Contrasts

In area and the size of its rural population, San Luis Obispo County is larger than many other rural jurisdictions. The local government is composed of a relatively balanced combination of advocates of traditional private property rights and those more concerned with public interests and environmental issues. This division has caused problems over the years, but there is disagreement more over methods than over goals. As the county's planning director put it, "We have a [current] county board here that is three to two for private property rights, but five to nothing for strong planning."

The fact that California Polytechnic has a very large school of architecture and urban planning has heightened interest in land-use and environmental issues and provided a ready pool of trained people to address them. San Luis Obispo County has had some sort of land-use planning for more than 30 years, and, like other California counties, operates under the guidelines of a general land-use plan. Under California law, zoning must be consistent with the general plan. Thus, when compared to some of the smaller and more remote rural areas dealt with in this book, San Luis Obispo appears well equipped to deal with and absorb the many changes now affecting its rural land market. But has it?

The Commitments

Certainly, San Luis Obispo County is committed to grappling with its changing land-use picture. The commitment appears quite strong. As one land planner told us:

> We don't particularly want any more rapid growth in this county, and we've made that known [to developers]... very well known.... If you come in here and try to do something that is very different from the general plan, you're really going to be in trouble.

The strength of the county's commitment to planning seems to be drawn from lessons of the past—for example, premature subdivision activity in such 1960s projects as California Valley. Recalling the problems resulting from this 26,000-acre fiasco in land sales, the county planning director stated:

> The lesson of California Valley is not just that we lost 26,000 acres of land, but also its impact on surrounding properties. In particular, agricultural land values rose, and surrounding farmers had to pay more [in taxes] than their land could produce in agriculture.

San Luis Obispo has long been committed to protecting commercial agriculture, and small-lot "paper subdivision" is not again likely to threaten its agricultural lands. But the problems of large-parcel land divisions and older subdivisions remain. For more than 20 years the county has explicitly recognized a distinction between "rural lands" and "agricultural lands," with the former demanding a higher level of services than the latter. Moreover, in 1961 San Luis Obispo was the first county in the state to establish "urban reserve lines," which distinguished between urban and rural areas according to varying standards, ranging all the way from curb and gutter requirements to dog-leash laws. The use of such lines is one of the reasons for the very sharp break in land use where a reserve line marks the edge of the city of San Luis Obispo—with almost completely built-up residential neighborhoods on one side and completely undeveloped grazing land on the other.

More recently the county has begun to distinguish between building permits to be issued for "rural residences" and "agricultural residences." The former are considered to be primarily "homesites together with accessory services such as hobby animals, incidental agriculture and open space."[61] "Agricultural residences," on the other hand, are those that are needed to support existing agricultural production. The county seems quite committed to distinguishing between the two types of residences as part of its general planning process for rural land. As a county planner told us:

> We're going to be looking more carefully at individual building permits. An agricultural residence is one that supports agriculture already on the land. If you own 100 acres and aren't using it and come in for a building permit, that's not an agricultural residence, it's a rural residence; and the services you are going to demand are likely to be quite different.

He added wryly: "The point is, if you're really a rancher, and your boots are dirty, that's one thing. But if your boots are clean and white, we're going to give you a hard time with securing a permit."

To stem further the conversion of productive agricultural lands into "ranchettes," the county has taken another rather bold step. In 1974 the concept of a "rural planned development" (RPD) was added to the zoning ordinance. In theory, the RPD combines the planning concept of residential clustering with the maintenance of large amounts of permanent open space or agricultural lands. Scale economies can be gained by maintaining large tracts in agricultural production; more efficient servicing for residential units can be gained through medium-density clustering.

The Conflicts

There is a feeling among many to whom we spoke that what is happening today in the San Luis Obispo County land market happened before—at the time when thousands of acres were prematurely subdivided and sold to owners now residing all over the United States. Although that kind of subdivision into very small lots will not be allowed again, many residents believe that the urge of urban people to own land in the county is similar to that which fueled the earlier land boom. One man, who has lived in San Luis Obispo County since 1914, said of the incoming population, "They see land up here—any kind of land—for maybe $500 to $1,000 an acre, and they see it as a tax dodge or inflation hedge. . . . They'll buy it sight unseen." One of the area's real-estate agents expressed concern that current land-use restrictions would have little, if any, more effect on the demand for land than the *lack* of regulation had in the old days of paper subdivision. As he put it, "People are coming from the cities. If they can get some land and it's reasonable, they'll buy it no matter where it is.... If the planning department says you have to have 10 acres to put a mobile home on, they'll go ahead and buy 10 acres."

In effect, San Luis Obispo County's increasingly strict land-use and building regulations have focused on avoiding a recurrence of the early land-boom years. But the regulations have encouraged a new kind of large-lot development that is even more wasteful of land. And, paradoxically, stricter controls have helped stimulate activity in the old subdivisions. As the general supply of rural lots dries up, because it is harder and harder to get county permits, the old subdivisions become more valuable and desirable. Combining a stricter permit process with zoning that increases the minimum lot size exacerbates the problem. The county has taken note of this unintended regulatory effect in a 1978 study which states:

> ... it is becoming increasingly apparent that increases in minimum parcel sizes alone, tend merely to increase the minimum acreage that new rural residents are willing to purchase to reside in rural areas. ... As minimum sizes for new rural residential parcels increase, there is an accompanying increase in the desirability of parcels in older and often premature subdivisions for residential development. Many of these older subdivision areas have even greater potential impacts on agriculture and, in addition, lack necessary improvements and services.[62]

San Luis Obispo County's commitment to manage rural land use is complicated by other factors, too—some beyond direct control. For example, as noted earlier, 42 percent of the entire county in 1978 was under Williamson Act agricultural tax-abatement contracts. The geographic distribution of the nearly 900,000 acres involved is significant. As is the case in many other areas, agricultural preserves in San Luis Obispo are heavily concentrated in the more remote portions of the county. Maps of the agricultural preserves clearly indicate that in the early to mid-1970s the preponderance of such lands was in the sparsely populated grazing and grain areas of the dry eastern part of the county.[63] At the same time, there was strong population growth in the western part of the county. Thus, the land most likely subject to pressure for conversion to nonagricultural uses—that is, rural land around the county's towns and its popular coastal areas—has been the least protected by status as agricultural or open space. The owners of such land have been reluctant to foreclose their development options by freezing it in a preserve.

San Luis Obispo's conservation program for agricultural land has also been weakened by the effects of tax-cutting legislation, namely, California's well-known Proposition 13, passed in 1978. By slashing all property taxes and limiting further tax increases, Proposition 13 reduced the tax-saving incentives of preservation programs such as the Williamson Act. Before Proposition 13, a farmer entering a 200-acre parcel in the Williamson Act program could cut his annual taxes from $3,000 to $900. Currently, his taxes even without a Williamson Act contract would be only $1,200 (they could be reduced to $400 under a contract).

In San Luis Obispo, new Williamson Act contracts averaged 80 per year between 1969 and 1977. Proposition 13 was passed in June 1978; there were only 4 new contracts in 1978 and only 2 in 1979.[64] To be sure, the large amount of land already in agricultural preserves probably contributed to the reduction in applications. But there also has been an increase in recent inquiries by owners who are interested in removing their land from the program. The tax savings are just no longer adequate inducements, given owners' other options in the land market. Evidence from other counties in the state has shown a similar dramatic drop-off in interest in Williamson Act contracts.[65]

San Luis Obispo County's concept of rural planned development (RPD) also has not gained an entirely favorable acceptance. Although recognizing RPD's potential value as a land planning tool, the county board of supervisors has approved only two small RPD projects and has balked at approving RPDs of any significant size at all. According to some county officials and many landowners, this style of development, with clustered residences and permanent open space, seems to threaten the county's rural atmosphere—particularly when the projects are large. Incremental urbanization of agricultural areas, by selling off parcels along the road, seems somehow less threatening. There has also been concern about how to ensure permanent management of the agricultural land and open space once an RPD has been created. Noting the concern over RPDs despite a general commitment by the county to the conservation of rural land, one planner told us, "The one thing we've had little trouble with here is getting people to think about keeping rural areas rural. There's been a good acceptance of that in the county. ...But RPDs will need some time yet."

The Contrasts

Finally, as in our other case studies, in San Luis Obispo contrasts can be distinguished between traditional, agriculturally oriented landowners and newer bidders now entering the land market. On one hand, many long-time residents want to retain agriculture, but are tempted by the land-value gains resulting from growth pressures. Any land-use regulation that might affect these potential gains is looked at suspiciously. Newcomers, on the other hand, whether young or in retirement, see stricter controls and regulations more positively—as necessary evils to protect the area's rural character. As one official put it, most of the newcomers "are people bailing out, cashing out of urban areas"; they do not want to see a recurrence of what they just left behind.

Consider the following set of contrasting comments from our interviews. A planning official:

> The older agricultural landowners perceive us as the enemy. We're cutting their options. The younger, newer owners tell us: "You're bureaucrats, but maybe you're the only ones who can help us."

A county official and long-time landowner:

> Maybe we should have shut the door when I came here [from Europe] in 1914. But they didn't keep me out, and I don't have the right to keep them out.

A well-known conservationist whose family arrived in covered wagons:

> Whenever I go down to the Board of Supervisors to raise questions about some subdivision, the only people who support me are those who have just moved here from Los Angeles. The [older] farmers are always on the other side.

The Future

Over the long run, a number of factors could reduce the strong population pressures felt by San Luis Obispo's land market. Perhaps most important will be the increasingly short supply of water.[66] To this may be added the relatively large public landholdings and lands tied up in agriculture preserves, although the latter are only temporarily reserved from development. California's well-known state coastal commission and the local coastal plans that have resulted from its mandates will limit the amount of change permitted along the county's coastal lands. And, finally, growth itself might spoil the rural charms that have attracted so many to the San Luis Obispo area, causing future demand to fall off.

Nevertheless, over the next few years population growth in San Luis Obispo is expected to continue, bringing with it more pressures and changes in the land market. County projections for the year 2000 show population increasing nearly 50 percent over the 1980 level.[67] If this projection holds, the county will have grown to more than four times its size a half-century earlier—averaging a 3 percent compounded annual rate of growth. Even with stricter land-use regulation and high land prices, what one resident called San Luis Obispo's "clean air and sense of community spirit" are likely to continue to be population magnets. Surely, the pollution and congestion will continue to drive some people out of their urban environments in more crowded parts of California. And a few more will retire to San Luis Obispo, where they may still own a lot or two in one of the old paper subdivisions.

The near-term future facing San Luis Obispo County can perhaps best be characterized in the complementary frustrations of two long-time residents. The first, a rancher and strong environmentalist, is concerned about continued growth and its effects on the land:

> If one were asked to enumerate San Luis Obispo County's prime resources, high on the list would be our greenbelt setting—pastoral and parklike. Yet nearly all the land providing this amenity is privately owned, and subject to the same economic pressures that affect any private property. [Pressures from rising prices and taxes] force land on the market prematurely...often from the hands of more enlightened owners who were reared on the land, who love it and want to keep farming it, into the hands of the promoter-types who buy it with the prospect of subdivisions, houses, pavement, development.

The other, a former rancher, is now one of the county's leading real-estate agents:

> You farm grain and you harvest a crop, but that's not guaranteed here. You have some failures, and somewhere down the line you're borrowing from the bank. Then you have a good crop and pay off the bank and start all over again. I just found I was on the wrong end of the thing. I wanted someone to pay *me* all that interest...so I went into real estate.

A Final Note

San Luis Obispo County differs from our other case-study sites because it is larger and more populous. In addition, the county population has increased steadily over the past three decades, in contrast to the kind of population turnaround other rural areas have only recently experienced. Nevertheless, the land-use issues that have surfaced in San Luis Obispo are very much like those found at our other sites. High levels of market activity, rising prices, parcellation, and new types of landowners are very much a part of the changing land market.

What distinguishes San Luis Obispo dramatically is its 30-year history of rural land-use planning, and its current commitments to broaden the types of planning tools to be used in the future. A proposed new version of the county's general plan retains some concepts already discussed—for example, the distinction between rural and agricultural residences and densities, the concept of rural planned developments, and agricultural preserves and open-space easement programs. In the new plan, lot-size requirements would be made equal both in and out of the county's agricultural preserves, to reduce the incentive for an owner to hold land outside a preserve. The plan also contains a broad new concept for land-use controls in agricultural areas—the use of land-capability standards, rather than predesignated zoning categories, to determine lot size. And, finally, further consideration is being given to using density bonuses for cluster development, and the transfer of development rights to encourage better-located development and promote the conservation of agricultural and open-space lands.

San Luis Obispo County clearly has been dealing with rural land-use issues longer than most rural areas, where only in the past decade has there been a revival of growth. The planning response has been strong, but tempered by political reality. The county planning director told us in 1978:

> We've got a number of different ideas just sitting on the shelf waiting for the day we can say, "Here it is," in response to some issue. The Board of Supervisors knows these things are there, but they don't want to see them yet.

In 1980, after more than 20 years as head of the county's planning program, and having completed the hearing drafts of the newly proposed general plan, the Planning Director resigned amidst heated controversies over how the plan should best be implemented. As a current staff planner summed up the situation, "Planning in rural areas will make it if we take small steps . . . go two steps forward, and one step backward.

VII

The case-study areas we have examined give further evidence of the widespread occurrence of the market trends described in chapter 1.

In each of the six very different areas, we found land prices sharply higher than they had been only 10 or 15 years ago. In each place, except for Douglas County, we found increased market participation by outside investors. We also found a broadening of the motives for rural landownership beyond the traditional motive of holding land for agricultural use. This was true even in Douglas County, where, although the amount of land owned by local farmers has not changed much, expectations about future capital gains have become a vital element in the farmers' decisions about buying or holding land.

The issues raised by land-market changes vary somewhat from place to place, but they typically involve a mixture of land-use and social impacts. In exurban Loudoun County, one finds concern that long-distance urban commuters and hobby farmers are bidding land away from commercial agriculture and changing the area's long-established rural character. In the Texas pineywoods and the Potomac Highlands, subdivision of land for rural residential and recreational use clouds the long-term future of the timber industry, even as it brings new people as well as new money into formerly depressed economies. In the upper Connecticut River valley and along the central California coast, the purchase of multiple-acre tracts by new residents is creating a new landscape, certainly not suburban, but no longer wholly agricultural. In East Central Illinois, there are still large tracts of uninterrupted farmland, but there is worry over how absentee landlords will manage their land and over the steadily rising cost of becoming a farmer. In many of the areas studied, there is concern about corporate and other absentee ownership, about aesthetic and public-service costs of new development, about access to land for hunting and fishing, and about the impacts of new residents on traditional rural society.

The places we have studied are very different in location, in topography, and in economic resources and prospects. But each has been touched by the cumulative impacts of thousands of individual decisions to buy, to sell, or to change the use of rural land.

REFERENCES

1. The alternative of taking a random sample of 50 or more rural counties was rejected because of the prohibitive cost of collecting original data (particularly landownership statistics) from such a large sample.

2. See U.S. Department of Agriculture, *A Dialogue on the Structure of American Agriculture: Summary of Regional Meetings, November 27-December 18, 1979* (Washington, D.C.: Government Printing Office, 1980), especially meetings in Sioux City, Iowa, and Sedalia, Missouri; Colorado Department of Agriculture, *Agricultural Land Conversion in Colorado*, vol. 1 (Denver: Colorado Department of Agriculture, 1979); George Van Otten, "Changing Spatial Characteristics of Willamette Valley [Ore.] Farms," *Professional Geographer*, vol. 32, no. 1 (1980), pp. 63-71.

3. San Luis Obispo County contains a fast-growing college campus, but its growth affects primarily the city of San Luis Obispo, excluded from our data wherever possible. Also a large nuclear electric power plant was built there during the 1970s, but its existence, including the employment created, does not appear to have influenced the local land market. Possible mineral discoveries in Hardy County had not influenced the land market at the time of our study.

4. Loudoun County Office of Economic Development, *The Demographic Survey of Loudoun County, Va., 1977*, Table 9, p. 11.

5. Thomas Grubisich, "Angry Taxpayers," *Washington Post*, July 23, 1978.

6. *Loudoun County Resource Management Plan* (Leesburg: Loudoun County Planning Department, May 1979), p. 68.

7. Grubisich, "Angry Taxpayers."

8. Piedmont Environmental Council, *County of Loudoun Environmental Resources Inventory* (Warrenton, Virginia: Piedmont Environmental Council, 1976), pp. 28-29.

9. U.S. Bureau of the Census, *Census of Agriculture* (1974 and 1978) (Washington, D.C.: Government Printing Office).

10. James Tyler, "Real Estate in Loudoun, Supply and Demand," *The Virginia Hunt Country*, 4th ed. (Middleburg, Virginia: The Country Books, Inc., 1977), p. 27.

11. Estimates derived from information and graphical presentations in Ibid., pp. 26-27.

12. James L. Short, "Dimensions of Land Use Change in Exurbia: Two Case Studies" (Unpublished study, funded by an environmental fellowship from The Rockefeller Foundation, The Conservation Foundation, Washington, D.C., July 1979).

13. Data obtained from reports filed with the U.S. Department of Agriculture under the Foreign Agricultural Investment Disclosure Act. Foreigners are defined as individuals who are not citizens or lawfully admitted into the United States for permanent residence, foreign-based corporations, and U.S.-based corporations in which foreigners have more than a 5 percent interest.

14. *Loudoun County Resource*, p. 39.

15. Ibid.

16. William R. Lassey, *Planning in Rural Environments* (New York: McGraw-Hill, 1977), p. 218.

17. Ibid., p. 220.

18. J.M. Earles, *Forest Statistics for East Texas Pineywoods Counties*, Forest Service Resource Bulletin (New Orleans: U.S. Forest Service, Southern Forest Experiment Station, 1976).

19. "Long Range Program for Tyler County," prepared by the Tyler County Program Building Committee, Revised 1978, p. 101.

20. U.S. Bureau of the Census, *Census of Agriculture (1974)—County Data* (Tyler County, Texas) (Washington, D.C.: Government Printing Office), Table 1, p. 80.

21. Land in farms, much of which was forested, fell from 219,000 acres in 1967 to 90,000 acres in 1974. Ibid., Table 2, p. 80.

22. "Long Range Program for Tyler County," p. 95.

23. A number of exclusions were made from our data base to represent the private, rural land market in the county. Public ownership and ownerships in the town of Woodville were excluded. Also, due to their size, landholdings of the major timber companies are not included here. We treat this special issue later.

24. The leasing of hunting rights, on both private and industry land, is, in fact, more common in Texas than in most other parts of the United States. See James G. Teer and Nathan K. Forrest, "Bionomic and Ethical Implications of Commercial Game Harvest Programs (1968)," in James A. Bailey, William Elder, and Ted D. McKinney, eds., *Readings in Wildlife Conservation* (Washington, D.C.: The Wildlife Society, 1974), pp. 109-118.

25. PL 93-439 was signed into law on October 11, 1974.

26. Land acquisition is under the direction of the Army Corps of Engineers. The data were given, as of July 1979, by the Real Estate Acquisition Division, Army Corps of Engineers, Washington, D.C.

27. These figures are from "Long Range Program for Tyler County," and the *Census of Agriculture* (1974).

28. Due to mergers, acquisitions, and name changes, it was difficult to make accurate comparisons of holdings between 1954 and 1976. This estimate is based on inspection of public land records and personal interviews.

29. Alvin Edward Moore, *History of Hardy County of the Borderland* (Parsons, West Virginia: McClain Printing Co., 1963).

30. *Champaign News-Gazette*, March 19, 1978.

31. John T. Scott, Jr., quoted in *Champaign News-Gazette*, July 7, 1979.

32. David A. Lins, "Inflationary Expectations and Land Values," in *Effects of High Farm Land Prices: 1978 Rural Policy Forum*, AE-4461 (Champaign-Urbana: University of Illinois, Department of Agricultural Economics, 1978); B. Delworth Gardner, "Issues Affecting the Availability and Prices of Land for Agriculture" (Paper presented to the California Chapter of the American Society of Agronomy, Fresno, January 26, 1978); Linda Snyder Hayes, "Investors in Farmland are on Dangerous Ground," *Fortune*, January 29, 1979, pp. 97-98.

33. The four eastern townships, which cover about 98,000 acres, roughly 35 percent of the county, were selected for analysis because they are not crossed by Interstate 57 and are unaffected by the unusual impact on landownership patterns of a large Amish settlement in western Douglas County.

34. A *holding* is defined as all land held in a single ownership within the boundaries of the four townships. A random sample of 100 landowners in the four townships analyzed indicates that 1 out of 15 may own additional land in Douglas County not reflected in the data.

35. Illinois South Project, Inc., *Who's Mining the Farm* (Herrin, Illinois: Illinois South Project, Inc., 1978).

36. Farm Credit Administration, *Characteristics of Federal Land Bank Loans, 1978*, Statistical Bulletin 23 (Washington, D.C.: Farm Credit Administration, Economic Analysis Division, November 1979), Table 10.

37. Margaret Bogue, *Patterns from the Sod,* Illinois Historical Collections, vol. 34, no. 18.

38. Harry Smith Wright, Jr., "The Principles of Setting Up a Special Extension Educational Program for Landowners in Pike County, Illinois" (Thesis, University of Illinois, Champaign-Urbana, 1969).

39. The townships are Hartland, Hartford, Woodstock, Windsor, and West Windsor, Vermont, and Lebanon and Plainfield, New Hampshire.

40. Ottauquechee Regional Planning and Development Commission, *Update: Ottauquechee Regional Land Use Plan, Interim Report* (Woodstock, Vermont: Ottauquechee Regional Commission, June 1977). See also Harvey Jacobs and Darby Bradley, *The Hartland Open Space Project* (Woodstock, Vermont: Ottauquechee Regional Commission, 1976).

41. Data provided by Federal Land Bank, White River Junction, Vermont.

42. Vermont Governor's Forest Taxation Study Committee, *Report,* September 17, 1976, p. 21.

43. Vermont requires more specific evidence of management than does New Hampshire.

44. Survey taken by Environmental Studies class, Dartmouth College, on file in Plainfield, New Hampshire, town clerk's office.

45. Calvin Wilvert, "The 'San-San' Gap: Land Use Changes Along California's Rural Central Coast" (Paper presented to the annual meeting of the Western Regional Science Association, San Diego, California, February 1980).

46. The regulations of the California Coastal Commission have, however, since 1972 placed severe limitations on nonagricultural development of coastal properties, so that nonagricultural value is based mainly on speculation about future relaxation of the regulations.

47. Wilvert, "The 'San-San' Gap," p. 6.

48. Urban/rural data are estimates obtained from the San Luis Obispo County Planning Department.

49. From figures cited in Wilver, "The 'San-San' Gap," p. 8.

50. State of California, Employment Development Department, *San Luis Obispo County Labor Market Bulletin,* various issues.

51. Wilvert, "The 'San-San' Gap," p. 7.

52. From information provided by the San Luis Obispo County Agricultural Commission.

53. San Luis Obispo County Planning Department, "Agricultural Issues and Opportunities," December 1978, mimeographed, p. 1.

54. Total numbers of parcels were taken from the property tax rolls in the County Auditor's Office.

55. During the 1950s, the Assessor's Office consolidated all separate but contiguous parcels under one ownership. Thus, the data here reflect total holdings rather than separate parcels.

56. Calculated from data in San Luis Obispo County Planning Department, "A Study of Non-Conforming Subdivision in Rural Areas" (Unpublished, November 1977).

57. San Luis Obispo, *Telegram-Tribune,* March 6, 1963.

58. Data from the San Luis Obispo County Planning Department.

59. Cited from Wilvert, "The 'San-San' Gap," p. 14.

60. Data from the San Luis Obispo County Planning Department. Differences between permits applied for and those granted could not be determined for the 1975-80 period.

61. San Luis Obispo County Planning Department, "Agricultural Issues and Opportunities," p. 4.

62. Ibid., p. 2.

63. From unpublished County Planning Department maps cited in Wilvert, "The 'San-San' Gap," pp. 12-13.

64. Unpublished data from the San Luis Obispo County Agricultural Commission. The reduced number of contracts in early 1978 can probably be attributed to anticipation that Proposition 13 would pass.

65. For example, in rural portions of San Diego County, Williamson Act contract applications averaged 60 to 80 per year prior to 1976. With the passage of Proposition 13, they dropped to only 15 in 1978. See Short, "Dimensions of Land Use Change in Exurbia: Two Case Studies," p. 73.

66. Wilvert, "The "San-San' Gap," pp. 15-21.

67. Estimates from the San Luis Obispo County Planning Department.

CHAPTER 6

Issues in the Rural
Land Market

The rural land market is an arena of private individuals and private interests. In buying and selling rural properties, millions of market participants independently exercise their good judgment and their foolishness; their exquisitely calculated financial schemes and their seat-of-the-pants guesses; their family obligations and their personal dreams. Land, the object of their activity, has been aptly described as "a commodity affected with a public interest."[1] But in the land market as we know it, private choices reign supreme.

Many people contend that the land market fails to protect the "public interest." There is no agreement, however, about what the public interest is. Some public goals affected by land, such as the continued production of food, fiber, and other products at reasonable cost, are accepted almost universally. Other goals are in dispute. For example, some people would like to see ownership of rural land, and therefore the power to decide how land is to be used, very widely dispersed. Others believe strongly that the right of the individual to accumulate property should take precedence.

In this chapter, we shall discuss a number of "public interest" issues. Each arises out of someone's contention that the unfettered operation of the land market fails to protect some interest other than that of the landowner. Each issue, moreover, is affected by one or more of the trends described in chapter 1: changing patterns of ownership, rising prices, and changing parcel sizes.

Essentially, the issues in the rural land market can be grouped into two categories, allowing for some overlap. One broad class of issues focuses on *land use*. These issues involve such matters as the relationship between land management and type of owner; whether the land market works efficiently in changing land from one use to another; and the possible impacts of land-market trends on the future availability of rural land for commodity production. For example, might increasing ownership of farmland by urban or other absentee owners cause land to be used in ways that reduce its future productivity?

A second set of issues focuses more explicitly on *social and political* questions. During the 1970s, a great deal of press attention was paid to who controls rural resources, raising questions about, for example, absentee ownership of rural land in Appalachia, foreign purchase of farmland, and corporate farming. More recently, a wide-ranging debate has begun on the "structure of agriculture," including consideration of the desirable size of farm units, the participation of nonfarm capital in agriculture, and the role of farming in a rural society in which farmers make up a small minority of the residents.[2] Concern has also been expressed about how population growth and the changing identity of rural landowners will affect traditional rural society and local government's ability to deliver public services.

Land-use Issues

At present, the United States has a rural land base unmatched worldwide in its combination of size and fertility—413 million acres of cropland, 505 million acres of nonfederal pastureland and rangeland, and 407 million acres of nonfederal forestland.[3] But projected growth in export demand for food and in domestic demands for lumber and paper suggest that, unless we markedly increase yields per acre, we could before long be using all of the land that can be made available.

Parcellation, changing ownership patterns, and high land prices may impede our future ability to expand commodity production. Perhaps the most important obstacle is parcellation, which affects tens of millions of acres of crop- and forestland, reducing their future economic possibilities as food or wood producers.

Obstacles to expanded commodity production—as well as some opportunities—are also presented by the changing pattern of landownership. This is especially true for the "nonindustrial private forests," those private woodlands not owned by the forest-products industry, which are increasingly controlled by urban residents and other nontraditional owners. Landownership may also affect rates of erosion, an important factor in the future productivity of cropland. Of particular significance is the high proportion of cropland held by absentee owners, who may not be able to supervise adequately their tenants' use of the land.

High land prices do not in themselves appear to stand in the way of future land availability, although, as we shall see later in the chapter, they have major implications for the distribution of wealth. However, land speculation, which is motivated by anticipation of price change, may tie up excessive quantities of potentially productive rural land, particularly on the fringe of expanding urban areas.

Parcellation

Parcel size is an important influence on rural land use because there are scale economies in farm and forest commodity production. Although there are gaps in our knowledge of what is the most efficient parcel size for various uses, there is surely some parcel size below which many otherwise feasible management practices are unlikely to be profitable.

Parcellation appears to be most worrisome with respect to forestland. We have already noted (in chapter 1) that 22 percent of forestland is in ownerships of less than 100 acres, and that 12 percent is in ownerships of less than 50 acres. Small tract size raises the costs of harvesting timber. A timber buyer for a large lumber company in Texas observes that:

> We have people coming to us all the time trying to sell timber in 2-acre, 3-acre, and 5-acre blocks. We just refer them someplace else. We hardly ever buy anything less than 25 acres, and we prefer 50 or more. Our contractor loses a day's work just moving his equipment to the next site.

Even more serious is parcellation's impact on the economics of applying productivity-raising management methods. Forest economist Clark Row calculates that tract size has substantial impacts on the financial returns to intensive forest management, and that scale economies are found as parcel size rises, up to at least 160 acres. He concludes that "where tracts are small, owners may accurately perceive that *for them* intensive timber growing would not be worth the effort, unless it facilitates other objectives."[4]

Moreover, even if a given type of management is profitable in terms of rate of return on investment, the total amount of revenue produced on a small tract may not be large enough to make a landowner take action. For example, few urban absentee owners would be motivated by a $100 per year return from thinning a hardwood timber stand, even if the percentage rate of return on investment were quite high. The same is true for such nontimber cases as leasing grazing land to an adjoining farmer, or leasing hunting rights or other kinds of access rights.

A recent study of forestland in Oklahoma demonstrated that parcel size had a measurable influence on the intensity of forest management.[5] The researchers found that styles of management tended to differ, depending on whether parcel size was in the range of 10 to 50 acres, 51 to 700 acres, or 700-plus acres. The acreage divisions between the groups were not arbitrarily fixed, but were set at the level at which the type of management began to change. As might be expected, the larger the tract-size group, the more likely was the owner to be interested in wood production, the higher was the intensity of management, and the greater was the probability of harvest.

Parcellation affects agricultural land as well. However, the effects are mitigated somewhat by the fact that agriculture is so varied that even rather small tracts can sometimes be used profitably—for vegetables, poultry, or orchard crops, for example. Modern Japanese agriculture demonstrates that it is technically possible to make small tracts quite productive. Nevertheless, American agriculture, as most widely practiced, is based on the realization of economies of large-scale production. For most crops, costs per unit of output drop as farm size increases, at least into the range of 100 to 300 acres.[6]

It is certainly safe to say that the division of high-quality farmland into the 2-to-10-acre building lots typically found in rural subdivisions precludes commercial agriculture of most currently practiced types. Nor do the larger 10-to-40-acre "farmettes" and "ranchettes" that have been created in so many rural places promise much commercial crop or livestock production. "Farmette" tracts frequently turn out to be more than the owner can take care of without substantial capital investment in farm equipment—an investment that would then likely be underutilized given the size of the "farmette" parcel. Formerly open fields in New England and the Middle Atlantic states, grown up in woods for lack of mowing or grazing, are visible evidence of new owners with more land than they can cultivate.

More than once during the course of our research we heard of new owners of small rural parcels who were willing to give away crops if a local farmer would just furnish the equipment and undertake harvesting. A Virgina official of the Soil Conservation Service

(SCS) told us of estate owners with alfalfa ready to cut and bale who did not have the machinery to do the job. Some owners had tried to get local farmers to share proceeds from the sale of hay, but most were willing to give it to anyone who would cut and bale it. In the words of the SCS official, "Those 10-to-20-acre people out there are hurting. They don't know what to do with that much land." And an urban-based owner of 37 rural acres told a similar story:

> There's a farmer down the road who has cut the hay in the field for the past three years. We let him keep the hay in return for cutting it. . . . It's much easier than mowing it ourselves. We have no equipment.

Urban buyers of rural land often have little idea of how much land they really want or need. As one New England dealer in recreational properties put it, "People are looking for more land than they are used to." To an urban or suburban buyer, accustomed to a quarter-acre house lot, a second-home parcel with five acres of forest may seem immense. Even after land has been subdivided, the new buyer often finds that he has acquired much more land than he can take care of.

Ironically, well-intended local and state land-use regulations have sometimes contributed to parcellation by causing lots used for development to be larger than they would otherwise have been. For example, many counties have zoned their rural portions so that building lots must be at least 5 or 10 acres. This requirement may inadvertently increase the total amount of land in medium-sized parcels, which are unnecessarily large for residential purposes, yet far too small for most agricultural uses. Similarly, Vermont's state land-use law (Act 250) exempts parcels of more than 10 acres from certain regulations. It is said that subdividers have chosen to avoid the costs of compliance with the law by creating lots just slightly larger than the 10-acre limit. A proliferation of 10.1-acre lots has also occurred in recreational areas in Michigan, where a state subdivision law has had a 10-acre cut off and where local 10-acre minimum zoning is common. According to one observer in that state, "What we have accomplished by this is thousands of lots where a person uses a half-acre for a house, while 9½ acres lie idle."[7]

A recent study of farmland loss in several counties near San Francisco described parcellation in that region as "the largest single consumer of farmland—taking more land, apparently, than does outright subdivision." The study also observes that this parcellation is accompanied by changing ownership patterns, compounding the impacts:

> Small farms can be highly efficient. But most of these little properties don't wind up as producing farms at all; they finish as rural "estates," hobby farms, or "ranchettes." Aside from removing land from production directly, they create real difficulties for serious agriculture around them.[8]

Farm operators are increasingly concerned that scattered rural residential uses will interfere with agricultural practices on nearby, undivided land. Where farms and residences are intermixed, the farmers face problems with dogs and vandalism, while the new residents complain to local officials about smells, noise, pesticide spraying, and slow-moving farm vehicles on the highways. The farmers are usually the losers in such contests. A study of land policy in Oregon notes that:

> In many respects, rural development presents an even greater, and less quantifiable, challenge to agricultural and timber productivity than does suburban development. A very few rural homesteads dotted through an agricultural area can have a surprisingly detrimental effect on a farming economy.[9]

The study concedes that, in the short run, parcellation may help a farmer stay in business by allowing him to sell off a parcel or two in lean years. But, in the long run, "each small subdivision undermines the productivity of the farm unit and makes it more likely that another parcel will have to be sold to subsidize the farmer in the future."[10]

Once rural parcels are divided, sold to diverse owners, and peppered with interspersed residential uses, they can be very difficult and expensive to recombine. Some indications of the cost and complexities of parcel recombination were evident in the experience of urban-renewal agencies during the 1950s and 1960s. The agencies incurred massive expenses as they purchased small, central-city properties and tried to recombine them into the large parcels needed for various projects.

Except on the urban fringe, much of the rural land being purchased by nontraditional owners for residential or recreational purposes has been marginal land not currently in demand for either agriculture or forestry. In the future, if commodity prices rise to considerably higher than current levels, these marginal lands may again be in demand. Once split and sold, however, such parcels may be effectively removed from the potential land base.

ISSUES IN THE RURAL LAND MARKET

Management of Nonindustrial Private Forests

Approximately 58 percent of the timberland in the United States is held by private owners other than the forest-products industry. About two fifths of this land is owned by farmers (whose holdings have been declining for many years); the rest belongs to what the Forest Service calls "other private" owners, a category that includes the newcomers and other nontraditional owners whose activities we have documented in earlier chapters. These nonindustrial private forests (NIPFs) include a considerable amount of potentially productive land; for example, they account for 71 percent of the timberland in the South. Because of their aggregate size and productive potential, the NIPFs will have to play an extremely important role if future timber demands are to be met.

Foresters have long bemoaned the alleged low productivity of the NIPFs, pointing out that NIPFs are growing wood at much less than biological potential and have not been fully participating in the movement toward intensive management that has become commonplace in the forest industry. One government report, for example, found that NIPFs were growing wood at only 49 percent of their productive capacity, compared with 59 percent for forest-industry lands.[11] Dozens of reports, task forces, symposia, and congressional hearings have considered the NIPF "problem."[12]

The reasons most frequently cited for the relatively poor performance of NIPFs are: (1) insufficient financial return to owners' investments in timber production; (2) owners' ignorance of opportunities in forestry; (3) owners' preference to use land to satisfy objectives other than timber production. The last two factors are directly affected by the changing composition of landowners.

It is difficult to fault landowners for not investing time and money in wood production when doing so would be unprofitable. But rises in wood-product prices, combined with possible profits from firewood production, appear to have improved the economics of timber management. One study by a forest-industry group identified 79 million acres of NIPF land in 25 states as offering "timber-growing opportunities producing an incremental rate of return of at least 10 percent after tax."[13] A task force of the Society of American Foresters reported that "virtually all studies reveal large-scale opportunities to improve [NIPF] management from the owners' and society's points of views."[14]

Given the apparent profitability of increased wood production, are NIPF owners prepared to respond? Economist Marion Clawson thinks so. He argues that, over the last 25 years, nonindustrial private forests have made substantial gains toward matching the forest-products industry's level of annual wood growth per acre.[15] He attributes the NIPFs' improved performance at least in part to the incentive of rising timber prices. Clawson argues bluntly that "for the nonindustrial private forests, the best public action is to leave them alone, aside from fire control."[16]

Others who have studied NIPFs put more emphasis on the role of owner ignorance and of the owner's nontimber objectives in reducing the investment response to rising prices. For example, the above-cited study by the forest industry notes as a "major restraint" to improved wood productivity the "lack of knowledge by small private owners concerning the benefits of forest investment."[17] Even Clawson concedes that economic models of timber output's response to price suffer "the very serious weakness that forest owners/managers may not respond to price or other stimuli in ways or to the degree that the analyst thinks would be rational."[18] The changing patterns of forestland ownership could thus become an important influence on investment in intensified forest management, and hence on future wood output.

Although there have been many surveys demonstrating that owners' personal characteristics affect their attitudes toward forest management and willingness to invest in it,[19] there have been very few studies relating both economic return and owner characteristics to the investment response. One study that did so for a sample of New Hampshire landowners found that the probability of timber harvest was strongly responsive to stumpage prices, but farmers were more than twice as responsive to price as nonfarmers. Owners of large parcels were found to be more likely to harvest wood than owners of small parcels. Thus, at any given price, both the trend from farm to nonfarm ownership and land parcellation lead to reduced timber supply.[20]

Factors influencing timber harvest are not necessarily the same as those influencing investment in growing trees. We can speculate that to the extent that nontraditional owners have higher incomes, and hence more to invest, as well as more education than traditional owners, they might be more receptive to taking advantage of profitable opportunities in tree planting or timber-stand improvement. Moreover, the new owners' environmental feelings might predispose them toward management options that would raise wood growth or that would improve the quality of such nonwood outputs as wildlife and water. Yet the idealistic desire to improve their land can falter when nontraditional owners face the hard work and expense that land management requires. One forester we spoke with claimed, "You can get [the newcomer's] ear a lot better than the old timer's." But a colleague added, "If it requires their own labor, you may as well forget about it."

Foresters who deal with the rural public believe that landowners who have purchased forest tracts for recreation or for investment are frequently misinformed about both the economics of timber management and how it might fit into their plans. Many new, urban-oriented owners tend to view resource protection in preservationist terms rather than in terms of "conservation for use." This leads the new owners to "conserve" the forest by not harvesting any of the trees on their property. Yet, in many parts of the country, foresters point out that the wood being conserved is of very low quality, the result of decades of "high-grading" (selective cutting of the best timber), and it will not be much improved by the passage of time. They believe that prudent long-term management would involve heavy immediate harvesting and regeneration in sounder trees and more usable species.

In part, the strong preservationist inclination of many new owners may reflect an ignorance of forestry; it may also, however, reflect basic motives for buying rural land. The trees that shade a wooded recreational site are likely to have greater value to the owner as scenery than they would to a logging contractor as sawtimber. Recently, some foresters have been advancing a new conception of "ecological forestry," in which selective harvesting is used to improve wildlife habitat and scenic quality, while producing salable timber products.[21] Perhaps this approach will begin to appeal to the owner who is not principally interested in timber production.

The impact of preservation-minded landowners on wood supply is also affected by the likelihood that intentions with regard to timber harvest may change.[22] A 1970 survey of Delaware woodland owners found that 58 percent said they had no plans ever to harvest timber. A 1974 resurvey found that, although the proportion of owners who said they would never harvest remained constant, 17 percent of the original respondents had changed from opposition to harvesting to a willingness to harvest. Moreover, some parcels had been transferred by sale or inheritance during the four years between surveys, increasing the possibility that any given parcel would at some point in its history come into the hands of an owner interested in harvesting timber. The authors of the study also noted that landowners unlikely to harvest tended to own smaller than average tracts, reducing the potential impact on wood supply. Despite the probability of eventual harvest, however, the productivity of at least some land is reduced during whatever time it is withdrawn from active timber management.

When they do decide to harvest, nontraditional landowners may contribute to poor forest management in yet another way. They may allow irresponsible timber operators to "high-grade" their land or to harvest in a careless and destructive manner. A West Virginia forestry professor points to two counties noted for new urban buyers as:

> ... good examples of people buying up land that they do not relate to in a stewardship sense. Much of our timber is nearing harvestable age and timber operators are approaching the landowners. We see a lot of harvesting done in a terrible manner. It makes a [substantial] and lasting water-quality problem; the land may be so eroded that it will take a long time to restore any cover; and it removes all economic value of the land [for forestry].

The recent revival of interest in cutting firewood provides an excellent opportunity in the eastern hardwood areas for upgrading forest quality by selective thinning. But, unless forestland owners seek professional guidance or educate themselves as to which trees to cut and which to leave, they may well find their timber quality even further degraded by poor harvest practices.

As in the case of parcellation, few of the impacts of poor timber management are likely to be felt in the near term. Little of the land purchased for recreational use (with the exception of some softwood areas of the South and Pacific Northwest) is currently a major source of wood-fiber supply. But lack of immediate need is no reason for complacency: it takes up to 30 years to produce good softwood sawtimber, and up to 100 for quality hardwoods. To the extent that owner ignorance or inattention causes underinvestment in nonindustrial private forestlands, future generations may face unnecessary shortages of wood products.

Management of Absentee-owned Farmland

At present, about one third of all farmland, approximately 300 million acres, is rented rather than owned by its operator.[23] Leasing is a long-standing practice in some parts of the country, including the Corn Belt. Some observers contend that leased land is more likely to be abused, particularly if the owner lives far away or knows little about farming practices and if the land is leased only for a year at a time. As a Maryland farmer put it:

> I can [pass] any farm along any road in this county and tell you if it's owner operated or tenant operated.... If it isn't yours, you put nitrogen on real heavy—you get the return [from that] right away, but you cut corners on the potash and the phosphorous.

In Virginia, a Soil Conservation Service agent observed that:

> A person leasing land is just interested in production. Most of the time he has only a 3 to 5 year lease. He does not have the interest in the land that the person who owns it does. You see a man who owns land who practices the best conservation [techniques], but when he rents land he is just out for what he can produce—it's only natural.

A New Jersey agricultural economist notes that, under the one-year cash rental arrangements prevalent in his state, a tenant who invests money in the land—even for so simple a practice as adding lime to the soil—may find next year's rent raised to reflect the added value.

Support for the "careless tenant" hypothesis also comes from a recent study in western Iowa which found that renters were losing an average of 20.9 tons per acre of topsoil annually to erosion, while owner-operators were losing only 15.6 tons.[24] On the other hand, early results of a study comparing national data on land leasing and erosion rates indicate no correlation between the two.[25] Additional research is needed before we can judge the wisdom of the proverb, frequently cited by land-reform advocates, "The best fertilizer for the land is the footstep of the owner."

Land Stewardship

There is a strong and widespread tradition in rural areas that a landowner has a moral obligation to use his land in a manner that husbands or protects its productive qualities, even in the face of economic incentives to do otherwise. This feeling of land stewardship arises from long-standing cultural and even religious values and is heightened by peer pressure among farmers and (to a lesser extent) forest owners. Of course, land stewardship is far from universal among traditional landowners. Some of the most wasteful land-use practices have been imposed by people who have had a long and intimate connection with their land. But there is no doubt that land stewardship has had a potent effect on behavior in most rural areas.

Voluntary programs for both soil conservation and forest management have relied on land stewardship. For example, the National Association of Conservation Districts and local soil and water conservation districts have since 1955 sponsored a yearly "Soil Stewardship Week." The literature used to promote this observance makes frequent use of ethical and religious arguments. Similarly, the American Tree Farm System, an industry-sponsored group that promotes forest management, has appealed to civic responsibility as well as to economics in its advertising. One promotional piece states, "There is really only one common characteristic that seems generally true of tree farmers across the country. That is a desire to fulfill an obligation to the land—an obligation that comes with ownership."[26]

Absentee ownership is only one of the land-market trends that some observers believe are reducing land stewardship in rural areas. Poet and essayist Wendell Berry argues that the increased scale of modern agriculture has also had an impact:

> The concentration of the farmland into larger and larger holdings and fewer and fewer hands . . . *forces* a profound revolution in the farmer's mind: once his investment in land and machines is large enough, he must forsake the values of husbandry and assume those of finance and technology.[27]

Others claim that rising land prices have brought subtle changes in attitudes. Over the last decade, the total increase in the market value of farmland has exceeded by a considerable margin the total net income from farming. This fact has not gone unnoticed by farmers, and some observers speculate that the experience has changed farmers' attitudes toward their land. One agricultural economist notes "the feeling among some young farmers that farming is just real estate investment. The land may be deteriorating a bit but it is still appreciating in value."[28]

Attitudes are by their nature difficult to measure, and statements about changing attitudes are difficult to prove. It is not hard to believe, however, that attitudes—as well as economics—are important determinants of land use and that the great changes that have recently come to the the land market have altered the context within which attitudes about land are formed.

Land-use Impacts of Ownership, Scale, and Technology

New owners, new scales of operation, and technological change frequently go together, and, in evaluating their impacts on land use, it is very hard to separate one force from another. Consider, for example, the "superfarms" that have been created in the last few years in coastal sections of North Carolina. Starting about 1970, corporations began to develop huge farming operations—the largest holding covered 370,000 acres—on what had been a virtual wilderness of swamps, bogs, and forests. Both U.S. nonfarm corporations and Japanese and Italian companies were involved. The clearing and draining of formerly waterlogged land has had substantial adverse impacts on terrestrial and marine wildlife, on water quality, and on the area's peaty organic soils, which literally burn away when the water table is lowered.[29] It is impossible to determine how much of the resulting environmental damage should be blamed on "unfeeling" corporations or foreigners, how much on the scale of operations, and how much on technological and economic forces that would have motivated even small-scale local farmers to use similar techniques, with similar results.

Very large-scale corporate owners have also been a major (though not exclusive) factor in the establishment of center pivot irrigation systems on tens of thousands of acres of the Mid-Columbia basin in Oregon and Washington. The result has been higher output and a change in the crop mix, but also increased pressure on energy supplies, pollution of surface water by herbicides and pesticides, and demands on the federal government to provide heavy subsidization for new sources of water.[30]

Yet another example of the interrelationship of scale, ownership, and land-use change is the tendency in some of the richest midwestern farming areas to replace a mixture of grain and livestock farming with a cash-grain monoculture. Dovring and Yanagida describe the resulting landscape as a "grain desert" that has "drained the rural landscape of other economic activity." They observe that in Illinois "the change to cash grain farming often means changing to larger operating units, sometimes also to larger ownership units."[31] Cash-grain farming may be especially attractive when land is owned by absentee owners, since it is less risky than livestock raising, and lease terms are easier to set. In this case, too, it is nearly impossible to separate ownership, scale, and economic forces favoring one use of land over another. Because cash-grain farming offers a good return for less drudgery and risk than is required in small grain-and-livestock enterprises, some conversion from one use to the other might well have occurred even if farm size were fixed and absentee ownership unknown.

Perhaps the relationship between ownership, scale, and technology can be most clearly illustrated by the 69 million acres of land owned by the forest-products industry. The industry owns much of this acreage in tracts of far larger than average size; it usually manages its land more intensively than either government or other private owners; and it is rapidly increasing its technical sophistication. From a wood-production standpoint, industry ownership is beneficial. Industry holdings amount to 14 percent of the nation's forest-land; because management is more intensive and the land is somewhat more fertile than average, these holdings account for 19 percent of annual wood growth. Some intensive management practices used by the industry, such as very large clearcuts, pesticide spraying, and conversions of hardwood to softwood plantations, have had negative impacts on the environment. On the other hand, the industry is probably more likely than the nonindustrial private owner to replant after harvest, to employ professional forest managers, and to try to maintain a healthy, fast-growing forest.

Because industry lands are often held in very large blocks, they have the potential to provide open space and visual amenity that could not be realized on small tracts of private land interspersed with various forms of development. Nearly all industry lands are open to public recreational access, occasionally with trails, campsites, or other facilities provided free of charge.[32] In many southern and New England states, a major part of the public's hunting opportunity is provided on industry-owned land. Although practice varies widely within the industry, a number of companies employ wildlife biologists and make some effort to minimize negative impacts on wildlife. Such attention is particularly important when large timber tracts are under intensive timber management, since uniformity may cause severe problems for wildlife diversity.[33] Some of the specific management practices of the industry have been deservedly criticized. But on many land-use criteria, the timber industry compares favorably with the scattered private ownership that is its most likely alternative.

ISSUES IN THE RURAL LAND MARKET

Land Prices and Land Use

Although, as discussed elsewhere in this book, there has been a manyfold increase in rural land prices during the last three decades, we see little evidence that high land prices, by themselves, have had much impact on the allocation of land among various uses. At current land prices, owners must content themselves with returns of perhaps 3 to 5 percent on the market value of their land. But this low return relative to land value does not seem to favor one use over another or to encourage keeping land idle. At any given point in time, an individual landowner will make his decisions on how to use his land on the basis of costs and returns in each alternative use, irrespective of mortgage interest or any other fixed costs that do not depend on how the land is used.

It is possible that the high price of land causes it to be held by people who (at a given level of return for each use) will respond differently from those who would be holding it if land prices were low. Thus, timber companies might be discouraged from buying land because of high prices; the urban-based investors who continue buying land may be less interested in or capable of practicing forestry. The extent of this phenomenon cannot be determined until we know more about (1) how high land prices affect the structure of landownership and (2) how various classes of owners react to land-use opportunities.

High prices may in the long run cause an intensification of land use. If land is expensive relative to labor or capital, land users will use less land and more of the other factors of production. Just as the low land prices that characterized the United States in the 18th and 19th centuries caused farmers to adopt land-extensive farming practices, the present high price of land is likely to cause future farmers and foresters to look for ways to use land more intensively. This has some advantages, not the least of which is greater focus on soil quality and, therefore, greater recognition of the need to protect it. There are, to be sure, some problems associated with intensification of land use, including water pollution from fertilizers and pesticides and damage to wildlife habitat. But most of these problems are not inevitable and can be dealt with through specific policies.

From the standpoint of land *use*, the overall level of land prices is much less important than the relative prices offered for land for each alternative use. Ideally, private market prices associated with devoting land to each use should reflect not only private returns but also any social costs (or social benefits) that might result. Although the free market is a quite remarkable institution, there are three types of cases in which market prices will *not* adequately reflect public interests.

First, many uses of rural land produce spillovers or "externalities" that affect other properties nearby (or, less frequently, farther away). These externalities are not reflected in the market return received by the operator and hence do not affect the price he is willing to offer to bring additional land into a particular use. For example, a farmer may raise cotton on erosion-prone land, earning a net annual return of $100 per acre. At a capitalization rate of 10 percent, this use would support a land value of $1,000 per acre. Yet the sediment carried off each acre of the cotton farmer's land may be producing annual damage to others (say, in the form of siltation behind a downstream dam) of $40. Thus, when both private and social returns are considered, the value of using the land for cotton may be less than its value as pastureland, which would produce much less erosion. Other externalities associated with rural land use include those affecting farmers when adjoining land is put into residential use, erosion caused by logging roads, and diminution of overall scenic quality when industrial, commercial, or recreational uses are introduced into areas with important landscape values. Sometimes people benefit from externalities, as when a timber company opens its land to the public for recreation.

All of the major traditional and nontraditional uses of rural land produce externalities, although the nature of the spillover varies greatly from one use to another. Because of externalities, market prices for various land uses do not fully reflect public interests. Sometimes the spillover causes government to intervene in the market with incentives or regulations; in many cases, spillovers are ignored.

A second source of divergence between private and social costs involves subsidies that promote one use of land over another. For example, agricultural use is artificially promoted by federal price supports for crops, the provision of water at below-market prices, and tax subsidies to farmers. Urban uses of land benefit from such subsidies as public provision of highways and sewer lines for which the landowner is not fully charged. Most subsidies are the result of deliberate public policy. Often, they are attempts to secure public benefits, such as gaining cheaper food by subsidizing agricultural water use. But sometimes subsidies are unintended or even work at cross purposes to one another. For example, one government agency may use preferential tax assessment to encourage farming in a given area at the very time when another agency is energetically extending utility lines there. Particularly at the urban fringe, the web of subsidies and externalities is so complex and pervasive that it is difficult to argue that the market's allocation of land is due to the "free play of private market forces."

A third source of divergence between private and public interests is the market's failure to take sufficient account of the interests of future generations. Suppose that a given piece of land currently yields $100 per year for agricultural use and $200 per year for urban use. If one assumes these incomes will continue into the future and capitalizes them, the land is clearly worth most as urban land, and the market would allocate it to that use.

Now, suppose that the urban value of the land will increase at a real rate of 3 percent yearly into the future, while future world food demands will raise the land's agricultural value at a real rate of 6 percent yearly. In 10 years, the land will yield $179 per year as farmland, and $268 as urban land. Most profit-conscious landowners confronting this prospect would likely convert the land from agricultural to urban use.

Yet consider values in each use 50 years hence. At that time, the land will yield $876 yearly for urban use, but $1,842 in agricultural use. Not until year 25 does the yearly agricultural income begin to exceed the yearly income from urbanization. Surely few speculators or other current owners would be willing or able to look so many years into the future.[34]

Even if future generations will have a significantly greater demand to use a particular piece of land in agriculture than they will for having the land in urban use, they may not make their future demand felt in today's market.[35] If the urbanization process is irreversible (or reversible only at very high cost), there will have been a real consumption loss to future generations. According to one economist, describing the role of the free market in allocating consumption over time, "the present generation is a dictator."[36]

Speculation and the Use of Land

An important issue related indirectly to land prices is whether land speculation leads to inefficient patterns of land use. The reader will recall that speculation was defined in chapter 2 as the holding of land primarily to profit from an anticipated change in use. While land is being "ripened" for its new use, owners may neglect investments in agricultural structures or equipment, or the land may even be idled completely.

We do not know whether professional speculators differ from farmers-turned-speculators in their behavior during the ripening period. Certainly a professional speculator might cultivate land during the ripening period in exactly the same way as a farmer who had held the land for many years. Often, the speculator hires the selling farmer or a neighbor to do the work. On the other hand, a farmer who begins speculating on a future change in use may drastically alter his patterns of land use, ceasing to invest in buildings, fences, and equipment and letting the fertility of the soil decline.

Lack of investment, or even disinvestment, in anticipation of a change in use is not necessarily a sign of inefficiency, either for the individual farmer or for society. Only a foolish farmer would invest in a barn with a useful life of 40 years when it is probable that within a decade or less his property will be sold for development. This reluctance to invest, sometimes referred to as the "impermanence syndrome," is in evidence in a wide band surrounding most of the country's large cities, and even some of its small, but expanding, towns.

The key issue is whether the amount of land involved in the impermanence syndrome is appropriate in view of actual demand for future development. If speculators (or speculating farmers) have guessed right about future urban land needs, they will have performed a useful service in easing land's adjustment from one use to another. But if they are overly optimistic about development prospects, they can create around our cities great rings of unused or lightly used land, land withdrawn from agriculture but perhaps never needed for urban expansion. As one agricultural economist put it:

> Chances for future development, no matter how remote, can affect the farmer's willingness to invest in the business. Far more land is affected by the possibility of development than can ever actually be used. The frequent result is that much land is prematurely pulled out of farming by unspecified development potential.[37]

Another economist thinks that the capital gains provisions of federal income-tax laws have increased the amount of land affected by speculation. He argues that "the fact that the return from holding land for future use is taxed as a capital gain encourages more land to be held for future conversion than would otherwise be the case."[38] Since that statement was made, capital-gains tax rates have been further reduced, increasing the tax advantage to the speculator.

The Department of Agriculture estimates that 24 million acres of land that could be used as cropland are being held for possible urban use.[39] Such land is "very near other land already in urban use and known to be held by a person or corporation for development." For example, says the Department, such a parcel might be a tract with a sign saying, "Owner will build to suit tenant—Zoned I-3."[40] This figure compares with a current rate of conversion of all land (including land with no crop potential) of 2.1 million acres per year. In addition to the land classified by USDA as held for development, there is likely to be an additional area, of unknown size, in which the *possibility* of development is inhibiting long-term capital investment for agricultural purposes.

Speculation has also been charged with creating distortions in the land market that can severely restrict the supply of land available for development and force home builders into inefficient patterns of leapfrog sprawl. For example, two distinguished land economists argue, "The sprawling nature of suburban growth is a direct outgrowth of private speculation in land."[41] Other researchers counter that speculative booms are by their nature short-lived, because "competitive market forces—the ability of developers to purchase land elsewhere—will tend to push land prices back toward equilibrium levels as long as the supply of developable land is not constrained."[42]

Finally, speculation can affect land use by leading to premature parcellation. One recent study found that, in U.S. fringe areas (of four cities) expected to develop in the next 10 years, 40 percent of the land is held in parcels of fewer than 10 acres. Even where development pressure was less intense, the study reported, more than one third of the parcels acquired since 1968 were smaller than 25 acres.[43] The "paper subdivisions" created in San Luis Obispo County several decades ago are another example of premature parcellation motivated in part by speculation. So are the many small-lot "recreational" subdivisions that were actively promoted in various parts of the United States during the 1960s and early 1970s. Millions of acres of these lands were made ready—divided into small parcels and laced with roads—for a change in use that never materialized. As a result, the land lies idle, in parcels ill-suited to any current or foreseeable productive use.

Rural Aesthetics

The rural landscape, which provides so much aesthetic enjoyment to people and which holds such an important place in American cultural mythology, is the product of nature, of the tastes and design traditions of rural landowners, and of the economics and technology of rural land uses. Within such natural constraints as topography and rainfall, rural landscapes depend on the type of crops raised; the proportion of cropland, pasture, and forest; the density and type of nonagricultural development; the layout of the highway network; and the architectural styles of houses, farm buildings, and fences.

In recent decades, rural landscapes have altered visibly. Affecting the most land, though sometimes unnoticed because the process has been gradual, have been changes in vegetation. In New England, the Middle Atlantic states, and the southern Piedmont, landscapes of open farm fields, no longer actively cultivated or grazed, have grown up in trees. In the Midwest and Great Plains, hedgerows and windbreaks have been bulldozed, allowing larger fields to be cultivated and making room for massive pieces of farm machinery to maneuver. In several parts of the South, "bottomland" hardwoods have been replaced by huge flat fields of soybeans and other row crops.[44]

Underlying economic factors probably have more to do with changing vegetative types than do the differing tastes of traditional and nontraditional landowners. To be sure, an agribusiness corporation is more likely to have 500 acres planted fence-to-fence in a single crop than are the five owners of adjoining 100-acre farms. But traditional landowners, reacting to the same economic forces as do corporations or absentee urban owners, have certainly played a major role in abandoning fields to brush and trees; small farmers in the South have been among those changing land from forest to soybeans.

A second, more easily noticed type of rural landscape change has been the scattering of urban-type structures and land uses over predominantly rural areas. The growth of the nonfarming rural population has led to a proliferation of houses along rural roadsides. Architecturally, these structures are frequently identical to those built in cities or suburbs, making them strikingly different from the local, traditional farm buildings. Some of these new structures are mobile homes, which in 1976 housed 8.8 percent of nonmetropolitan residents, up from 5.8 percent in 1970.[45] Strip commercial development along roadsides is also quite obvious in rural areas, although considerable progress has been made by many states in controlling billboards along major highways.

Second-home developments in rural areas range from the well designed, even picturesque, to the grotesque. One study notes:

> Second home projects can destroy a marsh vista, intrude on a skyline, or light up a mountainside that once loomed black against the night sky. Aesthetic impacts range from the "invasion" of wilderness by development to what the Nantucket Islanders simply call a "loss of charm" as small villages are transformed by growth and development.[46]

Preference for one landscape type over another is subjective, but there is evident concern in many parts of the country over the passing of traditional rural landscapes.[47] J.B. Jackson, for many years editor of *Landscape* magazine, was among the first to point out that the rural landscape "is undergoing a revolution in its way as radical as the revolution in the urban environment . . . [T]he family homestead . . . has vanished and along with it much of the 19th century landscape." The new rural landscape that was emerging, he predicted, would be composed partly of the mechanized, underpopulated landscape of modern farming—"with little to offer us in the way of pleasure or recreation"—and partly of the "city dweller's landscape of play."[48] Jackson, writing in 1966, believed that one solution was to separate the two landscapes, "engineering" attractive artificial landscapes for recreation. The revival of rural population growth, which has become evident more recently, makes such separation increasingly unlikely.

The increased interest in rural living has led to attempts to preserve older rural landscapes for entirely new, predominantly aesthetic, purposes. Many rural areas, particularly in the eastern half of the United States, which has been settled longer, contain plentiful examples of distinctive styles of architecture and construction methods. Barns, farmhouses, outbuildings, and even entire villages built in the 18th and 19th centuries are irreplaceable aesthetic and historic resources, providing insights into early construction techniques and life-styles. As a result of years of population decline, many such structures have been abandoned and left in disrepair. The U.S. Department of the Interior and private groups such as the National Trust for Historic Preservation and local historical societies have been addressing the problems of preserving these cultural resources, generally beginning by making local surveys of historic structures and important landscape types.[49] Local planners are grappling with the difficulties of reconciling the rights of private owners to build new structures, or tear down old ones, with the concerns of society to maintain a tangible link with its past. In many areas, preservation efforts are aided by affluent former urbanites who are actively seeking historic properties to rehabilitate, sometimes converting farm buildings to entirely new commercial or residential use.

Wildlife Habitat

Some of the same forces that are making land less available for commodity production are probably making it more suitable for wildlife habitat. For example, the abandonment of farm fields has favored species such as white-tailed deer, which flourish in a young, growing forest. The existence of many dead or rotten "cull" trees as a result of high-grading creates a habitat for cavity-dwelling species, such as wood ducks, raccoons, and woodpeckers. To the extent that small tract size means a multiplicity of interspersed uses, the total wildlife carrying capacity may be increased. On the other hand, wildlife suffers from some of the practices of large-scale commercial agriculture, particularly removal of hedgerows, crop and forest monoculture, and heavy application of pesticides.

Landownership patterns are difficult to relate to the quantity or diversity of wildlife. Large data gaps exist in quantitatively measuring habitat, in evaluating how land-use change affects habitat, and in describing how landownership is related to land-use change. It can be said that many recreation-oriented, nontraditional landowners are very much interested in wildlife, including "nongame" species, which have long been neglected by state and federal wildlife authorities. Unfortunately, beyond the few owners who build nesting boxes for bluebirds or who plant pasture in crops that provide wildlife with food and "cover," most owners, traditional and nontraditional, benefit wildlife more by inadvertence—particularly by lack of active land management—than by design.

Public Recreational Access

In many parts of the country, privately owned lands provide most of the public's opportunity for hunting, fishing, snowmobiling, and cross-country skiing. More than 66 percent of all hunting activity, for example, takes place on private land, with the figure reaching 87 percent in New England.[50]

Traditionally, local landowners have allowed one another to hunt or fish on each other's property. But this is changing, as rural land is being bought by new types of owners who have no ties to local people and who may have a personal dislike for some recreational activities. Posting of rural land against public use has become widespread.

A study of 28 New York townships, for example, found that the percentage of road frontage posted rose from 16 percent in 1963 to 29 percent in 1972.[51] Another, more recent, report notes that "there appear to be alarming trends away from the use of private property to satisfy public recreational uses and increased posting of private lands to deny access and prevent trespass."[52] Some owners have been angered by unauthorized use or vandalism; others fear liability for personal injuries. But the changing character of landownership is also playing a role.

The chief warden of the state wildlife department in Maine observes that:

> There are more and more people coming into the state all the time and a lot of them are buying up property. Often, land that has been open for years is suddenly posted by its new, out-of-state owner. I can understand why some people get a little angry.[53]

A West Virginia district forester, operating in a part of the state in which there has been considerable land purchased by absentee urban owners, relies on volunteers to help him fight fires. He has found that local residents are not eager to fight fires on land they do not own and on which they are not allowed to hunt.

The forces at work here may be more than just residents versus nonresidents. One study of posting found that nonresident owners did not post their land significantly more often than did local owners. However, among both resident and nonresident owners, there was a significantly higher rate of posting by those with metropolitan rather than rural backgrounds.[54] An official of the Wildlife Management Institute has stated:

> There's a different type of person inhabiting rural areas today. We have an increasing proportion of people who grew up in metropolitan areas. They are very protective of their "places in the sun."

Also, it seems probable that landowners with urban backgrounds, often neither familiar nor in agreement with the values others find in hunting and fishing, will not be inclined to allow free use of their property for the pursuit of such pastimes.

The rate of posting may also be affected by parcellation and by increased rural settlement. Small parcels make it very difficult for even the conscientious recreational user to seek permission from the many owners whose lands he may want to cross or use. This is likely to lead to more incidents of trespass, reinforcing a tendency toward posting property. The increase in scattered rural dwellings means that there will be more occasions when a hunter, fisherman, or snowmobile enthusiast risks disturbing someone's privacy.

Social and Political Issues

Objections to the concentration of landownership have formed the basis of social and political disputes since ancient times. The history of Athens and the other Greek city states was marked by recurrent struggles between the landed and the landless. Within the United States, there has always been an inherent tension between the Jeffersonian ideal of a nation of small landowners and the widely held belief that the market should be allowed to function, even if it means that the most successful market participants may accumulate large amounts of wealth in land. For most of our history, this tension seldom caused real conflict, because a high ratio of land to people, and the continuing disposal of land from the public domain, meant that land was fairly easily available to anyone who could make productive use of it.[55]

Today, land-market forces reflecting increased competition for all types of rural land are causing growing interest in social and political aspects of the structure of landownership. Critiques of concentrated ownership are frequently accompanied by advocacy of its opposite: ownership of rural land should be more widely available to those who are currently landless, particularly young farmers, small-scale farmers, and rural members of minority groups. During the past decade, concern over the distribution of landownership in rural areas has been reflected in numerous congressional hearings, legislation at federal and state levels, scores of exposés, and the formation of national and regional advocacy groups. Political scientist Frank Popper calls differences between landowners and the landless "one of the key social divisions in contemporary America."[56]

The fact that crop and livestock production are increasingly controlled by fewer and fewer farm operators has also surfaced as an

important issue even among people with few egalitarian sentiments. A major government study of the "structure of agriculture,"
conducted during 1978-80, revealed that the 50,000 largest farms,
which make up only 2 percent of all farms, accounted for 36 percent
of total farm receipts.[57] Even further concentration was predicted if
current land-market trends continue.

Land for Young Farmers

High land prices and greatly increased average farm size have made
it very difficult for young people, other than those who have inherited land, to enter the farming business. The beginning farmer has
neither the scale economies nor the borrowing power of the established, expanding operator. Moreover, since his operating income
initially will be low, he receives a smaller tax advantage from depreciation and interest deductions than does the high-income farmer or
the nonfarmer investor.

Interestingly, the availability of farmland on a rental basis offers
the principal opportunity by which a landless young farmer can
start out. Farm rentals are either on a crop-share basis or, unlike
purchase prices, are at levels that bear a reasonable relationship to
production prospects. The new farmer can invest his limited capital
in machinery, then, with luck, lease enough land to realize scale
economies. Eventually, he may be able to borrow on equity in the
machinery or accumulate enough savings to purchase some land
outright. Thus, the absentee owner or retired farmer offers the landless young farmer what is probably his only opportunity to enter
the business.

The "Family Farm"

The concept of the small farm that is family owned and operated is
part of American mythology. A nationwide Harris poll taken in late
1979 found that 60 percent of the public preferred a country with "a
relatively large number of small farms," with only 19 percent pre-
ferring "a relatively small number of large farms." And 67 percent of
the respondents said they would "support new federal controls on
farmland ownership if they helped increase the number of small
farms and farm owners in this country."[58]

These sentiments notwithstanding, today even the family farm
no longer fits the traditional image. The increasing size of the
average farm and significantly higher land prices have meant that

231

the successful, full-time family farm has become a large, highly capitalized, and complex business. For example, the National Grange defines a family farm as one needing no more than 900 days of labor annually. Yet, in the more fertile farming regions of the United States, using modern machinery, 900 person-days of labor would easily be enough to cultivate over 1,000 acres of corn or soybeans, requiring a land value alone well in excess of $1 million.

At present, the average family farm is not nearly so large. But continued farm expansion could result not so much in a nation of huge, highly capitalized corporate farms (seen as a major agricultural policy issue a few years ago), but in a nation of very large, highly capitalized family farms. One observer of the farm real-estate market has noted that "the greatest threat to the small-family farm may very well be the larger-family farm—intent on expansion and doing so from a solid financial base."[59]

Past rises in land values and access to national mortgage markets through the Federal Land Bank system have been among the forces enabling the aggressive farmer to expand the size of his operation. Part of the price of expansion through credit has been increased risk in times of falling crop prices or rising interest rates. As an Idaho potato farmer put it:

> The initial response [of farmers] to rapidly appreciating land values was positive, as it provided an unending source of credit, even though production returns were not keeping pace. However, the rapid increase in interest rates has now left many growers in the equity-financing trap, threatening their very survival as they attempt to generate enough capital to survive debt.[60]

Some observers are worried that farmers have incurred so much mortgage debt in their rush to buy land. They point out that a succession of poor crop years, or of bumper crops but poor prices, could put overextended farmers into a severe cash squeeze. Moreover, the variable interest rates charged on Federal Land Bank mortgages could rise to intolerable levels. Other observers see little reason to worry; they point out that farmers' debts may be large, but their assets are much larger. As one midwestern banker put it, "You're always going to have farmers who are in over their heads—and others who are too conservative and should be pushing harder."

On average, American farmers do not appear to have expanded to a financially dangerous extent. Overall, farm real-estate debt (1980) is only 12 percent of farm real-estate value and the leading lender, the Federal Land Bank system, typically requires the borrower to have a net worth equal to 50 percent or more of the loan amount. But the temptation to expand and to seek profit through land-value appreciation as well as commodity production has pushed some farmers, in some areas, into a situation in which they cannot survive a succession of years of low crop prices, or poor crops, or high interest rates.

Farmers who are unwilling or unable to expand have two options. They can leave farming, as some 2 million farm people have since 1970. Or they can become part-time farmers, supplementing their farm income with a part-time or full-time job in the expanding nonfarm sector of the rural economy. So many farmers have taken off-farm jobs that, in all but two years since 1970, the off-farm income of farm residents has exceeded their income from farming.

If current trends continue, University of Minnesota economist Philip Raup predicts that:

> The agricultural structure that will emerge will consist of a small number of large to very large units that can take maximum advantage of credit, tax and price support policies, and a large number of small or part-time farms whose owners will reckon their return on capital in terms of amenity values rather than monetary rewards.[61]

A recent USDA projection of future farm numbers and sizes coincides with Raup's expectation. It notes a "sharp distinction evolving between small and large farms, with little middle ground."[62] The projection indicates that by the year 2000 the country's largest 50,000 farms will account for 63 percent of all farm sales, up from 31 percent in 1974. Also projected is increased specialization by individual farms in a limited number of commodities.

Recent debate over the "structure of agriculture" has been fueled by charges that increased farm size has been heavily influenced by tax policies, price supports for crops, water-project subsidies, and an alleged scale-increasing bias of government-sponsored agricultural research.[63] Small-farm advocates point out some of the costs of expanded scale in agriculture—displaced farmworkers, inferior product (the machine-adapted tomato, for example), and heavy dependence on fossil fuels. These advocates contend that a smaller-scale agriculture, or one with units of very diverse sizes, might be as efficient a food producer as an agricultural system that is continually expanding.

Minority Ownership

Blacks and Hispanics make up 17 percent of the nation's population; they own only 1.6 percent of the nation's land. A number of advocacy groups[64] have focused on this disparity, pointing out that these minorities are thereby prevented from sharing in land's traditional role as a source of economic and political power. Particular attention has been paid to the case of southern blacks, whose control of rural land has fallen significantly during this century.[65] In 1910, black farmers owned over 15 million acres in the South; by 1970, they owned only 6 million. This loss of land has in many cases been a byproduct of individual betterment, as black owners migrated from tiny subsistence farms toward the higher incomes and educational opportunities available in northern and southern cities. Unfortunately, by leaving the land, black owners have missed sharing in the enormous capital gains that have accrued to rural landowners during the last three decades.

Many minority owners who remain on the land face the classic problems of small-scale operations, with low productivity and lack of capital for expansion. In many parts of the South, black owners are also beset with the problem of clouded title, since the occupant actually doing the farming may share legal ownership with a large number of relatives scattered around the country. Without the consent of all these people, the property cannot be bought by the occupant, sold to someone else, or used by the occupant as collateral for housing or agricultural-expansion loans. Moreover, any single owner—sometimes at the behest of a speculator who wants to acquire the property—can request a "partition sale" at which the land is auctioned and the proceeds distributed among all the heirs. Often, the current occupant is unable to compete with outside bidders and thus loses land that he may have cultivated for many years. One estimate puts the amount of such "heirs property" at one third of all land owned by blacks in the rural South.[66]

Migrant workers, many of whom are blacks or Hispanics, find that high land prices make it nearly impossible for them to buy enough land to cultivate profitably. They frequently work in areas (such as California or South Florida) in which the average farm size is extremely large, and in which very capital-intensive operations predominate. Without either the funds for a cash purchase or the equity to obtain a large mortgage, the migrant workers are unable to make the transition to owner-operator.

Absentee Control

It is frequently charged that absentee ownership of an appreciable amount of an area's land leads to an impoverishment of the surrounding community. An absentee owner is assumed to be more likely to bank, buy supplies, and spend for personal consumption in a distant city, not at local businesses. Almost invariably cited is anthropologist Walter Goldschmidt's 1947 study of two rural California towns, carefully matched except that one was surrounded by corporate farms and the other by small, family operations. Although Goldschmidt found the total volume of agricultural production was the same in both areas, he concluded that family farms generally supported a "healthier rural community," with "more institutions for democratic decision making...a measurably higher level of living [and] better community facilities."[67] For example, the family-farm town had twice as many business establishments as did the corporate-farm town. Goldschmidt's findings were replicated in a more recent study of a much larger sample of California farm towns and in a study of communities in rural Alabama.[68]

Absentee owners with large holdings, particularly corporations, have also been charged with dominating the local political system. As one southern Illinois citizen group put it, in pointing to the holdings of corporate coal interests, "We believe that whoever controls the land will ultimately control the people."[69] Even local real-estate brokers have shown concern over possible absentee control. A West Virginia land dealer told us, "I think that big corporations should be controlled in what land they buy.... They're getting richer and more powerful every day.... Think what they can do with all their resources."

Appalachia, with its history of outside ownership of land and of economic and political backwardness, is frequently cited as evidence that there is a direct connection between the two phenomena.[70] Absentee-landowner interests in that region have also been charged with controlling state and local governments so as to favor lax regulation of mining practices, anti-union policies, and unfairly low property-tax assessments for mineral-bearing lands and timberland. One Appalachian land activist notes that a foreign-owned coal trust, which holds 44,000 acres containing coal and timber in Claiborne County, Tennessee, finds most of its land appraised "at about $25 an acre—an amount far less than the cheapest farmland in the county." He concludes that the company

> ...is like a colonialist, extracting wealth from Claiborne County and leaving behind poverty, environmental ruin and low property tax revenues. The valley from which it derives its wealth and the county courthouse are its colony, lacking the power, money, or ability to challenge the colonizer.[71]

A significant increase in absentee control over a community's land could have a major impact on the functions of ownership, management, and labor. At the extreme, there might be a situation where a nonfarm, nonlocal corporation or investment syndicate owns the land; a professional (probably nonlocal) management firm is hired to oversee production; and a landless local labor force actually works the land. One Nebraska research group, noting the increasing scale of farming in that state, and the growing use of professional farm managers, has observed that, if current trends continue, "it is possible to forecast the development of a Corn Belt class structure rigidly defined along owner-manager-worker lines."[72] Similar fears that an increase in farmland ownership by nonresident capital would turn U.S. farmers into a "new generation of share-croppers" were cited during congressional hearings on the 1977 "Ag-Land Trust" proposal.

Ownership of rural land by residents of foreign countries raises all of the issues of absenteeism with an added dash of nationalism. Because many foreign purchases are for investment, rather than for some obvious agricultural or industrial purpose, they tend to seem mysterious, and hence more disturbing. It is perhaps for this reason that the relatively small, albeit perhaps increasing, foreign farmland purchases in the United States have received so much attention in the press and even in Congress. Resentment of OPEC may also play a part, although evidence to date indicates that the foreign owner is less likely to be an Arab sheik than a Canadian timber company or a European investor trying to protect his wealth in a time of economic uncertainty.

Some Americans recoil from the idea of *any* foreign ownership of U.S. farmland or timberland. Others say that it is tolerable only in small quantities, one writer arguing that "foreign investment is like foreigners: a sprinkling does not hurt and will often be beneficial, but large concentrations may be disturbing to national life." Still others believe that it is far better for even potentially hostile foreigners to own fixed (and hence expropriable) assets, such as land, within the United States than it would be for them to continue to hold huge quantities of U.S. currency and government securities, which can be shifted rapidly in ways that might threaten the nation's monetary stability.

A recent nationwide poll of farmers found them to be split over the issue of foreign ownership. Of those responding, 41 percent believed that "no foreign ownership of farmland should be permitted." Another 42 percent argued that foreign ownership should be allowed only if foreign owners are taxed on an equal basis with American farmers and if the foreign-owned farms cannot be used as tax shelters. Only 6 percent endorsed the proposition that "the property owner should be able to sell to whomever he chooses," while 10 percent felt foreign ownership "should be closely controlled by state and federal government."[73]

Concentration and Competition

Concentration of land in the hands of a few owners, whether corporations or individuals, U.S. residents or foreigners, has at least the potential for fostering anticompetitive practices. This potential is increased when the major landowners also control the facilities needed for storing or processing the commodities produced by the land, such as feedlots, pulp mills, sawmills, or grain elevators. Landowners might use their market power to raise the price of their product to consumers, to keep smaller producers from entering the market, to hold down input prices, or to put the local labor force at a bargaining disadvantage.

There is probably very little *monopoly* power in the rural land market.[74] It is difficult to think of cases in which a *single owner*—except for the federal government—controls enough rural acreage in an area to single-handedly control labor or product markets. On the other hand, there are quite a few instances in which a relatively small number of owners control most of the locally available forestland, rangeland, or, less frequently, cropland. These owners would have to collude, formally or tacitly, before they could effectively control market outcomes.

Of all the states, Maine probably has the greatest degree of concentration of private landownership. Seven paper companies own

6.5 million acres of land in Maine, about one third of all the land in the state, and an even higher proportion of the land suitable for growing pulpwood.[75] In 1974, a Ralph Nader study charged that:

> Through selected harvests on their huge landholdings, the [paper] companies can control the supply and demand of pulpwood in the state. While this control keeps the price of pulpwood low for the mills, it also works extreme hardships on the men who harvest and deliver the wood.[76]

The study also charges that, by concentrating the use of their extensive land resources on pulp and paper production, the companies have discouraged the emergence in Maine of independent firms in other branches of the wood-products industry.[77]

Land-reform advocates have also expressed concern about control of rural land and mineral rights by large, energy-related companies. Much attention has been paid to the tendency for large, cash-rich companies to purchase the land and mineral rights of smaller firms and to rearrange holdings so as to have a stake in multiple sources of energy. Thus, a firm that has traditionally been only in the oil business may now own extensive coal-bearing land, oil-shale deposits, uranium-rich land, and perhaps even land with geothermal potential. Some energy firms also have large holdings of land suitable for producing metals and other hardrock minerals, and a few have taken over mineral-production companies. However, there seems to be a sufficient number of firms involved in each branch of the energy business to make some form of collusion among them a prerequisite for exercising market power.

It is not within the scope of this book to evaluate the role of rural landownership as a source of economic power in input, labor, or product markets. There certainly is a concentration of landownership in a few hands in some areas of the country. Often, however, there is even greater concentration of control of production or marketing facilities than of land. Thus, if owners wished to collude, they might draw most their market power from control of mills or marketing facilities, not from land. (Of course, concentration of landownership in the hands of existing producers may discourage potential competitors from building mills in a given area.)

Concentrated landownership can lead to possible anticompetitive practices in another, more indirect way. The economic power derived from land is frequently used as a source of political power. This can be translated into a variety of government-provided benefits for the favored owners. Thus, large-scale rural landowners have been accused of using their political power to obtain government-subsidized water from irrigation projects (this has recently become a major issue in central California, in Arizona, and in the Columbia River basin), crop price supports, "marketing orders" that fix farm-product prices, and favorable farm labor legislation.[78] These benefits give the recipients a competitive edge relative to producers who do not receive them—for example, producers in other states or other river basins.

Newcomers and Social Change

Even before the recent revival of rural population growth and the arrival of newcomers from urban areas, the social fabric of the American countryside was changing. Through the 1950s and 1960s, levels of income, education, and health care were edging toward, though not reaching, national averages. Housing had improved, and the interstate highway system made rural areas much less isolated from the stores and services enjoyed by urbanites. Television beamed the same programs and the same advertisements into rural homes as into cities and suburbs.

But newcomers, whether permanent residents or weekend visitors, have made marks on rural society—some positive, some not so positive. The higher incomes and expensive possessions of newcomers have been the source of some resentment; yet some of their money has gone to local businesses. Local jobs have been created, though many of these jobs, especially in recreation-oriented communities, are low-paying or seasonal.[79] It would be interesting to compare the range of retail stores available in towns where many newcomers have settled with those in rural towns of equal size that have been less affected. Based on our own travels in rural communities, we have come to expect more, and more varied, shops and restaurants in the migrant-affected town, particularly if the town is a vacation center or has many urban retirees. It is ironic that one's chances of finding good "country style" cooking appear to be highest in places with the most urban settlers. One would likely find a wider selection of magazines on newsstands in the migrant-affected town, perhaps a bookstore, almost certainly one or more stores selling handicrafts. Local hardware stores would be more likely to carry such items as riding equipment or imported wood stoves.

Newcomers often start rural businesses or revitalize old ones. It is widely known that some affluent and highly educated newcomers are interested in purchasing country inns and rural newspapers, often pouring money into them far out of proportion to the financial return.[80] Less frequently remarked are the people who see growing rural areas as a good place to start a small business and to make money. Rural industrial and mining growth have not only created jobs directly, but have helped open new opportunities in retail trade and in personal and professional services.

Newcomers are frequently hobby farmers, some raising a limited amount of products for market (honey, maple syrup, wine grapes, sheep, fruit), while others aim at diversification and self-sufficiency. Newcomers frequently express themselves by building houses—sometimes of modern or nonconventional design—or by restoring classic farm structures. They are often eager to experiment with solar power, composting toilets, or organic gardening.

It is difficult to document precisely how settlers from urban areas are changing the character of rural society. One rural sociologist predicts that, as a result of urban-to-rural migration, we should anticipate

> ...problems of social integration...for community boundaries, both social and geographic, will be disturbed by the inmigration of new people. Old political alliances and status hierarchies are inevitably upset...[C]ommunity solidarity may be threatened by conflicts over goals, rate of development, and allocation of community resources.[81]

He notes, however, that some of the influx will be either former residents returning to the rural community or people who will have gained familiarity with the community prior to moving there. To the extent that these people already share rural values, or have established social ties, their impact on rural society will be reduced.

Other newcomers will be dissatisfied urbanites who seek a place in which they can start all over. The cities have historically served as a sort of "escape valve" for those in rural areas who found conditions at home—perhaps personal, perhaps economic—not to their liking. Current trends of urban-to-rural migration may be partially an expression of just the opposite—an "escape" to *rural* environments by those either not willing or able to continue to cope with urban life-styles and economic pressures.

A recent analysis of surveys of rural values and beliefs concluded that rural America "differs from urban, especially from large city ...America in the emphasis given to major values, in value-related beliefs and behavior and in general outlook." It noted that this was contrary to earlier expectations that, due to population mobility and mass communications, rural and urban places would become homogenized into a uniform mass culture.[82] Commenting on this finding, sociologist Thomas Ford speculates that perhaps the new urban-to-rural migrants "are not the bearers of the culture of the cities but rather dissenters from the urban way of life."[83] If this is true, rural-urban value differences could persist indefinitely, with people gravitating selectively toward places congenial to their values and life-styles.

One source of conflict between newcomers and traditional rural residents pertains directly to the land market. New residents can afford to pay more for choice rural parcels, and, because prices seem low by urban standards, they are often willing to do so. Consider the following account by an urban owner of land in rural Virginia:

> We paid something like $30,000 for 37 acres. That was more than the prevailing price of land, but we liked the general setting of the farm so much that we didn't quibble on price. I think that the prevailing price of land in large tracts was about $300, and smaller tracts about $600. So we paid [about] $800 for it.

This kind of transaction may delight the seller, especially the seller who makes more money from disposing of his land than he did in a lifetime of cultivating it. But the price rise can cause real problems for others in the community, such as the young person looking for a homesite, or the farmer who must bid for productive land against urban recreationists or hobby farmers.[84]

Traditional and nontraditional owners also may differ in their attitudes toward land-use change. Coming anew to a seemingly pristine rural setting, the new owners may feel that what they see is the way the land has always been, and hence automatically merits preservation. The long-time owners, on the other hand, may remember that a dense forest was once an open field or (as in our Texas case) that the woods were once dotted with oil derricks. In many parts of the country, long-time residents have almost certainly witnessed the ability of a forest to regenerate itself after a clearcut or a fire. Thus traditional owners are likely to have a greater appreciation than newcomers of the ability of the rural landscape to absorb change and to recover from environmental damage.

Long-time residents also may have known hard times in the past, when people and capital fled to the cities. They may have watched local commerce and public services decline as a direct result of falling population. Thus, the prospect of new highways, new public works, and new population growth is a welcome one. But many new owners, having observed the effects of unplanned, land-consuming growth in suburban settings, seek fervently to avoid seeing the process repeated in their new surroundings.[85]

At one of our case-study sites, a recent arrival, with 25 years of city life behind him, lamented his rural community's lack of concern over managing its new growth: "The economic sense of this area for many years has been poverty; now along comes this growth and for the first time in their lives people have a chance to make some money and they jump." A local resident whose family had lived in the area for several generations looked more to the positive, short-run aspects of growth. As he stated it, "We've sat here while this place was nothing....We're going to grow now." And down the road a local participant in real-estate development noted with a smile, "People want to come here, and we're glad to fix 'em up."

Impacts on Local Governments

Local governments derive revenues from rural lands, but also must provide public facilities and human services. Much of the revenue comes from property taxes. These vary greatly from state to state, averaging $3.34 per acre (for farm real estate, 1978) nationwide, but ranging as high as $25.96 per acre in Rhode Island and as low as $0.26 per acre in New Mexico. Counties containing federal land receive payments in lieu of taxes of at least $0.75 per acre, and sometimes, in mineral- or timber-rich areas, several dollars per acre.[86]

Rising rural land prices would be expected to increase property-tax revenues, although assessments of rural properties often lag far behind actual market values. When assessments do change, the new buyer is likely to be most heavily taxed: his property will probably be assessed on the basis of the purchase price or on the construction cost of a newly built structure. An adjoining property that remains vacant and has not turned over may continue to be assessed at the low value of past years. Local people, county assessors included, often feel that it is only reasonable that a low-income local farmer should pay less property tax than an obviously prosperous outsider. The newcomer or nonresident is likely to make little complaint—but only as long as his total tax bill is low by urban standards. Thus, an urban-based owner we spoke with purchased 70 acres of land a few years ago in rural Virginia and built a recreational cabin, for which he now felt he was being unfairly taxed:

I felt that a cabin which I had built at a cost of $1,000 was not reasonably assessed [now] at $5,000 . . . . Before that I did not think the taxes were onerous because they were about a dollar per acre per year. [Now] I feel strongly about this because there are no county services. And I mean none! The only thing the county has to do with that mountain is assess the property and get the taxes.

Against the tax revenues must be set any new public service costs incurred by local government. Rural counties and townships typically provide far fewer public services than do urban jurisdictions. Some services, such as central water and sewer, are not needed; others, such as highway patrol and certain public health functions, are provided by state agencies. Those services that are offered tend to be relatively inexpensive because of the reduced level of service (for example, volunteer fire departments) and the low wages paid to rural public employees.

Purchase of rural land by outsiders has little or no immediate effect on public costs, and local governments may enjoy a fiscal dividend from the property-tax revenues. This is generally true of second-home and retirement communities as well.[87] But rural population growth can eventually bring new costs, which sometimes mount faster than new revenues. As one authority on fiscal impacts puts it:

. . . in the immediate short-run, per capita public costs tend to drop because of the slow response of government to population growth and economic development. In the long run, as new development becomes mature, costs rise. But people who are long-time residents are used to paying low taxes and don't want expensive new services.[88]

One of the first costs to rise is police protection, insofar as the influx of new people strains the capacity of informal systems of social control. School costs increase if second homes are converted to full-time family residences. Older people who have moved to the area for retirement require medical and other social services that are expensive to provide to a low-density population. Former urbanites begin to press for services that they had become accustomed to in urban areas. One Vermont local official complains, for example, that owners of vacation homes insist fresh snow be cleared from rural roads immediately, day or night. "People don't go to sleep when it snows like they used to," he says.

The capacity of local government is strained by rural growth in other ways as well. Many rural counties have only a few thousand people; the major units of local government in rural New England often contain only a few hundred. Frequently, the only public employees are teachers, clerks, and maintenance workers. There is rarely a professional administrator or planner. Such an arrangement may work very well in providing the same governmental services year after year. It is severely tested, however, when new and more complex government functions must be introduced.

Since the early 1960s, regional councils made up of several adjoining counties have been formed in most rural parts of the United States. They provide valuable (and in many cases the only) staff assistance to local governments, and sometimes have allowed multicounty provision of more sophisticated services. But the councils' functions are mainly advisory, and they have had chronic difficulties in persuading local elected officials to take advice on how to deal with new growth.

The response of local governments to change is also affected by the lack of good models for managing rural growth and for providing modern services to small, dispersed, but growing populations. For example, Doherty notes "the irrelevance of much existing planning literature and legal precedent to small town and rural country conditions," while a presidential policy statement observes that "large-scale urban-oriented technologies are often not economically feasible when applied to small towns and rural areas."[89]

Like most forms of major social and economic change, rising levels of activity in the rural land market and increasing population bring both problems and opportunities. On most counts, the revival of interest in rural land and rural living must be preferred to the long period of economic stagnation and population decline experienced by so many rural places during the period from 1920 to 1960. Growth is almost inevitably accompanied by problems—but it also tends to supply the financial resources and the social dynamism required to mitigate them.

Slowly Developing Problems

Some of the land-market issues we have raised here are currently quite troublesome; others are likely to pose problems only in the very long run. Some have been the intellectual object of researchers and the political object of decision makers and advocacy groups, while others are neither widely recognized nor well articulated. We believe that the more slowly developing problems are potentially the most worrisome, for the long time needed for them to build up is likely to be matched by a long time to deal with them effectively.

If large quantities of potentially productive rural land are devoted to urban, residential, or recreational uses; if parcel sizes become too small for efficient management; or if land and timber are neglected or abused by their owners, it may take decades to cope with the results. We have a policy choice to make. On one hand, we can wait until slow but steady trends result in immediate crises. Or, we can continue to monitor land-market trends, try to understand them, and take some relatively modest precautions to avoid future problems. Some of the precautions we might take are the subject of the following chapter.

REFERENCES

1. Richard F. Babcock and Duane A. Feuer, "Land as a Commodity Affected with a Public Interest," in Richard N.L. Andrews, ed., *Land in America* (Lexington, Massachusetts: D.C. Heath, 1979), pp. 99-125.

2. U.S. Department of Agriculture, *Structure Issues of American Agriculture* (Washington, D.C.: Government Printing Office, 1979); U.S. Department of Agriculture, *A Time to Choose: Summary Report on the Structure of Agriculture* (Washington, D.C.: Government Printing Office, 1981). Although the USDA's "structure of agriculture" study ended with the Carter Administration, the issues continue to be addressed in the farm press and in the literature of agricultural economics.

3. Data are from the 1977 Soil Conservation Service National Resources Inventory.

4. Clark Row, "Economics of Tract Size in Timber Growing," *Journal of Forestry*, vol. 76, no. 9 (September 1978), pp. 576-82.

5. Richard P. Thompson and J. Greg Jones, "Classifying Nonindustrial Private Forestland by Tract Size," *Journal of Forestry*, vol. 79, no. 5 (May 1981), pp. 288-91.

6. Bruce F. Hall and E. Phillip LeVeen, "Farm Size and Economic Efficiency: The Case of California," *American Journal of Agricultural Economics*, vol. 60, no. 4 (November 1978), p. 591.

7. Interview with Raleigh Barlowe, Department of Resource Development, Michigan State University, May 1980.

8. People for Open Space, *Endangered Harvest: The Future of Bay Area Farmland* (San Francisco: People for Open Space, 1980), p. 50.

9. H. Jeffrey Leonard, *The Politics of Land-use Planning in Oregon* (Washington, D.C.: The Conservation Foundation, forthcoming), MS. chapter 4, p. 17.

10. Ibid., p. 21.

11. Data from President's Advisory Panel on Timber and the Environment, *Report* (Washington, D.C.: Government Printing Office, 1973), p. 36.

12. See studies cited in Roger Sedjo and David Ostermeier, *Policy Alternatives for Nonindustrial Private Forests* (Washington, D.C.: Society of American Foresters and Resources for the Future, 1978), Appendix I. See also U.S. Forest Service

and National Association of State Foresters, *Proceedings of the National Nonindustrial Forestry Conference* (November 26-27, 1979), General Technical Report WO-22 (Washington, D.C.: Government Printing Office, 1980).

13. Forest Industries Council, *Forestry Productivity Report* (Washington, D.C.: National Forest Products Association, 1980), p. 40. This is the *incremental* return on investment in forest management, not the *total* return on the capital invested in the land.

14. Society of American Foresters, *Improving Outputs from Nonindustrial Private Forests*, Task Force Study Report (Washington, D.C.: Society of American Foresters, 1979), p. 1.

15. Marion Clawson, "Strategies for Future Forest Production" (Paper presented at Resources for the Future Conference on Forest Land Use, Washington, D.C., March 30, 1981).

16. Ibid., p. 54.

17. Forest Industries Council, *Forestry Productivity Report,* p. 45.

18. Clawson, "Strategies for Future Forest Production," p. 35.

19. See William B. Kurtz and Mark B. Lapping, *The Small Forest Land Owner: Ownership and Characteristics,* Exchange Bibliography No. 1113 (Monticello, Ill.: Council of Planning Librarians, 1976).

20. Clark Shepard Binkley, "Timber Supply from Nonindustrial Private Forests: An Economic Analysis of Landowner Behavior" (Ph.D. dissertation, School of Forestry and Environmental Studies, Yale University, 1979), chapter 4.

21. See Leon Minckler, *Woodland Ecology* (Syracuse: Syracuse University Press, 1975).

22. Brian J. Turner, James C. Finley, and Neal P. Kingsley, "How Reliable Are Woodland Owners' Intentions?" *Journal of Forestry,* vol. 75, no. 8 (August 1977), pp. 498-99.

23. See chapter 4, footnote 34.

24. John F. Timmons and Wade Hauser, *Soil Erosion Control in Western Iowa: Obstacles and Remedies* (Ames: Department of Agricultural Economics, Iowa State University, forthcoming).

25. Linda K. Lee, "Impact of Landownership Characteristics on Soil Conservation," *American Journal of Agricultural Economics,* vol. 62, no. 5 (December 1980).

26. American Forest Institute, *Green America,* Spring 1974.

27. Wendell Berry, *The Unsettling of America: Culture and Agriculture* (New York: Avon Books, 1977), p.45.

28. Statement of Earl Heady, Iowa State University, at Resources for the Future Conference on the Adequacy of Agricultural Land, Washington, D.C., June 19-20, 1980.

29. See Mary Joan Manley Pugh, "Superfarms and the Coastal Environment," *Carolina Planning,* vol. 2, no. 2 (Summer 1976), pp. 34-42.

30. A. V. Krebs, *Roll on, Columbia: Corporate Agribusiness in the Mid-Columbia Basin,* rev. ed. (San Francisco: Agribusiness Accountability Publications, 1979).

31. Folke Dovring and John F. Yanagida, *Monoculture and Productivity: A Study of Private Profit and Social Product on Grain Farms and Livestock Farms in Illinois,* AE-4477 (Champaign-Urbana: Department of Agricultural Economics, University of Illinois, 1979), p. 7.

32. One recent study estimated that 84 percent of corporate-owned acreage was open to the public for recreational use, much of it with no restrictions. This compares with 56 percent of noncorporate land. The study notes, however, that "most of the acreages represented by these percentages are not actively managed for recreation, nor are people encouraged to use them." Harold K. Cordell, Michael H. Legg, and Robert W. McLellan, "The Private Outdoor Recreation Estate," in U.S. Department of the Interior, *The Third Nationwide Outdoor Recreation Plan*, Appendix IV (Washington, D.C.: Government Printing Office, 1979), p. 51. See also, "Public Recreation on Private Lands," entire issue of U.S. Department of the Interior, Bureau of Outdoor Recreation, *Outdoor Recreation Action*, no. 35 (Spring 1975).

33. In 1980, the National Wildlife Federation brought a stockholder action against the Weyerhaeuser Company, charging that wildlife habitat was being degraded by timber cutting and species conversion on the company's 900,000 acres of land in Oklahoma. The company agreed to modify management plans to preserve some of the hardwoods on its land and to allow a "blue-ribbon" committee to study the question. See Dick Cook, "Weyerhaeuser and Wildlife: NWF Finds a Key," National Wildlife Federation *Leader*, May 1980, p. 13.

34. The market's inadequate provision for the future does not occur simply because no speculator can live long enough to reap the eventual reward; for one could imagine a succession of speculators, each selling (at an increasing price reflecting the nearness of the payoff) to the next. Rather, the market fails because of the inability of the first speculator in this line to be confident of the future payoff.

35. The role of markets in allocating nonrenewable resources over time has been the subject of lively debate among economists for many years. Among the issues are (a) whether observable market rates of interest adequately reflect the social opportunity cost of capital; (b) whether traditional decision rules (for example, maximize discounted net present values) adequately account for the needs of future generations, given that the present generation makes all the decisions; (c) whether technological change will greatly change future production and consumption functions. Two of the more enlightening contributions to this literature are John V. Krutilla and Anthony C. Fisher, *The Economics of Natural Environments* (Baltimore: Johns Hopkins University Press for Resources for the Future, 1975), especially pp. 60-75; Raymond F. Mikesell, *The Rate of Discount for Evaluating Public Projects* (Washington, D.C.: American Enterprise Institute, 1977).

36. Alan Randall, "Contemporary Issues in Natural Resources: Discussion," *American Journal of Agricultural Economics*, vol. 60, no. 2 (May 1978), p. 291.

37. Lawrence W. Libby, "Land Use Policy: Implications for Commercial Agriculture," *American Journal of Agricultural Economics*, vol. 56, no. 5 (December 1974), p. 1144.

38. Richard F. Muth, "Urban Residential Land and Housing Markets," in Harvey S. Perloff and Lowdon Wingo, Jr., eds., *Issues in Urban Economics* (Baltimore: Johns Hopkins University Press for Resources for the Future, 1968), p. 315.

39. U.S. Department of Agriculture, Soil Conservation Service, *Potential Cropland Study*, Statistical Bulletin 578 (Washington, Government Printing Office, 1977).

40. Ibid., p. 14.

41. Marion Clawson and Harvey S. Perloff, "Alternatives for Future Urban Land Policy," in Marion Clawson, ed., *Modernizing Urban Land Policy* (Baltimore: Johns Hopkins University Press for Resources for the Future, 1973), p. 236.

42. H. James Brown, Robyn S. Phillips, and Neal A. Roberts, "Land Markets at the Urban Fringe: New Insights for Policymakers," *Journal of the American Planning Association* (forthcoming).

43. Ibid., MS. p. 25.

44. See, for example, Trusten H. Holder, *Disappearing Wetlands in Eastern Arkansas* (Little Rock: Arkansas Planning Commission, 1970).

45. James Mikesell, "Mobile Homes: More, but Where, for Whom, Why," *Rural Development Perspectives*, March 1980, pp. 40-42.

46. U.S. Council on Environmental Quality, *Subdividing Rural America* (Washington, D.C.: Government Printing Office, 1976), p. 56.

47. See the dozens of papers on the subject in *Our National Landscape* (Proceedings of a Conference on Applied Techniques for Analysis and Management of the Visual Resource, April 23-25, 1979, Incline Village, Nevada), General Technical Report PSW-35 (Berkeley, California: U.S. Forest Service, Pacific Southwest Forest and Range Experiment Station, 1979).

48. J.B. Jackson, "The New American Countryside: An Engineered Environment," *Landscape*, vol. 16, no. 1 (Autumn 1966); reprinted in Ervin H. Zube and Margaret J. Zube, eds., *Changing Rural Landscapes* (Amherst: University of Massachusetts Press, 1977), pp. 27-38.

49. Organizations concerned with historic preservation are increasingly finding that their efforts in rural areas should not be limited to identifying and protecting individual buildings, but should also encompass landscape and even cultural features. See Jane Silverman, "Rural America: Love It or Lose It," *Historic Preservation*, vol. 33, no. 2 (March/April 1981), pp. 24-31.

50. U.S. Department of the Interior, Fish and Wildlife Service, *National Survey of Fishing and Hunting, 1970* (Washington, D.C.: Government Printing Office, 1972). The 1975 National Survey of Hunting and Fishing, the latest available, showed a similar figure for total hunting activity, but did not offer a regional breakdown.

51. Bruce T. Wilkins and Eugene C. Erickson, "Private Lands Available for Wildlife in Central New York," *Proceedings of the 38th North American Wildlife Conference*, 1973, pp. 322-26.

52. W.L. Church, *Private Lands and Public Recreation* (Washington, D.C.: National Association of Conservation Districts, 1979).

53. Portland (Maine) *Press-Herald*, August 30, 1977.

54. Tommy L. Brown and Daniel Q. Thompson, "Changes in Posting and Landowners' Attitudes in New York State, 1963-73," *New York Fish and Game Journal*, vol. 23, no. 2 (July 1976), p. 121.

55. One exception was in the South, where a variety of social and economic factors perpetuated a system first of slave-operated plantations, then of sharecropping.

56. Frank J. Popper, "Ownership: The Hidden Factor in Land Use Regulation," in Andrews, ed., *Land in America*, p. 131.

57. U.S. Department of Agriculture, *Structure Issues of American Agriculture;* U.S. Department of Agriculture, *A Time to Choose.*

58. Poll taken in fall 1979 by Louis Harris Associates, Washington, D.C., for the U.S. Soil Conservation Service.

59. Marvin Duncan, "Farm Real Estate: Who Buys and How," *Monthly Review of the Federal Reserve Bank of Kansas City*, June 1977, p. 5.

60. Statement of Allen Wood, Caldwell, Idaho, in U.S. Department of Agriculture, *A Dialogue on the Structure of American Agriculture: Summary of Regional Meetings*, November 27-December 18, 1979 (Washington, D.C.: U.S. Department of Agriculture, 1980), p. 82.

61. Philip M. Raup, "Some Questions of Value and Scale in U.S. Agriculture," *American Journal of Agricultural Economics*, vol. 60, no. 2 (May 1978), p. 307.

62. Thomas McDonald and George Coffman, *Fewer, Larger U.S. Farms by Year 2000—And Some Consequences*, U.S. Department of Agriculture, Economics, Statistics, and Cooperatives Service, Agriculture Information Bulletin No. 439 (Washington, D.C.: Government Printing Office, 1980), p. 5.

63. See footnote 57.

64. Organizations concerned with minority ownership of rural land include the NAACP's Project Rural (New York), the Rural Advancement Fund/National Sharecroppers Fund (Charlotte, North Carolina), the Emergency Land Fund (Atlanta), and the Central Coast Counties Development Corporation (Aptos, California).

65. See Leo McGee and Robert Boone, *The Black Rural Landowner— Endangered Species* (Westport, Connecticut: Greenwood Press, 1979).

66. C. Scott Graber, "A Blight Hits Black Farmers," *The Nation*, vol. 226, no. 9 (March 11, 1978), pp. 269-72.

67. Walter Goldschmidt, *As You Sow: Three Studies in the Social Consequences of Agribusiness* (Montclair, New Jersey: Allanheld, Osman & Company, 1978).

68. Isao Fujimoto, statement before the U.S. Congress, House, Subcommittee on Family Farms, Rural Development and Special Studies, in *Obstacles to Strengthening the Family Farm System*, 95th Cong., 1st sess., October 28, 1977; Ginny Looney and Duna Norton, "The Case for Small Farms," *Southern Changes*, December 1979.

69. Quoted in Brian J. Kelly, "Energy Giants Amassing Land Here," *Chicago Sun Times*, August 24, 1978.

70. Appalachian Land Ownership Task Force, "Land Ownership Patterns and Their Impacts on Appalachian Communities" (Report submitted to the Appalachian Regional Commission, Washington, D.C., February 1981).

71. John Gaventa, "Property Taxation of Coal in Central Appalachia," in Steve Fisher, ed., *A Landless People in a Rural Region: A Reader on Land Ownership and Property Taxation in Appalachia* (New Market, Tennessee: Highlander Center, 1979), p. 78.

72. Center for Rural Affairs, Walthill, Nebraska, in Peter Barnes, ed., *The People's Land* (Emmaus, Pennsylvania: Rodale Press, 1975), p. 49.

73. Jan Broadhurst and Donna Harper, *The Farmer Speaks: National Survey of Opinions on Farm Issues* (Manhattan, Kansas: Agricultural Experiment Station, Kansas State University, 1981).

74. Monopoly power does exist for owners of sites with unique physical characteristics (the top of the highest local mountain) or locational characteristics (the land surrounding the county's only interstate highway exit). Because no piece of land is identical to any other, it might be said that all landownership constitutes a

kind of monopoly. But this sort of monopoly power rests on the special characteristics of relatively small parcels of land, not on concentrated ownership of a broad class of land.

75. William C. Osborn, *The Paper Plantation* (New York: Grossman Publishers, 1974), p. 1.

76. Ibid., p. 3.

77. Ibid., pp. 178, 209.

78. Robert Fellmeth, *The Politics of Land* (New York: Grossman Publishers, 1973); various publications of National Land for People, Fresno, California; Agribusiness Accountability Project, San Francisco, California; Rural America, Washington, D.C.

79. Some studies of job creation associated with rural second-home projects are summarized in U.S. Council on Environmental Quality, *Subdividing Rural America*, pp. 70-75.

80. John Kenneth Galbraith offers an amusing analysis of the economics of country inns in *The Liberal Hour* (Boston: Houghton Mifflin, 1960), pp. 169-77.

81. Harry K. Schwarzweller, "Migration and the Changing Rural Scene," *Rural Sociology*, vol. 44, no. 1 (Spring 1979), pp. 7-23.

82. Olaf F. Larson, "Values and Beliefs of Rural People," in Thomas R. Ford, ed., *Rural U.S.A.: Persistence and Change* (Ames: Iowa State University Press, 1978), pp. 91-114.

83. Thomas R. Ford, "Contemporary Rural America: Persistence and Change," in Ford, ed., *Rural U.S.A.*, pp. 3-18.

84. See Appalachian Land Ownership Task Force, "Land Ownership Patterns and Their Impacts on Appalachian Communities," especially pp. 149-58.

85. Houstoun argues, however, that blue-collar, urban-to-rural migrants, motivated more by job growth and housing costs than amenities, are likely to join with indigenous ruralites in welcoming growth and change. Lawrence O. Houstoun, Jr., "The New Nonmetropolitan Growth: People, Markets and Development Options" (Unpublished paper, September 1980), p. 12.

86. The payments, made under P.L. 94-565 (1976), are determined by a complicated formula involving acreage, population size, and federal revenues generated by the land.

87. See studies cited in U.S. Council on Environmental Quality, *Subdividing Rural America*, pp. 61-70.

88. Interview with Dr. Thomas Muller, The Urban Institute, June 23, 1980.

89. J.C. Doherty, "Public and Private Issues in Nonmetropolitan Government," in Urban Land Institute, *Growth and Change in Rural America* (Washington, D.C.: Urban Land Institute, 1979), p. 78; Carter Administration Small Community and Rural Development Policy (Washington, D.C.: The White House, December 20, 1979), p. 4.

CHAPTER 7

Toward New Policies
for Rural Land

The fact that rural land is important to society does not at all diminish the importance of this land to individuals. The millions of people in the private sector who make choices about buying, selling, or using rural land are unlikely to welcome social controls on their activities, particularly when no land resource crisis seems imminent. This distaste for control will probably be expressed in political resistance. The most successful policies for rural land, therefore, are likely to be those that safeguard public interests while interfering minimally with individuals' desires and aspirations.

In the following pages, we discuss land-use policies that are intended to allow people to continue to repopulate the countryside and to continue to invest in rural property, but with minimum disturbance to rural land's traditional productive and environmental functions. Our policy suggestions do not constitute a complete program for managing rural growth.[1] Rather, they are a sort of menu from which can be chosen those approaches best suited to local conditions. The land-use policies emphasize innovative methods for dealing with the consequences of the three land-market trends discussed throughout this book—parcellation, rising prices, and changing patterns of ownership.

In addition to land-use policies, this chapter considers some ways of reducing inequalities in the distribution of ownership of rural land, as well as ways to protect public interests where concentrated ownership or absentee ownership exists. While there seems to be some consensus in society that protecting rural land's productive and environmental functions is an acceptable social goal, there is no such agreement on goals regarding the distribution of landownership. Therefore, our discussion will focus less on the appropriateness of ends than on the efficiency of means. We analyze the advantages and disadvantages of a number of frequently suggested policies for dealing with social and political consequences of land-ownership, and sometimes offer suggestions of our own that might reach the same goals more efficiently or more effectively.

The Policy Context

Several general observations that can be drawn from chapters 1 through 6 have shaped our thinking about rural land policies. First, rural areas have not only changed, they have changed appreciably in recent years. The image of rural America as an isolated, somewhat idyllic place, inhabited chiefly by hardworking but financially strapped farmers, is increasingly incompatible with reality. Only 1 rural resident in 10 now lives on a commercial farm. More often than not in recent years, over half the income received by farmers has come from off-farm sources. The construction of the interstate highway system not only dramatically improved access to shopping, educational and health facilities, and jobs for people in rural areas, it made the countryside more accessible to urban dwellers. The rural landscape and way of life have been altered remarkably by the changing economics and new technologies of agriculture and forestry.

These new realities have had a profound impact on physical development in rural areas. No longer are these areas occupied almost exclusively by full-time farms and scattered commercial towns. Urban migrants and longtime rural residents alike have been creating a settlement pattern that simply does not fit many of our traditional ideas of what a "rural" area is or should be. The result has been described as "buckshot urbanization," the "countryfied city," and as part of "an urban civilization without cities."[2] Policymakers do not yet have a widely accepted vocabulary to characterize the emerging pattern of people and land uses, much less a clear idea of what that pattern ideally might become.

Researchers are just beginning to provide arguments in support of various policies for rural settlement. There are advocates of the European model, which (with some variation from country to country) strives for the maximum possible separation of agricultural and nonagricultural land uses. In Bavaria, for example, sharp legal distinctions are made between areas designated for development (*Innenbereich*) and those reserved for traditional rural uses (*Aussenbereich*). Only within a development area does a landowner have a legal right to subdivide or build nonfarm residences on his land.

Others have argued that the United States, with its extensive and fertile land base, can accommodate a great deal of low-density, dispersed settlement, so long as careful planning is done to direct that settlement toward lands of poorer quality and to minimize conflicts among uses. Moreover, many people believe that Americans will not consent to policies that prohibit a highly dispersed settlement pattern. As one rural land expert puts it:

> [It] simply is not practical to think in terms of chasing the nonfarmers out of [rural] areas any more than it is worthwhile to try putting legal fences around the suburbs. . . . Rural areas have an intermingled pattern of heterogeneous land uses. The best we can do is work on means for facilitating the pleasant and productive coexistence of the elements in this intermingled pattern.[3]

Another observation worth making is that, even though rural areas have been changing, they remain very different from urban areas. Solutions to land-use problems that have worked in the suburbs cannot simply be transplanted to the countryside. The most obvious difference between rural and urban areas is density. Historically, urban land-use controls have been oriented toward managing the externalities that arise when people live together at high densities. Rural areas have enough space to absorb many of these impacts and thus do not need the same degree of public control over them. But rural areas have some unique problems of their own: how to protect a system of commodity production that requires huge quantities of land; how to provide public services to a dispersed population; how to manage aesthetics in a situation in which the features of land, not buildings, are the dominant visual elements; how to maintain the functions of natural systems that are relied on for services (for example, water and sewage disposal) supplied artificially in cities.

It is time for planners, and planning educators, to begin to put together a unified body of knowledge about rural planning.[4] Planning for rural areas must, of course, borrow from urban planning, but it should also incorporate the insights of agricultural economists, geographers, foresters, regional scientists, and rural sociologists, all of whom have been considering the changing structure of rural land use and rural society.

A third observation is that we must become more aware of the diversity of interests, motives, and goals in rural areas. This diversity is strongly manifested in divergent attitudes toward growth, which vary from place to place and from one group of rural residents to another. For example, newcomers from urban areas may perceive a need to "pull up the ladder" to protect their newly acquired tranquility. But longtime, traditional landowners in the same area may strongly oppose any program that calls for reducing the rate of population growth or limiting the ability to make land-use decisions. Over the years, the longtime owners may have watched the value of their land escalate, causing some problems (for example, higher taxes and difficulties in expanding agricultural operations), but also raising the owners' wealth and dramatically improving their prospects for retirement income. These traditional owners, whatever their feelings for the land and love of the country environment, cannot be expected to ignore the economic benefits of selling land to newcomers. Indeed, many a farmer or rancher views his land as a "bank account," to be tapped whenever circumstances warrant.

Whether attitudes for or against growth dominate often depends on the area's past economic and social circumstances. For example, in San Luis Obispo County, California, the economy was generally prosperous prior to the substantial growth that has occurred recently. People in the county have been receptive to land-use programs attempting to control further growth and change. On the other hand, in Tyler County, Texas, and in Hardy County, West Virginia, two areas marked by a lack of prosperity, economic growth is perceived more positively. Residents of these counties are likely to be quite cool toward land-use planning unless it contains a commitment to economic growth.

Attitudes toward growth and social controls on land use may also be influenced by differing degrees of dependence on agriculture, differing intensities of nonfarm demand for land, and differing rates of population growth. As noted, longtime residents of a prosperous farming county may be more prone to adopt regulations limiting the urbanization of agricultural land than would residents of another county where agriculture has long been declining. In a fast-growing exurban area adjoining suburban jurisdictions that have already experienced fiscal and environmental strains as a result of land-use change, attitudes may differ considerably from those in a more remote area that has no such neighbors and where population pressures are less. Because of these differences, some jurisdictions may be willing to accept regulatory approaches to land use, while other jurisdictions may wish to rely on very selective interventions or even on wholly voluntary programs.

Another important difference among rural places is administrative capacity. A rural county of 50,000 is more likely to be able to support a professional planning staff than is a county of 5,000. This does not mean that the smaller place cannot have effective land policies, only that it must rely more on the efforts of citizen-staffed planning boards or on state-provided technical assistance than on its own employees.

Coping with Parcellation

As we have shown in earlier chapters, there is a tendency today for rural property to be held increasingly in smaller units. Land previously owned in large tracts, mainly by farmers, is being broken up to meet the new demands for smaller parcels. Nonetheless, despite the considerable parcellation that has occurred, 83 percent of the private land in the United States continues to be held in units of 100 acres or more—generally units large enough to continue the efficient production of food or fiber (see chapter 1). Parcellation thus confronts policymakers with two distinct kinds of problems: first, how to manage land that has already been divided; second, how to limit further parcellation.

Managing Divided Properties

There can be no single prescription for managing properties that have already been divided into small parcels. Some parcels, particularly these containing fewer than 10 acres, will probably have to be written off as commercial commodity producers, at least under present economic and technological conditions. For these parcels, public policy should focus on mitigating the environmental and public-service problems that arise when land is used for residential sites. For medium-sized properties (say, 10 to 100 acres, depending on fertility and topography), there are still significant opportunities for commodity production. But these opportunities can be realized only if there are production incentives for the owner, and if new institutional arrangements are created that will allow economies of scale through common management.

Remote Subdivisions. From an environmental and public-service standpoint, some of the most troublesome examples of small-lot parcellation can be found in the thousands of recreational subdivisions laid out during the 1960s and early 1970s but still mainly vacant. In most of these projects, structures are being built at a very slow pace. But, in a region that is very remote and that may have severe limitations on either water supply or waste disposal, even a relatively small amount of development can be excessive. Many of these projects are concentrated in a few booming Sunbelt and western states, and despite the remoteness of the subdivisions it is possible that they will attract more settlers in the future. For example:[5]

> In Arizona, 2,565 remote subdivisions take up 943,460 acres of land, and are platted into 742,829 lots—an average of 1.3 acres each.

> In New Mexico, 81 subdivisions encompass more than 1 million acres, broken into 342,341 lots—an average of 3 acres each.

> In Colorado, there are some 200,000 remote subdivided lots covering about 2 million acres of land—an average of 10 acres each.

> In California, there are reported to be some 3 million acres of land that has been transformed into "subdivisions without homes."

Fortunately, for both the environment and for local governments, actual habitation in many such large-scale subdivisions has tended to cluster in only one portion of the property, generally in a "showcase village," where public services and recreational facilities were provided at the outset by the developer. Often, developers have made it possible (sometimes encouraged by a court order) for those buyers who wanted to build to apply payments made on a remote lot toward the purchase of a site in a developed area.[6]

The current low build-out rate and the tendency toward clustering do not lessen the need for public policies to cope with the present stock of small-lot rural subdivisions. Local governments will eventually bear most of the consequences of such developments and should begin to take this responsibility seriously. Like the 50-year-old "paper subdivisions" in San Luis Obispo County, the lots created in past land booms will not just disappear. Local governments should start thinking about which services to provide to such developments and which to withhold, about how to price services, and about the future location of dwellings. They should plan not for the optimistic population forecasts of the original developer but for realistic estimates of the number of people who will actually want to build.

Reparcelling and Consolidation. Occasionally, building out subdivided rural land may threaten immediate environmental or aesthetic damage. For example, during the early 1970s, the construction of scattered houses in small-lot subdivisions along the California coast began to degrade scenic views from the coastal highway, even though the total number of houses involved was not large. In such cases, the public sector may intervene directly in the development process by reparcelling or consolidating the land involved.

This is one of the roles of California's Coastal Conservancy, a state agency created in 1976.[7] The Conservancy was set up by the California legislature to augment the planning and regulatory work of the California Coastal Commission, an agency with powerful authority over a band of land that generally extends 1,000 yards inland along the state's entire length. In the course of its work, the Coastal Commission faced many situations in which previously subdivided lots in coastal areas were too small and poorly located for construction to be allowed within the commission's environmental guidelines. One of the reasons for the creation of the Conservancy was so that an alternative could be provided both to the harsh, politically unpopular, and possibly unconstitutional option of prohibiting construction in existing coastal subdivisions and to the expensive and needlessly restrictive option of having the state buy the land for permanent parkland.

The Conservancy began its operations in 1977, with a state-allocated budget of $7 million, and by 1980 had under consideration three lot-consolidation projects—one in southern California and two in the northern part of the state. In the Santa Monica Mountains, outside Los Angeles, the Conservancy proposed to acquire and consolidate some 200 small lots for resale as 16 larger parcels, covering a total of about 40 acres. In northern California, one of two smaller projects provided for consolidation of 72 lots into 50 units under a redesigned building plan; the other called for the purchase of 35 subdivision lots on 22 acres and subsequent transfer of their development potential to some other approved area.

In addition to the small-lot reparcelling program, the Conservancy is charged with facilitating the preservation of coastal agricultural land, in part by consolidating small tracts into units large enough for continued food production. According to California state statutes:

> The Conservancy may acquire fee title, development rights, easements, or other interests in land located in the coastal zone in order to prevent loss of agricultural land to other uses and to assemble agricultural lands into parcels of adequate size permitting continued agricultural production. . . . [And it] shall take all feasible action to return to private use or ownership, with appropriate use restrictions, all lands acquired for agricultural preservation.[8]

The Conservancy's agricultural land program has had difficulty getting under way. Through mid-1980, no purchases or leases had been finalized on any of California's coastal agricultural lands, although the Conservancy continued to look for such a project.

In our case-study county of San Luis Obispo, the Conservancy attempted to purchase 46 acres of cropland on which it planned to record a permanent agricultural easement.[9] This land was then to be transferred to an adjoining farmer who, in return for the land, would place an agricultural easement over his own 192-acre parcel. The result would have been a contiguous 238-acre parcel of permanently preserved agricultural land. The project fell through, however, because the farmer who owned the larger parcel would not accept the Conservancy's appraisal of the value of the land, and the Conservancy chose not to exercise its power of eminent domain. Other agricultural projects are now under consideration.

The failure of the San Luis Obispo project points up two of the difficulties faced by reparcelling programs such as the Conservancy's. First, it is very difficult politically to exercise eminent domain to carry out a mandate like the Conservancy's. Although California law allows the agency to condemn property, a Conservancy official told us that the preferred method is to implement programs by stressing to existing owners the significance of a given project— what he called the "willing owner" approach. Second, although parcel recombination and resale is cheaper than permanent state acquisition, it is still very expensive. Based on research and field experience, the Coastal Conservancy estimates that the resale of purchased land would only recoup half of each acquisition dollar after suitable restrictive easements are imposed on the land.[10] Moreover, the Conservancy estimates that *each* of its projects probably will require an acquisition budget of $1.5 million; yet in 1980 a total of only $1 million was allocated for the Conservancy's entire farmland preservation program.

Given these problems, reparcelling is likely to be attractive only for lands of unusual scenic quality or wildlife value (where the alternative is outright acquisition) or where the government has already acquired most of the parcels through tax default.

Common Management of Fragmented Tracts. A second approach to dealing with the legacy of past parcellation would focus not on combining ownerships into larger units, but rather on consolidating the *use* of several contiguous or nearby parcels so that they could reach the scale necessary for production efficiency. This approach would be most applicable to medium-sized tracts of land—say, tracts of 20 to 100 acres—that have been created by the division of larger parcels.

There are a number of possible methods for bringing together individually owned parcels under common management. Although the following examples are predominantly drawn from the field of forestry, their general principles are applicable to cropland and grazing land as well.

One opportunity is provided by professional management services. These services are available from individuals, such as consulting foresters and farm managers, as well as from larger firms that may manage land in several states.[11] For forestland, management firms can provide advice to forest owners, draw up management plans, contract to improve timber stands, and plan the harvest, marking the trees to be cut. With several nearby clients, management firms are sometimes able to put together a joint timber sale, improving the chances of attracting competitive bids from timber purchasers. Professional managers cannot solve the problem of scale diseconomies in physically performing forestry work on small parcels, except in those situations where they can organize several contiguous or nearby parcels in a common timber sale or stand improvement. But they can help to overcome the limitations that small scale imposes on obtaining information and making management decisions. They also make it easier for land held by absentee owners to be put to productive use. Because much of their income comes from arranging timber sales and marking trees to be cut, the interest of professional management firms in small parcels is likely to be directly related to the current price of stumpage.

Management services are also available to small-scale owners from public and nonprofit agencies, which tend to be more sympathetic than are professional consultants to the needs of owners with small tracts or owners who have dominant objectives other than wood production. State foresters and extension foresters give free advice and even financial assistance to landowners, generally concentrating on ownerships of fewer than 500 acres. In fact, there is some concern that the various government subsidy programs may be overemphasizing the very small parcel, offering subsidies for timber investments on tracts that are too small (for example, under 10 acres) to be profitably harvested.[12] The Boston-based New England Forestry Foundation offers landowners in the region all the services of a consulting forester on a nonprofit, fee-for-service basis. Executive Director John Hemenway notes that, although the average area managed by the Foundation is 100 to 200 acres, "we deal with properties right into the suburbs of Boston."

Government and nonprofit programs have made it possible for small-tract owners to obtain management services otherwise difficult or expensive to procure. But these programs typically have promoted coordinated management of contiguous tracts more on an opportunistic basis than as a matter of policy. Whether there is a market for a more coordinated approach is uncertain. A survey of owners of nonindustrial forestland in East Texas recently tested interest in several alternatives for forestry-assistance programs.[13] The most popular options were technical assistance aimed at improving nontimber as well as timber values and a requirement that loggers post performance bonds that would compensate landowners for damage done during harvest. The survey found that hypothetical programs involving coordinated management among a group of landowners were less than half as popular as programs in which attention was directed toward a single parcel and the government shared management costs with the owner. However, owners who were younger, had higher incomes and educational levels, and who came from urban backgrounds showed a greater than average interest in the group-oriented programs.

The small-tract problem in forestry has been approached by the forest-products industry through programs variously called "landowner assistance programs," "Tree Farm families," and "cooperative forest management programs," which are sponsored by lumber and paper companies.[14] For example, International Paper Company offers landowners within hauling range of its mills a free field inspection and written forest-management plan, then recommends a contractor to provide needed services. If a contractor is not available, the company performs the services at cost. In return, the company asks for right of first refusal when the landowner eventually wants to sell his timber. By 1980, International Paper had about one million acres enrolled in its program. Other firms' attempts to assist small landowners have also grown dramatically during the last five years, reflecting the companies' uncertainties about future wood supplies and their difficulty in purchasing land in places where land prices have begun to reflect development value.

Perhaps the most direct approach to consolidating management of fragmented parcels is through timber cooperatives, often organized by the owners themselves. Cooperatives of this sort are not a new idea. Some were formed during the 1930s,[15] but the idea never really caught on, probably because stumpage prices were low and many owners had no interest in producing wood. Lately, higher wood prices, the increasing demand for wood energy, and greater general interest in renewable resources have rekindled discussion of cooperatives. One example of the new interest is Associated Woodland Owners of Western North Carolina (AWO). AWO is a member-owned cooperative formed by a group of small-tract forestland owners in four North Carolina counties. Most private forest holdings in this area are in tracts of fewer than 100 acres. Thus, AWO was formed so that its members would have better access to the management, marketing, and technologies available to owners of larger tracts. Incorporated in 1979 by 11 owners of small forestlands, the cooperative has grown to include 19 members and has some 7,500 acres of forestland under management. About a third of the members are out-of-state owners for whom AWO is providing timber-management services. In its first nine months of operation, the cooperative initiated sales of about one million board feet of lumber. AWO's forester told us that many of the owners "just did not know what they had or how to present their timber to potential buyers." The cooperative is also studying the possibility of developing a firewood program, taking advantage of general interest in wood heat throughout the area. To do this, AWO needs to identify how much low-grade hardwood is available on its members' lands, how to get it out of the woods, and at what cost. The cooperative is also attempting to meet the multiple demands of some of its members. The forester told us:

> Overall, the landowners have a desire to manage their timber for overall yield. But some of them want to preserve wildlife habitat and have a few hiking trails, too. I think they have realized they can have all of this and still do some managing to increase the yield from the land.

Regulating Further Parcellation

Many state and local governments fail to foresee the problems that can result from parcellation and therefore see little reason to limit it. This is particularly true if there has not yet been much build-out in an area or if only medium-sized parcels are created.

Perhaps governments would take a tougher stance if they were aware of experiences such as California's problems with vacant building lots around Lake Tahoe. During the 1960s, tens of thousands of rural homesites were created on the California side of this scenic lake. They produced property taxes for local government, and many remained unoccupied long after they were laid out. Over the years, as more and more homes were built, it was apparent that the pristine water quality of the lake—one of its outstanding tourist attractions—could not sustain such a population level, even with the help of expensive sewage-treatment measures. In 1980, California's Water Resources Control Board prohibited building on 7,100 unoccupied lots. The board anticipated that the state would have to pay $131 million in compensation to the lot owners. The Tahoe experience, like so many cases of premature or excessive rural subdivision, underlines the fact that an immediate benefit to subdividers, real-estate agents, and local tax rolls can be outweighed by environmental and financial impacts, some of which may not become visible until decades later.

Even in communities where there is concern about the consequences of parcellation, it may be difficult to limit the practice. A major obstacle is land value. Because of the considerable demand for small-to-medium-sized parcels, land is worth far more in the market when subdivided than when it remains in a large tract. Thus, there is a community of interest uniting owners and buyers against controls that restrict land divisions.

Perhaps the easiest kind of parcellation to control is the "premature" residential or recreational subdivision, typically consisting of many small lots in a remote location. There are two general approaches to this kind of control. The first is to enact regulations that deny permission to create rural residential subdivisions grossly exceeding the demand for dwelling units. INFORM, a research organization that has studied premature subdivisions in Florida and the West, recommends that state and local authorities require a prospective large-scale subdivider to produce market studies verifying an anticipated build-out rate of 80 percent in 10 years.[16]

An alternative approach to premature subdivision has been suggested by both INFORM and by the authors of the influential report *The Use of Land* (1973). This alternative has become the basis for state subdivision laws passed during the 1970s in several states, including some of those in which remote subdivision projects have had the heaviest impact.[17] The approach requires developers of recreational small-lot subdivisions to provide basic services (such as water, roads, and sewage disposal) to each lot and to comply with environmental protection standards. *The Use of Land* recommended, for example, that "recreational home developments should be required to satisfy the same environmental and land-use policy standards that ought to apply to first-home developments."[18] Such policies, in addition to reducing adverse environmental impacts, would tend to raise the price of lots in recreational subdivisions, thereby discouraging purchasers who are not serious about putting their lots to use. Minimum development standards such as these can be effective, provided they do not go beyond what is truly necessary to create usable building lots and to protect the environment. Those that do go beyond that point waste consumers' money, while seeking ends that could be achieved more directly by linking the rate of new subdivision to the rate of build-out.

It is ironic that, in many states and localities, the most effectively regulated type of rural land division is, in fact, the massive remote subdivision, a type of parcellation not presently much demanded in the marketplace (see chapter 2). Most state and local subdivision laws, where they exist at all, do not effectively regulate land division that creates only a small number of parcels at any one time or that creates parcels each of which exceeds a certain size—for example, 10 acres. Rural people have traditionally thought that these kinds of land divisions were not proper concerns of public policy. Yet the division of a 100-acre tract of timberland into 20-acre recreational or "investment" plots, or the splitting off of a couple of house lots whenever a farmer needs cash, may have as much impact on the future productivity of land as do the more obvious "subdivisions" regulated by local or state laws.

Regulation of minimum lot size is a form of land-use control that is apparently growing in popularity in rural areas. In some rural jurisdictions, minimum parcel sizes are set at 5, 10, 25 acres, or even larger—far more than the 1 or 2 acres that some communities require so that each lot's water well can be separated from the drain field of the lot's septic tank.

Sometimes, setting a large minimum for parcel sizes is specifically intended to preserve agricultural land.[19] This can be an effective measure, provided that the minimum parcel size is large enough that few people will be interested in buying a lot for residential purposes. Thus, in DeKalb County, Illinois, where the minimum lot has been set at 40 acres, the smallest available parcel would cost (at an average 1978 farmland price of $2,747 per acre) $110,000; in nearby McHenry County, the minimum 160-acre parcel would cost nearly $400,000. (These very large lot sizes do not, it should be noted, extend over the entire county, but are imposed in those areas where agriculture is the intended use.) "Lots" of this size are too large to interest most residential users and, in any case, are so expensive that few could afford them.

Such very large lot-size requirements, though growing in popularity, are exceptional. More typically, the minimum lot size is sufficiently small, or the land's per-acre value sufficiently low, that large numbers of residential buyers are still willing to buy the minimum-sized lot. Often, 5- or 10-acre minima are adopted by county governments as a kind of compromise between those who want to stop development on agricultural land and those who are opposed to any controls that reduce a farmer's opportunity to sell for residential use. Consequently, when residential demand for land is strong, such compromises do not prevent "land-busting," but rather direct it toward producing larger lots. Thus, one finds a proliferation of nonfarm homes on 7-acre lots in Plainfield, New Hampshire; on 10-acre lots in Loudoun County, Virginia; and on 20- and 40-acre lots in San Luis Obispo County, California.

In taking a fresh, close look at policies affecting rural land divisions, one major goal should be to assure that parcel size is appropriate to the intended land use. If the land is to be residential, the buyer should not be forced by law to purchase more land than he wants or needs. But if the land is to be considered part of a community's farm or forest base, it should not be permitted to be divided into parcels too small for economic use.

There are practical means available by which governments can achieve this goal. In most states, local governments are enabled—and occasionally required—to enact zoning and subdivision regulations. But many rural public officials, looking at the complexities of zoning and subdivision controls in the suburbs, feel no need for such laws, except perhaps within town boundaries or when large-scale developments are contemplated. This attitude is partly correct, partly mistaken. *Suburban* controls are not needed—but new, simplified *rural* zoning and subdivision controls are.

Consider controls on uses. A typical suburban zoning ordinance may have a dozen or more separate categories, each with a detailed list of permitted uses, parcel sizes, and setback requirements. To protect rural lands against urban and suburban development, a rural community has little need for so many requirements. Local law might instead prohibit any division of agricultural land, regardless of size or number of parcels, that would interfere with the economic use of the land for commodity production. Thus, a farmer would be free to split off a parcel for sale to a neighboring farmer, or even to one down the road, provided that it could be shown that both the parcel split off and the seller's remaining ownership unit were economically viable for commodity production.

The idea of flexible parcel-size requirements linked to land use is not novel. It has precedent in rural zoning requirements of two of the nation's most ambitious land-use regulatory programs, California's coastal zone program and Oregon's statewide land-use program. The California program, set up by a voter initiative in 1972, began very early simply to prohibit rural land divisions that would preclude future productive use of agricultural land. The California legislature confirmed this policy in the 1976 California Coastal Act, which, among other things, provided that future coastal land regulations (to be implemented by local governments) "assure that all divisions of prime agriculture lands . . . shall not diminish the productivity of such prime agricultural lands."[20] Another section of the same law provides for protecting commercial timberland along the coast by barring divisions into "units of noncommercial size" except where necessary to provide for timber processing and related facilities. These goals are not just toothless policy declarations, for they are to be used as the basis for state review of local regulations and for citizen appeals to the state coastal commission and to the courts.

Oregon's land-use program, begun in 1973 and twice upheld by the state's voters, provides for identification by local governments of agricultural land not needed for future housing and for zoning that land for "exclusive farm use." Under the Oregon program, the state does not require local governments to adopt a specific minimum parcel size within the agricultural zone, but requires that "such minimum lot sizes as are utilized for any farm use zones shall be appropriate for the continuation of the existing commercial agricultural enterprise within the area . . . ."[21] Forestland must be "retained for the production of wood fiber and other forest uses," but the method of protection is not specified, nor is any reference made to parcel sizes.

Oregon's "performance zoning" for farmland is particularly useful in a state with products ranging from wheat and cattle, for which hundreds or even thousands of acres may be needed to constitute an economic unit, to high-value crops such as seeds, vegetables, and cherries, which can be grown commercially on small parcels. The state's Land Use Board of Appeals and the state courts have taken an active role in reviewing the consistency of local zoning and subdivision regulations with the continuation of commercial agriculture. An increasingly large body of administrative and judicial case interpretations now exists to guide local governments in rural areas.

In one recent decision, for example, a state appeals court upheld a state administrative decision that prohibited splitting 12 parcels of 40 acres each from an 860-acre tract of grazing land.[22] The tract was in an area where at least 200 to 250 acres were necessary for a viable agricultural unit. In another case, the division of an 82-acre parcel into 6 smaller tracts was allowed, after the county government demonstrated that individually owned hobby farms would lead to greater agricultural use of what had been essentially uncultivated land.[23] In a third case, the division of 479 acres into 92 rural homesites was struck down because, according to the state appeals court:

> ...the relevant finding by the Board [of County Commissioners] ...does not give us enough information to determine whether the purposes of [the Agricultural Goal] could be met by the developer's proposal.[24]

Further refinement, and probably more litigation, is needed before Oregon finds a way to, as one observer put it, "offer a standard for minimum lot sizes that effectively screens legitimate farm-related development from those that seek to call rural residential developments farms."[25] But the flexibility offered under the agricultural goal has led Oregon far beyond the old style of rural zoning, which countenanced any division of productive land into building lots, provided only that the lots were sufficiently large.

The protection of forestland has been described as "one of the most important and least resolved elements of Oregon's land use program."[26] There has been to date less case-by-case interpretation than for farmland, either by the state land-use authorities or by the courts, on how strict local authorities must be in limiting the division of forestland into smaller parcels or the construction of houses in forest areas. One very significant unresolved problem is to what extent owners of already subdivided tracts of forestland will be permitted to build.[27]

Alternatives to Parcellation

Because so many people want to buy rural land, regulatory limits on parcellation could easily result in a vast unmet demand for land and hence to intolerable political pressures to change the regulations. To relieve such pressures, we must invent some realistic alternatives to parcellation.

A first step in that direction should be to note the primary reasons why someone might want to own a piece of rural land. Certainly, some land buyers want a multi-acre tract because they have use for it, either productive or recreational. But many people buy more land than they can use because (1) they want to protect their view or their privacy; (2) they want to hold the land as an investment; (3) they get psychic pleasure from the idea of controlling a large tract; or (4) local regulations prevent creation of smaller lots.

We believe that demand for parcellation could be greatly reduced if new forms of land development and ownership made it possible for people to satisfy objectives of protection, investment, and the enjoyment of property without breaking land into smaller tracts. If new forms of development and ownership could be devised, society would not have to rely entirely on regulations limiting parcellation. Some of these new arrangements could also allow landowners to garner parcelling value without actually dividing the land.

Mixed-use Developments

One alternative is the "mixed-use development," which allows traditional productive uses to coexist with new residential or recreational uses within a single planned development. Under this arrangement, the more intense forms of development are concentrated on lands of lower productivity, leaving large contiguous tracts of the more fertile land available for continued productive use in crop, animal, or wood production. Happily, it appears that the productive use can sometimes become an amenity, actually enhancing the aesthetic and recreational qualities of the developed land. In concept, a rural mixed-use development resembles a suburban "planned unit development," except that productive agricultural or forestry use replaces the golf course or lake as the focus of open space.

The mixed-use development can be contrasted with the present pattern of piecemeal rural growth. The latter also mixes different types of uses, but in an uncoordinated and mutually unsatisfactory way. For example, one may find 10- and 20-acre "farmettes" alongside smaller 2-to-5-acre rural homesites, and both groups intermingled with commercial agricultural operations. There is little coordination among the uses, nor are the uses matched to the characteristics of the land.

The idea of deliberate mixed-use development in rural areas is quite new, and there is not yet enough experience with it to determine either its market appeal or its possible side effects. Nevertheless, several interesting examples—most of them from the private sector—suggest the wide range of possibilities for the creative mixing of rural uses.

One of the pioneers of the mixed-use concept is Farmcolony, in Greene County, Virginia. Farmcolony contains a total of nearly 300 acres, in the center of which are 150 acres of farmland used for growing crops and raising cattle. Included in the project are 48 homesites, each between 1.5 and 3.5 acres, and a 40-acre wooded nature preserve. The homesites are located in wooded or unfarmable areas at the fringe of the development. Purchase of a homesite carries with it automatic membership in a homeowners' association, which owns and operates all common land in the development. The project combines clustered rural development with the possibility for productive use of farmland, resulting in a "rural condominium" concept.[28] According to one of the landowners, the concept "gives the private sector a viable alternative to aid [in keeping] as much of the agricultural land in farming as possible while using the remainder of nonfarm land for residential development."[29]

Yet another project of this type is a residential development proposed for a 300-acre site in Frankford Township, New Jersey, a rolling area of farms and forest. If a standard subdivision layout were used, each of 110 homes would be placed on its own 3-acre lot, making agricultural use impossible and giving the land an intensely developed look. But according to the proposal of developer Karl Kehde, all of the residential units would be constructed in a series of clusters of 4 to 8 homes concentrated on a small portion of the site. The best agricultural land (about 140 acres) would be leased or sold to farmers, subject to a permanent prohibition of development. Other wooded portions of the site would be open to residents for common recreational use. Moreover, treated sewage effluent from the houses could be used to irrigate the project's farmland, saving water, energy, and fertilizer costs.[30]

The idea of mixing uses has also been applied to large tracts of land with aesthetic and recreational values. Near Mountain View, Missouri, in the Ozarks, a group of local landowners practiced what they call "cooperative land stewardship" as they sought to preserve 600 heavily wooded acres bordering on the Ozark National Scenic Riverways from clearcutting by a lumber company. The idea was to sell about 30 percent of the land as homesites, using the money to purchase the remaining acres as common forest area for members of the cooperative. In 1979, the group used a $5,000 donation as "earnest money" to persuade the owner of the land not to sell it to a lumber company during a period when money from sales was being accumulated to pay for the entire tract. By mid-1980, sales of the homesites, supplemented by a small loan from a local bank, proved sufficient to purchase the whole 600 acres. At the same time, an adjoining 40-acre parcel was acquired, and the entire project now totals 640 acres. Of the 23 proposed homesites, 17 have been sold, the majority in 10-acre parcels (at $12,500 each), and over 400 acres remain in commonly held forest and wilderness lands. Each new buyer automatically becomes a member of the Greenwood Forest Association, which governs use and management of the entire project, including setting development standards for the homesites and determining use of the common areas. Most restrictions are ecologically focused—for example, use of composting toilets is required, as is the recycling of waste water, and there is a limitation on clearing trees on the homesites. Each year, members "thin" 10 acres of the common forest area for use as firewood in their homes. Greenwood Forest thus combines cooperative ownership with a mix of residential, recreational, and minimal forestry uses of the land.

There was a somewhat similar endeavor at one of our study sites in West Virginia, where nearly 3,000 acres of heavily wooded land are held by the Chestnut Woods Association. The association is a partnership among 14 families who sought to prevent the land from being subdivided into smaller blocks for recreational use. Wary of growth in the area, 9 partners initially purchased some 2,200 acres in 1972, followed in 1975 by 700 more acres, as 5 more families were added to the association. Each participant purchases a share in the association and is granted a 12-acre tract, with improvements limited to only 4 of those acres and no further subdivision possible. The remaining 2,784 acres are held in common by members of the association, who have put conservation plans into effect and leased a portion of the area to local farmers for grazing. The main purpose of the association is to give people who want to own land a means of acquiring and preserving in its natural state a relatively large parcel. Along with this purchase, the member gains hunting and recreational access to a much larger tract than would be possible on an individual basis. Under the partnership form of ownership, individual interests in the association may be sold, with capital gains accruing to the individual shareholder. At the same time, however, further subdivision is precluded by terms of the partnership.

We are unaware of any mixed-use development that tries to mix recreational or permanent residences with active timber management. In some ways, this would be more financially attractive than mixed-use farm development, because large tracts of forestland are available at per-acre prices much lower than those for farmland. Moreover, the kinds of physical incompatibilities that pose management problems when farms and homes are mixed (for example, loose animals, vandalism) are much less likely to occur in the case of mixed residential and forestry use.

How can local government's planning and regulatory powers be used to further mixed-use development? Such policies could not only preserve resource-based uses on much of the land but could reduce future public-service costs by promoting concentration of rural residential development.

Local governments might identify potential large acreages for which the mixed-use concept could be applied. Private land development or subdivisions could be funneled into such areas, with the requirement that large identifiable portions of the land be permanently used for agriculture, forestry, or other desirable functions. By judicious use of open-space buffers, development could be allowed around the preserved acreage at densities compatible with aesthetics and the ability of the land to absorb septic effluent. Use-value assessments could then be applied to the open-space, agricultural, or silvicultural lands, with the developed portions assessed at full market value.

One version of the mixed-use concept has been part of the land-use control system of San Luis Obispo County since 1974. The county's zoning ordinance provides for a category of "rural planned development" (RPD) analogous to the "planned unit development" (PUD) commonly used in urban areas.

As noted in chapter 5, the RPD concept thus far has been used only twice in San Luis Obispo, once to encourage clustering in a residential project on the edge of the county seat (preserving a mere 30 acres of "open space") and the second time for a tiny 3-unit cluster project. County supervisors have turned down several larger RPD proposals.

One of the disapproved projects in San Luis Obispo was proposed in 1973, before RPD was officially adopted. In 1972, the county board had turned down the application of a southern California developer to subdivide a 10,000-acre cattle ranch into 1,800 recreational campsites. The following year, the developer returned with another proposal. The entire parcel would be divided into 350 "investment units," but residential uses would be clustered on only 750 acres of the site. A guest ranch, with facilities for horse shows and rodeos, would also be developed. But the bulk of the land, though commonly owned, would remain open and would mix grazing, horse trails, and "incidental camping."

Another large mixed-use development was proposed in 1977 for 852 acres of the 3,000-acre "Varian Ranch." Under current zoning, the ranch owner could have divided this land, which was used for grazing cattle, into 42 parcels of 20 acres. He proposed, however, to create an RPD consisting of 42 lots of 1 acre and a single 810-acre parcel. The 1-acre lots were to be laid out carefully in a particularly scenic valley on the property. For approximately $100,000 each, purchasers would acquire both a house lot and joint ownership in the larger parcel, which would be subject to a permanent open-space easement. The ranch owner then intended to lease the larger parcel back from the shareholders, giving him close to his original 3,000 acres. The project, he maintained, "would allow for a combination of single-family development and for the retention of prime grazing land."

The county government's main objection to these two projects was that they would place large numbers of new residences in areas that were outside town limits and wholly agricultural. The fact that current zoning permitted an equal number of units was not persuasive, since that kind of growth happens only incrementally and hence seems less worrisome. County officials were also concerned about providing public services to these new households, which would have been located well beyond the present boundaries of such services.

Other problems, too, must be faced if mixed-use development is to succeed in rural places. First, there is a question whether individual development projects can be large enough to obtain scale economies in the operation of the common productive acreage. Such scale may be possible where 10,000-acre ranches are common, but may not be in locations where 100-to-300-acre farms predominate.

Second, even if large enough in total acreage, the mixed-use project would still have to contain a sufficient number of homesites to make the entire project economically feasible for the developer. This, in turn, could make it difficult for the sites to be absorbed by the local market at a pace fast enough to meet the developer's financial requirements. Farmcolony, for example, was begun in 1974, yet six years later a quarter of the 48 sites remained unsold, and fewer than 15 homes had been built. Such a slow absorption into the market puts substantial financial strains on private developers, many of whom would not be able to carry a project for so long a period. A greater degree of success might be achieved by starting with a smaller project and fewer homesites. This alternative, however, raises questions about production efficiencies on the common lands to be farmed.

Finally, conflicts between residential and productive uses must be prevented. Although clustering residences helps reduce some forms of conflict, the fact that residents also own the productive land will probably result in demands for recreational access and other privileges that may be incompatible with the needs of a farmer leasing the land. One wonders, for example, how the Varian Ranch project could reconcile continued cattle grazing with the desire of 42 new families to ride horses on "their" open space. Conflicts of this type are similar to those faced by any condominium or neighborhood association that manages common facilities. The problems are not insurmountable, but their resolution requires a high level of management skill.

Other Forms of Clustering

In addition to the mixed-use development, there are several other methods to encourage clustering. One of these bears the unwieldy name "fixed area-based allocation" agricultural zoning.[31] It stipulates that owners may build houses in proportion to the amount of land they own—say, one house per 40 acres. This type of zoning differs from ordinary zoning, however, in that each house does not need to stand on a separate 40-acre lot but may be built on a relatively small lot, preferably clustered with other houses along a road or on an unproductive part of the property. A variation uses a sliding scale ("sliding scale area-based allocation") so that the number of units allowed per acre falls as farm size rises. For example, in Shrewsbury Township, Pennsylvania, the owner of a 20-acre parcel would be allowed to build three (presumably clustered) units, while the owner of 100 acres would be allowed six units.[32]

Another method of clustering involves density transfer from one property to another. In its most formal variant, this method of zoning is called "transfer of development rights" (TDR). Under a TDR zoning ordinance, each landowner in a defined region is assigned a certain number of development rights (for example, each receives the right to build one house for every 20 acres he owns).[33] These rights can only be exercised in a defined "development receiving area" where clustered development would be suitable. In theory, owners of land in the receiving area would buy development rights from other landowners and transfer them to their own property, thus leading to clustering of development. The TDR idea has been much discussed, but little implemented, in both suburban and rural areas.[34] Among the obstacles to TDR are its relative complexity, the lack of a ready cash market for the "development rights," and the potential difficulty in identifying suitable receiving areas.

In addition to formal TDR programs, density transfer might be used more informally by encouraging adjoining farm owners to pool the density allowed under fixed-area or sliding-scale zoning and to cluster all the units on that portion of their properties with the least agricultural potential. Local government might give a density bonus for such multiple-owner clusters, or might provide central water and sewer service under favorable terms.

Reviving Towns and Villages

Another means of avoiding parcellation is to redirect rural growth away from open land to existing towns and villages. These already developed areas vary tremendously in the quality of their housing stock, in their range of retail and public services, and in their general attractiveness. Some are reviving along with the countryside; many continue to stagnate. Towns and villages will not provide a satisfactory living environment for persons whose interest in rural areas focuses on living in the open countryside or on cultivating a hobby farm. But they can represent a pleasant alternative for persons looking for a less-hurried way of life, lower housing costs, and a sense of community.

Today, rural towns are being subjected to two kinds of economic stress. Even in high-growth areas—perhaps *especially* in such areas—old central business districts are losing trade to shopping centers. The new competitors may be either regional shopping malls at the edge of medium-sized regional centers (the so-called "middle markets") or they may be simply roadside clusters of new retail buildings at the edge of a smaller community. In both cases, small-town retailers are forced out of business. As a result, town dwellers experience a reduction of opportunities for shopping and socializing close to their residence. This reduces one of the primary attractions of small-town life and makes low-density rural living a relatively more desirable alternative. The long-standing trend in rural counties toward consolidation of schools, post offices, and other public-service outlets has also contributed to a declining quality of life in the small towns where these facilities were once located.

A second source of stress for small towns is the obsolescence of housing stock and lack of suitable sites for new homes. A young couple seeking housing in a rural region often finds it more attractive to buy a vacant rural parcel and build a house or site a mobile home there rather than renovate an older in-town dwelling. Often, the local banker, too, is much more amenable to the former than to the latter.

The time may now be appropriate for builders, local officials, and consumers to try to revive rural towns and villages. Physically, this will involve the refurbishing of residences and commercial buildings; more importantly, it will involve a changed perception of the role of this type of community. Just as the open countryside has acquired a new, more positive image in recent years, the function of the town and village as a desirable living and shopping environment might be revived.

In most areas of Western Europe, farmers have by tradition lived in villages rather than on the parcel of land that they cultivate. In recent years, the proportion of farmers in the rural population has fallen, just as it has in the United States. But land-use controls in Europe have been used to continue to concentrate people in village centers, rather than allowing everyone to spread out at low density. Edge-of-town shopping centers have seldom been permitted. The result has been not only an attractive and productive countryside, but prosperous villages. The United States, which has a historical tradition of each family living on its own farmstead, would do well to study and emulate the European "village model" for housing new, nonfarm rural growth.

More speculatively, it may be possible to create entirely new, small-scale, medium-density rural communities. One planner has suggested "scaled-down, compact versions of the carefully planned 'neighborhoods' of Columbia, Maryland . . . mixed use communities . . . composed of one or two hundred homes at six to twelve units per acre."[35] It has yet to be established if there is much consumer demand for housing in such planned neighborhoods. Nor is it known how these communities will relate to the retail and public-service functions of existing rural settlements.

One possible prototype of this kind of settlement is The New Village, which styles itself as "a new *small* town." Located on a 180-acre site near Uniontown, Pennsylvania, The New Village is intended eventually to consist of a settlement of about 600 people, along with a commercial center and small industries. Initiated in 1978 by the Institute on Man and Science, a nonprofit educational center, the project gives heavy emphasis to reducing housing costs by self-help construction of houses, cooperative provision of infrastructure, and energy-efficient buildings. Other goals are to obtain a diversity of residents and to encourage resident participation in designing and managing the site's development. The New Village is attempting to reduce land conversion by clustering all buildings on 78 acres of the site, leaving the rest for "open space and productive use."

By mid-1981, New Village members had nearly completed rough roads, sewers, and a common building, and were working on the first model home. Interestingly, the county planning commission reacted negatively to the idea of special zoning for a "new town," but gave permission for a mixture of residential, business, and agricultural zones that will result in clustered development and residual open space.

New Forms of Landownership

Still another alternative to parcellation may be found in exploring new approaches to landownership. These may or may not involve mixing types of development. Because people have so many diverse motives for buying rural land, a truly creative rural policy will encourage a variety of ownership forms, ranging from allowing people to use land, without owning it, to providing vehicles for land investment, without personal use.

Use without Individual Ownership. In some cases, rural land use would be more efficient if institutional arrangements existed that allowed land to be used by more than a single individual owner. For example, many people want to use rural land for farming or forestry, but are unable to buy it because its price has been driven up by speculation and inflation hedging to a point far above its current use value. One way for these people to gain access to land is through a community land trust. This is an institution by which land is perpetually owned by a nonprofit group, but rented to individuals for farming or homesites under long-term lease.[36] Typically beginning with a donation of money or land, a community land trust acquires an initial property which it leases to a potential user for as long as 99 years. The user pays a periodic rental to the trust, generally an amount lower than it would have cost either to rent or buy the land. The trust, in turn, uses this income to pay property taxes and to create a revolving fund for the purchase of additional land. The trust is also able to impose lease conditions that prevent the user from building superfluous structures, or farming the land in ways that might damage the soil.

The user is allowed to own any buildings or other improvements that he might place on the land, and usually he can pass the lease on to his heirs. He is not allowed to sell or sublease the land itself, which remains permanently owned by the trust.

Unlike a private organization holding land in common, such as the owners' association at Farmcolony or the Chestnut Woods Association, a true "community" land trust is open to anyone and does not have individual memberships or shares that can be bought and sold. Robert Swann, director of the Institute for Community Economics and closely identified with the land-trust concept, argues strongly that community land trusts should have an open-ended and expanding membership and should not be controlled by those using land owned by the trust. This, he says, avoids creating a group that might eventually feel a private ownership right in the land and perhaps even try to sell it and divide the profits.

Some community land trusts are interested in protecting agricultural land and in providing low-cost rural homes, still others in allowing access to land for blacks, women, or migrant workers. Many trusts own little or no land or never get beyond the organizing stage. But a survey taken in 1979 identified 14 trusts, scattered across the United States, with holdings averaging 260 acres.[37] Among the oldest and best known is the Earth Bridge Land Trust in southern Vermont, where 35 people occupy 12 leaseholds on 5 parcels totalling 400 acres. Another is New Communities, Inc., founded in 1968 to provide land for poor blacks in Lee County, Georgia. It owns more than 5,000 acres of cropland, pasture, and forestland.

The most serious problem faced by a community land trust is getting enough initial capital to buy land. Even if bank loans are available—and they are hard for such a group to obtain—the interest on the mortgage debt will require the leaseholders initially to make payments much higher than would be required to rent similar land. We noted in chapter 2, for example, that average rent-to-value ratios for farmland are less than half the current mortgage interest rate. Of course, over time, the lease payment could be held constant, while land rents would tend to rise. It may also be possible to subsidize agricultural lessees with revenues obtained from leasing small residential lots on less-fertile parts of the property. Another problem for community land trusts, however, is ensuring continuity of management, which is difficult with an open-ended membership whose views of proper land use may change over time.

Distinct from the community land trust is the conservation trust, in which the idea is not to keep the land productive, but simply to preserve it as open space. National groups such as the Nature Conservancy and the Trust for Public Land have been active in projects of this sort, as have local groups stretching from the Berkshires to

Big Sur. Conservation trusts make considerable use of the induce-ment federal tax law gives to donors by allowing the value of the land gift to be deducted from taxable income. However, since open-space land yields no income and there are some management expenses, conservation trusts often prefer eventually to sell or donate their holdings to some public agency that will make the area permanent parkland.

Another method of allowing land to be used by more than an indivdual owner is to encourage such forms of recreational devel-opment as hotels, day resorts, guest farms, time-sharing, and second-home rental arrangements. These alternatives are particu-larly relevant to rural scenic areas where individual second homes—occupied for only a small part of the available time—threaten to overwhelm the landscape.[38] Such a policy has been followed by the California Coastal Commission, which early in its existence began making permit decisions favoring hotels over second homes in scenic coastal areas and which since 1976 has operated under a legal mandate to give "visitor-serving commercial recreational facilities" (defined as those providing accommodations, food, and services) priority over private residential development.[39] The commission has also encouraged the development of a string of hostels to pro-vide low-cost vacation housing along the coast.

Visitor-serving facilities in rural areas may include resorts, lodges, inns, and motels, all of which are not only more intensively used than second homes but create more jobs for local people. In some parts of the country, particularly New England, there has been a long tradition of renting second homes themselves for the months in which they are in peak demand; elsewhere, resort developers increasingly offer to manage and rent out units not being used by their owner. The resort "time-sharing" concept, which involves outright sale of the right to occupy the facility for a specified period each year, is a logical extension of this. While time-sharing presents formidable consumer-protection and management problems, it appears from an environmental standpoint preferable to the sale of individual housing units.

In some instances, visitor-serving uses can actually be integrated into commercial agricultural operations. Traditionally, many west-ern guest ranches have been working cattle ranches. Some eastern states, among them West Virginia and Pennsylvania, maintain lists of farms that will receive paying guests. One large-scale example of an integrated operation is to be found in Syria, Virginia, a two-hour drive from Washington, D.C., where the Graves family has for five generations owned 2,000 acres of corn, grazing, and orchard land. The farm, which adjoins scenic Shenandoah National Park, is in an area where demand for second homes is competing strongly for agricultural land. The Graves family takes advantage of the demand, offering visitors accommodations in an attractive collection of cabins, farm houses, and more modern units scattered in several locations on their property. The extensive farm operations, particularly apple picking in the fall, are themselves a major feature of interest for the tourists. The wide-open agricultural landscape of the Graves property contrasts sharply with other areas in that part of Virginia where individual subdivision development has taken land out of production and clutters the visual scene.

Providing people who live in urban areas with abundant and varied opportunities for rural recreation will not eliminate the desire to own second homes, but it is likely to reduce it. It will also make it easier to justify the equity of regulations that make second-home construction more difficult. And, properly handled, it can be a way of bringing urban money into rural communities, without interfering with resource-based uses.

Divided Ownership without Divided Land. At the opposite pole from the "use without ownership" of the community land trust and the guest farm is the possibility of allowing people to purchase investment interests in rural land without dividing the land. This idea is a controversial one, for it does facilitate absentee ownership, a condition with potential land-use and social impacts that we discussed in chapter 6. Many farmers and social activists objected to the Ag-Land Trust proposed by Continental Illinois Bank and Merrill Lynch (see chapter 2); some people would likely object to investment syndicates holding timberland. Yet consider the example of an environmentally oriented rural investment group, Timber Owners of New England (TONE).

TONE began in 1953, when a dozen investors jointly purchased 600 acres of southern New Hampshire forestland.[40] Over the years, more investors were added, and more land purchased, so that today the group has more than 100 shareholders holding 3,300 acres of land. Between 1953 and 1975, the venture sold some 2 million board feet of lumber, while substantially increasing the quality of the standing timber stock. Although some of TONE's profits have been paid out to shareholders, most are reinvested. As a result, the book value of its membership shares has gone from $10 per share in 1953 to about $30 per share currently.

In addition to its investment goals, TONE provides for recreational use of its property. A group of 44 persons, most of them TONE members, makes up "Wildlife Conservation Trust," which pays TONE a yearly fee for hunting and fishing rights and recreational use of various buildings on the land. The effect, as one observer has put it, is like a "combination tree farm and conservation trust."[41]

At present, a person who wants to invest in rural land has two choices. He can purchase land outright, often in a smaller than optimal parcel. Alternatively, he can purchase stock in a publicly held company known to be a large landholder—railroads, lumber companies, and a few agribusiness firms are typically used for this purpose. More creative use of landownership forms would give investors greater opportunity for rural land investment, while keeping the land undivided and productive.

Improving Land Management

Even when land-use opportunities are not limited by small parcel size or interspersed residential settlement, rural land may not be managed to its full potential. Often, opportunities for uses that are profitable or socially beneficial are impeded by owners' lack of knowledge, lack of motivation, or short-term thinking.

In some cases, improved land management means more intensive use—intensive in the sense that more labor and capital are applied to a given parcel of land. It would be foolish to suggest that every holding of rural land should be intensively used to produce food or wood. There is not, at present, a sufficient market for the additional products to justify the massive financial investment that would be required. Moreover, the adverse impacts on the environment, on wildlife, and perhaps on landscape aesthetics, would be enormous. Yet there are many instances in which it would be useful to return currently unused rural parcels to producing commodities or to increase the intensity of use.

More intensive use of certain currently unused lands would take some of the pressure off portions of the land base where demands are overconcentrated. For example, the fact that timber stocks on nonindustrial private forestlands are so poor has encouraged the timber industry to plan greatly intensified management of its own land and to press for expanded cuts of old-growth timber on the national forests. Likewise, lack of hunting and fishing access to private land has crowded recreationists onto public lands. More intensive management of some land would also generate incomes and job opportunities within rural communities, particularly in traditional resource-based sectors that are associated with cherished life-styles.

Improved land management may also mean *less*-intensive management. Some rural land is so carelessly cultivated that erosion will eventually lower its productivity. Other land is used in ways that are permanently damaging wildlife habitat or other natural systems. In many cases, this socially irresponsible management is deliberate, the result of economic incentives that produce a divergence between what is profitable for the owner and what is beneficial for society. But, in other cases, damage is being done inadvertently, contrary to the owner's intentions or without his knowledge.

Accommodating Landowner Objectives

Often, in our talks with urban owners of rural land, people indicated that enjoyment and price appreciation, not production, were the primary reasons for having bought a rural parcel. These owner values are likely to affect even properties on which uses are not restricted by parcellation. How can owners with these motives be encouraged to practice better land management? Much higher prices for wood or for agricultural rentals would no doubt have a major impact on owners' motivations, but unpleasantly high price levels for commodities are not the only way to bring this land back into production. As an alternative, a combination of education, penalties, and incentives might make a significant contribution even now to keeping land productive.

Rural land can be used for commodity production while meeting—or even enhancing—owners' desires for enjoyment and price appreciation. Speaking of the "suburban forests" of New York State, one writer has noted:

> It is clear that the owners of the suburban forest will want something besides commercial timber management recommendations. They will want some combination of recommendations for creating woodland that is pleasant, interesting, and enjoyable with recommendations that can lead to saleable timber.[42]

As mentioned earlier, in recent years foresters have begun to develop and test methods of "ecological forestry" which emphasize long rotations and harvesting individual trees or groups of trees, rather than clear-cutting.[43] Such methods do not maximize wood production, but they allow the production of premium-grade products without interfering with the owner's recreational or aesthetic enjoyment of his land. Adoption of these methods will be psychologically wrenching for many foresters, for their traditional forestry education has ill-prepared them to deal with owners with dominant nontimber objectives. This unfortunately applies even to some government foresters who are supposed to aid small landowners. As a recent report on the future of New England forests puts it:

> Thousands of management plans proposed [by extension foresters] for small woodland owners will never be implemented because of their often narrow and singleminded [wood oriented] approach to forest management.[44]

But resistance is likely to come, in particular, from private consulting foresters and from logging contractors, many of whom simply do not personally identify with nontimber values. The process of educating landowners about wood production is likely to require a parallel effort to broaden the view of forestry professionals.

Better Management of Leased Land

Another land-management priority is to ensure that cropland leases take adequate account of erosion control and soil-fertility improvement. Leases for residential and commercial buildings invariably provide that the tenant refrain from abusing the property; often, tenants are required to assume responsibility for performing (although not necessarily paying for) specific maintenance functions. Similar provisions are rarely found in lease agreements for rural land. A significant educational effort will have to be made to persuade nonoperator owners—who now own 40 percent of U.S. farmland—that clauses requiring effective soil conservation and the maintenance of fertility are important to protect their interests.

Some examples of leases with such provisions are available and may serve as models. The form used by Massachusetts in leasing state lands for farm purposes[45] requires that the state's land be returned at the end of the lease period "in at least as good condition as it was at the begining of such period." The lease also requires that a farm plan be submitted, that the farmer prevent "soil erosion, siltation of waterways, pollution, or nuisance," that a record be kept of all fertilizer and pesticide applications, and that, if agricultural use terminates, the land be seeded to permanent cover. Alaska's lease form requires that the prospective tenant submit a farm conservation plan and map, including soil-conservation practices to be used, for review by the Soil Conservation Subdistrict and the Director of the State Division of Agriculture.

State and county extension agents might also pay more attention to getting absentee owners of farmland interested in soil steward-ship. This is not easy. Besides being spatially dispersed, absentee owners are likely to be less susceptible to the combination of peer pressure and pride of good management that have been so impor-tant in persuading resident farmers to use soil-conserving practices, with no immediate financial payoff. As an official of a midwestern farmers' organization puts it, "Voluntary conservation programs are very dependent on an owner-operator situation." Indeed, the existence of high absentee ownership may create a new need for a regulatory rather than voluntary approach to soil conservation.

Lack of incentive aside, absentee owners may simply not know that their land has an erosion problem. One approach to dealing with this recently has been pursued by the Soil Conservation Dis-trict in Baltimore County, Maryland. If the operator of leased land is losing large amounts of topsoil, the district may send him a letter reminding him of that fact. If the tenant refuses to take action, the district notifies the landlord directly.

Improved Management and the "Impermanence Syndrome"

A significant obstacle to good land management on the urban fringe is the possibility, however remote, that land will be converted to residential, commercial, or industrial uses, which are generally more profitable than commodity production. As population growth has decentralized, this possibility has begun to affect even land well beyond the fringe. To the extent that rural land actually will be converted, it may be socially efficient for it to be managed at a low level of capital investment during the interim period. But, as we noted in chapter 6, many people believe that the amount of land currently subject to this "impermanence syndrome" is well in excess of the actual demand for land.

Public policymakers cannot foresee the future; nor can they always influence future events. But they can take steps to reduce at least somewhat the uncertainty about future patterns of develop-ment. By designating the most fertile land in the jurisdiction for agricultural use, and then preventing its division into parcels of uneconomic size, local governments can send an important message to landowners. That message can be reinforced in decisions about the extension of roads and sewers. If firm policies on development control are implemented over a sufficient period of time, land-owners will begin to change their expectations about the future, and, therefore, their behavior.

Ideally, under these circumstances, land designated as agricultural would increasingly come into the hands of serious farmers. The same would be true of land designated for forest management. The remaining land would become the focus of attention for speculators and developers, and their activities would help move it more rapidly into its intended use.

Tax Policy and the Rural Land Market

At several places in earlier chapters, we noted the impact that tax policy has on the use and ownership of rural land. Some tax policies are deliberately designed to affect rural land—for example, preferential assessment of farmland and capital-gains treatment of proceeds from timber sales. But many of the most significant impacts of taxes on the land market are secondary impacts, incidental to the principal purposes of the tax.

We need to be more aware of these unintended impacts of tax policy on the rural land market, and we need to avoid them where avoidance does not conflict with other important public goals. To do this, it will be helpful to have an ideal conception of how tax policy should affect the rural land market.

Ideal Tax Policies for the Rural Land Market

In addition to meeting the normative standards that all taxes should meet,[46] ideal tax policies affecting rural land should have the objectives of encouraging productive use, penalizing nonuse, and subsidizing particular types of use or types of ownership only when significant public benefits result. The present tax system falls far short of these goals.

Probably the most important tax provision presently affecting the rural land market is the fact that profits on the sale of land held for more than one year qualify for federal and often state taxation at capital-gains rates. For taxpayers in higher brackets, this is a large saving indeed, and its impact is magnified by the fact that interest on loans used to buy the land can be deducted from taxable income during the holding period.

Much attention has been paid recently to modifying federal tax laws so as to encourage productive investment; one frequently suggested approach is reduction of capital-gains taxes. Such reductions would produce significant tax savings to persons realizing profits from the sale of rural land. From the standpoint of encouraging productive use of rural land, however, proposals for lower capital-gains taxes overlook a critical fact: capital gains achieved by rural landowners are almost invariably due to general price inflation or to circumstances beyond the control of the landowner (for example, completion of a highway improvement or an increase in the demand for scenic properties). Price appreciation is seldom the result of any action that the landowner himself has taken to improve the productivity of his property. The industrious landowner who plants trees on barren land or who by wise husbandry improves the quality of his pasture receives capital-gains treatment of his profits when he sells the land. But so does the owner who holds his land idle, waiting for inflation to raise its market value. The tax code, in short, rewards unproductive and productive activity equally.*

We believe that, as applied to undeveloped land, a further reduction in capital-gains tax rates would be unnecessary and unwise. In fact, if the purpose of the reduction is to encourage the creation of new productive assets, such a policy could actually be counterproductive, for it could siphon away funds that would otherwise be invested elsewhere in the economy.[47]

Instead of rewarding landholding, ideal tax policies would reward long-term investments that maintain or improve the productive potential of land—soil-conservation practices, for instance, or reforestation and timber-stand improvement. In 1980, President Carter signed a law providing for a 10-percent investment tax credit and amortization over a seven-year period of up to $10,000 yearly of reforestation expenditures. This measure remedied a long-standing inequity that had allowed an investment tax credit and accelerated depreciation to people making long-term investments in machinery, but not to those investing in trees.

Quite the opposite of favorable tax treatment of capital gains from raw land sales has been the idea of state taxes on "speculative" land profits. There have been legislative proposals of this sort in

---

*The federal tax law passed in August 1981, while this book was in production, in general moves the tax code even further from the ideal policies discussed here. In particular, the law reduces the maximum capital-gains tax rate from 28 to 20 percent; on the other hand, the reduction in tax rates applied to ordinary income does give some additional incentive to those using rural land to produce income.

Hawaii, Maine, Massachusetts, Montana, New Jersey, and Washington; in 1973, a land-gains tax law passed the Vermont legislature.[48] Under Vermont's program, the rate at which land gains are taxed increases with the percentage gain, and is higher for shorter holding periods than for longer ones. The highest rate, 60 percent, applies to land sold after a holding period of less than one year, with a price increase of more than 200 percent. Land held more than six years is not subject to the tax.

The Vermont tax had the dual—and mutually contradictory—purposes of raising revenue and dampening land speculation. To date, the tax has not been very successful as a revenue raiser. During its first four years, revenues went steadily downward, from $1.3 million in 1973-74 to $660,000 in 1976-77. Subsequently, revenues rose somewhat, reaching $913,000 in 1979-80.[49] Very few transactions have been subject to the tax's highest rates; on average, tax payments have amounted to less than 6 percent of the value of unimproved land.[50]

Baker and Anderson, who studied the impact of the tax on the land market, found it difficult to draw strong conclusions, in part because the Vermont land market has since 1973 been so deeply affected by economic forces other than the land-gains tax. They feel that the tax "may have caused some degree of subdivision reduction," but believe that "the most emphatic impact is its apparent influence on investors, particularly from out of state, to withdraw from the Vermont land market."[51] Their survey of Vermont landowners revealed "what appears to be a significant increase in the proportion of property being bought by landowners for their own use rather than for investment."[52]

Although the Vermont tax may have been justified by the circumstances—it was imposed in the midst of a period of rapid land turnover and widespread speculation—we believe that land-gains taxes that vary with the length of ownership are not a wise policy for most rural jurisdictions. In the land markets that we studied, the principal land-use problems—parcellation, poor land management, residential scatteration—had little to do with the length of time land was held. Most nontraditional owners in our case-study counties were purchasing land with the intent of holding it indefinitely; many of those subdividing land had held it for several years or were acting as agents for longtime holders. A Vermont-style tax penalizing rapid turnover would have had very little impact on their actions.

We see no justice or rationality in putting a heavy tax burden on the gains of short-term holders, while those who hold land for a longer period—perhaps without putting it to any use—go untaxed. Less favorable capital-gains treatment of sales of undeveloped land, as we have suggested, would tax away part of the gain from both groups, without artificially favoring those land investors who were willing to hold onto their land for some prescribed period of time.

Another very large tax subsidy currently affecting rural land is preferential treatment of farmland (and sometimes forestland) for local property-tax purposes. State legislation permitting such favorable treatment is now on the books in all but two states.[53] Generally, these programs provide for reduced or deferred property taxes if land is kept in some productive or open-space use as defined by the particular program. If the land meets the program's minimum requirements, the owner receives the full tax benefit. If the land is taken out of that use, or the owner fails to meet all the requirements of the program, the benefits of lower taxes are lost. It is an all-or-nothing proposition.

An ideal approach, we believe, would provide landowners a range of incentives to manage their land productively and to provide benefits for the public. This approach would take as its first step a careful, fair-market-value assessment of all rural properties. Unlike assessment practice in many rural areas, which sometimes assigns the same (generally low) value to all farmland and another to all forestland, these assessments would take into account the effects on value of parcel size, urbanization potential, fertility, and any applicable land-use restrictions. Ideal tax regulations would allow owners of working farms and forestlands to defer any property-tax payment that amounted to more than, say, 5 percent of their annual net income. This deferred tax liability would become a permanent lien on the land, payable with interest when the land was sold. The policy would allow traditional farmers to continue working their land, even if its rising price made potential property taxes very high. And it would make owners of idle property (who would not qualify for the tax deferral) pay a greater share of rural taxes. Linking farm property taxes to income, called a "circuit-breaker" policy, is already a feature of farmland tax laws in Michigan and Wisconsin and has been proposed in other states. But we must emphasize that our ideal policy would defer the tax liability, not forgive it.

If assessors were instructed to take into account the impact on market value of land-use restrictions, owners of land with restricted urbanization potential would face much lower assessments than those with land that was zoned for future residential use. This is unlikely to make the former welcome use restrictions, but it would at least reassure them that they would pay lower taxes than those with unrestricted urbanization opportunities. Conversely, the prospect of high tax assessments would give owners of land realistically zoned for development an incentive to put it on the market immediately. This would increase the land supply at the urban fringe and, at least theoretically, would help prevent leapfrog development.

After rural land has been assessed at fair market value, carefully targeted tax incentives could be given to reward owners who were managing their land in a socially beneficial way. For example, a percentage tax reduction could be given to those owners of productive forestland who actively managed their land for wood products.[54] Similarly, a tax reduction could go to those farmers who operated their land under a soil-conservation plan approved by their local Soil Conservation District. Or a reduction could go to owners who complied with landscape-protection rules devised for scenic or historic districts.

Tax incentives could also be given owners who open their land for public access. As noted earlier, as new owners come to rural areas, there has been a tendency for lands once open to hunting and other recreation to be posted against public use. We would like to see owners who open their land rewarded with a tax break. New Hampshire's use-value assessment program addresses this issue. In addition to use-value assessment, lands open to public recreation without entrance fee are accorded an additional 20 percent reduction in tax assessment. Moreover, New Hampshire's fish and wildlife department offers rural owners who open their land special signs with which they can post the area around any buildings, provided lands away from the buildings are made available for hunting.[55] (Yet another positive incentive for providing access should be revisions of trespass and liability laws,[56] including perhaps a state fund to compensate landowners for damages caused by public use.)

Another tax affecting rural land is the estate tax. In recent years, there has been considerable pressure from farmers for either reduction or deferral of these taxes. We agree that the burden of estate taxes is indeed a problem for some families seeking to keep family farms in business over more than one generation. But it is also true that sales of land by estates are one of the primary sources of the supply of farmland to the market. Further liberalization of estate-tax laws, particularly increases in the amount exempt from tax, would help some farm families but is likely to restrict even further the opportunities for young, landless farmers to buy land.*

We are quite aware that real-world policymakers would have to tailor the ideal tax policies just described to fit political realities and to take into account social objectives other than that of improving land use. One obvious issue would be who would make up the difference if local property-tax deferrals due to the "circuit breaker" reach high levels. Because the benefits of better land management and public access extend well beyond the individual community, we think that the state government should provide funding to local jurisdictions adversely affected by these policies. State funding of local revenue losses is already a feature of the farm-assessment law in California, while Wisconsin and Michigan provide for state financing through state income-tax credits for the participating landowner. Also, tax changes should be phased in slowly so that owners do not face precipitous tax increases or reductions in any single year.

It is likely that an incremental approach would also be needed in moving legislatively toward a tax system that has fewer negative impacts on the land market. One place to start might be to improve the general quality of tax assessment in rural areas, and to raise taxes on vacant urban-fringe properties already zoned for development. Whatever the legislative strategy chosen, the direction of tax reform should be toward providing public subsidy only when there are identifiable public benefits.

Inflation and the Land Market

Taxes are not the only aspect of the overall U.S. economy that can have perverse secondary impacts on the land market. Inflation—and the efforts of investors to avoid inflation—also has an extremely important influence on the price of land and on patterns of land-ownership. Inflation has distorted market signals, has increased the use of land investment for capital preservation and tax avoidance, and has changed the distribution of wealth. Government policies aimed at controlling inflation, therefore, are likely to have beneficial effects on a number of land-market problems. The benefits for

---

*The 1981 federal tax law provides for major reductions in estate-tax rates, increases in the minimum value subject to tax, and more liberal estate-tax treatment of family farms and forestland.

the rural land market of controlling inflation are best illustrated by describing the problems that high rates of inflation have recently caused.

First, inflation has distorted market signals, directing the attention of landowners away from the price signals given by the normal competition among uses. Inflation has been only one element of the overall increase in the price of land, but it has been an important one. We noted earlier, that when farmers and forest owners gain more from yearly appreciation in the price of their land than from commodity production, undesirable changes may occur in their attitudes toward land and in their investment behavior. Past inflation also makes owners form expectations, sometimes unrealistic, about the future price of their land. This makes them reluctant to sell land (see chapter 3), even though another owner might put it to more productive use. As a result, the quantity of land supplied for sale becomes less responsive to demand increases than it otherwise would be.

Second, inflation increases the attractiveness of land investment for people whose primary objective is not using the land for production or personal enjoyment, but as a means of hedging against inflation. Among other things, inflation has pushed taxpayers into higher marginal tax brackets, making it extremely attractive to buy land with borrowed money, deduct the interest and any operating losses, then enjoy capital-gains treatment of the proceeds from the land's eventual sale. By creating an incentive for investment, inflation may have increased the purchase of land by "nontraditional" owners and hastened the increase in farm size.

Finally, inflation changes the distribution of wealth. As prices increase, people who hold cash or fixed-dollar investment, or those who own no assets at all, suffer declines in real wealth relative to people owning tangible assets, such as land. Inflation has made it increasingly difficult for low-income people, including young people, to purchase land for farming or other types of use.

There are many good reasons for reducing the current rate of overall price inflation. Impacts on the rural land market offer yet another reason.

Policies Affecting the Distribution of Landownership

The question of how land should be distributed among various owners is often emotional and always value-laden. A recent increase in public concern about rural landownership has been reflected in

scores of policy initiatives—many proposed, and a few implemented—at the state and national levels. Most of these initiatives
may be classified as taking one of two general approaches: (1) policies designed to increase access to land by small-scale, low-income,
or beginning farmers; or (2), alternatively, policies designed to restrict or discourage large-scale, corporate, foreign, or absentee ownership of land. Most of the interest to date has centered on farmland
rather than forests.[57]

In 1979-80, bills aimed at increasing young or low-income
farmers' access to land were introduced in 14 state legislatures and
in Congress.[58] Prohibition or restriction of foreign ownership of
farmland was considered in 21 states; 5 considered bills relating to
corporate ownership.[59] Bills were introduced in Congress taking a
variety of approaches to both these subjects. Meanwhile, the
Department of Agriculture held nationwide hearings on the "structure" of agriculture, a term that encompassed concerns with both
the size of the farm operating unit and the character of ownership
patterns.

Regardless of how the land is used, it seems to matter very much
to people whether land is controlled by absentee owners, or by a
small number of local land barons, or by a relatively numerous class
of small owner-operators.

But there are considerable differences in attitudes within society
about the conflicting values connected with landownership. Some
people give highest place to the Jeffersonian ideal that "the small
landholders are the most precious part of the state," a notion that
has carried over into a glorification of the family farm. Others are
more likely to applaud and try to protect the entrepreneurial drive
that impels the successful farmer to continual expansion of the scale
of his operations. Landownership by large "agri-business" corporations is anathema to some observers, while others note the long
acceptance of corporate dominance in most of the nonfarm economy. Even the concept of the family farm is subject to some dispute:
some question whether a family-operated business with assets in the
millions of dollars is deserving of public protection or public
subsidy.

In many cases, conflicting values are operating in a situation of
limited information. For example, nearly everyone would agree that
U.S. agriculture should provide a dependable, low-cost supply of
food and fiber. But there is considerable uncertainty about whether
scale economies in agriculture are inevitable, or simply the result of
a business and government system that encourages bigness in scores

of subtle ways. Moreover, even if large or corporate-owned farms (or mines or timber operations) are lower-cost producers, people differ in the price they are willing to pay to avoid concentration.

We cannot resolve these issues here. Continued public debate is needed on the most desirable structure of agriculture and on the more general issue of the overall distribution of rural landownership. In the meantime, it is desirable to review some of the principal varieties of proposed policies and to look at their advantages and disadvantages in reaching the objectives they assume.

Increasing Access to Landownership

There have been many proposals, mainly for state or federal legislation, to help small-scale or beginning operators gain access to land. Most involve helping young farmers who want to buy farmland.[60] The most popular approach is to make credit available to such buyers under favorable repayment schedules or at subsidized interest rates. For example, under a program started in 1978 by the Farmers Home Administration, "limited resource" farmers and ranchers can get loans at concessionary terms in order to buy land. During a recent period in which the rate on ordinary FmHA farm ownership loans was 12.25 percent, "limited resource" buyers could borrow for as long as 40 years at an interest rate of only 5 percent.[61] There are also provisions for deferring or rescheduling payments if the borrower runs into short-term financial hardship. During the program's first two years, some 7,439 loans were approved for a total amount of $628 million. Needless to say, the demand for such loans far outstrips the supply.

Several states also have subsidy programs for limited-resource buyers. Minnesota's Farm Security Program offers both state loan guarantees and a state interest-rate subsidy to farmers with a net worth below $75,000. By early 1980, more than 180 farmers had been enabled to purchase 30,000 acres of land. North Dakota initiated such a program in 1978, with loan guarantees and the interest-rate subsidy provided through the state-owned Bank of North Dakota. Texas approved a state loan-guarantee program in 1979. Bills calling for similar programs have been introduced in several other states, while a bill providing for federal guarantees of loans made under state programs for beginning farmers was debated, but not passed, by Congress.[62]

A very recent innovation is the "Aggie bond," a state-issued bond the proceeds of which are reloaned to farmers at below-market interest rates.[63] Because interest on the bonds is exempt from state and federal income tax, the state is able to borrow at extremely favorable rates. For example, in 1980 Louisiana sold $25 million in Aggie bonds carrying interest rates of 6.5 to 7.6 percent. Because of the low interest rate, the state could relend money at very attractive rates.

Another approach is to focus government subsidy on the land *seller*, encouraging him to sell (or in some cases to lease) his land to a beginning farmer. For example, Minnesota and North Dakota make it possible for persons selling land to beginning farmers to avoid state income tax on the mortgage interest received. This gives sellers an incentive to deal with a beginner, and probably to give him favorable loan terms. Proponents of this approach argue, moreover, that subsidizing the seller, rather than the buyer, prevents the subsidy from having an upward influence on land prices.[64]

Yet another frequently suggested approach is for the government to purchase farmland, then lease or sell it on favorable terms to low-income or beginning farmers. The Canadian province of Saskatchewan has had a program of this type for nearly a decade. It now affects nearly a million acres of land, which are leased to limited-resource farmers. Lessees are given the option to purchase after five years at market value (minus a "homestead refund" of up to $5,000). Legislation promoting this approach has also been introduced in the U.S. Congress.

A major problem with all of these subsidy policies is that they cost the government money and distribute their benefits narrowly. The true cost of many of these programs is difficult to estimate, because most rely on the government's borrowing power or foregone tax revenue, rather than a direct appropriation. Nevertheless, the costs to the government are real.[65] A tax break for a land seller is money lost to the state treasury; a state bond guarantee eventually will raise the state's cost of borrowing money.

Thus far, the total amount of money spent under beginning-farmer subsidy programs is fairly small—but so is the number of farmers aided by them. If the subsidy per participant is large, as it has to be to help the farmer operate in today's land market, one must ask whether beginning farmers are more deserving of public help than are all of the other worthy people and causes making claims on society's purse. It is ironic that the unremarked objective of beginning-farmer subsidy programs is to enable the buyer eventually to get enough equity to compete in the land market without subsidy—that is, to join the drift toward largeness and concentration.

We think that there are better ways to help small-scale farmers get—and keep—productive land. We need to make the small operator a more profitable agricultural producer, and, therefore, a stronger competitor in the land market. One way to do this is to tilt federal farm programs in favor of the smaller producer. For example, presently the government sets "target prices" for several major crops (among them wheat, corn, and cotton) and makes a cash payment to producers when prices fall below this level. A tilt toward small operators might involve setting a target price that varies inversely with a producer's total output.[66] Another way to help small producers is to redirect agricultural research away from scale-increasing technology toward techniques suitable on small farms.

We also need to see if more creative credit arrangements can make unsubsidized loans more available to limited-resource farmers. There may be lessons to be learned from the attempts of financial institutions to accommodate first-time homebuyers in the recent period of high home prices and soaring interest rates. A wide variety of variable interest-rate and variable payment-level mortgages have emerged in the residential sector. Most of these are not appropriate to agriculture, because they assume that the borrower can count on his income going up uniformly over time—not a safe bet in farming. But one very promising new residential mortgage instrument is the "shared appreciation" mortgage.[67] Under this scheme, banks will make a loan to a homebuyer at the lower-than-market interest rate in exchange for a share in the future appreciation in the price of the dwelling. At the end of, say, 10 years, the arrangement is renegotiated. If the price of the house has risen, the borrower uses his own share of the appreciation as equity for a new conventional mortgage, paying off the bank for its appreciation share. If the house has not gone up in value, the bank gains nothing beyond the interest already received.

Applied to the farm real-estate market, the shared-appreciation mortgage could have several advantages. We pointed out in earlier chapters that a significant part of the current price of farmland is the capitalized value of future expected price appreciation. Because of this, a farmland purchase can almost never be justified entirely on the basis of its current output. Under a shared-appreciation mortgage, a beginning farmer could give up some of his future price appreciation in exchange for a concessionary interest rate. One potential source of such mortgages could be the federal government, through the Farmers Home Administration, for example. In the private sector, insurance companies, pension funds,

293

foreign investors, and others interested in hedging against inflation are also very likely to be interested in lending through shared-appreciation farmland mortgages, for such financial instruments would enable them to participate in the farmland market without actually owning land.[68] (This arrangement would also avoid abuses that might come from direct absentee control of the land.)

Just as in the case of a shared-appreciation home mortgage, if the farmland's price went up, the operator could refinance with conventional financing. If the price did not go up, the person or institution issuing the mortgage would have no gain on its share of the appreciation, but would have successfully hedged against inflation.[69]

Limiting Ownership

Many policies have been suggested for affecting the structure of landownership by restricting or prohibiting some types of ownership or by trying to make such ownership less profitable. These policies are variously directed against corporate owners, foreign owners, absentee owners, very large-scale owners or operators, and operators with substantial nonfarm incomes. Particularly in the last two cases, policy is directed not at penalizing such owners but at removing public subsidies that have heretofore given them a special advantage in the land market.

One of the oldest and most sweeping laws limiting ownership is found in North Dakota, which in 1932 prohibited participation in farming or the holding of farm real estate by domestic and foreign corporations. The law has apparently changed ownership patterns from what they would have been in its absence. According to the 1978 USDA landownership survey, in the North Central region as a whole, family corporations owned 3.6 percent of farmland and ranchland, and nonfamily corporations owned 1.1 percent. But ownership of these types was almost nonexistent in North Dakota. Oklahoma has long had some less-stringent limitations on corporate ownership, as well as a prohibition on ownership by foreign individuals.

During the last few years, several other states, all in the Midwest, have limited corporate ownership or have required such owners to report their holdings.[70] Many states, such as Iowa and Kansas, distinguish family corporations and corporations with only a few shareholders from other corporations and treat the former more liberally. More than a dozen states substantially prohibit nonresident aliens from permanent ownership of rural land.[71] Some make

294

such ownership subject to a time limit (six years in Illinois) or to an acreage limit (320 acres in Indiana; an astonishing 500,000 acres in South Carolina). We have already noted the large number of bills affecting either foreign or corporate ownership that have been introduced in state legislatures. Most of these bills have not been enacted, although in 1979 Iowa, North Dakota, and South Dakota passed laws greatly restricting foreign ownership; Iowa put further restrictions on acquisition of farmland by certain nonfamily corporations.

Bills limiting landownership have also been introduced in the U.S. Congress, which in 1978 passed a law requiring disclosure of foreign agricultural land investment. Subsequently, Senator McGovern's Agricultural Foreign Investment Control Act (S. 194, 1979) would have essentially restricted foreigners from owning more than a minority interest in a single farm unit. Senator Bayh's Family Farm Anti-trust Act (S. 334, 1979) would have prohibited persons or corporations with nonfarm business assets of more than $15 million from "controlling or attempting to control . . . the production of raw farm products through the ownership or long-term leasing of agricultural land." Neither bill was enacted.

There have been very few policies enacted or proposed to discriminate against absentee owners who are not corporations or foreigners. Such policies would have a difficult time politically, for the largest single group of absentee owners of rural land in many farming areas is retired farmers and farm widows, who depend on income from their land as a retirement annuity. Moreover, there would be consitutional difficulties if a state chose to limit ownership by out-of-state residents or to subject them to tax penalties not imposed on residents.

Some states do make a distinction for property-tax purposes on the basis of whether or not the owner makes his permanent residence on the land being assessed. Usually these distinctions take the form of "homestead exemptions," which reduce the assessed value of owner-occupied property by some fixed dollar amount. West Virginia taxes owner-occupied residences, owner-occupied farms, and the minerals beneath them, at rates that are generally half those applied to property owned by people who do not live on the premises. The impact of this distinction is limited, however, by the fact that West Virginia property taxes are extremely low for all classes of property. Minnesota, which has fairly high tax rates, also levies higher taxes on farm properties owned by people who do not live on the parcel or within a specified distance of it.

There have also been some attempts to relate property taxes to the size of holdings. Homestead exemptions have this effect in that they result in a greater percentage reduction in the tax burden for persons whose taxable holdings are less valuable. Land-reform groups have suggested that even stronger distinctions be made on the basis of size of holding. For example, a Nebraska group has proposed requiring certain corporations to pay an "excess land tax" on agricultural landholdings exceeding an assessed value of $50,000.[72] A North Dakota farm group has proposed a tax on any landholdings beyond what is considered a viable family farm. The group suggests that the tax "should be sufficiently graduated to insure that larger-than-family-sized farm units are significantly economically disadvantaged."[73] The same group has also called for a graduated lease tax imposed when land is leased to large-scale operators. The intent would be to encourage the landowner to lease farmlands to smaller producers.[74]

An alternative to trying to control the composition of landownership or influence it by taxation is to regulate the specific undesirable activities in which absentee, corporate, foreign, or other classes of landowners are alleged to engage. Because some of the activities may also be associated with landowners who do not fall into these categories, specific regulations may have a greater impact than would controls on ownership.

For example, as already noted, regulations or incentives could be designed to control erosion and other forms of neglect of the soil. These might deal with neglect caused by absentee ownership, as well as erosion caused—perhaps for different reasons—by local owners. Similarly, forestry practices of corporate owners, if deficient, might be regulated within the framework of state forestry acts applied equally to all classes of owners.

The exercise of *economic* power by large landowners may already be regulated to some degree by existing federal antitrust laws.[75] For example, the Sherman Act is probably applicable to cases of price-fixing, whether the basis of the monopoly power derives from ownership of a processing plant (such as a paper mill) or from ownership of a large amount of land. Invoking that law in one well-known case in 1957, the Supreme Court held that the Northern Pacific Railroad could not use the market power implicit in its huge ownership of rural land in the Northwest to require persons leasing or purchasing land to ship products on the company's railroad lines.[76]

Specific regulation can probably do less in cases in which particular types of landownership lead to a concentration of *political* power. To be sure, limitations on campaign contributions may reduce the connection between economic and political power, but experience to date has shown these laws are of limited effectiveness. Cases in which landownership leads to disproportionate political influence probably represent the strongest argument for controls on the size or concentration of landholdings.

Impacts of particular forms of landownership on an area's *social structure* probably cannot be ameliorated except by direct controls on ownership. But there is inadequate documentation of the links between these impacts and various forms of ownership, and even less consensus on their desirability. The congressional debate over foreign ownership of farmland that took place in the late 1970s (see chapter 2) indicates both a lack of documentation of impacts and lack of consensus about their seriousness. It is interesting to note that the major legislative outcome of that debate was not regulatory legislation, but a mandatory disclosure and reporting requirement.[77]

Embracing a Land Ethic

A great deal of human decision making is based on self-interest. In the case of land, owners make consumption decisions on the basis of what is best for themselves and their immediate families. Owners make investments, economists tell us, on the basis of the value to themselves of the future benefits of the investment, discounted to the present by an appropriate interest rate.

But even economists recognize that many investment and consumption decisions are also motivated, or at least influenced, by altruism and by ethical codes that go beyond immediate self-interest.[78] For example, many farmers spend money to control erosion not because they fear damage to soil productivity during their lifetime, but because they wish to hand the resource unimpaired to future users. Similarly, landowners may allow public recreational access to their land because they feel it is unfair to do otherwise.

There has been a modest amount of writing about the idea of an ethical basis for land use.[79] The undoubted master of thinking about this subject, Aldo Leopold, argued that:

> economic feasibility limits the tether of what can or cannot be done for land . . . [but the fallacy] which we now need to cast off, is the belief that economics determines *all* land-use. This is simply not true. An innumerable host of actions and attitudes, comprising perhaps the

297

bulk of all land relations, is determined by the land user's tastes and predilections, rather than by his purse. The bulk of all land relations hinges on investments of time, forethought, skill, and faith rather than on investments of cash.[80]

Broad discussions of a "land ethic" can be stirring, and may even motivate landowners to action. But are there any concrete things we can do to promote altruism in the use of rural land? We think that it would be quite helpful, and of only minor cost to the government, if those who purchased rural land, identified from county property-transfer records, were to receive a letter from the state governor along the following lines:

You have recently joined the community of approximately 100,000 people who own rural property in West Virginia (or Texas, or Oregon). By becoming a landowner, you have gained a number of rights to use and enjoy your land.

As a rural landowner, you also join a group with great responsibilities to your neighbors and to society as a whole, including citizens yet unborn. You should learn as much as possible about your land and its capabilities and limitations. Then you should consider taking some steps that will benefit others and increase your own pride of ownership:

● Rural land is a source of jobs in your community. Consider whether more actively managing your forestland would make it possible to harvest lumber or pulpwood or firewood, creating useful products and jobs for your rural neighbors. If you have fields but don't intend to use them, find out if a local farmer might wish to rent them for grazing.

● Rural land is a source of recreational opportunity in your community. Ask the state department of fish and wildlife about programs for controlled public use that can reduce vandalism, limit your liability, and prevent trespass around occupied buildings. If you permit public access, you may be eligible for state funds to increase wildlife on your land, or even for a special tax subsidy.

● Rural land is intimately connected with your community's distinctive landscape and scenic qualities. Get to know the history of your community and the style of rural buildings and land uses that have made it different from other parts of the country. The rural landscape that you enjoy is not formed randomly, but by deliberate land-use choices, past and present. Your county and state historical society can help you find out

*why your area has developed in the way it has. When changing
land uses or building new structures or fences, ask yourself,
"Would I be pleased if many other owners in the county made
this kind of change?"*

*● Finally, rural land is a source of food. Despite all of mod-
ern farming's advances, we still rely on naturally productive
soils. Protect them from erosion and cultivate them wisely.*

*There are many state and federal sources of information,
technical assistance, and even financial subsidies that can help
you get more profit or enjoyment from your acquisition.
Among these are the county extension agent, who can provide
advice on agricultural techniques and on building rural residences and farm buildings; the county and state foresters, who
can counsel you about forest management and perhaps provide
low-cost seedlings or other tangible help; and the representatives of various soil-conservation agencies who can assist you
with erosion and water management problems. Addresses of the
closest office of each of these agencies are enclosed. In addition
to personal help, these agencies can supply thousands of useful
publications on all areas of rural living and land management.*

This sort of letter appeals both to self-interest and to altruism.
Above all, it tries to make the new owner aware that his land is not
just a personal possession but is part of a community. Understanding that fact may help nontraditional owners to self-regulate their
use of land and thereby minimize the need for expensive subsidies or
coercive regulation.

Research and Monitoring

We cannot conclude a discussion of policies related to the rural land
market without pointing out the need for research and for continuous monitoring of market behavior. In writing this comprehensive
book about the rural land market, we have become very much aware
of the gaps in our own knowledge and of our own unanswered
questions.

A clear priority is for the federal government to collect data on
how the ownership of nonfarm property is changing over time. The
1978 USDA national landownership survey is an invaluable tool,
but a similar survey should be taken at periodic intervals so that a
record of changes over time can be compiled.[81] Information about
ownership should also be as closely integrated as possible with the

land-use data collected by the Soil Conservation Service and the Forest Service so that more can be learned about how ownership affects changes in land use.

There is also a need for more monitoring of prices of forestland, recreation land, and urban-fringe development land. This may be done either by individual concerned agencies—much as USDA now collects data on farmland prices—or as part of a comprehensive price index for all forms of undeveloped land. The latter poses difficult conceptual and operational problems, but is now being studied by a federal interagency committee.

A third data-collection need is for better information describing the physical and economic availability of land for various uses. For example, it would be helpful to be able to describe the area of timberland not only by land quality and tree species, as at present, but also by size of parcel, size of "stand condition" (the area of trees of similar species and age), size of the owner's nearby holding, and the owner's harvest intentions. Similarly, it would be useful to monitor the amount of farmland that is annually surrounded or "leap-frogged" by urban development. We should point out that such monitoring does not have to involve the annual collection of massive quantities of data. Rather, existing field employees could annually check for land-use and ownership changes in a scientifically chosen sample of representative parcels. Similar procedures are now followed by the Soil Conservation Service and Forest Service in their current, more limited, monitoring efforts.

Data collection and monitoring will tell us more about what is going on in rural America. But some research is needed to better understand problem areas. One research priority is gaining a better understanding of the timber-production opportunities for nonindustrial private forestlands, particularly studies that simultaneously evaluate returns on investment and the constraints imposed by parcel size and ownership patterns.

We also need to learn much more than we now know about scale economies in all types of rural land use. To what extent—and in what way—are large farms or timber operations really more productive than smaller ones? And if there are differences in productivity, or in profitability, are they due to technological factors or simply to business practices or government subsidies that favor the large operator over the small? Some fresh research is also needed with regard to the impacts of ownership concentration on rural communities. There has been quite a bit of work—though much of it by parties with an ax to grind—on impacts of corporate owner-ship of Appalachian coal lands. But there has been relatively little good research on the impacts of corporate farming, and hardly any on the advantages or disadvantages of concentrated industry owner-ship of forestland.

A final subject where research is needed is rural landscape change, including landscape aesthetics, wildlife habitat, and his-toric preservation. Planners and land-use experts do not yet have a good conceptual structure or even a vocabulary adequate to describe what is happening to the rural landscape. They are thus almost forced either to borrow planning concepts from cities and suburbs (minimum lot sizes and separation of uses, for example) or to look only at land's productive function. Conceptual research on rural landscape changes will make it possible eventually to measure such changes and then to frame policies to discourage those which are undesirable.

In this book, we have tried to bring together what others have written about the land market, newly available government data, and the results of our own investigations in six widely separated local areas. Above all, we have endeavored to show that land-market activity touches an extremely large number of current rural issues—the rural population revival, agricultural land preservation, the "farm structure" debate, and nonindustrial private forest manage-ment, to name just a few. The study of the land market, we believe, illuminates the complex interplay of economic forces and personal tastes that ultimately determines land use, and points the way toward policy innovations that can protect public interests in a time of rapid rural change.

REFERENCES

1. For example, we have given relatively little space to methods for identifying and preserving productive agricultural land, a subject of much current interest to both researchers and policymakers. However, we discuss at length a neglected area of agricultural land policy, the prevention of parcellation. The brief treatment given to other aspects of agricultural land policy is not a downgrading of their importance, but recognition that others have presented them well. An up-to-date bibliography of this work is National Agricultural Lands Study, *Agricultural Land Retention and Availability: A Bibliographic Source Book* (Washington, D.C.: Government Printing Office, 1981). For a summary of state and local poli-cies toward agricultural land, see Robert E. Coughlin, John C. Keene, *et al., The Protection of Farmland: A Reference Guidebook for State and Local Govern-ments* (Washington, D.C.: Government Printing Office for National Agricultural

Lands Study, 1981). We will also not dwell on such important rural planning issues as the provision of infrastructure and public services, transportation, energy, and low-cost housing. For discussion of some of these broader rural planning issues, see Judith Getzels and Charles Thurow, eds., *Rural and Small Town Planning* (Chicago: American Planning Association, 1979) and William R. Lassey, *Planning in Rural Environments* (New York: McGraw-Hill, 1977).

2. These terms are used respectively in *Land and Food: The Preservation of U.S. Farmland,* American Land Forum Report No. 1 (Spring 1979), p. 15; J.C. Doherty, "Public and Private Issues in Nonmetropolitan Government," in Glenn V. Fuguitt, Paul R. Voss, and J.C. Doherty, *Growth and Change in Rural America* (Washington, D.C.: Urban Land Institute, 1979), p. 56; and Irving Kristol, "An Urban Civilization Without Cities," *Current,* November 1972, pp. 3-14.

3. Howard E. Conklin, *Planning for a New Distribution of Rural People,* Staff Paper No. 79-37 (Ithaca: Department of Agricultural Economics, Cornell University, November 1979).

4. For recent examples of thinking on rural planning, see Vernon P. Deines and Ann D. Watts, "A New Mood for Rural and Small Town Planning" (PAS Memo no. 80-6, American Planning Association, Chicago, June 1980); Lee Nellis, "Planning with Rural Values," *Journal of Soil and Water Conservation,* vol. 35, no. 2 (March-April 1980), p. 69; and Ann D. Watts, "We Don't Teach Rural Algebra: Why Should We Teach Rural Planning?" (Paper presented to the annual meeting of the American Planning Association, Baltimore, Maryland, October 1979).

5. From information presented in Larry K. Stephenson, "Primary Markets, Secondary Homes, Tertiary Locations: Subdividing the Southwest" (Paper presented at the Association of American Geographers Conference on Land Use Issues of Nonmetropolitan America, University of Maryland, June 23-25, 1980).

6. Leslie Allan, Beryl Kuder, and Sarah L. Oakes, *Promised Lands:* (vol. 1) *Subdivisions in Desert and Mountains* and (vol. 2) *Subdivisions in Florida's Wetlands* (New York: INFORM, 1976, 1977).

7. The Conservancy's six areas of responsibility are: preservation of agricultural land, coastal restoration, coastal resource enhancement, resource protection zones, reservation of coastal resource areas, and public access to the coast.

8. Section 31150, Ch. 1441, California Statutes, 1976.

9. Charles E. Little, "Farmland Conservancies: A Middleground Approach to Agricultural Land Preservation," *Journal of Soil and Water Conservation,* vol. 35, no. 5 (September-October 1980), p. 206.

10. Ibid.

11. Examples of the latter are Doane Agricultural Service (farmland, St. Louis), James Vardaman Co. (timberland, Jackson, Mississippi), and Oppenheimer Industries (ranches, Kansas City).

12. Thomas J. Mills, *Cost Effectiveness of the 1974 Forestry Incentives Program* (Fort Collins, Colorado: Rocky Mountain Forest and Range Experiment Station, 1976).

13. Clifford A. Hickman and Randy J. Gehlhausen, "Landowner Interest in Forestry Assistance Programs in East Texas," *Journal of Forestry,* vol. 79, no. 4 (April 1981), pp. 211-13.

14. Howard S. Muse, Jr., "Helping Private Landowners Help Themselves," *American Forests,* July 1978, pp. 27-28.

15. A review of this history is found in Charles H. Stoddard, *The Small Private Forest in the United States* (Washington, D.C.: Resources for the Future, 1961).

16. Allen, Kuder, and Oakes, *Promised Lands*, vol. 2, pp. 427-29.

17. Nelson Rosenbaum, *Land Use and the Legislatures* (Washington, D.C.: Urban Institute, 1976), pp. 21-23.

18. William K. Reilly, ed., *The Use of Land: A Citizens' Policy Guide to Urban Growth* (New York: Crowell, 1973).

19. An excellent discussion of large-lot agricultural zoning may be found in Coughlin, Keene, *et al.*, *The Protection of Farmland*, chapter 6.

20. California Coastal Act (1976) sec. 30241(e).

21. Oregon Land Conservation and Development Commission, *Statewide Planning Goals and Guidelines*, rev. ed. (Salem: Oregon Land Conservation and Development Commission, 1976), Goal 3 (Agricultural Lands).

22. Flury v. Land Use Board of Appeals, 50 Or App 263 (1981). See also S.O.D. v. Douglas County, Oregon Land Use Board of Appeals 80-121 (1981).

23. Meeker v. Board of Commissioners of Clatsop County, 287 Or. 665, 601 P2d 804 (1979).

24. Hood View Neighborhood Association v. Board of County Commissioners of Clackamas County, 43 Or App 869, 604 P2d 447 (1979).

25. H. Jeffrey Leonard, *The Politics of Land-use Planning in Oregon* (Washington, D.C.: The Conservation Foundation, forthcoming), MS. chapter 4, p. 65.

26. Ibid., p. 54.

27. In City of Scappoose v. Board of County Commissioners of Columbia County, 50 Or App 483 (1981) the court ruled that county government could not automatically issue building permits for small lots in previously subdivided forestland. Instead, the county must show that the land is "irrevocably committed to non-farm or non-forestry uses."

28. Currently, the legal form of ownership of the common lands is that of a land trust. As initially sold, each buyer purchased title to a homesite which automatically gave him an undivided 1/48th interest in the common acres. During the development, some concern was expressed that the Securities Exchange Commission might consider these undivided shares as securities, so the development was reorganized in the form of a land trust.

29. Joseph H. Nash, Jr., "Farmcolony: A Development Alternative to Loss of Agricultural Land," *Urban Land*, February 1976, p. 12.

30. Middlesex-Somerset-Mercer Regional Study Council, Inc., *Planning for Agriculture in New Jersey* (Princeton, New Jersey: Middlesex-Somerset-Mercer Study Council, 1980), p. 30.

31. Coughlin, Keene, *et al.*, *The Protection of Farmland*, p. 116.

32. Ibid, p. 119.

33. See John J. Costonis, *Space Adrift* (Urbana, Illinois: University of Illinois Press, 1974).

34. A national survey found that by 1980 only ten municipalities and two counties had adopted TDR for the preservation of farmland and other open space. Only five TDR transactions, involving 184 acres, had taken place. See Coughlin, Keene, *et al.*, *The Protection of Farmland*, pp. 174-79. One of the nation's most ambitious agricultural TDR programs was adopted by Montgomery County, Maryland, in 1980. See *Plowing New Ground: Questions and Answers, Montgo-*

mery County, Maryland, Agricultural and Rural Open Space Preservation Program (Silver Spring, Maryland: Montgomery County Planning Board, 1981).

35. Lawrence O. Houstoun, Jr., "The New Nonmetropolitan Growth: People, Markets and Development Options" (Unpublished paper, September 1980), p. 15.

36. See John Blackmore, "Community Land Trusts Offer a Hopeful Way Back to Land," *Smithsonian*, vol. 8, no. 3 (June 1978). Community land trusts frequently are set up in the legal form of a nonprofit membership corporation, rather than as a "trust."

37. Survey taken by Institute for Community Economics, reported in telephone interview with Robert Swann, February 20, 1981.

38. The average second home is used only 53 days of the year and only 6 percent are used more than half the year. U.S. Bureau of the Census, *Second Homes in the U.S.*, Current Housing Reports, Series H-121, No. 16 (Washington, D.C.: Government Printing Office, 1969).

39. California Coastal Act, 1976, sec. 30222.

40. Richard Wein, "Who Owns These Woods," *Country Journal*, vol. 4, no. 3 (March 1977), pp. 68-74.

41. Ibid.

42. Howard E. Conklin, "The New Forests of New York," *Land Economics*, vol. 42, no. 2 (May 1966), p. 204.

43. See Leon Minckler, *Woodland Ecology* (Syracuse: Syracuse University Press, 1975).

44. Carl H. Reidel, *The Yankee Forest: A Prospectus* (New Haven: Yale School of Forestry and Environmental Studies, 1978), p. 28.

45. Lease provisions of Massachusetts and other states are surveyed in Elizabeth G. Carpenter, *Summaries of States with Agricultural Leasing and/or Buy Back Agreements* (Trenton: New Jersey Department of Agriculture, July 1980).

46. Among those standards are fairness, adequacy of revenue production, ease of administration, and willing compliance.

47. The same argument could, of course, be made with respect to capital gains from holding gold, diamonds, coins, and other "unproductive" assets.

48. Robert G. Healy and John S. Rosenberg, *Land Use and the States*, 2nd ed. (Baltimore: Johns Hopkins University Press for Resources for the Future, 1979), pp. 69-72; R. Lisle Baker and Stephen Andersen, "Taxing Speculative Land Gains: The Vermont Experience" (Unpublished manuscript, Environmental Law Institute, Washington, D.C., 1980).

49. Information from Vermont State Tax Office.

50. Baker and Andersen, "Taxing Speculative Land Gains," VII-6.

51. Ibid., VII-11.

52. Ibid., VIII-9.

53. Coughlin, Keene, *et al.*, *The Protection of Farmland*.

54. This would not have to involve any new public institutions. For example, Vermont's 1979 Use Value Assessment Act presumes that forestland is under active management if it is a part of the American Tree Farm System (a private organization), is so certified by the county forester, or has participated in the last five years in a federal cost-sharing program.

55. *New Hampshire Times*, January 4, 1978, p. 18.

56. See W.L. Church, *Private Lands and Public Recreation: A Report and*

Proposed New Model Act on Access, Liability and Trespass (Washington, D.C.: National Wildlife Federation, 1979).

57. There has been considerable public concern about the ownership of mineral-bearing lands, but little legislative activity.

58. Conference on Alternative State and Local Policies, *New Initiatives in Farmland and Food Policy—A State Guide 1979-80* (Washington, D.C.: Conference on Alternative State and Local Policies, 1981).

59. Ibid.

60. An excellent sourcebook on several existing and proposed programs is Jay Sherman and Lee Webb, *Assisting Beginning Farmers: New Programs and Responses* (Washington, D.C.: Conference on Alternative State and Local Policies, 1980).

61. However, borrowers are reexamined every two years to see if they can afford to pay higher interest rates.

62. See U.S. Congress, Senate, Committee on Agriculture, Nutrition and Forestry, *Family Farm Entry Assistance Act: Hearing on S.582*, 96th Cong., 1st sess., April 3, 1979. A similar bill (H.R. 2977, the Beginning Farmer Assistance Act) was introduced in the 1981 Congress by Rep. Berkley Bedell (D-Iowa).

63. Lawrence Ingrassia, "Tax-Free 'Aggie Bonds' Help Farmers Buy Land at Below-Market Interest Rates," *Wall Street Journal*, December 1, 1980.

64. A subsidy to the buyer moves the demand curve for land rightward, which (*ceteris paribus*) raises the market price. A subsidy to the seller moves the supply curve rightward, lowering the market price.

65. For example, if the Farmers Home Administration charges only 5 percent interest on a loan, when the free market rate is 12 percent, the true program cost applied to an outstanding loan volume of $628 million is about $45 million annually or $6,000 per borrower per year.

66. Present law provides for a maximum on the total payment (excluding disaster aid) received by an individual farmer. The 1978 limit of $40,000 per individual affected only 1,184 farmers, or 0.2 percent of program participants. The limit reduced total program payments by 1.33 percent. U.S. Department of Agriculture, *A Time to Choose: Summary Report on the Structure of Agriculture* (Washington, D.C.: Government Printing Office, 1981), p. 103.

67. Shared-appreciation home mortgages have been written by several savings and loan associations and mortgage banking firms. In 1979, the California Legislature provided (AB 333) for a $7.5 million demonstration program using the shared-appreciation concept to make housing more accessible to low- and moderate-income people.

68. It is also possible that a secondary market for such mortgages, or even for the appreciation rights alone, could be set up.

69. As used here, hedging is the practice of making counterbalancing transactions so that the loss on one offsets the gain on another. Widely used to protect one's financial position from uncertain events, it is the money manager's equivalent to betting both sides of a football game. A shared-appreciation mortgage provides the lender with a hedge against inflation, regardless of what happens to land prices. If inflation rates accelerate, land prices would most likely increase rapidly, giving the lender a profit from the appreciation right. If inflation slows down, the appreciation right might be valueless, but the lender would most likely realize a substantial capital gain on the conventional fixed-income securities (such

as bonds and ordinary mortgages) that make up the rest of his portfolio of investments.

70. A survey of laws limiting corporate ownership can be found in Council of State Governments, *Corporate Farming and the Family Farm* (CSG Research Brief, Council of State Governments, Washington, D.C., July 1976). Recent legislative activity is surveyed in Conference on Alternative State and Local Policies, *New Initiatives in Farmland and Food Policy*.

71. See list in Howard Zaritsky, "Foreign Ownership of Property in the United States: Federal and State Restrictions," in U.S. Congress, Senate, Committee on Agriculture, Nutrition and Forestry, *Foreign Investment in United States Agricultural Land*, 95th Cong., 2nd sess., January 1979, pp. 191-203.

72. Center for Rural Affairs, Walthill, Nebraska, cited in Council of State Governments, *Corporate Farming and the Family Farm*, p. 14.

73. North Dakota Farmers Union, *Report of the Family Farm Commission* (Jamestown, North Dakota: North Dakota Farmers Union, 1978), p. 29.

74. Ibid., p. 24.

75. William E. Perry, "The Sherman Act and Land: The Interstate Commerce Requirement," *Columbia Journal of Environmental Law*, vol. 3, no. 2 (1977), pp. 306-343.

76. Northern Pacific Railway Co. v. United States, 356 U.S. 1 (1957). The majority noted that "the undisputed facts established beyond any genuine question that [Northern Pacific] possessed substantial economic power by virtue of its extensive landholdings which it used as leverage to induce large numbers of purchasers and lessees to give it preference, to the exclusion of its competitors, in carrying goods or produce from the land transferred to them. . ." Interestingly, the court ordered the railroad to eliminate this "tie-in" requirement in land leases and sales, but did not order it to divest landholdings.

77. The resulting law is the Agricultural Foreign Investment Disclosure Act of 1978.

78. Kenneth E. Boulding, *The Economy of Love and Fear* (Belmont, California: Wadsworth, 1973).

79. Among recent writings are Wendell Berry, *The Unsettling of America* (New York: Avon Books, 1977) and Piedmont Environmental Council, *Toward a New Land Use Ethic* (Warrenton, Virginia: Piedmont Environmental Council, 1980).

80. Aldo Leopold, *A Sand County Almanac* (New York: Oxford University Press, 1966), p. 240.

81. Efforts should also be made to increase response rates, a major problem with the first survey.